NEITHER CONFIRM NOR DENY

John Ware has been a journalist since 1971; from 1974 to 1977 he was based in Belfast. He has since covered the Northern Ireland conflict and its aftermath across print, radio and TV, mainly for BBC *Panorama*. In 2001, he was named Television Journalist of the Year by the Royal Television Society for his documentary *Who Bombed Omagh?*, and in 2004 he was awarded the prestigious James Cameron Prize for 'work as a journalist that combined moral vision and professional integrity'. In 2020, the BBC described him as a 'reporter with an extraordinary record of excellence at *Panorama* for investigative journalism in the public interest'. He is the author of *Mengele: The Complete Story*, a biography of the Auschwitz concentration camp doctor, which has been published in over a dozen countries. Although he lives in England, over the years John has spent so much time in Northern Ireland that he regards it as his second home.

NEITHER CONFIRM NOR DENY

BRITISH INTELLIGENCE, LAWLESS AGENT RUNNING AND THE SUPPRESSION OF TRUTH

John Ware

MERRION PRESS

First published in 2026 by
Merrion Press
10 George's Street
Newbridge
Co. Kildare
Ireland
www.merrionpress.ie

978 1 78537 580 4 (Paper)
978 1 78537 594 1 (eBook)

A CIP catalogue record for this book is available from the British Library.

Typeset in Minion Pro 11/16 pt

Cover design by Fiachra McCarthy

Front cover image: © Pacemaker Press Intl

Merrion Press is a member of Publishing Ireland.

CONTENTS

ACKNOWLEDGEMENTS

Many of those who gave so much of their time providing me with the information that has gone into this book cannot be named for obvious reasons. They know who they are, and they are all honourable servants with inquiring minds and respect for facts and truth. As to those who can be named, first and foremost are my former steadfast BBC colleagues – Geoff Seed, Amanda Farnsworth, Eamon Hardy, Sarah Mole, Nick London and Celia Watson, and the wisest of owls, Barney Rowan. Advice and help was always available from David McKittrick, for years the *Independent*'s much-respected Ireland correspondent. Jane Winter, the director of the NGO British Irish Rights Watch (now known as Rights & Security International), was invaluable with her advice and scrupulous attention to detail. Jane's appetite for research, analysis and advocacy about the Northern Ireland conflict and its aftermath was enormous, and this book and the historical record owes her a special debt. The same is true for the genial, encyclopaedic and ever-helpful Kevin Winters and Liam Diver of KRW-Law. I am grateful too for the judicious insights of my good friend Alasdair Palmer and for his support of the work that I and Geoff Seed did when Alasdair was on the *Sunday Telegraph*. Finally, apologies and gratitude to my family for putting up with many, many months of absence over the years across the Irish sea.

LIST OF ABBREVIATIONS

ACC	Assistant Chief Constable
ACOS G2	Assistant Chief of Staff, Army Intelligence Section
CCRC	Criminal Cases Review Commission
CF	Contact Form
CHIS	Covert Human Intelligence Source
CIA	Central Intelligence Agency
CID	Criminal Investigation Department
CLF	Commander of Land Forces
CO	Commanding Officer
CRU	Central Resettlement Unit
CWIED	Control Wired Improvised Explosive Device
DPP	Director of Public Prosecutions
FRU	Force Research Unit
GHQ	General Headquarters
GOC	General Officer Commanding
HET	Historical Enquiries Team
ICRIR	Independent Commission for Reconciliation and Information Recovery
INLA	Irish National Liberation Army
IPCO	Investigatory Powers Commissioner's Office
IPT	Investigatory Powers Tribunal
IRA	Irish Republican Army

ISU	Internal Security Unit (IRA)
JSG	Joint Support Group
KC	King's Counsel
LVF	Loyalist Volunteer Force
MISR	Military Intelligence Source Report
MoD	Ministry of Defence
NCND	Neither Confirm Nor Deny
NIFSL	Northern Ireland Forensic Science Laboratory
NIO	Northern Ireland Office
NIPB	Northern Ireland Policing Board
OC	Officer Commanding
OPONI	Office of the Police Ombudsman, Northern Ireland
ORBAT	Order of Battle
'P' cards	Personality cards
PII	Public Interest Immunity
PIR	Passive Infra-Red Sensors
PIRA	Provisional Irish Republican Army
PPS	Public Prosecution Service
PSNI	Police Service of Northern Ireland
QC	Queen's Counsel
RUC	Royal Ulster Constabulary
SIO	Senior Investigating Officer
SPOC	Single Point of Contact
TCG	Tasking and Co-ordinating Group
UDA	Ulster Defence Association
UDR	Ulster Defence Regiment
UFF	Ulster Freedom Fighters
UVF	Ulster Volunteer Force

PREFACE

'... amid the clash of arms, the laws are not silent. They may be changed, but they speak the same language in war as in peace.'

THESE WERE THE WORDS OF Lord Atkin during the Second World War, when he dissented from his fellow law lords that a man should be detained without trial simply on the word of the home secretary. They were echoed during the Northern Ireland conflict in 1983 by Lord Chief Justice Lord Lowry, and again in 1991 by Attorney General Sir Patrick Mayhew in a lecture entitled 'The Rule of Law in Northern Ireland': 'In the interests of maintaining confidence in the administration of justice, they [Lowry's words] can hardly be proclaimed too often – provided they are true ...'[1]

For the most part, the rule of law did apply to the overt arm of the Northern Irish counter-insurgency, on the streets and in the courts. It did not, however, apply to everyone, despite Margaret Thatcher's injunction that it must. The law was mostly silent over how the state's covert arm was run.

To be clear, no state can fight terrorism successfully without some compromise of the legal and moral standards we take for granted in peacetime. High grade, actionable, human-sourced intelligence about terrorists' plans is best secured from agents inside those organisations. The closer to the action, the more reliable the intelligence. As one ex-head of the Royal Ulster Constabulary's Special Branch memorably observed, 'Good intelligence on terrorists doesn't come from milkmaids.'

The three intelligence-gathering agencies – military intelligence, Special Branch and MI5 – accepted that their agents had to act the part. The inevitable consequence of this was that the state was drawn into extremely serious criminality, including murder. Time and again. Sometimes even the murder of police officers and soldiers.

It is the scale of criminality on which the rule of law was silent that helps explain why the undercover war's legacy remains, to this day, an obstacle to reconciliation through truth. That legacy has its roots in the state's embrace of the 1981 recommendation by a senior MI5 counter-terrorism officer, Patrick Walker, that intelligence gathering should have de facto primacy over criminal justice.

A vast number of agents and informers were recruited, affording the intelligence services a clear picture of who in republican and loyalist terrorist organisations was doing what, and when. The understandable desire to keep building this picture led to the services turning a blind eye to the very serious crimes in which the intelligence gatherers were necessarily engaged, because that was the only way they could keep supplying the pieces of the picture. With spying taking precedence over locking people up, a premium arose on protecting agents, and often their close associates, at all costs from criminal investigation and prosecution, irrespective of the seriousness of their crimes. Source protection became *the* deified priority, along with a marked reluctance to pull agents out, even those repeatedly involved in murder.

Patrick Walker – who went on to become the director general of MI5 – was an intelligence officer, not a police officer. One of the unintended consequences of his legacy has been a failure to this day to solve some of the 1,200 unresolved conflict-related killings. This book is a forensic chronicle of this legacy told through the prism of two intelligence agents, codenamed 6137 and 6126, who were, respectively, Brian Nelson and Freddie Scappaticci.

These names are well known today, for much has been written about the two agents as a result of inquiries into how they were run. However, these inquiries were conducted in the teeth of opposition from officials in the more shadowed reaches of the state, who have seen themselves as the rightful custodians of history with a duty to delay, obscure and sometimes blatantly hide the facts. Their approach has been symbolised by the decades-long government protocol known as 'Neither Confirm Nor Deny' (NCND), deployed when governments prefer to evade awkward intelligence-related questions. In Northern Ireland, NCND has been applied to numerous criminal, civil and inquest proceedings relating to the 1,200 unsolved killings. A Cabinet Office Guidance Note describes NCND as 'a mechanism used to protect sensitive information', which 'applies where secrecy is necessary in the public interest and where this mechanism avoids the risks of damage that a confirmation or denial would create'.[2]

Yet even the current chief constable of the Police Service of Northern Ireland (PSNI), Jon Boutcher, acknowledges that the automatic application of NCND to conflict legacy cases has, over the years, 'assumed a totemic status within government and the security forces' and has 'become an implacable dogma or mantra with the qualities of a stone wall'.[3] One of this dogma's most striking manifestations has been the refusal by previous governments, on the advice of MI5, to even acknowledge that Freddie Scappaticci was the agent known as Stakeknife, despite his involvement in thirteen murders and fifteen abductions, some involving torture, and the fact that he died in 2023. That, at least, remains the position at the time of this book going to press, as the families of his victims await the Northern Ireland Secretary Hilary Benn's promised final word on the matter.[4] In the decade in which Boutcher has been investigating legacy cases – first as head of Operation Kenova and now as chief constable – he has found that the automatic application of NCND to those cases has been used to cover up 'dreadful things' by state agents;[5] or, as the former head of Police Scotland, Sir Iain Livingstone, who succeeded him as head of Kenova put it, to 'protect agents who commit grotesque serious crime, leaving victims and families ignored and their demands for information and answers dismissed'.[6]

The irony is that NCND is often applied more strictly today than it was during the insurgency itself. It is as if those who see themselves as the custodians of the conflict's historical narrative are more determined to keep their version intact in the face of new and embarrassing revelations that increasingly seep out – as inevitably, in a free society, they will. After initial resistance from officials, generals, police officers and ministers, much more has emerged about the activities of Brian Nelson since he was unmasked in the 1990s than had materialised by 2026 about Freddie Scappaticci. Had it not been for the tenacious efforts of Boutcher and Livingstone, the public and the relatives of Scappaticci's victims would be even more in the dark than they are today.

Included in this book are the attempts over the decades – mostly by government officials and lawyers working both with or for MI5 – to limit disclosure of the full extent of the state's moral compromises over agents 6126 and 6137. It draws on many unpublished documents and the first-hand accounts of confidential sources, who, I'm satisfied, were in a position to know the facts.

Due to the scale of agent recruitment, it is a reasonable assumption that compromises of the gravity that were made in the cases of Nelson and Scappaticci were also made with many of their fellow agents. Given the blind eyes that were turned day in and day out to the activities of both agents by all three intelligence-gathering agencies – the army, Special Branch and MI5 – it seems unlikely to have been otherwise.

That said, it is not the purpose of this book to dignify the narrative that holds the security forces to be corporately devoid of morality, when very many who served were deeply moral men and women. Many lives were saved thanks to agent-source intelligence by interdicting murders and bombings on countless occasions. The criminal justice system also functioned: some 25,000 republican and loyalist terrorists were jailed.

My purpose, rather, is to tease out in all its complexity the moral maze that the state knowingly ventured into by consciously choosing to elevate agent protection over the rule of law. It is for others to judge whether there was a better way of fighting terrorism and whether the moral and legal compromises that were made were acceptable. Or whether, as Lord Atkin adjudged eighty-three years ago, there are some principles which remain forever inviolate, irrespective of the provocation.

History requires those of us who chronicled this conflict to provide as full and accurate a record as we can, told more with dispassion than emotion, deeply distressing though many of these events are. I hope this account makes a useful contribution to that end.

Chapter One

Agent 6137 – Recruitment

ON 4 MAY 1984, A thirty-six-year-old part-time skip driver, seeking excitement from the dull routine of his life, telephoned the British Army at their headquarters at Thiepval Barracks, Lisburn, County Antrim, asking to speak to someone in the intelligence service. Over the course of two phone calls, Brian Nelson offered his services to spy for British military intelligence.[1]

The army was intrigued, so he was invited to a meeting the following day in Cranmore Park, in South Belfast. In full spring bloom, the park provided suitably dense vegetation for cover. There, just before noon, Nelson met members of the army's secret source handling agency, the Force Research Unit (FRU), recently established to centralise intelligence gathering from the military's many agents scattered around the six counties. The FRU had four detachments or 'dets', one for each region: North Det in Ebrington Barracks, on the east bank of the River Foyle, Derry; South Det in Bessbrook Mill, South Armagh; West Det at RAF St Angelo, near Enniskillen; and East Det at Palace Barracks in Holywood, East Belfast. Nelson was run by the last of these. Each det was commanded by a lieutenant or captain, assisted by a 'Field Source Control Officer', who had a team of eight or ten handlers of ranks varying from sergeant to warrant officer 2, as well as a clerk and a collator.

Cover for the FRU's first meeting with Nelson – what the official record described as a 'rolling pick-up' – was provided by three armed operatives, whose job it was to satisfy themselves that Nelson had not been followed and that this was not an ambush. Nelson was then taken five miles south by van to the car park at Drumbo church, the site of one of Ireland's oldest religious foundations, including the Drumbo round tower, dating back to the early medieval period, with its panoramic view of the Lagan Valley. In the security of the van, he was given a brief credibility test by being asked to identify key members of the loyalist paramilitaries; he passed comfortably.[2] Asked why he was volunteering, Nelson explained that he wanted some 'excitement to his life'.[3] Such were the first tentative steps of a relationship that, over the next five and a half years, would develop into one of agent and spymaster, and involve assassination and all manner of serious criminality. It was not, however, a one-off.

Throughout the three-decade-long Northern Ireland conflict, the entire agent-running regime for all three intelligence-gathering services knowingly operated well outside any legal framework. Although the conflict ended over a quarter of a century ago, the repercussions of the way Britain chose to pursue the clandestine side of its counter-insurgency strategy reverberate to this day. The strategy has contributed significantly to the failure of the nationalist and unionist communities to reconcile their differences over the past.

The FRU's first impression of their latest candidate for recruitment was favourable. They were impressed that Nelson hadn't asked for money or even a bus fare, so they gave him £2. They also noted that his 'background' suggested he had 'excellent potential as a source' within the Ulster Freedom Fighters (UFF), nom de guerre of the largest loyalist paramilitary organisation, the Ulster Defence Association (UDA).[4] They also seem chuffed that Nelson showed 'no wish to work for' the Royal Ulster Constabulary (RUC),[5] consistent with the tense inter-agency rivalry that existed between the FRU, Special Branch and MI5. This rivalry became 'most apparent in the often strained relationship' between the FRU and the branch, which was especially apparent over the recruitment of Nelson.[6]

The favourable 'background' that potentially made Nelson such suitable spy material was the fact that he had been both a 'major' in the UDA and, before that, a private in the British Army. No matter that both careers had ended disastrously. Having been born and brought up in Belfast's Shankill, Nelson had joined the Royal Navy as a boy entrant after leaving school just shy of his sixteenth birthday. After initial training, he was sent to the Royal Naval Air Station HMS Condor, at Arbroath near Dundee. He fairly soon decided the navy was not for him and joined the Territorial Army.[7] When he turned eighteen, he joined the regular army, serving with the 1st Battalion Black Watch, with postings in Germany, Malaya, Cyprus, Canada and Libya.[8] His regular army career was also short-lived and saw him face frequent detentions in military prisons for disciplinary breaches, such as going AWOL and causing wilful damage to Ministry of Defence (MoD) property, which included crashing a Land Rover.[9] On leave, he was seen walking up the Falls Road, recklessly shouting, 'We are the Brits.'[10] By February 1970, at the age of twenty-two, he was suffering from duodenal ulcers[11] and was offered the option of being medically downgraded with a reduction in pay or a medical discharge with a small pension. He chose the latter.[12]

Nelson returned to Belfast and became a furniture van driver. He met his wife, May, in September 1970 in a local bar while a riot was going on outside, and they were married the following March. Wanting to 'defend Ulster', as he put it, he joined the UDA after it was established in September 1971 and was sworn in while sitting in the back seat of a car.[13] The UDA's declared goal was the defence of Protestant loyalist areas, but while combatting the Irish Republican Army (IRA) was part of that goal, its pursuit of this was blatantly tribal, with the murder of some 431 victims, the vast majority Catholics.[14] Because he'd been in the regular army, Nelson was soon put in charge of weapons training for the West Belfast UDA. The weapons available were self-loading rifles, sub-machine guns, handguns and a few antiques.[15]

Particularly terrifying for Catholics in the 1970s was the ever-present risk of being abducted and taken to a room above a pub or drinking club, where the victim would learn they were to be 'rompered' – played with, as the term suggests, though not in the carefree manner of boisterous children but in a drawn-out, sadistic ritual of torture, sometimes as a precursor to their murder. On 25 March 1973, two young UDA assailants, one aged seventeen, the other eighteen, led by 'Major' Nelson, then twenty-five, went hunting for Catholic prey. They found forty-two-year-old Gerry Higgins, who was so poorly sighted that he was registered as blind, walking past North Queen Street police station. The father of five, who enjoyed crooning Bing Crosby songs in his spare time, was bundled into a car at gunpoint and taken to a drinking den in the Shankill area.[16] There, he was pistol-whipped, his hair set on fire, and he was electrocuted. His hands were wetted before electrodes were attached and electric shocks administered by turning the handle of a box – the quicker the turn, the greater the shock.

The ringleader of this gang was reported in court to be 'Major' Brian Nelson,[17] not playing only a 'peripheral role', as his barrister Desmond Boal QC would plead two decades later when Nelson was in court as a state agent having been charged with multiple murders and conspiracies to murder.[18] His conduct was at odds with how he had been brought up, as Nelson later acknowledged. 'My father had many Catholic friends,' Nelson told me in 1991. 'As kids, if we had used the word Fenian we'd have got a cuff round the head.'[19]

Higgins pleaded with his torturers that he had a heart condition and begged to be allowed to take his medication. This was refused, and he suffered a heart attack.[20] 'People will be reading about you in the papers in the morning, but you will not be one of them,' his captors told him, before taking him outside and attempting to bundle him into a car. By good fortune, a patrol of the Coldstream Guards was passing and arrested them, then handed them over to the police.[21] Higgins was taken to hospital, where he was not expected to live. His son Gary recalled visiting him there: 'His face was black and blue and covered in burn marks, and to see that just terrified me.'[22] While Higgins did survive, his daughter Elaine says he 'never recovered from this horrendous ordeal. His life was left in tatters, his faith in humanity destroyed.'[23]

It seems very likely that had it not been for the soldiers, Higgins would have been taken to a place where he could safely be shot. Nelson's seventeen-year-old accomplice was found to have a 0.22 revolver in his waistband, along with nine bullets.[24] Despite this, the charge of conspiracy to murder against Nelson was dropped and he was fortunate to get a relatively light sentence of seven years.

On 10 August 1977, Nelson was released from jail and, according to Special Branch, 'avoided contact with the UDA and lived a quiet lifestyle' until 4 May 1984, when, 'after a lot of soul searching', he telephoned Lisburn garrison, offering to work for military intelligence by rejoining the UDA and reporting on their activities.[25] His future handlers recorded that, having been a 'major' in the UDA and having served time for kidnapping and possession of a firearm, Nelson was assessed as having 'the right pedigree for reinvolvement. At present his access is limited to low-level "eyes and ears" information from friends.'[26]

That would soon change. After a mere month-long assessment, the FRU took on Nelson as an agent and gave him a code number: 5054.[27] His spymasters knew that he was working the double by driving for a skip hire firm while also claiming the dole. Even so, they raised his weekly payment for handler meets from £10 to £15, describing him as 'security conscious'.[28] That too would change. At a wedding reception in February 1985, with his sister Carole, who was extremely drunk, he telephoned the FRU asking to be patched through to his handler, whereupon he put his drunken sister on the phone. Whether this was to impress her, or as a prank, is unclear, but it was an early sign of his reckless approach to security. At his weekly handler meeting, Nelson was given a dressing down, but his weekly retainer nonetheless rose to £25.[29]

Such drunken episodes would become a feature of Nelson's reporting and carried a serious risk of him blurting out his clandestine role to fellow UDA members or even some random person. The following month, having antagonised several members of the Ulster Volunteer Force (UVF) as he left a Saturday night party, he was beaten up. The FRU record doesn't say what triggered this, but judging by the ferocity of the fracas, drink may well have played a part again. As Nelson and his wife, May, walked down the garden path, he was dragged to the ground by the hair from behind, then beaten about the head and face. May, rather courageously, tried to fend off his attacker before her brother came to the rescue. Nelson suffered cuts and bruising around the nose and eyes.[30] His wife appears to have been more of a scrapper than him, losing three teeth and being badly bruised in another fracas later that year, when she again came to her husband's rescue and received a 'kicking whilst trying to defend him'. Fortunately, her missing teeth were 'not her front teeth', a handler observed.[31]

This pattern of life would have been familiar in the raucous, densely populated, drink-fuelled world of the Shankill in the 1970s, replete with patriotic graffiti paying homage to the Crown. Nevertheless, Nelson was generating a great deal of trust with the UDA leadership. He earned kudos by using his regular army experience to become one of three instructors for the UDA 'Silver Wings' course – the training up of a militia of fighters in preparation for a doomsday scenario whereby Britain would finally lose patience with this restive corner of the United Kingdom and leave Northern

Ireland to its fate.[32] For that summer's training course, he ordered twenty-five pairs of boots and training shoes.[33] Included on the course were some of the UDA's most active gunmen, including Johnny Adair, Matt Kincaid and William 'Winkie' Dodds.[34] Dodds was revered in the UDA as 'The Big Evil'; he was certainly evil and also very obese.

In April 1985, when Nelson was asked by his UDA bosses to join them on a recce of potential targets to bomb in the Irish Republic, his handlers encouraged him to go, despite Nelson being 'slightly worried' he might get caught by the Garda Síochána. He was reassured that the trip would 'only increase his standing amongst UDA hierarchy', as indeed it did.[35] And his standing had been rising. The previous month, he had been appointed UDA intelligence officer for West Belfast.[36] By May, his FRU code number had changed from 5054 to 6137.[37]

Nelson had been taken into the confidence of the UDA leadership to such an extent that in May 1985 they entrusted him with a mission to Durban, South Africa, to buy weapons from ARMSCOR, the army procurement agency of the then apartheid regime.[38] On his return, his handler remarked that he seemed 'tired and withdrawn and under pressure'. Nelson appeared to 'want to get away from it all', which perhaps was not a surprise since the trip had been a bit of a disaster.[39] Ignoring his host's advice to avoid walking at night on unlit streets, Nelson had promptly been mugged taking a shortcut back to his hotel. When he fought back, he was stabbed in the shoulder and lost his watch and glasses.[40] He also told his handlers that, while in South Africa, he was treated in hospital for venereal disease, presumably acquired from an ill-advised sexual liaison.[41] As for the purchase of an arsenal of 9mm pistols, assault rifles and an automatic shotgun called the 'Striker' designed for bush warfare, which Nelson thought would be perfect for 'house-cleaning operations' in Belfast, nothing came of it.[42]

On his return to Belfast, Nelson met the UDA's two top leaders – Andy Tyrie, the UDA's self-styled 'supreme commander', and John McMichael, a UDA 'brigadier' – in Tyrie's summer holiday caravan in Newtownards.[43] Tyrie, McMichael and their fellow UDA commanders were satirised by Special Branch as 'The Doomsday Boys' because they would go off to Tyrie's caravan for the weekend, 'convince each other they are about to be overrun, then they'd come back on a Sunday and get totally drunk. And nothing much would happen.'[44] They blew hot and cold on the weapons shipment too. Having told Nelson before his trip to Durban that the money was there, they now told him it wasn't there after all. Any shipment would likely have been a waste of money anyway. Had it gone ahead, there were plans in hand to intercept the weapons en route to Northern Ireland.[45]

One of Nelson's jobs was to drive UDA members to collect protection money from building sites.[46] Uncomfortable at having to be part of the extortion team, he fretted that he might be caught by the RUC.[47] That possibility was also causing his handlers some anguish, and an incident in the summer of 1985 shows why. The anti-racketeering squad had persuaded a courageous director of a joinery firm to covertly tape a meeting with the UDA, which the RUC had asked him to arrange in the hope of secretly recording admissions of the UDA's extortionate demands. The director was terrified the tape might make a clunk after half an hour, because that's what had happened on the test run when it switched off. The recorder was also weighing down one side of his jacket, where it was secreted in the pocket. The detective chief inspector running the operation suggested he weigh his other pocket down with an extra clip of ammunition for the personal protection weapon he'd been licensed to carry. Adding to the director's anxiety, he caught a glimpse from the meeting place of an RUC photographer in an upstairs window of a nearby building and fretted that the UDA might see him too. Still, he secured a rich batch of admissions, including those, as he recalled, from a man who 'resembled Nelson and who talked about "how I needed to protect my Catholic workers"'. Fortunately for Nelson, the entire exercise turned out to be a futile waste of time because the tape failed to work.[48] One UDA gangster, James Pratt Craig, involved in extortion was so confident he was untouchable that he would make veiled threats in person to the detective chief inspector running the anti-racketeering squad.[49]

Of course, Nelson's greatest collision with the law was his role in targeting republicans for assassination, into which the UDA was increasingly drawing him. According to him, the UDA had some 200 index card files on potential targets, and targeting was conducted very much on a 'hit and miss basis and resembled the actions of a headless chicken'.[50] One morning the 200 index cards 'mysteriously' appeared at the UDA's Shankill Road office, 'ostensibly' for Nelson's use, and he spent some time trying to update them by cross-referencing the details with the electoral register, Kelly's street directory and the telephone book.[51]

John McMichael, then commanding the UDA's South Belfast Brigade, wanted to upload the information on these index cards to a central computer installed at the UDA's Gawn Street headquarters in East Belfast. Nelson was told that targets from the UDA's four 'brigades' – North, South, East and West – were to be fed into this computer. All updates would be fed back to each of the four brigades, so that all brigades would have a full picture. As the intelligence officer for West Belfast, Nelson was given funds to purchase the computer.[52]

At first, Nelson's computer was housed at the UDA's West Belfast office, which made it impossible for him to share the intelligence with his FRU handlers. However, he managed to persuade the West Belfast commander, Tommy 'Tucker' Lyttle, to allow him to take the computer home and work on it from there, which meant he could share 'his own information for targeting by the UDA' with his handlers without risk of being caught.[53] To what end, however, is unclear. Over the four and a half years that Nelson was active as an FRU agent, there is little in the FRU files to show that his intelligence was exploited for saving lives, the FRU's main justification for its existence. When this intelligence was passed on to Special Branch – as it usually was, albeit only occasionally in sufficient detail to be actioned – the branch rarely acted on it by ensuring those being targeted were warned or by interdiction from the security forces flooding an area where an attack was planned. Nelson's pre-eminent purpose seems to have been to help satisfy the insatiable intelligence gatherers' appetite for 'building a picture', in which every piece of the intelligence jigsaw was seen as an essential contribution to countering the insurgency – the template MI5 had inherited from the Cold War.[54] 'Building pictures' became a Special Branch mantra especially, and it was often judged to be more important than locking people up, although it is only fair to note that very many people were locked up.

On 1 August 1985 came the inevitable: the British state, in the person of Agent 6137, was required by members of the UDA – whom his handlers had tasked him to get alongside – to engage in a series of conspiracies to murder. Nelson was ordered by Lyttle to draw up a list of Sinn Féin councillors to target for assassination. The IRA's 'Armalite and ballot box' policy was on the march, its political wing (Sinn Féin) having won seven Belfast city council seats in the previous May's local elections, one ahead of the nationalist Social Democratic and Labour Party (SDLP), which opposed violence.[55] This marked the start of what, in the years to come, would be an irreversible shift within Northern Ireland's nationalist population from the SDLP to Sinn Féin. As a first step in his role, Nelson was to supply photographs of potential targets to help the gun team identify their prey. Lyttle also made it clear that the final choice of targets was a matter for Nelson. 'A difficult position for 6137 to find himself in,' observed the FRU dryly.[56]

In the event, it appears that Lyttle chose the first target: a Sinn Féin politician who had stood in the elections, a docker called Harry Fitzsimmons, aged forty-seven and a father of four.[57] The UDA assassin 'Winkie' Dodds – sometimes known as 'Stinky Winkie' due to his malodorous personal habits, in preference to his other nom de guerre 'The Big Evil'[58] – had established that Fitzsimmons had a clockwork-like routine: at 7.30 a.m. on the button every morning he'd open the door of his ground-floor apartment in the Unity Flats complex, North Belfast, to a friend. Both men would then leave for work at the docks, with Fitzsimmons calling at a newsagent's just around the corner.[59] The plan was for Dodds to imitate the 'friend' by knocking on the door at 7.20 a.m. First, though, he wanted Nelson to make 'certain that he had the right person'.[60] On the morning of 17 September, Nelson went into the newsagents to buy cigarettes. As he left, he 'all but bumped' into Fitzsimmons, who had just entered the shop. The individual Nelson identifies in his journal as the 'commander' of the UFF, Eric McKee, a position corroborated by numerous references in Sir Desmond de Silva's report (albeit under the acronym 'L/28'), said he was 'delighted' at Nelson's confirmation and told Nelson he was now looking for a silencer to give Dodds.[61]

Ten days later Dodds arrived on the pillion of a motorcycle, rang Fitzsimmons' bell at 7.20 a.m. and, when Fitzsimmons opened the door, shot him in the chest, shoulder and hand – 'blood pumping everywhere' as Dodds later recounted proudly to Nelson, adding with relish that he 'was just lying there, screaming, "get me a priest, get me a priest"'.[62] As Dodds jumped back on the bike, it stalled, so the pair had to push-start it, laughing as they sped away, according to witnesses.[63] Back at UDA headquarters, Nelson was with McKee when the morning news bulletins reported the shooting. 'McKee was ecstatic,' said Nelson, 'he was over the moon.'[64]

By the time of the shooting, the FRU had sent seven Military Intelligence Source Reports (MISRs) to Special Branch on the developing threat to Fitzsimmons' life, including one warning that the UDA had confirmed his daily morning routine.[65] While obvious to Special Branch that a murder attempt was imminent, no effort was made by the police to prevent the attack or even to warn Fitzsimmons. But this was not uncommon where threats to life of members and associates of armed groups were concerned, most especially republicans, because the protection of agents – or 'source protection' as it was known – was afforded such a high priority, and, if the intelligence services were going to risk compromising a valuable human asset, they weren't going to expend the capital on supporters and activists of terrorist organisations that wanted them dead anyway. Fortunately for Fitzsimmons, he survived.

In his 2012 forensic review of the activities of the FRU, the late Sir Desmond de Silva QC, a distinguished criminal barrister and international lawyer, found that prioritising the protection of all agents – including those who had gone rogue (as Nelson would) – instead of withdrawing them, was a feature not just of the FRU but also of Special Branch and MI5.[66] This meant 'playing God' with the lives not just of members of a terrorist group but also of their supporters who were being targeted. It was these latter recesses of the moral maze into which the agencies had ventured that became increasingly hard to justify.

Many of the debacles or moral compromises (depending on your preference) associated with source protection – such as the failure to both prevent and investigate crimes during the conflict, including murder – can be traced back to Britain's counter-insurgency strategy in the Northern Ireland conflict undergoing a radical change in 1981 on the recommendation of a senior MI5 officer, Patrick Walker. From February that year, intelligence gathering was given pre-eminence over the criminal justice system, an 'unhelpful separation', as diplomatically adjudged today by the current PSNI chief constable, Jon Boutcher.[67] The fatal shooting in November 1982 by undercover police of Michael Tighe (17), in a hayshed used by the IRA to store explosives, graphically illustrates why.

Unknown to Detective Chief Superintendent George Jackson, who was in charge of the Criminal Investigation Department (CID) investigation into Tighe's shooting, MI5 had installed a listening device in the hayshed. Jackson was told by Special Branch officers junior to him that the crime scene would be out of bounds even to him for ninety minutes. In that time the listening device was removed, effectively extracting the evidence that no warning had been given to the boy before he was shot, despite the officers who shot him claiming otherwise in statements on the instructions of Special Branch.

Although branch officers were busy at the scene, their presence or purpose was not questioned. Moreover, Jackson did not attend the post-mortem, 'where valuable and significant information should have been gleaned regarding the trajectories of the bullets fatal to Tighe'. The officers who fired the shots and their weapons were not made immediately available to members of the CID; instead, they were debriefed by Special Branch officers before CID could conduct any interviews. Cartridge cases generated by the shooting were not recovered at the scene and appear to have been removed by officers not from the investigating CID team.[68]

In short, the unintended consequence of Walker's radical recommendation in 1981 – that CID become subordinate to Special Branch – led in many notable cases to the corruption of the criminal justice system. It certainly led to a vast amount of intelligence being gathered, much of it never acted upon because it was withheld from the CID, so much so that, in the view of Jon Boutcher, the RUC became 'deskilled'.[69] Walker later became director general of MI5,[70] but the legacy of unsolved crimes involving state agents that his changes bequeathed extends to the present day, as set out by Boutcher in March 2024 in his interim report on Operation Kenova's investigation into the FRU agent codenamed Stakeknife.[71]

With the RUC's decisive separation of Special Branch from CID, came an acceleration of agent recruitment. Over the two decades that followed, hundreds more agents went onto the books, mostly for Special Branch but also for the FRU and MI5. During the third investigation by Sir John (now Lord) Stevens into alleged 'collusion' between state agents and proscribed loyalist and republican organisations, one of his detectives asked for the number of registered informants currently in north-west Belfast. The figure returned was 110.[72] So faithfully was the Walker doctrine applied that, for the most part, the preservation of these sources overrode criminality and sometimes even life itself.

Prioritising source protection meant that intelligence about very serious crimes was often withheld from CID detectives for fear that it might compromise the source's cover. The former police ombudsman, Baroness Nuala O'Loan, has given her assessment of the cost of this legacy: 'hundreds and hundreds and hundreds of people died because those people were not brought to justice and weren't stopped in their tracks'.[73]

Under Walker, the CID was required to hand over agent running to the branch, as well as to pass on potential agents for recruitment. The branch was also to be involved in deciding if a suspect should be charged with a criminal offence, even if they had admitted it, in case they were a recruitment intelligence prospect. Moreover, all arrests had to be checked with the branch to ensure that no police, FRU or MI5 agents were involved. The way Walker was interpreted led to a 'cabal of Special Branch self-interest that was fiercely resistant to any form of scrutiny or oversight based on claims about a paramount need for secrecy'.[74] Inevitably, this led to state agents breaking the law on a grand scale but, at the time, the agencies saw no alternative. 'You weren't going to get intelligence on terrorists from milkmaids,' as Ray White, the former head of Special Branch in Belfast put it. 'If asked to plant a bomb, you can't say, "I'll make the tea, but I don't do bombs."'[75] He has a powerful point.

Yet in public, the mantra repeated through the second half of the conflict by prime ministers and chief constables alike was that the counter-insurgency was all about establishing the rule of law for everyone.[76] Sir Jack Hermon, chief constable throughout the 1980s, couldn't have put the position more clearly when I pressed him in 1992 for a BBC *Panorama* programme:

> JW: Might there not be circumstances sometimes, occasionally, when it really is impossible to save a life, because if you do act on the information, the finger of suspicion will automatically fall on the informant, and you blow his cover?
>
> JH: If cover were blown in those circumstances, then he has to be given a new identity. But there cannot be the use of the word impossibility to prevent murder. There cannot be.
>
> JW: It is always possible to try and prevent it?
>
> JH: Yes, it must be so. It must be so.
>
> JW: It is never justifiable in your judgement, to allow a crime of that kind to take place to protect an agent?

JH: It cannot be justified to allow that crime to take place.

JW: If the threat is against a known, active member of the Provisional IRA, might that not be a temptation to let that go? Should it be? Is it understandable?

JH: I don't think we're talking about temptations. We're talking about the rule of law and its application.[77]

Yet in the decades both before and after Walker, the record shows that exceptions to the rule of law were made time and time again by the intelligence services, including Special Branch.

To the extent that police guidelines on agent handling existed, they dated back to a 1969 Home Office circular drawn up for 'criminals in a mainland context, rather than for coping with terrorists'. These required agents to 'never counsel, incite, or procure a crime' and to participate only if the agent didn't 'engage in planning and committing it'. Even then, they were to be involved only if, by 'playing a minor role', it would result in arrests before anyone was harmed.[78]

The guidance for FRU handlers and agents was entirely contradicted by the practice: on the one hand a 1986 directive from the commander of land forces (CLF) said, 'All operations are to be conducted within the Law and members of the FRU remain subject to Military and Civilian Law at all times'.[79] Moreover, 'Instructions for Source Control and Handling in Northern Ireland' stated, 'It is unlawful for any person to authorise an illegal act …'[80] Yet the mere fact of recruiting an agent to become a member of a proscribed organisation was a breach of the CLF's directive, never mind their targeting people for assassination or, as in other cases, storing weapons or, say, going on a bomb run – all tasks in which the most deeply embedded agents would sooner or later find they had to participate.

As for MI5, a former head of the service in Northern Ireland told me that of the three intelligence-gathering agencies, MI5 was the most ethical 'by a stretch'.[81] There is evidence that MI5 paid more observance to the law, with 'elements of reasonable oversight' and 'legal input and governance', than either Special Branch or the FRU.[82] That said, when Sir Patrick Walker went on to become MI5's director general, he made it clear that he did not consider the service to be bound by the 1969 Home Office guidelines,[83] although de

Silva reported that MI5 lawyers in practice provided regular advice and guidance on agent-running operations, something apparently not readily available to the FRU or Special Branch in the 1980s.[84]

In a journal written by Nelson in 1991, while he was awaiting trial for murder and other serious crimes, he invites us to believe that his first intimate encounter with the murderous consequences of his role as a state agent – the cold-blooded attempt to assassinate Harry Fitzsimmons – caused him to have 'serious doubts' about continuing to work for the FRU. 'I didn't feel so good about the whole affair,' he wrote. He'd hoped 'possibly something would be done to pre-empt' the attack and that at his next meeting with Sergeant Mick Brown, his FRU handler, Brown had sensed his 'subdued' mood as they fished side by side for trout on the banks of the picturesque Six Mile Water, a County Antrim river that is in fact twenty-six miles long and flows into Lough Neagh.[85]

Sir Desmond de Silva QC didn't buy this. In his review, he said he was 'inclined to treat as highly suspect any doubts on [Nelson's] part as to the morality of what he was engaged in.'[86] As de Silva notes, there was no reference in the contemporaneous FRU files reflecting the misgivings Nelson claimed he hoped Sergeant Brown had picked up on during their fishing trip; Nelson makes this claim some six years later in his highly exculpatory journal. Just a decade before his alleged 'misgivings' over Fitzsimmons, as the leader of a romper room gang he'd been prepared to take the partially blind Gerry Higgins to his death after torturing him, yet in his journal Nelson suggests that the Fitzsimmons attack drove him to 'search for a way out' of his life as a spy.[87] When the opportunity arose a month later, with a job offer in Germany as a floor layer at a new BMW plant, he wrote, 'I was more than grateful for this timely offer.' At his next meet with Sergeant Brown, Nelson informed him he was bidding goodbye to Belfast.[88]

FRU records tell a different story as to Nelson's motive for leaving Belfast. They are extremely detailed and, in my view, broadly credible as a contemporaneous record of Nelson's exchanges with his handlers. They show that the contract in Germany being offered to him was worth almost £50,000 in today's money – several times more than he was netting from the FRU, the dole and odd skip-driving jobs. Between May 1984 and October 1985, his income from the FRU was today's equivalent of approximately

£6,000 in retainers over the course of sixty handler meets. Financially, there was no contest between staying in Belfast and moving to Germany, which presumably explains why his wife, May, 'urged him to take the job'.[89]

It is also clear that, despite leaving, Nelson wanted to keep a foot in the FRU, since their records document him telling his UDA bosses that he eventually intended to return to the UDA, his 'ultimate goal' being to 'become a member of its Inner Council when this opportunity arose'.[90] It was a goal the FRU fully expected him to achieve, since he had 'the brains to outshine the majority of UDA members'.[91] Given that within nine months, Nelson had managed to work his way up to being 'the most trusted intelligence officer in West Belfast', the FRU assessed that 'in the present political and military climate access and scope for development is high'.[92]

The 'climate' being referenced by the FRU was the instability generated by fierce loyalist opposition to the Anglo-Irish Agreement, which the British and Irish prime ministers had signed in November 1985, a month after Nelson had decided to leave Belfast. The Agreement granted the Irish government a consultative role in Northern Ireland on matters relating to security, legal affairs, politics and cross-border co-operation, and it enraged loyalists. 'Never, never, never, never …' bellowed the Reverend Ian Paisley outside Belfast City Hall to 100,000 protesting loyalists.[93] Just days earlier, the then secretary of state for Northern Ireland, Tom King, was physically attacked by loyalists as he arrived for a function at Belfast City Hall.[94] In December, all fifteen Unionist MPs resigned their seats at Westminster. Menace was in the air. Both the FRU and the UDA were desperate to retain Nelson's services, the former to report on the UDA's plans to destabilise the province, the latter to exploit that opportunity.[95]

By Christmas the FRU was actively trying to persuade Nelson to leave the job in Germany he'd started just two months earlier. So too was the UDA, whose leaders Andy Tyrie and John McMichael had been 'stunned' by his departure, telling him there would always be a job for him on his return.[96] Despite the greater remuneration his new German job was providing, Nelson appears to have been seriously tempted to give it up. According to FRU records, he suggested he might 'stage an accident which would render him useless and forcing his firm to send him home'. The FRU ruled this out as being impractical, because it 'could result in serious injury to the source'.

Instead, it suggested that if he couldn't come up with a better story, he should 'bluff a back injury, which normally cannot be proved one way or the other'. Meanwhile, the FRU offered him 'an attractive financial package', which persuaded Nelson to give his verbal agreement to return early in 1986, by which time, he said, he would be entitled to a rebate from the German exchequer for the tax he had paid.[97]

When, just after Christmas 1985, Nelson told Eric McKee that he'd be back in Belfast by March 1986, McKee's 'eyes lit up', telling him that the UDA's intelligence had 'gone downhill' since he'd left.[98] It was McKee who had constantly selected him for targeting because, based on Nelson's key role in the attempted murder of Harry Fitzsimmons, he 'knows he gets results'.[99]

The irony is that, at this stage, the FRU does not appear to have wanted Nelson to actively engage in targeting but instead limit his role to simply being the repository for intelligence files. Their records show that in his first phase of employment, his handlers had quite properly sought to minimise his criminality. A week after the Fitzsimmons attack, the FRU noted McKee had 'led him into acts of conspiracy which neither he nor the handler are happy with'.[100] Debriefed in the rear of a blue Renault Trafic van over drinks and snacks, Nelson had told his handler that McKee wanted him to target another Sinn Féin councillor, Paddy McManus. This had brought 'a stern rebuke' from the handler, a message that was repeated the following week.[101] When his handlers learned that he had passed the names of potential targets to the UVF, he was told not to do 'this again or anything similar unless told to do so by his UDA commanders'.[102]

Despite Nelson having undertaken to return to Belfast early in 1986, in the event it would be a whole year before he returned to the FRU. When he did, a very different regime awaited him. He was now to be actively encouraged to 'professionalise' the UDA's targeting. Unlike his previous spymasters, the FRU was also no longer troubled by him disseminating his targeting files to other loyalist death squads, such as the UVF and Red Hand Commando, because he hoped their assassination attempts might succeed where his UDA comrades had failed.

The stage was now set for the British Army's rendezvous with one of the most disastrous agent-running operations of the conflict.

Chapter Two

6137 – 'Bitten by a bug'

THE FRU WAS COUNTING ON Nelson's new handler, Warrant Officer Ronnie Anderson, to ensure that Nelson kept his promise to give up his well-paid job as a floor layer in Germany and return to Belfast by March 1986.[1] As a fellow Ulsterman, they hoped Anderson's 'friendship and a combination of ex-military and Irish protestant propinquity' would generate a bond between the two men.[2] Privately, Anderson sensed that Agent 6137 was not reliable agent material who would respond obediently to handling.[3] That disquiet was reinforced when March came and went with no word from Nelson.

On 1 April, Anderson telephoned Nelson at his home in Belfast to see if he'd actually returned. Satisfied that the voice answering was Nelson's, because he gave the correct code as protocol required on an insecure line, Anderson waited for his agent to return the call using the FRU's 'reverse contact procedure'. But no call came.[4]

Over the next few days Anderson telephoned the same number but got no further answer until the seventh day, when the phone was answered by a man who gave his name as David Creighton, Nelson's brother-in-law. 'You're too late, Brian has been and gone,' said Creighton. 'Who are you anyway?' Anderson passed himself off as 'Ronnie Watson', saying he and Nelson had done some casual HGV driving in the past. Creighton said that Nelson had no plans to return until the summer.[5]

The FRU had unwisely taken Nelson at his word without bothering to get his German telephone number from him, although they had his address in

Neutraubling, the Bavarian town in southern Germany to which he'd moved. A call to international directory enquiries bore no fruit. The unit was forced to conclude that something had caused Nelson to have a change of heart, but it didn't know what.[6] The pressure was on to get him back. Loyalist opposition to the Anglo-Irish Agreement was growing and there was widespread loyalist intimidation, with paramilitaries increasing attacks on Catholics and mobs in Portadown attacking Catholic homes.[7] RUC officers were also being attacked and even shot at.[8] Although the FRU had some hundred agents in republican armed groups, they had zero coverage on the loyalist side now that their only agent inside the UDA seemed to have done a runner.[9] The FRU was determined to find out why Nelson had changed his mind; moreover MI5 was also now showing an interest in recruiting him, Nelson having impressed them with intelligence-gathering missions with which MI5 had tasked him in 1985.[10]

On 21 May, a member of MI5 and Nelson's previous handler, Sergeant Mick Brown, who knew Nelson better than Ronnie Anderson, flew to Munich. There they hired a car and drove north to Regensburg, where they found a hotel. Their itinerary proudly records that a 'substantial meal was consumed'.[11] First stop the following day was the large BMW car plant in Regensburg, where Nelson was laying the floor for a new extension. The plan was for the two operatives to approach him away from his family because they knew his wife, May, had no idea that he'd spent most of the previous two years spying for the British Army.

Unfortunately for them, the BMW factory was vast and the odds of spotting Nelson leaving work were tiny, so the two men abandoned that option and drove the ten kilometres to Neutraubling, where they took up positions in the garden of a café opposite the entrance to the block of flats where he was living. They hoped to catch him as he got home, but with no sign of him arriving by 7.30 p.m., Sergeant Brown decided to check if he was already home. He pressed the bell next to Nelson's name plate, hoping he would answer, but as he climbed the stairs he instead came face to face with May, whom the two intrepid spies had been trying to avoid. May was waiting outside the flat with one of her sons for the mystery visitor who'd rung the bell. Brown pretended to have got the wrong apartment and continued climbing the stairs. Rejoining his MI5 colleague in the car a few minutes later, they concluded that meeting Nelson on his own was 'virtually impossible'. The mission was aborted, and they flew back to London none the wiser as to why 6137 had appeared to go cold on them and noting dolefully that he 'does possess the potential to go far should he return and carry on from where he left off'.[12]

The truth is that Nelson and May had decided to give Germany a go. They were enjoying a lifestyle and standard of living that Belfast couldn't match, and, as Nelson later wrote, 'our future in Germany was secure in every sense'.[13] Judging by what Nelson's sister Carole had to say, it was easy to see why. The family had become 'very well established in Germany and had a beautiful apartment. They had lovely neighbours. The children were at good schools. They were doing very well. Obviously, she had no desire to come back to Belfast.' May had also been learning German.[14]

There the matter rested until December 1986, when a new commanding officer (CO) was appointed to run the FRU, a Scotsman, Lieutenant Colonel Gordon Kerr, who was well versed in the darker arts of espionage. As a rising star in the Intelligence Corps, between December 1979 and February 1982 he had served as the commander of an intelligence-gathering detachment along the border, which won him the Queen's Gallantry Medal.[15] During that tour, Kerr is said to have 'gravitated towards' a legendary Special Branch officer in Southern Region, Detective Superintendent Frank Murray, who, in 1975, as a detective sergeant had lost a leg, a hand and an eye when a booby-trapped desk he opened exploded, injuring him and killing his colleague.[16] Despite his injuries, Murray was renowned for his boundless energy and was crowned the 'bionic man' by admiring colleagues. In exchange for access to Murray's extensive network of intelligence, Kerr was sometimes able to facilitate Murray's access to the Special Air Service (SAS).[17] Kerr had not, however, endeared himself to senior members of the RUC. Assistant Chief Constable (ACC) Wilf Monahan is said to have intervened when he heard that Kerr wanted to dig up the graveyard of a church in the town where Monahan lived to search for weapons.[18]

After leaving Northern Ireland, Kerr became a frontline Cold War warrior in Berlin, taking command of 3 Intelligence and Security Company (3 Int & Sy Coy), whose job during the Cold War was to protect British forces within the British sector of Berlin from penetration by Soviet and

East German agents. Under his command, the 'Three I-Spy', as 3 Int & Sy Coy was known, is reported to have conducted more 'flag tours' – secret intelligence-gathering missions – than the Berlin-based French and US military intelligence missions combined. Kerr was 'pointlessly aggressive and confrontational', one officer who served with him is reported to have said.[19]

News of Kerr's return to Belfast in late 1986 was greeted by the RUC hierarchy with foreboding. Senior officers were told to avoid social functions with him. At that level he was in effect persona non grata, such was his reputation from his earlier days along the Irish border. Even elements in Special Branch mistrusted him. 'Once SB [Special Branch] stopped trusting you, you became the enemy,' as the former RUC head of CID, Detective Chief Superintendent Eric Anderson, put it.[20] A former head of Special Branch in Belfast eventually refused to have him in his office.[21] Former RUC Chief Constable Sir Jack Hermon also told me that one of his deputy chief constables who had dealings with Kerr in the early 1980s had called him a 'liar, cheat, manipulator' with 'no integrity in his approach'.[22] To the head of RUC Special Branch, the late ACC Brian Fitzsimons, Kerr was a dangerous 'crusader'.[23] A 'dour Scot' was how an officer senior to Kerr saw him: 'Not exactly the kind of person you'd ask to a diner party for entertainment. But clever.'[24]

In contrast, his own soldiers were unstinting in their admiration of Kerr. The following sample of comments are a fair reflection of the respect in which he was held: a 'superb man';[25] an 'extremely good bloke, well-liked by everyone';[26] 'very personable' and 'ambitious';[27] 'probably the closest thing to James Bond';[28] 'very professional';[29] the 'best commanding officer the FRU has had'.[30] FRU operatives liked his talk of 'taking the war to the enemy'.[31] According to former FRU handler Ian Hurst, 'We had an email go round and ask us to detail what kit we needed to make our job easier … Resources were there, plentiful. Basically, the unwritten guidance given by Kerr is that the gloves are off.'[32]

Whatever the truth about digging up graves and the like, Kerr's grasp of the complexities of agent running in Northern Ireland, judging from his extremely detailed statements, suggest a highly astute individual, at least on paper. In practice, however, the way he appears to have allowed Nelson to be run was a mess. According to the first of John Stevens' three inquiries into FRU agent running, under Kerr's command Nelson became an 'agent provocateur', recommending targets to be shot by 'close quarter assassination squads', partly as a consequence of Nelson's terms of reference not having been 'clearly defined' and his handlers not having been trained in the 'complexity of law in dealing with, and supervising agents'.[33]

Money seems to have been no object when it came to Kerr's determination to re-recruit Nelson from Germany. At a meeting with MI5, Kerr said he was prepared to offer Nelson a 'sizeable financial incentive' and instructed FRU Operations Officer Major David Haydock and the East Det FRU commander, Captain Peter Simpson, to start preparing one.[34] Meanwhile Ronnie Anderson was told to try and contact Nelson again. This time he succeeded,[35] persuading Nelson to fly back for a meeting in London on 14 January 1987.[36] He promised 'a good day out at the expense of the firm'.[37]

Greeting Nelson at Heathrow were Simpson and Anderson, who drove him to the nearby Excelsior Hotel. There they were joined by a member of MI5, Richard Marshall.[38] From the hotel, Nelson phoned his wife, lying to her that he'd had an early start and was away for the day running an errand for his American boss.[39] At the start of the meeting Nelson was 'quite adamant that he and his family were perfectly happy in Germany', but by the time he had to fly back to Germany that evening, after a 'substantial quantity of vodka', he 'appeared very keen on the idea of returning'. The FRU agents reported that although they hadn't met Nelson for a year, it was as if they'd never been out of touch; they found him 'easy going, amenable and likeable'. The meeting 'was enjoyed by the entire party,' reported Simpson.[40] The lights were turning green.

Boarding the aircraft for his return to Germany, having been 'awash' with drink for several hours at the Excelsior, Nelson admitted to being 'totally intoxicated'.[41] Once back, he soon decided that if he didn't return to Belfast, he was 'ducking out of the fight against terrorism', as yet oblivious to the role that the new FRU regime had in mind for him, which would mean that he himself would be playing an active role in terrorism. As to the guilt he claimed to have felt for his part in the Harry Fitzsimmons shooting, he had somehow 'long since' absolved himself. The blame for that, he said, 'lay somewhere else' and, anyway, he was 'bitten by a (spying) bug', the explanation for which is worth quoting in full because it is one of the passages in Nelson's largely exculpatory journal that rings entirely true:

> … hooked is probably a more appropriate word. Working at the level at which I did within the organization, one became enmeshed in a web of intrigue, conspiracies, confidences, danger and the power of being aware of things that others around you want, the deadly game of working undercover and pitting your wits against those who seek you, who you seek to compromise, which, in my case, brought me into contact with both main protagonists. The list goes on, but this phenomenon acts like a drug, and the more you experience it, the more you want it, regardless of the moments of intense fear and terror.[42]

The immediate task that the FRU/MI5 set Nelson was to persuade May to return to Belfast. His journal perfectly articulates his dilemma: 'How does one tell one's wife or ask her to give up a nice apartment, a good job, a secure future, a comfortable lifestyle, to return to Belfast and to return to no job, no prospects, not to mention disrupting our sons' education all over again?'[43] How indeed, but Nelson's mind was made up. When he finally disclosed his secret life to May, she at first thought he was suffering from 'some sort of delusion', so he phoned Ronnie Anderson and said, 'Talk to her. She doesn't believe me.' Fortunately for Nelson he had a 'totally devoted wife', who, he says, told him: 'You know, I've never stood in your way no matter what you wanted to do. I've always stood by you and always will. And I would do, and I will do if you want to go back, just so long as you're sure it's what you want to do.'[44]

Delighted at the news, the FRU observed that Agent '6137 was pleased to be back in contact' and that his 'main motivating factors are his love of excitement which he gains from his involvement with this office … his work with this office does boost his ego'.[45] However, FRU records also suggest that Nelson's wife was not quite as on board as his journal suggests. On 6 February Nelson telephoned Anderson in Belfast and told him May wanted to speak to the FRU about the move. She asked Anderson to come to Germany the following weekend because she was looking for 'reassurance', afraid that her husband was using the FRU offer as an excuse to 'get back to his old friends in the UDA' for whom she seems to have had little time.[46] Kerr instructed Anderson and Simpson to get over to Germany the following weekend to placate her.

Kerr's decision to send them both without a member of MI5 triggered a monumental row with the service, which had been harbouring plans to recruit Nelson for itself. After meeting Nelson at the Excelsior hotel, on his day trip to Heathrow, MI5's Richard Marshall had told Colonel Kerr he'd been 'very impressed by 6137' and thought he had 'great potential'.[47] So did Kerr, who was utterly determined that the agent the FRU had recruited in the first place should continue to work 'solely under FRU direction'.[48] But MI5 was so determined to get a piece of the action that it was prepared to compromise by running him jointly with the FRU if it couldn't get him exclusively. This was despite experience having shown that joint handling was often problematic, with competing priorities over agent tasking. MI5 also harboured a barely concealed disdain for the army's agent-running operation, an attitude shared by Special Branch. Neither the branch nor MI5 were convinced of the army's need to run their own agents in the first place. For its part, the FRU dismissed MI5 as a 'small organisation with its fair share of officers of dubious quality'.[49]

One of the pervasive myths of the Northern Ireland conflict is that MI5 was omnipotent and could exercise control over both military intelligence and Special Branch. It is certainly true that since 2007, when MI5 assumed primary responsibility for national security intelligence in Northern Ireland, it has exercised through ministers a veto over the disclosure of classified material in the many conflict-legacy cases still coming before the civil and coronial courts more than a quarter of a century since the Good Friday Agreement. Also, from the 1980s, MI5's most senior officer in Northern Ireland, the director and coordinator of intelligence (DCI), has held the important role of setting the intelligence-gathering priorities for Special Branch and the FRU.[50] Nonetheless, in the 1980s, MI5 was still the junior intelligence-gathering partner, in the sense that it ran fewer agents than the army and police, and those it recruited were mainly tasked with building a strategic picture of the conflict, rather than delivering day-to-day tactical intelligence. All three agencies were also autonomous, which fuelled fierce institutional rivalry. The feud between MI5 and the FRU over Brian Nelson was a case in point.

The one card MI5 could play in their effort to appropriate Nelson as their agent was that the FRU CO Colonel Kerr needed the service's authority for his soldiers to meet an agent on foreign territory, since protocol between allies usually required the host intelligence service to be informed, in this case the German domestic intelligence agency, the Bundesamt für Verfassungsschutz (BfV). Kerr had instructed Captain Simpson to prepare to fly with Nelson's handler Ronnie Anderson to Germany on 13 February.[51] MI5 saw the opening and while telling Kerr that far be it for the service to be 'poaching', MI5 headquarters seems to have been scheming to do exactly that, having 'it in mind to offer 6137 full time employment'.[52] A territorial punch-up loomed as Kerr snapped back, 'I do consider that poaching.'[53]

MI5 offered a compromise: they would authorise the trip provided MI5's Richard Marshall replaced Simpson.[54] Kerr – rightly it would seem – saw this as a sly attempt to 'wrest control' of the case from the FRU. With Kerr's senior emissary excluded, he feared Marshall would have more influence with Nelson and his wife, so Kerr stuck to his guns: both Simpson and Anderson had to go, he insisted, and if Marshall wanted to tag along that was fine with him.[55] Playing for time, MI5 responded that in principle they approved, subject to Kerr submitting an 'operational plan for clearance' by MI5 headquarters.[56]

By Wednesday 11 February, Kerr still had not had MI5's answer, so he ordered Simpson and Anderson to confirm with Nelson that the weekend meeting would go ahead.[57] The next day, a senior member of MI5, Tony Rundell, came into Kerr's office and bluntly stated that he feared 'blood was going to be spilled' over the case.[58] Rundell then put his cards on the table: MI5 headquarters was 'extremely interested' in recruiting Nelson because it was thought he had 'great potential and might be able to work his way up to the top of the UDA and join MI5's three agents they had in place including one at the very top'.[59] Rundell said it made much more sense for Nelson to be run by MI5 because he would be in a position to provide vital 'strategic and political intelligence', which was MI5's principal intelligence-gathering role. Kerr wanted output from Nelson (known as 'product') too, but also the day-to-day tactical stuff: when, where and who would the UDA strike next?

Nonetheless, Rundell told Kerr he was sure Sir Patrick Walker, by then MI5's director general, would be able to 'put together a convincing case' for the service hiring Nelson and that 'he would probably succeed'.[60]

The row reached boiling point. In that case, blood would indeed be spilled, responded Kerr, and he emphasised that Nelson would be providing information of 'supreme interest to the army and RUC'.[61] (Events would prove otherwise; Nelson's product seems to have been of very little interest to the RUC, since Special Branch rarely acted upon it.)[62] Rundell then made it clear that MI5 would oppose the FRU even meeting with Nelson's wife, and it dawned on Kerr that the real game was for Marshall to secure Nelson's support for switching from the FRU to MI5 by personally selling the idea to her.[63]

Friday 13 February arrived with still no approval for the mission from MI5. Convinced that MI5 was deliberately stalling, Kerr decided to ignore this and ordered Simpson and Anderson to get on the plane to Munich. When the news reached Rundell, he was furious, telling Kerr he had broken all the rules, that Sir Patrick Walker was also 'very angry', and that he would be contacting the 'General', meaning Northern Ireland's CLF, Major General Tony Jeapes.[64] Too late, replied the wily Kerr. Jeapes had already been briefed and 'saw no reason' for MI5 to take over the case.[65]

For all his bristling machismo, however, Kerr knew that he had probably broken protocol by not having secured MI5's authority for a recruitment pitch on the soil of an ally. Knowing this, Kerr told MI5 that although Simpson and Anderson were now airborne, en route for Germany, they would not physically approach Nelson without clearance from MI5.[66] A second abortive FRU mission to Germany beckoned.

The row was descending into farce. Rundell said he didn't believe Kerr would keep to his word and neither did MI5 headquarters. Kerr replied that his soldiers would absolutely obey his orders and suggested that, instead of meeting Nelson, they should telephone him when they got to Germany as if they were speaking to him from the FRU office in Belfast.[67] Rundell countered that even that was breaking the rules.

Kerr later assured his immediate boss, the assistant chief of staff of Army Intelligence (ACOS G2), that Simpson had carried out his instruction not to meet Nelson[68] and had instead invited him and his wife by telephone to come to Belfast. Nelson said that would not be possible because they had no childcare, but he agreed to drive back to Belfast with his wife and sons the following weekend and stay for a week's holiday to catch up with friends and family.[69] However, Kerr's own statement four years later to the Stevens 1 Inquiry gave a different account, admitting that his soldiers had, in fact, met Nelson: 'One of my officers went to Munich where he had a meeting with Nelson and his wife and persuaded them to return,' wrote Kerr.[70] It seems Rundell's scepticism that Kerr would keep his word may have been justified.

Whatever the truth, the FRU had beaten off MI5, which reconciled itself to defeat, although the service would later attempt to rewrite history, claiming in 1993 that it considered Nelson's re-recruitment to be 'inadvisable'[71] – a thoroughly disingenuous statement from the head of MI5 in Northern Ireland, given the enthusiasm and guile with which his service had tried to get Nelson to spy for it, if not exclusively, then at least in partnership with the FRU. MI5 appears to have applied the 'retrospectoscope' by deciding Nelson's re-recruitment to have been inadvisable only when it realised it had dodged a bullet as it reflected on his three years of spectacular law-breaking, murder and multiple conspiracies to murder.

The control a handler has over their agent is tenuous at the best of times, but in Nelson's case, exercising this proved to be completely impossible – something that became obvious to the new FRU regime running him on his return to Belfast for a brief holiday to start organising with the FRU the logistics of rehiring him as an agent. On this trip to Belfast, so keen was Nelson to get stuck back into action that he also met up with Eric McKee, leader of what the FRU referred to as the UDA's 'Close Quarter Assassination' teams,[72] which used the UFF nom de guerre. The UDA was not proscribed until 1992, despite the fact that in practice it and UFF were 'one and the same', as former SDLP politician turned columnist Brian Feeney succinctly put it.[73] McKee was 'overjoyed' at the prospect of Nelson's return, while the UDA's West Belfast 'Brigadier' Tucker Lyttle's response was also 'more than favourable'.[74] 'There is no question,' observed the FRU, '6137 thoroughly enjoys the clandestine and exciting role as an agent for military intelligence. He has obviously missed this aspect of his life during his stay in the FRG [Federal Republic of Germany]. Indeed, it is almost certainly the single motivating factor in this case.'[75]

You could say that again. So excited at being back in the bosom of the FRU was Nelson that he suggested to Lyttle he might smuggle four handguns back to Belfast in the furniture he'd be moving from Germany. The response from Nelson's handlers was less than favourable. 'This over enthusiasm and self-tasking' and 'freelancing' would not be tolerated, the FRU told him.[76] And yet it was – on many more occasions to come.

The 'substantial' financial package offered by the FRU to Nelson to match the standard of living he'd enjoyed in Germany was considerable. It included:

- A new £22,000 home in Ballysillan, North Belfast, secured with a £2,200 deposit
- £1,000 initial furniture grant
- £4,000 to buy a taxi and Public Service Vehicle insurance, the taxi being his cover to engage in targeting operations in republican areas of the city (as Nelson had arrived back from Germany with a car made conspicuous by its left-hand drive)[77]
- £6,200 initial capital expenditure, plus removal expenses
- £200 weekly payments (the equivalent of around £30,000 per annum in today's money)[78]
- A £1,300 loan to help him settle his debts in Germany, to be paid off at the rate of £50 per week from his £200 weekly salary from the FRU[79]

The house-buying had some interesting moments. Ronnie Anderson and handler Martin Callan, who would shortly take over from Anderson as Nelson's main handler, had found a suitable property for Nelson and his family to move into on their permanent return two months later. Nelson went to view it and, over a cup of tea, the owner commented that the two previous visitors had seemed like policemen. 'Without choking on my tea,' Nelson explained that they were his cousins, shortlisting suitable properties for him. A similar security lapse happened when the solicitor doing the conveyancing said that when he'd been talking to Ronnie on the phone, 'all he could hear was the noise of voices speaking over radios' in the background. 'Are youse guys with the security forces?' asked the lawyer. Nelson deftly explained that Ronnie owned a taxi firm.[80]

To keep Nelson's wife on board, East Det FRU boss Captain Simpson took her out to dinner at the sixteenth-century Old Inn in Crawfordsburn, fifteen minutes outside Belfast. This was at Nelson's urging to 'finally allay any suspicion or fears she currently holds concerning his terrorist involvement'.[81]

Nelson returned with his family to Germany to work out his notice, coming back to Belfast in late April, before making one last trip back to Germany on his own in late May to collect the family's belongings.[82] Within two days of his return in April, he told his handlers that the UDA had appointed him intelligence officer for the entire organisation, not just West Belfast, as in his previous spell.[83] That same day, 30 April, would see him up to his neck in targeting a prominent republican.[84] 'McKee soon sought me out to assist him on what he regarded as an important hit,' wrote Nelson.[85]

Just before Nelson had gone to live in Germany in 1985, his handlers had warned how McKee's trust in Nelson as the 'only man' who would 'provide results' was drawing him into the danger zone. It had 'led him into acts of conspiracy which neither he nor the handler are happy with'.[86] Yet the new FRU regime in 1987 regarded Nelson's proximity to McKee as a major asset:

> In the past when 6137 targeted people for the UDA he, of course, would be aware that the victim would be hit some time or other based on his information. However, he never knew the hit team or when they would strike. It is to be hoped these arrangements will continue as it leaves 6137 virtually above suspicion if a job goes wrong.[87]

To ensure that Agent 6137 remained above suspicion, lessons in basic tradecraft followed: secure telephone procedures, cover stories for his absences at handler meetings, counter-surveillance drills for handler pick-ups and drop-offs – usually by van – for his weekly debriefing sessions. The abort signal was the passenger side sunshade in the vehicle up; down meant the coast was clear.[88] They also provided him with a hollowed-out spirit level in which he could conceal targeting documents at vehicle checkpoints. When he had to move a Starlight night-vision scope for a rifle – which he had been hiding for the UDA – his handlers gave him an escort to ensure a smooth run through such checkpoints.[89] Nelson's brother-in-law David Creighton said he occasionally saw him carrying a weapon.[90] He also owned a gas pistol, which he gave to Eric McKee to convert into a 0.32 pistol that fired six rounds from a magazine. McKee test-fired the gun into sandbags at UDA headquarters on the Shankill Road.[91]

These arrangements, intended to ensure Nelson remained above suspicion, would eventually fail, leading detectives from England to his and the FRU's door three years later. For most of those three murderous years, however, they remained intact, during which time Nelson was encouraged by his new FRU spymasters to 'professionalise' the UDA's targeting but to make himself scarce when the target was actually hit. The FRU repeatedly records that this goal was shared enthusiastically by their agent:

- Nelson wanted the 'UDA to attack legitimate targets which means proper planning and targeting must be done. This has not happened in the past and is only just beginning to happen with 6137 in his current position as Intelligence Officer.'[92]
- Nelson wanted to 'see UDA as a professional organisation and wants rid of those people who are only in the UDA for their own gain as criminals or racketeers. 6137 wants the UDA only to attack legitimate targets and not innocent Catholics.'[93]
- He wanted to 'see an end purely to sectarian murders and to concentrate on specific targeting of legitimate Republican terrorist targets.'[94]
- He wanted 'a prestigious target to be hit by the UDA but he is being over-enthusiastic in his quest to gain intelligence.'[95]
- He did 'not like sectarian killings and as the Intelligence Officer for West Belfast Bde UDA ... wants to see specific targeting carried out on legitimate targets.'[96]
- He 'would like to see the UDA as a professional organisation active against Republican terrorists and not a body made up of racketeers and criminals lining their own pockets.'[97]
- He wanted 'to see the UDA carry out professional operations against targets.'[98]

Inevitably, facilitating a more 'professional' targeting regime for the UDA drew Agent 6137 into murderous criminality on a vast scale. But in the lawless post-Walker counter-insurgency, this was seen more as an occupational hazard than an obstacle, and certainly not a reason for pulling him out.

Sir Patrick Walker's 1981 recommendation to prioritise intelligence gathering over the criminal justice system had put a premium on source protection for all three intelligence-gathering agencies – the FRU, Special Branch and MI5 – not just by overriding the law, but also by disregarding threats to the lives of others, if that is what it took to keep the agent in place. That may not have been Sir Patrick's intention, but it became the practice. The FRU's policy was never to retire an agent, irrespective of what that agent did. 'I can think of no scenario where Nelson's involvement in criminality would have been sufficient for the FRU to desert him,' his handler Martin Callan later candidly admitted to the first of Stevens' three inquiries.[99]

Chapter Three

6137 – 'A bad bastard'

'NELSON IS A BAD BASTARD, unreliable and dangerous,' one of MI5's trusted agents told his handler, sometime after Nelson had been arrested in 1990 by detectives from the Stevens 1 Inquiry. The agent had had direct dealings with Nelson, so he knew his character. 'I could have told you this a long time ago and saved you all a lot of trouble.'[1] The 'trouble' that followed Agent 6137's re-recruitment into the FRU in early 1987 is a case study in the perils of an agent-running operation freighted with foreseeable risks.

The FRU had taken on an agent with a zeal to kill what he deemed to be 'legitimate' targets, recruited by a new crusading CO, Colonel Gordon Kerr, and run day-to-day by subordinates with only a basic six-week agent-handling course under their belt. This sometimes left them either unable or unwilling to realise when Nelson was operating beyond permitted limits.[2] And when they did realise it, they seemed less concerned about their agent endeavouring to stay within the law than they did about the risk of him being caught by the law.

One of the FRU's more experienced handlers did, however, glimpse the future. Although Ronnie Anderson had been ordered to try to tempt Nelson back from Germany, he was 'not keen on Nelson returning to work for the FRU. In my judgement he was unreliable.'[3] That re-recruitment order from Colonel Kerr still begs some questions: what exactly drove Kerr's determination to reactivate 6137? And why was he so determined to win the turf war this had started with MI5?

In late 1986, the then secretary of state for Northern Ireland, Tom King, complained that the army needed to up its intelligence-gathering game. Armed and masked loyalists had overpowered guards at the Ulster Defence Regiment (UDR) base in Coleraine in February 1987 and stolen guns and ammunition. Special Branch had received advance warning of the raid but hadn't told the army.[4] The RUC made amends by quickly capturing the thieves as they made their getaway on the M2 motorway, but this raid and other mishaps had tinged the British Army with a 'Dad's Army' image. To King and the top brass, that was no laughing matter.[5] Moreover, when Nelson went to Germany, they'd lost their only agent within the loyalist paramilitaries.

So, Nelson's re-recruitment seemed logical. Also, bringing him back to Belfast would give Kerr additional political kudos at his regular meetings with the Intelligence Review Committee (IRC), which reviewed the intelligence effort against both republican and loyalist paramilitaries. The IRC was chaired by MI5's director and co-ordinator of intelligence at Stormont and was attended by senior representatives of the army, police and all three intelligence-gathering services.[6] And Kerr was regarded as a very political operator.

The case Kerr made to his boss, ACOS G2, for Nelson's re-recruitment was that Nelson was so well placed he would provide 'information of supreme interest to the Army and RUC'.[7] The explanation Kerr gave to Stevens after Nelson's arrest in 1990 was more specific. He said Nelson had been tasked to 'prevent – or at the very least limit' the 'murderous activities' of loyalist paramilitaries. 'There was a desperate need for operational intelligence on the Protestant terror groups who were successfully targeting individuals for assassination on a seemingly ad hoc basis,' Kerr told Stevens.[8] ACOS G2 gave the same justification: 'The whole purpose of continuing to run Nelson as an agent was to prevent murders.'[9] Yet as events would show, Nelson's intelligence was by no means exploited to save lives. Only three lives at most can be shown to have been saved during his four and a half years as an agent. Besides thwarting weapons thefts from British Army bases and political kudos for the FRU, the only tangible benefit to the state seems to take us back to 'building pictures' – in this case, a picture at the heart of the UDA's killing machine.

That said, Nelson's revived spying career began with the saving of a very high-profile life. The target for which Nelson says Eric McKee sought his assistance, on his first day as the UDA's chief intelligence officer, was the Sinn Féin candidate campaigning to become the MP for Belfast West in the June general election, Gerry Adams. McKee had learned that Adams' ex-RUC bulletproof Ford Cortina drew up outside a Housing Executive office in Murray Street every Wednesday morning between 9.30 and 10.30. He asked Nelson to hatch a plan that would enable the UDA to 'have a crack at Adams'.[10]

Venturing into Murray Street the following day in a suit, carrying a clip-board and with the confident air of a public official, Nelson spied the ideal spot: opposite the Housing Executive was an office block with scaffolding covered by plastic and canvas sheeting. He couldn't see any workmen, so he climbed a ladder to the first level and found it offered 'an ideal firing point' at about fifty metres distance. Back home, Nelson sketched out his plan: one copy went to McKee, another to his handler Ronnie Anderson. Nelson says Anderson told him that his boss – the officer commanding (OC) of the FRU's East Det – had wanted Nelson to 'drop everything to do with it'. But, according to Nelson, Anderson had argued that because Adams was a 'prestige target' and McKee had invested such faith in Nelson, it 'would look bad' for Nelson were he to opt out and not 'show eagerness in an opportunity to get Adams'. This argument, that the attack should be allowed to help Nelson 'get off to a good start … appeared [to have] carried the day – at least for the time being'.[11]

With the hit planned for 6 May,[12] Nelson joined McKee at his home awaiting news from the gun team. At 10 a.m. the phone rang. 'That's it,' said a despondent McKee. 'He's not coming.'[13] Adams, appropriately, had gone to someone else's funeral.[14]

A few days later McKee told Nelson he'd secured a limpet mine with a four-second fuse. The plan now was for a pillion rider on a motorcycle to stick it to the roof of Adams' car. Adams wouldn't survive the blast, whereas he might survive a bullet since he was known to wear body armour. 'They won't stand a chance,' McKee told Nelson. 'They'll be blown to fucking pieces.'[15] McKee ordered Nelson to attend a full rehearsal the day before the operation. The attack was fixed for 13 May. However, it seems that Colonel Kerr was in two minds as to whether this attack should be stopped and sought the opinion of the CLF Major General Bob Hodges, who told me, 'Kerr came into my office undecided; he was "shall we, shan't we?"' Hodges told Kerr that under no circumstances should the attack be allowed to proceed.[16] In the event, Adams was a no show once again, being at yet another funeral.[17]

The following Wednesday, 20 May, the target area was saturated with security forces although, again, Adams didn't show. Loath to give up, McKee now set his sights on 27 May but was told by the UDA's Inner Council (its decision-making body) to abandon the attack. Two days later, the limpet mine was recovered by the security forces from a UDA arms dump in a lock-up garage in Woodvale.[18] The intelligence on its whereabouts had not, however, come from the FRU via Nelson.[19]

Aside from the initial wobble over whether or not to allow the attack, this had been a near textbook operation in exploiting intelligence to safeguard both life and the long-term national interest. The FRU had warned Special Branch of the plot in a timely fashion, as they were obliged to do, and the branch had responded by telling the UDA leadership that it was aware of the plot and to ensure it was aborted.[20] Within the intelligence services, there was a consensus that Adams' life was worth saving, since he'd shown clear signs of trying to edge the republican movement onto a constitutional path and bring the more hawkish Martin McGuinness with him. Having finally wrested control of the IRA from the old guard in the Republic the previous November, both leaders had taken the key step of ending Sinn Féin's long-standing policy of abstaining from standing for election to the Dáil. Nelson says his handlers told him that the FRU had ultimately concluded that had Adams been assassinated, it would have been 'totally counterproductive, particularly considering the delicate balance of power within Sinn Fein'.[21]

Despite the success of this operation, Nelson's time as Agent 6137 over the next thirty-one months would see only two further tangible examples of his intelligence being exploited by the RUC to prevent an imminent assassination. And it was the RUC who had the ultimate say since, under the 'normalisation' policy of police primacy, the RUC and not the army had been the lead counter-insurgency force for over a decade. As with Adams, exploiting Nelson's intelligence to save the two additional lives appears to have been motivated by hardheaded pragmatism more than basic humanity. One of the targeted individuals may have been a police informant in a republican organisation.[22] The other was a senior IRA commander, Harry Maynes, against whom the attack in May 1988 had to be aborted because Nelson was going to be an active participant on the ground signalling when it was clear for the gun team to strike, which meant there was a very high risk of him being caught.[23]

On 19 May, Nelson told his handlers that the UDA intended to shoot Maynes the following day. Maynes worked for a taxi company, and from Nelson's observations in his own taxi he'd established Maynes' morning routine. Nelson's role was that of 'trigger man', signalling to the gun team hiding in a nearby house when Maynes was in the office. The attack was abandoned by the UDA when the area was saturated with security forces. Nelson, however, had positively begged the FRU to allow the attack to take place and says his handlers later told him that they had 'argued until four in the morning' for the attack to happen 'without interference'.[24] The official FRU record says Nelson was 'upset that the CQA [Close Quarter Assassination] on Maynes did not take place'.[25] His handlers sought to console him by saying that had he not been involved, the attack would have gone ahead,[26] presumably because they would have turned a blind eye.

In the case of Adams, MI5 suspected the FRU had been 'pushing 6137' to 'implement' the attack 'speedily as a way of re-enforcing his standing with the UDA'.[27] The service criticised the FRU for not properly thinking through the politically nuclear consequences had Adams been shot and Nelson's involvement become known. Never mind that Gerry Adams was identified by the intelligence services as a member of the IRA's ruling Army Council. The government would have been accused of conspiring to murder 'a prospective MP with all the attendant adverse consequences'.[28]

MI5 also issued a stern rebuke directly to Kerr and the head of Army Intelligence for not initially restraining Nelson's enthusiasm for the Adams attack, no doubt tinged with a degree of satisfaction after its humiliating defeat at Kerr's hands the previous February in its own attempt to recruit Nelson. The service in Northern Ireland assessed that the situation was now 'contained', but that is not how MI5 headquarters in London saw it. A telegram responded that running Agent 6137 was fraught with the risk of 'going off the rails', while also doubting that words of advice to Kerr from their MI5's Belfast colleagues would 'have the slightest effect'.[29]

Events would prove London right, yet beyond giving advice to the FRU, the service was impotent to enforce change. It had no command and control over the FRU, which was the master in its own house as a result of the autonomy given to each of the three intelligence-gathering services, despite the RUC having 'police primacy' and the main responsibility for prosecuting the counter-insurgency and maintaining law and order. Indeed, so autonomous was the FRU that it hadn't even informed the RUC that it intended to rehire Nelson, as etiquette, if not the rules, required. The first time Special Branch knew he was back in Belfast as an FRU agent was when his name began to surface in reports from the branch's own agents inside the UDA.[30] This sits ill with Kerr's claim to have 'carefully developed Nelson's case in conjunction with [RUC SB]'.[31]

On the other hand, the FRU's extremely detailed records (known as contact forms) of their dealings with their Agent 6137 show that at least once a week, the FRU sent Special Branch a 'wealth' of MISRs based on Nelson's reporting, including sometimes 'valuable tactical intelligence'.[32] This meant the MISRs contained sufficient detail for the RUC to respond by mobilising security forces to disrupt a planned UDA assassination, should they wish to and should resources permit. The MISRs were summaries of the contact forms (CFs), which were themselves composed from tape recordings of the agent's meetings with his handlers and covered the meeting place, routes to and from the contact point, a diary of events and activities of the agent since the last meeting, with a section on specific issues the handler wanted debriefed by the agent.[33]

The 2012 Conservative government-commissioned review by the late Sir Desmond de Silva QC into the assassination of the Belfast solicitor Patrick Finucane is at odds with the earlier inquiries led by John Stevens over how this material was used. Some detectives in Stevens' team put much of the blame on the FRU for the failure to exploit Nelson's intelligence to save lives, arguing that their MISRs were often vague and lacked detail.[34] RUC Chief Constable Sir Hugh Annesley concurred, putting the blame squarely on the FRU for not providing lifesaving intelligence.[35] While that was true on several notable occasions, both de Silva and the 2004 Labour government-commissioned inquiry into alleged state collusion with terrorists by the late Justice Peter Cory of the Canadian Supreme Court, found that in the main it was Special Branch that failed to action FRU MISRs. Contrary to Stevens, de Silva found the MISRs 'contained a wealth of potentially life-saving intelligence' in sufficient detail to have allowed the RUC to act.[36] And as Cory said, 'Special Branch paid virtually no attention to his [Nelson's] intelligence reports … there is only an occasional reference to Nelson in the Intelligence book …'[37] De Silva corroborates this point with forensically detailed charts showing what intelligence the FRU passed to the branch and when.[38]

Certainly, Nelson's intelligence was high grade and the FRU awarded it B2 status, meaning it was 'actionable, and the source reliable'.[39] Yet, with the exception of the aborted attacks on three people – Adams, Maynes and the unnamed 'individual who had assisted the police'[40] – de Silva finds that the branch showed a spectacular lack of interest in FRU MISRs sourced from Nelson, despite these MISRs on some occasions being so detailed that the branch must have realised that the UDA had 'completed their targeting' and an attack was imminent.[41]

One thing seems clear: if Kerr's reason for re-recruiting Nelson was to save lives, his intelligence didn't seem to be having that effect. Save for the three isolated cases mentioned, none of the threats from Nelson to dozens of republicans he targeted were recorded in the Belfast Special Branch's Threat Book, even though loyalist armed groups generally were responsible for 45 per cent of murders (most of them civilians) in Greater Belfast while Nelson was active between 1987 and 1989.[42] Yet the number of threats recorded in the Threat Book from agents within the IRA against individuals belonging to what broadly could be called the unionist community – typically, members of the security forces, the judiciary, civil servants, prison service personnel and some politicians – was twenty times higher (730 threats to 'unionist' targets compared to 36 to 'republican' targets).[43] And whereas the RUC took little or no action on Nelson's FRU reports, the branch did take action twenty-six times in response to FRU reports of threats against the security forces and public officials coming from its agents within the IRA.[44]

For many nationalists and republicans, this striking bias in favour of protecting the lives of one community (unionist) in Greater Belfast over the other (republican) might most obviously be explained by RUC sectarianism. Yet sectarianism isn't reflected in the RUC charge rates of loyalists and republicans across Northern Ireland as a whole. Indeed, there is compelling evidence that in the thirteen-year period between 1983 and 1996, when the murder of civilians by loyalist paramilitaries reached a peak and the number of civilians murdered by loyalists and republicans in that period was almost identical (279 compared to 270), the charging rate against loyalists was almost double that of republicans (41 compared to 22 per cent).[45] So, as de Silva also finds, the RUC's response to the West Belfast UDA during the period 1987–89 is in stark contrast to the overall pattern.[46]

Some former Special Branch officers in Belfast have explained the RUC's lack of actioning Nelson's MISRs as a consequence of the fierce competition for security force resources. Threats assessed as immediate and real were prioritised for obvious reasons.[47] Responsibility for deciding on the priority of those threats was down to the Tasking and Co-ordinating Group (TCG), which was staffed by experienced branch officers with attachments from the army and MI5. Resources were finite and often constrained the TCG from authorising more than, on average, ten 'tasking sheets' (i.e. operations) per day.[48]

This reason aside, Special Branch doesn't appear to have judged Nelson's intelligence as actually worth acting on. The former head of the RUC Source Unit in Belfast told the first of Stevens' three inquiries that he couldn't think of a single 'individual whose life has been saved as a direct result of Nelson's information.'[49] Seemingly unaware of the three cases previously mentioned, he dismissed Nelson as a 'low-level informant', while his successor considered most FRU sources to have been 'rubbish.'[50] A senior MI5 officer who liaised with the FRU said the RUC 'always gave less credence to FRU sources' and that the relationship between the branch and the FRU was 'not harmonious.'[51] The branch also suspected that Nelson 'might be fabricating or withholding intelligence.'[52]

Dismissing so comprehensively the value of Nelson's intelligence reeks of a corrosive inter-agency rivalry between the branch and the FRU, and the former's strongly held belief that the army didn't need to have its own agent-running unit in the first place, since the field was already crowded with both branch and MI5-run agents. As one former senior branch officer put it: 'If we did this again, we'd be better off with only one intelligence-gathering unit, not three.'[53] Within the branch, there was also antipathy and mistrust for Colonel Kerr. 'I reached the point where I would no longer have Kerr in my office,' another senior branch officer told me.[54]

Still, none of this adequately explains the RUC's disproportionate focus on threat intelligence directed at the broadly unionist community in Greater Belfast, as compared to their relative disinterest in threat intelligence from Nelson against republicans. What adds to the puzzle is that MI5 had a similar experience to the FRU: the service confirmed to de Silva that they had no record of Special Branch having responded to threat intelligence against republicans from their own agents inside loyalist terrorist organisations.[55]

This conundrum was addressed by de Silva. He agreed that compared to threats from republican groups, the RUC had taken 'comparatively very little exploitative action' in response to threats from loyalists.[56] His explanation unsurprisingly included the fact that there were a greater number of threats originating from the IRA and other armed republicans than from loyalists, and that many of those in the republican community had paramilitary 'traces' provoking a natural reluctance by the RUC to safeguard individuals who may have celebrated the deaths of soldiers and police officers, or who were, at least, untroubled by their deaths.[57] However, de Silva finds the principal reason for the disparity was the overriding priority given to source protection to ensure an agent's cover remained intact, even at the expense of someone else's life.[58] The RUC was especially reluctant to provide warnings to individuals in a community broadly considered to be untrustworthy because of its hostility to the state, fearful that they would make political capital out of it.[59] 'There was always the risk of the targeted person going up the road to Sinn Féin and publicising the warning,' as a former senior Special Branch officer put it. 'Pretty soon the loyalists would be asking "This was only known to four people, so which one is a tout?"'[60] Members of the security forces and public officials being targeted by the IRA, on the other hand, could be trusted to receive warnings without publicising them.

So far, so unsurprising. Once again, terrorism had compelled the state to compromise the legal and moral standards otherwise taken for granted in peacetime. Put bluntly, source protection was being elevated over the state's obligation to protect all of its citizens' lives under Article 2 of the European Convention on Human Rights (ECHR). And yet, while the universality of this obligation may be laudable, it would be odd if some members of the security forces hadn't felt that applying it equally to people determined to blow them up was a right they were not always predisposed to offer. Moreover, while the obligation may have existed under international law, the ECHR had not yet been incorporated into domestic statute. That only happened in 1998 under the Human Rights Act, and so the Convention had nothing like the status it has assumed today.

A further question concerns the FRU's response to the fact that the branch was so obviously disinterested in MISRs summarising Nelson's intelligence. Despite Colonel Kerr's insistence at Nelson's trial five years later that his principal purpose in enticing him back from Germany was to save the lives of innocent Catholics being targeted by the UDA, there was no response from the FRU to the RUC's non-response to their 700 plus MISRs. De Silva found no evidence that the FRU had ever challenged the branch as to why Nelson's intelligence was not being exploited, even though it must have been obvious to the FRU that their MISRs were being largely ignored.[61] Yet this seems not to have troubled the FRU, even though it would have been a simple matter for this issue to have been raised with the Belfast TCG. The moral imperative that Kerr claimed for re-hiring Agent 6137 on paper does not seem to have been quite as acute in practice.

In what way, therefore, was Kerr – as he so emphatically claimed – using Nelson to save lives by 'limiting the murderous' activities of the UDA? At a glance, the remit set by the UDA and by the FRU appeared identical. The UDA had tasked Nelson to 'build an efficient intelligence network to enable the Association to properly target known Republicans for possible execution.'[62] The FRU, as noted in Chapter 2, had tasked him to 'professionalise' UDA targeting, 'enabling him to make sure that sectarian killings are not carried out but that proper targeting of PIRA [Provisional IRA] members takes place prior to any shooting.'[63] It's easy to see why this was interpreted not just by republicans but others (including me) as the FRU intending to use Nelson as a proxy assassin to kill leading IRA members.[64] Hunting down and killing the enemy is what armies do, after all. But was this actually the FRU's agenda?

Clearly it was Nelson's, as another CF recorded: '6137 … wants the UDA to attack legitimate targets which means proper planning and targeting must be done. This has not happened in the past and is only just beginning to happen with 6137 in his current position as Intelligence Officer.'[65] The FRU records include multiple entries in this vein. This appears to have been the basis on which some of the detectives working on the three Stevens inquiries concluded that the FRU's military objective was indeed identical to Nelson's: that they were using him to direct the UDA towards senior PIRA targets whom the FRU wanted the UDA to kill because they were a threat to the state. 'The FRU were playing God,' said one senior Stevens detective. 'No doubt about that.'[66] It was 'about honing targeting,' said his colleague.[67]

Yet, while this was clearly Nelson's agenda, Kerr has repeatedly denied that using Nelson as a proxy assassin was also the FRU's agenda. In referring to the several handler comments in the CFs about the importance of Nelson 'professionalising' the UDA's targeting, Kerr says the handlers 'may not always have chosen the right expression, clause or turn of phrase'.[68] And while he has acknowledged that the FRU's policy was to use Nelson to steer the UDA towards targeting the IRA, where he parts company with Stevens and fellow accusers is in his insistence that this was a conventional distraction tactic aimed at dissipating the UDA's time and energy by channelling them into pursuing far harder targets, which demanded more reconnaissance and planning, thus reducing their ability to mount 'ad hoc targeting of Catholics'.[69]

On this de Silva gives Kerr the benefit of the doubt – and for several reasons which are worth setting out. First, he found that the tactic was not without precedent: both Special Branch and MI5 had tasked a jointly handled loyalist agent to use a similar distraction tactic in the 1980s.[70] Second, if the FRU had actually intended to use Nelson pro-actively to ensure that his choice of 'legitimate' targets were assassinated, why – as he and Cory agree – did the FRU pass so much of his intelligence on to the RUC by way of MISRs?[71] This is a fair point. After all the RUC was the organisation supposedly tasked with protecting those very targets. Third, if using Nelson as a proxy for state assassinations was the FRU's real purpose, wouldn't the FRU have been expected to regularly give Nelson up-to-the-minute intelligence on the movements of the intended targets, rather than relying on leaked documents?[72] Fourth, why did the UDA kill so few leading republicans?[73] While several attempts were made to kill some of the most active members of the IRA's Belfast Brigade, none were actually killed. And finally, a new handler assigned to Nelson in April 1989 – Colour Sergeant Ben Lawrenson – repeatedly 'expressed concern at Nelson's behaviour' and, for the first time, as recorded in the CFs, 'discussed the options of exploiting Nelson's intelligence to prevent attacks'.[74]

These seem to me to be fair counters to the view that Kerr was engaged in a proxy assassination campaign, and it is right that the historical record reflects that. On the other hand, it is impossible to say whether Kerr's distraction strategy did *actually* save lives. Entrusted to an agent who very much saw his role as a proxy state assassin of republicans, whether or not they were in the IRA, the strategy was reckless. As the FRU acknowledged, '6137 initiates most of the targeting.'[75] This led to chaos and multiple deaths, with none of the victims known to be active members of the IRA. How many deaths, exactly, is again impossible to say.

De Silva found that Nelson played some part in 'at least four murders, ten attempted murders and numerous conspiracies to murder'.[76] The Stevens 3 Inquiry concluded he had been involved in 'over 50' criminal conspiracies, mostly murder.[77] My own records indicate at least six individuals were murdered after being actively targeted by Nelson, but it is possible that he contributed to more, perhaps many more.[78] That is because an unknown number of victims whose details he painstakingly compiled on what he called his 'P', or personality, cards were later murdered by the UDA and other loyalist murder gangs like the UVF and Red Hand Commando, to whom he had incontinently disseminated his 'P' cards without objection from his handlers.

In the journal Nelson wrote in jail, which I and my BBC colleague Geoffrey Seed acquired in 1992, he listed eight murders and thirty-four conspiracies to murder against the names of the 'persons or places I was involved with, or because of my position in the UDA was made aware of …'[79] At his trial in 1992, the prosecution brought thirty-four counts against Nelson, including two of murder, four of conspiracy to murder, and two of aiding and abetting murder, before a deal was done whereby the murder charges were dropped in exchange for him admitting to five counts of conspiracy to murder.

Also at Nelson's trial, Colonel Kerr said he had provided lifesaving intelligence on 217 individuals, intending, no doubt, for the public to interpret that as 217 lives saved.[80] In 1998, government sources put an actual figure on the lives they claimed Nelson's intelligence had saved: they told UN

Special Rapporteur Param Cumaraswamy it was 'about 70 lives'.[81] Having examined the entirety of the Stevens documentation and relevant RUC documents, de Silva found both of these claims to be baseless.[82]

Using a zealot like Nelson for the objective that Kerr says he had set him – to distract the UDA from shooting ad hoc Catholics by steering them towards the more time-consuming targeting of leading IRA members – was always going to be high risk. Inevitably, Nelson was drawn into multiple conspiracies to murder that ended in the deaths of innocents. But was he also encouraged to be involved in those conspiracies, one of Nelson's first handlers was asked when interviewed by Stevens. 'Yes, at our behest,' Martin Callan replied.[83]

It was a task that Nelson set about with enthusiasm. 'It is obvious that 6137 does want a prestigious target to be hit by the UDA but he is being over-enthusiastic in his quest to gain intelligence,' the FRU recorded in August 1988.[84] 'In my time Nelson put a large amount of information on targeting for use by the UDA's Close Quarter Assassination team,' Callan told Stevens. 'The mystique of the job gave him an adrenaline boost. He liked to think he was part of the "team". Throughout the time I handled Nelson he was always unpredictable' and would 'carry out actions without clearance from the FRU office'.[85]

While, as de Silva has concluded, it may not have been FRU's intention to use Nelson as a proxy assassin of active IRA terrorists, there were certainly times when the FRU's actions not only facilitated that goal but gave tacit approval to it. The net effect was to significantly increase the UDA's ability to commit murder. That process began with the FRU's help to Nelson in refining and updating a vast quantity of old UDA targeting files that Nelson handed over to them. Eighty-five per cent of these files had been leaked to the UDA by rogue members of the security forces in the first place.[86]

Chapter Four

6137 – 'What did he really achieve at the end of the day?'

AT 8.02 P.M. ON THE evening of 14 October 1987, a blue Ford Sierra and a silver Hyundai merged with the evening traffic coming out of north-west Belfast, one in front of Nelson's car, the other behind for protection, driving in convoy for a few miles, then pulling into a lay-by on the Hightown Road. From the boot of his car, Nelson quickly handed over a large suitcase and carton bulging with photographs and files of potential UDA targets. The handover took only three minutes.

Most of the files had been leaked over the years by rogue members of the army and police. They'd been handed over to Nelson in a large egg box when he rejoined the UDA.[1] One much-valued UDA source was a Special Branch officer who alone had provided fifty files.[2] The files included Order of Battle (ORBAT) sheets given to mobile and foot patrols of soldiers and police to help them identify leading IRA members. They also included no fewer than 1,000 'RUC P [personality] file cards of various nationalist personalities', files on a senior UDA man, 'various' military maps of Belfast, photographs of 'military Ops. room or Int. cells walls … Garda reports on national personalities' and 'photographs of various targets in Eire'. The FRU recorded the purpose of this clandestine transfer as being merely 'copying and evaluating' Nelson's store of intelligence.[3]

Nelson seemed to have envisaged a more subversive purpose. He was seeking his handler's help in refining the files because he couldn't face ploughing through the mountain of documents. 'I baulked at the thought of having to go through and evaluate every scrape [*sic*] of paper,' he wrote in his journal. It would have taken 'me weeks if not months to get through it all'. According to Nelson, his handlers weeded out the files of IRA members and suspects who were either dead or no longer active. A few days later, he received back 'a much pruned ... amount of documentation'.[4]

Not only did the FRU copy everything Nelson handed over that day, but from then on it also received copies of all the new intelligence collated by Nelson from the 'innumerable amount of information' about 'personalities within Republican organisations' that was leaked to the UDA.[5] From this, Nelson fastidiously produced several hundred 'P' cards, containing details such as addresses and car registration numbers, which would assist UDA assassination teams to locate, follow and kill their targets.

At the request of his handlers, Nelson found a flat in the Glencairn area of Belfast to securely store his intelligence dump, including the 'P' cards. His handlers were given three sets of keys to the property, the location of which they also registered with Special Branch to ensure it was out of bounds to searches by uniformed security force patrols.[6]

When it came to Nelson distributing his 'P' cards to UDA/UFF murder gangs, he no doubt interpreted the FRU's failure to object – and sometimes positively support – as signalling their tacit approval for them to be used to target and kill those whom Nelson deemed 'legitimate targets'. How else can the evidence from the FRU files of Nelson's handlers knowingly permitting him to repeatedly disseminate scores of his 'P' cards in batches, not just to the UDA's most active gunmen, but also beyond the UDA to the UVF and Red Hand Commando, be interpreted? John Stevens' inquiries recovered Nelson's 'P' cards from no fewer than twelve loyalist dumps, one as far away as Derry.[7]

Special Branch was 'fully aware' of Nelson's involvement in the extensive dissemination of his lethal targeting through 'P' cards, but it doesn't appear to have objected. In failing to even attempt to exercise control over this proliferation, both the RUC and the FRU had irreversibly lost control of how the very targeting material they'd helped him update and refine was subsequently used. Of course, had Nelson been ordered by his UDA masters to hand out batches of ‘P’ cards to multiple assassins, he would have had little choice but to obey, albeit with a token batch, to preserve his cover. But FRU records show that the initiative to disseminate was actually his and that he told the UDA on one occasion that he could only do so much targeting because he was ‘tied down with too many briefs and paperwork to be able to confirm or deny any targeting’.[8] In other words, the job of targeting needed to be shared out more equitably.

By sharing his ‘P’ cards with the UVF, Nelson appears to have been motivated by his frustration with the UDA for failing to kill two leading republicans: Thomas Keenan and Alex Maskey. Agent 6137 ‘feels that if the UDA are not going to act then it is better that the UVF do it than no one,’ recorded one FRU CF. ‘Although the UVF are not particular about their targets, they appear to be more aggressive.’[9] That was an understatement, as Nelson knew very well. One FRU report has him describing the UVF’s quartermaster as ‘an absolute animal, a psychopath’ who, during a row with his wife, had pushed her head down the toilet.[10]

There was ‘ample evidence that the UVF were living off Nelson – and increasing its strike rate as a result,’ observed Detective Chief Superintendent Vince McFadden, senior investigating officer (SIO) for the first Stevens inquiry.[11] Nelson gave the UVF copies of his ‘P’ cards on at least four occasions.[12] In return, the UVF gave the UDA a limpet mine. Nelson’s handlers approved, noting that if this trade was ‘successful, it will enhance 6137’s standing, particularly if the UVF did attack one of the targets for which he provided information’.[13] This is hardly consistent with the claim made to the Stevens 1 Inquiry by the OC East Det FRU, from where Nelson was run, that the FRU’s mandate was to prevent ‘imminent danger to life or property’.[14]

The FRU quite properly informed Special Branch, via MISRs, whenever Nelson had copied large batches of his ‘P’ cards to the UDA and UVF, but this was a near-pointless exercise, and the FRU must have known it. Rarely did the MISRs include the scores of names in the handed over ‘P’ cards now at risk of being shot and, anyway, on several occasions there were so many that Nelson himself couldn’t remember them. As with almost all of the Nelson-sourced MISRs, the branch showed no interest, and the FRU showed no interest in their lack of interest.[15]

FRU records document some sixteen occasions when Nelson gave copies in bulk of his 'P' cards to the UDA or UVF. There is no evidence in those records of Nelson's several handlers and co-handlers restraining or admonishing him for the lethal anarchy gifting his 'P' cards had unleashed. The only record that I have come across of a handler expressing concern is Martin Callan, though whether he did that while in post is unclear. Callan did, however, tell the Stevens 1 Inquiry in 1990 that Nelson had 'killed the one thing that he had tried to create, namely that he was the only source of intelligence data for the UDA.'[16]

It is impossible to know how many individuals who featured on Nelson's disseminated 'P' cards became his victims because of this. All one can say with confidence is that from Nelson's return to the UDA in May 1987 up to February 1992, dozens of people whose names were later recovered by Stevens from his intelligence dump were the victims of attempted murder. At least five whose names in his handwriting were on 'P' cards were the victims of murder and attempted murder by the UVF or UDA.[17]

To Colonel Kerr, Nelson's mass dissemination of his targeting material was 'relatively insignificant.'[18] He even accused the Stevens 1 Inquiry of making a 'political accusation' with their perfectly justified accusation that by allowing Nelson to proliferate his targeting files, the FRU had put lives at risk on a long-term basis.[19] One of Kerr's successors as FRU CO is thought to have vehemently disagreed. The unnamed colonel is believed to have been the author of a highly critical MoD review of the way Nelson was handled, condemning the proliferation of his P cards as 'extremely dangerous as Nelson would no longer have control over targeting material. The spreading of such material greatly enhanced the UDA's potential for murder with no possible warning from Nelson.'[20] The colonel also noted that Nelson's handlers made 'no comment on this action.'[21] By its silence, the message the FRU was sending Nelson was decidedly mixed: on the one hand, it wanted him to professionalise the UDA's targeting, thereby increasing that organisation's capacity to kill; on the other, it wanted him to desist from getting too close to the action even though it knew that killing 'legitimate targets' is what Nelson was desperate to achieve.

When Kerr was asked by de Silva how exactly the FRU had communicated this to Nelson, he danced round the question: 'I think the best way of answering that is to say that as a rule, we would not normally discuss with our agents our full strategy for the running of the case. The important thing, as far as Nelson was concerned, was that he was tasked to report everything he possibly could ...'[22]

The FRU records indicate that there were several occasions when Nelson could have been forgiven for thinking that his handlers were happy to facilitate his goal of assassinating targets he deemed 'legitimate', even if they were not proactively striving for it. For example, when Nelson sought information from Martin Callan about a 'legitimate target' he was actively targeting, Callan acknowledged that he would sometimes respond by saying 'perhaps you don't have that wrong'.[23]

In January 1988, Nelson's handlers gave him the vehicle registration number associated with Brendan Hughes, the IRA's legendary OC of the Belfast Brigade in the early 1970s until he was jailed in 1974.[24] Hughes had been back in Belfast since 1986, and Nelson was actively targeting him and wanted him dead. Two months later, Nelson's handlers gave him the vehicle registration numbers of cars being used by two more PIRA men, one of whom was Pat McGeown. The FRU had been asked by the RUC to use Nelson to help them identify a rogue police officer who had been disclosing names and addresses to a UDA contact seeking checks on vehicle registration numbers from the police. The FRU told Nelson to pretend to the UDA contact that he was seeking the names of the owners of registration numbers of cars he had logged leaving a Sinn Féin centre. Nelson did this, but he also used the information to update his own 'P' cards on Hughes, McGeown and the third IRA man,[25] as his handlers might well have guessed he would. In the case of Hughes, the UDA man came back with Hughes' address, which Nelson's handler confirmed was correct.[26] Nelson then used this information to target all three.

In July 1988, Nelson's handler again confirmed the registration number of a car, this time one used by Sinn Féin councillor Alex Maskey, in advance of a plot to shoot him in a restaurant. Initially, Maskey had been spotted by a UDA man having Sunday lunch with his wife at a hotel.[27] What appeared to be his car, a beige Lada, was parked outside. Nelson raced off to try to find a gunman, then returned to stake out the hotel pending his arrival. To his exasperation, he watched Maskey depart before two tooled-up assassins could arrive. Nonetheless, he was so pumped up with excitement that he telephoned his handler to say he'd had an 'exciting day' because Maskey had 'just missed death by about 20 seconds', proudly boasting that he, Nelson, had been 'involved up to my neck with a Mister Heckler' – meaning a Heckler and Koch gun.[28] There was no comeback from the handler, which suggests the fact that Nelson was 'up to his neck' in a murder conspiracy came as no surprise.

Nelson also informed his handler that if Maskey came back for his lunch the following Sunday, he would be shot. To be certain that he was in the hotel without having to check inside, Nelson needed confirmation that the beige Lada was Maskey's car. 'Can you give me a read out … if I give you a [registration] number?' asked Nelson. The handler responded, 'Yeah, go on.' The handler then called Nelson back with the answer. The car wasn't registered to Maskey, but 'it's probably used by him though'. The handler then enquired, 'What's going to happen now?' to which Nelson responded, 'If he's there next Sunday, he's going down.'[29] Again, no criticism was levelled at Nelson. Fortunately for Maskey, he didn't return to the hotel the following Sunday.[30]

Similarly, in targeting two senior IRA men, Brian Gillen and Anto Murray, the Belfast Brigade's operations officer, Nelson said that in the case of the latter, his handler traced an outline of Murray's house on a piece of paper for Nelson to give to the UDA's 'military' commander Eric McKee, because the location was too dangerous for a safe stake-out.[31] In the case of Gillen, Nelson claimed to have been given his address because his handler wanted to convince him it was too dangerous to stake out.[32]

The following month, August, Nelson was again targeting Harry Maynes, whom he had marked down as the PIRA's OC 2nd Battalion. This followed Nelson's abortive attempt the previous May to act as trigger man for the UDA gun team to shoot Maynes at the taxi office where he was based. Once again Nelson was given a helping hand when he called his handler.

Nelson: 'Can you check something for me?'
Handler: 'What's that?'
Nelson: 'Two cars.'
Handler: 'Why?'
Nelson: 'It's just to eliminate them.'
Handler: 'What is it connected with?'

Nelson: 'The taxi driver.'
Handler: 'Go on.'
Nelson: 'JXI 1290 Blue, TIA 7148 Gold.'
Handler: 'Wait a minute … what do you expect them to be?'
Nelson: 'Friends of his.'
Handler: 'Yeah, they probably are, looking at where the owners live.'[33]

Targeting David Clinton, a member of the Irish National Liberation Army (INLA), Nelson was helpfully told by a handler that he was wasting his time looking for him in Belfast because he'd moved to Downpatrick.[34] Had the UDA decided to pursue him, they now knew where to look.

When, later that year, Nelson objected to an order from UFF commander Eric McKee to target Father Des Wilson, whom they regarded as a close ally of Gerry Adams, his handler suggested he should 'leave Wilson' and propose another target from 'Sinn Fein or [the] PIRA hierarchy'.[35]

Nelson, who had just turned forty, had progressed in one sense since his 1973 sectarian foray into UDA romper-room sadism, when he led a gang of thugs who electrocuted and beat up the partially sighted Gerry Higgins. The files portray a man now apparently repelled by his UDA comrades shooting Catholics simply and solely because they were Catholics. So, when he learned that, on the basis of his targeting, shortly after 10 p.m. on 10 May 1988, the UDA's revered 'Big Evil' Winkie Dodds had barrelled into 4 Newington Street in North Belfast and shot dead an innocent father of two, twenty-nine-year-old Terence McDaid, in front of his wife, parents and children, he frantically telephoned his handlers in the early hours: 'It was one of ours but they got the wrong man.'[36]

When Dodds burst into the McDaid family's living room, Terry's wife, Maura, was 'screaming at them to stop it, to stop shooting'. Woken by the commotion, their two daughters saw it all from the top of the stairs.[37] 'I remember being told, "Don't look, don't look"', said Tracy, who was eight at the time. 'So I looked and saw my daddy laying just like a stone on the floor, with my mummy standing over him.'[38]

Nelson made four panicky calls to his handlers that night because, more accurately, it was he, not Dodds, who had 'got the wrong man', since it was he who had given the wrong address to Dodds five days before the assassination, and also to Eric McKee on the day of the murder.[39] Later that day Nelson's handlers felt able to assure him that Terence McDaid was 'traced as PIRA' after all, at which point his handlers noted that Nelson became 'quite content'.[40] However, it wasn't true that Terry, unlike his brother Declan, was in any way involved with the PIRA. This was confirmed by Detective Chief Inspector Kieran Lagan, who told Terry's inquest that he had 'no paramilitary connections'.[41]

Whether Nelson's handlers had contributed to this catastrophe remains unclear to this day. Declan had been marked out by the UDA as a target before Nelson returned to Belfast in the spring of 1987. An old 'P' card correctly gave his address as 22 Oceanic Avenue, a four-minute walk from 4 Newington Street, but this card had been updated in Nelson's handwriting, saying, 'now staying with sister … at Newington Street'.[42] According to Terry's widow, Declan had visited her house two days before Terry was shot, although he was not living there.[43] So how would Nelson have known 4 Newington Street was where Declan's 'sister' – who was in fact his sister-in-law – lived?

Nelson's explanation to the Stevens 1 Inquiry was that from over a month of visual sightings of Declan McDaid at his home at 22 Oceanic Street, he'd discovered he spent 'quite a lot of time' at 4 Newington Street. When he checked the address on the electoral register at Belfast central library, he found Maura McDaid's name there.[44] Yet this area in North Belfast was strongly nationalist/republican and residents were particularly alert to strangers, since it interfaced with the staunchly loyalist area of Tiger Bay. Stevens' inquiries were sceptical that Nelson had been able to spend long hours sitting in a car or standing on a street corner observing 22 Oceanic Avenue, waiting for Declan to emerge so he could follow him. Unfamiliar faces would not have lasted long in that closed neighbourhood 'before being clocked', said Detective Sergeant Nicky Benwell. 'Our RUC liaison officer said you'd barely have time to deliver a summons.'[45] Three years later, Nelson would intimate that he did get some assistance from the FRU (see Chapter 14).

The murder of Terence McDaid was one of four arising from Nelson's targeting in which children either witnessed the moment of their father's execution or saw him bleeding out, the air thick with cordite and hysterical screams of terror and torment.[46] On each occasion the FRU or Special Branch had had ample warning of the UDA's murderous plans, either from

Nelson or the branch's own agents. All such warnings went unheeded. In three of those murders, no member of the murder gangs reliably linked to them was arrested, let alone charged. Not for the first time, this failure begs the question: what was the state getting out of protecting agent criminality over locking up the known perpetrators of cold-blooded murders?

Not nothing, argue defenders of that regime. It at least allowed the intelligence services to 'build a picture' from inside the rival terrorist groups: 'who was up, who was down, long-term strategy, that kind of thing', as one former branch officer put it. 'Building a picture was very much an MI5 cultural thing,' he explained. 'Gathering intelligence, building pictures, developing information, even if it was never going to see the light of day.' The counter-argument is that the moment an agent crosses into serious criminality, that agent should be withdrawn. 'In which case you're pretty soon going to run out of agents,' the former officer explained.[47] In Nelson's case, Stevens concluded that building pictures was more of a priority than saving lives. 'Decisions were made on the basis of expediency rather than life saving as the FRU's primary purpose,' said Detective Inspector Sarah Bynum. 'I think the primary goal, was to have information from whatever sources.'[48] Justice Cory had concluded likewise. Nelson's 'involvement in violent activities was of concern to his handlers only to the extent that this exposed him to risk of apprehension by the police.'[49]

Another child to intimately witness the result of Nelson's targeting was nine-year-old Sean Slane. At the sound of repeated gunfire at 4.15 a.m. on 23 September 1988, he saw his father Gerard 'just dropping at the top of the stairs'. The family had been woken by glass being smashed as gunmen forced their way into the house, past a child's bike, shooting up at Gerard, a painter and decorator. Then the sound of a car, tyres squealing as the attackers made their getaway. Slane died trying to fend off his assassins by hurling a ladder at them. His last words to his wife were, 'Theresa, it's the Orangemen.'[50] 'He's dead, they've killed him,' Sean heard his mother screaming out. His young brother Gerry was so hysterical that he was jumping up and down on the broken glass, cutting his feet. Sean remembers 'just seeing my dad lying with all tea towels over his chest where the gunshots were and just all blood'.[51] Afterwards, one of the gunmen proudly described how his partner's bullet had caught Slane 'right in the head … you couldn't get any better than that could you?'[52]

Slane was murdered after Nelson had been tasked by the UDA with finding the killer of a UDA racketeer, Billy Quee, whose murder was claimed by a dissident offshoot of the INLA, the Irish People's Liberation Organisation (IPLO). An eyewitness identified Slane from a photograph, but the police said there was nothing to suggest he'd been involved.[53] No matter. Nelson gave Slane's address and his photograph to the gun team. 'Is this the chappie?' Jim Spence, allegedly one of the assassins asked Nelson. 'I'll soon deal with him.'[54] Even though Nelson reported this on 21 September, the FRU 'almost certainly' didn't send a MISR to the branch until after Slane was shot on the 23rd. But even had the FRU dispatched it in time, it would have been useless, since it referred only to the fact that 'IPLO members' were being targeted, without naming Slane or the fact that the attack was imminent.[55] Spence was not arrested by the RUC, despite Special Branch being told by the FRU that he had 'planned the murder of Gerard Slane',[56] and, the following February, that he played 'a critical role in directing and organising the murder' of the Belfast solicitor Patrick Finucane, as, indeed, did Agent 6137.[57]

It was 7.25 p.m. on a Sunday evening as the thirty-eight-year-old lawyer sat down to dinner in the kitchen with his wife and three children, John (8), Katherine (12) and Michael (17). Two gunmen kicked in the front door and ran down the hall. The lead gunman, wearing black with a camouflage jacket tied round his waist, opened fire through the kitchen's glass-paned door as Finucane tried to close it. Finucane's wife, Geraldine, activated a panic alarm, then was hit in the ankle by a ricocheting bullet. She fell against the dining-room door, putting her hands over her head at the continuous blasts of gunfire. Two or three bullets hit Finucane in the chest and stomach, and he fell back, helpless, on the floor. More shots followed – around twelve in all – now slower and more deliberate, aimed at his head and neck.[58] The post-mortem report showed that one or more of the bullets had been fired from just 15 inches away.[59] Finucane's eldest son Michael's memory of that Sunday evening is, unsurprisingly, 'not a place I care to visit very often, but I know it's there'.[60]

Finucane was considered by many in the police and army to be 'a thorn in the side' of the security forces because many of his clients were members of the IRA whom he'd defended. He had, for example, brought a successful habeas corpus application to get Brian Gillen released from police custody after the RUC burst his eardrum while he was being questioned over the murder of a police officer. The case highlighted the danger of associating a lawyer with his clients, for Gillen had a legitimate claim that was settled in the mid-1990s on advice by a senior counsel, Pat Coughlin QC, who later became a High Court judge.[61]

In the run-up to Finucane's murder, he was reported to have received several death threats from police, mainly delivered via his clients when they were being interrogated. One client said he was told to tell Finucane that he was a 'thug in a suit, a person trying to let on he is doing his job, and that he, like every other Fenian bastard, would meet his end'.[62] Two months before he was shot, police officers interrogating a prominent UDA gunman for murder urged him to focus his efforts on Finucane. One officer is reported to have said it would be 'a bad blow for the Provos [the IRA] to have Finucane removed'.[63] The following month, three clients of Finucane's – including his brother Seamus – were told 'he's a dead man', 'he would meet his end' and 'fucking Finucane's getting took out'.[64]

At the same time, Nelson's stock had been falling with both his UDA and FRU masters. Both were complaining he'd failed to deliver any targeting intelligence worth exploiting since the attempt on Harry Maynes the previous May, which, as the FRU reminded him, 'had to be aborted because 6137 managed to get himself involved'.[65] His handlers were also disturbed by his cavalier approach to security. Thanks to a tip-off prior to the uniformed RUC raiding Nelson's house, he'd only just managed to move a 'lot of incriminating material, like an infrared weapon sight, a counter eavesdropping device, radio scanner and intelligence material on Sinn Fein/PIRA members'. At the same time his tax-free income – from his FRU salary and other perks, jobs on the side, his UDA salary, his unlawful claim of benefits and his wife's income – gave him a total annual income of £27,000, today worth around £74,000.[66] 'The time has come for 6137 to be faced with the facts,' recorded an exasperated FRU note.[67] His handlers were also wearying of his 'history' of phoning the office after 'getting drunk'. At their next meeting, his handlers planned to ask him what he was doing with his 'spare cash' and 'what he believes he does for this office and his motivation for doing it'.[68]

Simultaneously, the UDA was blaming Nelson for a 'lack of intelligence and incorrect targeting' after a series of failed hits.[69] Based on Nelson's targeting, since October 1988, masked gunmen had burst through three front doors to find only terrified wives and children at home.[70] In one of the attacks, Marion Kelly and her three children were confronted by a gunman in her hallway, while another stood over her seventeen-year-old son who was cowering on the floor. They demanded to know if a man called Patrick Monaghan was in the house. They fled only when it was clear the Kelly family didn't know who they were talking about. Five days later, Barbara Morgan and her three children faced a similar ordeal. Two gunmen broke into their house planning to kill Barbara's husband, James. In both cases, Nelson had personally provided the gunmen with the names and addresses. In Monaghan's case, Nelson's 'intelligence' was inaccurate, despite him having assured the would-be-assassins that it was 'very up to date'.[71]

Nelson had also begun to worry much more about his own security within the UDA. In one of the UDA's bouts of febrile paranoia the previous August, he had briefly – and falsely – fallen under suspicion for passing information to the IRA and was interrogated and apparently electrocuted with a cattle prod. This followed a tip-off from a UDA Special Branch source that someone close to a senior UDA man, Moby Bickerstaff, was passing information to the IRA. Nelson was suspected because he was known to be close to Bickerstaff.[72] He also feared he might have come under suspicion again because he'd opposed the targeting of Father Des Wilson, and the UDA told him the RUC had also got wind of the plot to kill the priest.[73]

It was against this background that Nelson appears not to have disclosed to his handlers the fact that Patrick Finucane was being targeted and that he had reconnoitred the Finucane family home.[74] Nor is there any record of him telling his handlers that he had passed Finucane's 'P' card to the 'military' commander of the UDA, Eric McKee,[75] and a notorious gunman, Ken Barrett. When Barrett saw it, he said, 'Fine'.[76] Barrett drove the getaway car for the two gunmen who shot Finucane a few days later.[77]

However, in both his first statement to Stevens and in his journal written in jail, Nelson claims to have told the FRU two months before Finucane was murdered that the UDA were 'showing an interest in this solicitor'. On the basis of Sir Desmond de Silva's analysis of the available material, Nelson's claims are unconvincing. Might the FRU have sanitised the record by deleting the CFs in which they believe Nelson forewarned his handlers? The existing CFs are extremely detailed in their reporting of what Nelson told them during his entire period as an FRU agent, much of it highly compromising for both him and them. Had there been a plan to sanitise the CFs, one might not have expected this material to have survived.[78] Operation Kenova also found that FRU handlers were trained 'not to embellish or diminish information they received', reinforced by Kenova's discovery that 'frank' confessions by agents to their handlers of 'involvement in serious criminality', including murder, were also retained by the FRU.[79] On the other hand, Stevens 3 was unable to find potentially incriminating telephone transcripts with Nelson in the McDaid murder, so sanitisation in some cases cannot be entirely excluded.[80]

The fact that there was nothing in the FRU CFs to show that Nelson had forewarned them about the attack on Finucane suggested to his handlers a loss of trust in him by the UDA. He was summoned to a rare 'boss' meeting with the OC of the East Det FRU.[81] It seems the FRU did not consider Finucane to be a member of the IRA, so there was no obvious motive for the FRU to collude with Nelson in his murder. 'We knew who was on the Provisional IRA Army Council, Northern Command and Belfast Brigade,' said Colonel Kerr. 'Patrick Finucane did not figure.'[82] By contrast, Army Headquarters Northern Ireland (HQNI) appears to have considered Finucane to have had some affiliation with the PIRA, as the words 'PIRA P2327' were tagged to his name in a handful of FRU files. Kerr, however, explained that this was not an FRU designation but was based on records from the army's All-Source computer and that the number 'p2327' referred to an HQNI file.[83] Detective Superintendent Alan Simpson, who investigated Finucane's murder at the time, made it unambiguously clear that the RUC had

> no evidence to suggest that Mr Finucane was a member of the PIRA. The police refute the claim that Pat Finucane was a member of the Provisional IRA. He was another law-abiding citizen going about his professional duties in a professional manner. He was well known both inside and outside the legal profession. He was regarded in police circles as very professional, and he discharged his duties with vigour and professionalism.[84]

Former Chief Constables Sir Ronnie Flanagan and Sir Hugh Orde have also exonerated Finucane of IRA membership in the face of assertions by others,[85] including former RUC Chief Constable Sir Jack Hermon, that Finucane was 'associated with the IRA'.[86] Four weeks before Finucane was shot, a briefing by Hermon and other RUC officers that some solicitors in Northern Ireland were 'effectively in the pockets of terrorists' led Home Office Parliamentary Under-secretary Douglas Hogg to tell MPs that a number of solicitors were 'unduly sympathetic to the cause of the IRA'.[87] An RUC note from January 1989 referred to Finucane 'associating closely with Gerry Adams' during the H-Block hunger strike and stated that he 'continued to support the Republican cause using his expertise in an advisory capacity and associating closely with PIRA/PSF [Provisional Sinn Féin] personnel'.[88] None of this, however, shows him to have been a PIRA member, nor is it to deny the 'shocking levels of state collusion' in a horrific murder, as finally acknowledged in 2012 by Prime Minister David Cameron, following the publication of de Silva's report. Much of the report was based on the vast amount of material gathered by the three Stevens inquiries, although de Silva says he had access to a 'significant amount of material' that was not available to Stevens or Justice Cory.[89] Cameron also cited the failure of Special Branch to act on threats to Finucane that, unlike Nelson, their agents *had* warned them about.[90] Notably, he made no mention of Finucane having been targeted by MI5's 'propaganda initiatives', an unwise initiative introduced in the 1980s without political clearance to counter republican propaganda. Information was disseminated through MI5's agents in the UDA, of which there were at least three, including 'one at the very top'.[91] The purpose of these initiatives was to discredit and 'unnerve' leading republicans. In Finucane's case, the UDA published a spoof edition of the IRA's weekly newspaper *An Phoblacht*, which it called *An Phobcrapt*; it featured Finucane with his client, IRA man Pat McGeown. While the parody no doubt raised laughs within the UDA, it also irresponsibly helped inflame loyalist sentiment against the solicitor.

An incident reported by Nelson nine months after Finucane's murder underscores the widespread belief within the RUC that the solicitor was a PIRA asset. On his release from RUC interrogation, one of the suspects for the murder, Winkie Dodds, remarked how friendly their questioning had been and that their interrogators had 'congratulated' the UDA on a 'fine job' with only one reservation: that the assassination should 'not have been done in such a fashion, i.e. in front of Finucane's wife and children'.[92]

There may, of course, be yet more to discover about the role of the state in Finucane's murder. A public inquiry into it was announced by the Labour government in September 2024 – a full twenty-three years after the Tony Blair government made a solemn commitment to hold one. De Silva's review of all the material accumulated by Stevens and Cory, as well as other classified material not disclosed to either inquiry, was intended by David Cameron as a substitute for the public inquiry that Blair had failed to deliver. Running to 829 pages, de Silva's review was forensic and comprehensive, although critics – and they include Pat Finucane's widow, Geraldine – saw it as a 'whitewash' and a 'sham'.[93] There are certainly many in nationalist West Belfast who suspect the plot to kill Finucane extended to Whitehall, Margaret Thatcher and her Cabinet. Against that is the fact that a review in 2012 by a senior Stevens officer of all the Cabinet minutes from 1988 to 1991 showed that neither Finucane nor his murder was ever mentioned.[94] A fertile area for the inquiry to explore, however, would be MI5's foolish propaganda initiatives.

As for the FRU and Nelson, the CFs show that, in the last nine months of his time as Agent 6137, his main handler, Sergeant Margaret Jones, was replaced by Colour Sergeant Ben Lawrenson. The FRU records suggest a marked effort at tighter control over Nelson at this time. He was sharply reprimanded for seeking information,[95] a service that even the MoD later observed seemed to have been 'rendered to him in the past'.[96] Nelson was also chastised by Lawrenson for lax security by 'frequent acts of recklessness',[97] having already been reminded that he was part of a team whose principal purpose was saving lives.[98] He needed 'careful monitoring,' said Lawrenson.[99] This tougher regime appears to have constrained Nelson's appetite for targets, mirrored in references in the CFs to Nelson's 'total failure to show any initiative', his 'lack of spark' and that he was just 'coasting'.[100] Gone too were references to the FRU's original goal for Nelson to professionalise the UDA's targeting.

All the danger signs picked up by Lawrenson had been flashing red from the first day Nelson was re-recruited two years earlier. Ronnie Anderson, the handler who managed his transition from the first FRU regime to the second, had adjudged him 'unreliable'.[101] His enthusiasm for the proposed assassination of Adams, and the suspicion that the FRU would have allowed this had MI5 and Special Branch not intervened, albeit for political expediency rather than the principle of saving a life, led MI5's head office in London to comment that running Nelson 'threatens to get out of control'.[102] A year after the Adams incident, the FRU itself acknowledged Nelson was going after PIRA targets without telling his handlers[103] and that it was a 'constant battle to persuade 6137 to refrain from becoming too involved'.[104] Martin Callan, Nelson's main handler in 1987, said he 'frequently voiced my concerns' about Nelson's level of criminality to the OC East Det FRU but was 'always told that I was "bomb proof" and not to concern myself with Nelson's activities but to purely report them'.[105] In his desperation to see 'legitimate targets' shot,[106] Nelson's 'cowboy' attitude to targeting had even led him into hostile bars, sitting within earshot of a hostile target, deluding himself that he wouldn't be spotted.[107]

The FRU's CO, Colonel Kerr, has been widely held to be principally responsible for the Nelson debacle. Clearly, as the soldier who so determinedly brought him back from Germany and who led the unit that ran him, Kerr bears a considerable liability. De Silva, however, does not accept that Kerr should be held solely responsible or accountable as, he says, has been 'implied' by Stevens and Cory.[108] It is certainly true that, while the army's senior chain of command to whom Kerr was directly responsible (ACOS G2 and the CLF) was probably unaware of the extent of Nelson's day-to-day criminality, they signally failed to ensure he was properly monitored after MI5's warning from when he returned to the FRU that he was unreliable and that the operation was likely to 'go off the rails'.[109]

There again, as long as the FRU's priority was protecting Agent 6137 as a source, irrespective of the extent of his criminality, running him as an agent was always going to be more about listening to him than exercising control over him. Criminality was the inevitable price of winning the trust of the UDA killers he'd been tasked with getting alongside to 'professionalise' their targeting.

The same applied to agents run by all three agencies. The handler met his agent on a Monday; he had no control over what the agent did on the Tuesday or any day until next they met. Even then, the agent dictated what he told his handler. The agent was in control. The handler listened. And had the handler reacted by sending in the cavalry to thwart every attack the agent told them about, the agent was likely to have a very limited lifespan. If, on the other hand, an agent was removed every time they got drawn into serious criminality, the intelligence services would pretty soon have run out of agents. At least, this is the Catch-22 defence offered by the spymasters accused of 'playing God' during the conflict by choosing who was to be saved, who might have to be sacrificed, which crimes were to be prosecuted and which were to be ignored.

There is a compelling, if chilling logic to this defence, particularly if you believe that to defeat terrorism you need to penetrate the terrorist organisations responsible, which the state, clearly, has a duty to do. Equally, the state has to show it's getting the much better end of the bargain, and that depends upon how much criminality the state is prepared to tolerate. The extent of the moral compromises allowed by the state has been *the* question that, more than any other, has so vexed the legacy of the Northern Ireland conflict, for the answer of what is acceptable is almost an entirely subjective one, such that consensus is never likely to be reached on the matter.

'What did he really achieve at the end of the day?' asked Lord Justice Kelly of Nelson's counsel at his sentencing hearing in 1992. 'Did he save lives?' The question cut through the proceedings like a knife. The answer was three, offset by many more deaths, while materially increasing the UDA's capacity to target republicans they deemed deserved to die.

There was a fourth life Nelson's handlers were determined to save: an extremely well-placed FRU agent embedded at the very heart of the PIRA. This was Agent 6126, licensed by the IRA to delve into almost any aspect of that organisation to protect it from penetration by British agents just like him. And licensed by the British state to do whatever it took to maintain his cover, which arguably involved even greater moral compromises than were allowed in running 6137.

Chapter Five

Agent 6126

CONWAY MILL IN THE HEART of West Belfast was the last of Belfast's linen-producing factories to close in the 1970s, a vast magisterial structure of white glazed bricks and vaulted floors supported by cast-iron pillars. It was left to rot for almost a decade, until it was reborn as the beating heart of cultural republicanism a decade later. Led by the veteran republican and small business entrepreneur, the late Tom Cahill, the not-for-profit Conway Street Community Enterprises Project Ltd was established in 1985 to provide, as Gerry Adams put it, 'education, self-help and local employment opportunities'.[1] As volunteers restored parts of the derelict building known simply as 'The Mill', it performed all of those functions – and a few more besides.

Cahill and Adams were both veterans of Cage 6 in Long Kesh, along with legendary IRA figures from the 1970s such as Brendan 'Darkie' Hughes.[2] With the rebels now in charge of a mill that once sweated labour, Conway Street also became an 'alternative centre for radical ideas' – and not the kind the Northern Ireland Office (NIO) was prepared to assist with charitable funds. Besides hosting a people's public inquiry into a fatal shooting by the RUC, 'The Mill' also became a centre for Sinn Féin press conferences and a general 'refuge' for republicans.[3]

It was an obvious venue, then, for the UDA's chief intelligence officer, FRU Agent 6137, to keep eyes, from a secure distance, on who was coming and going, and their vehicle registration numbers. Brian Nelson would often try his luck by asking his handlers to give him the owners' names and addresses, and he would occasionally succeed. Failing that, there was a friendly police source with access to the vehicle database on whom the UDA could usually rely.

Within the FRU, one of the vehicles logged by Nelson in November 1987 put the 'breeze up vertical' as the old Second World War saying goes. Nelson's handlers were alarmed to find it belonged to a long-serving member of the IRA, who was more prized by the FRU as an agent than even Nelson, or indeed any of the FRU's hundred other agents. This agent – Agent 6126 – was the 'golden egg' as General Sir John Wilsey, former general officer commanding (GOC) Northern Ireland put it. 'It was the one thing that was terribly important to the army.'[4]

So prized was 6126, in fact, that from 1982, when the FRU was formed, an entire team of handlers, support staff and soldiers was dedicated solely to running this agent, with a phone line also dedicated exclusively to him and staffed round the clock.[5] This team was based in a Portakabin at army headquarters in Lisburn.[6] It became known as 'The Rathole', not in appreciation of the rat-like cunning that successful espionage requires, but due to the unpleasant working environment.[7] Agent 6126's handling was directly overseen by the FRU CO, with his intelligence (and that of other FRU agents) accurately filed by an administrative support officer.[8] A bespoke intelligence database, known as 'Bog Rat 3970' or 'Osbourne', was also created to handle his reports.[9] Agent 6126 was Freddie Scappaticci, codenamed Stakeknife, a member of the IRA's Internal Security Unit (ISU) tasked by the organisation with protecting the republican movement from being penetrated by spies just like him. IRA volunteers referred to the ISU as the 'nutting squad', because after a confession had been wrung from a suspected agent they were shot in the head; typically a bullet would be fired by each of two executioners, so that both were implicated in the murder.[10] Following Nelson's sighting of 6126's car at Conway Mill on 18 November 1987, an anxious FRU reported, 'if 6137 finds a trace on 6126 on his files, he may well, due to ease of access, begin to target 6126 at his home address'.[11]

Nelson's handlers were also worried about the risk of him targeting other FRU agents in the IRA without telling them. With about a hundred agents in republican armed groups on the FRU's books, that risk was high. Worse, there was nothing to stop the UDA's 'military' commander, Eric McKee, targeting them without telling Nelson. Agent 6126 in particular was one life that absolutely merited the FRU pulling out all the stops to ensure he was safe.

By placing an agent at the heart of the ISU, the British had secured eyes and ears at the point where all the IRA's paths intersected. The ISU has been likened to the IRA's 'electrical junction box through which every wire must flow'.[12] Perhaps not every wire – some operations, and some units were hermetically sealed even from the security department. Nonetheless, through Scappaticci, it's fair to say the 'British really had the wedding tackle of the IRA firmly in their hands', as former IRA man Anthony McIntyre put it.[13] This was no exaggeration. The ISU had access to members of the IRA's ruling Army Council, having been appointed by senior members of its newly established Northern Command. ISU operatives also had the freedom to roam most places, ask any questions, probe any weakness precisely because of the trust that had been placed in them by the leadership.

The ISU was established in 1978 – the same year that Scappaticci was recruited by military intelligence. It was the product of a restructured IRA, whose principal architects were Ivor Bell[14] and Gerry Adams.[15] The plans were drafted while both were serving jail sentences in Long Kesh internment camp, Adams for trying to escape while interned and Bell for helping him.[16] The creation of Northern Command, which wrested control of the IRA from Dublin, was central to its so-called 'Long War' strategy. This held that if the Provos just kept bombing and shooting, they would eventually sicken the British out of the north of Ireland. To maximise this renewed war effort, penetration by British agents and informers had to be minimised. Until the formation of the ISU, suspected 'touts' had been dealt with autonomously by each brigade, and the record had not been pretty. Most of the IRA's death penalty victims had not been IRA members and they included a fifteen-year-old boy with a mental age of eight, who was left with a placard saying 'Tout' pinned to his chest;[17] a sixty-two-year-old retired poultry dealer;[18] and a widow and mother of ten children, Jean McConville.[19] McConville, along with, at the very least, sixteen other suspected informers, was 'disappeared' – abducted, murdered and secretly buried – to hide the IRA's embarrassment at the scale of British penetration.

The newly formed ISU's job was to ensure the security of the IRA at every level: if members walked into a bar, a chill would descend. Besides flushing out anyone from agents to ordinary nationalists who might give the time of day to a British squaddie, they also vetted new recruits and interrogated volunteers released from interrogation by Special Branch. Internal Security's priority was to find out exactly what the branch knew about an operation that had gone wrong, and what the volunteer had actually told them, as opposed to what the volunteer was saying they had told them. The slightest inconsistency risked raising suspicion that the volunteer had been released conditionally after agreeing to inform on their IRA comrades in exchange for not being charged.

In such cases, a psychologically nerve-racking ordeal, sometimes physical, awaited the volunteer, facing the wall with a hood on in a cold upstairs room. Of all the ISU's interrogators, Scappaticci, with his blend of psychological and physical menace, was one of the most feared and effective. 'People felt intimidated by him,' said McIntyre, 'even when he didn't intimidate. People felt very uncomfortable in his company.'[20] One source, the former IRA man Seán Maguire, who became a key member of Sinn Féin's communications team, once quipped that his 'worst nightmare would be to be interviewed by Freddie Scap. If you fall under his suspicion, you'd wet yourself.'[21]

The state paid a high moral price in running Scappaticci. Those handling him, as well as those in Special Branch and MI5 who knew his prized position, can have been in no doubt whatsoever as to what he would need to do to ensure his cover remained intact. This was not an agent simply reporting on the activities of the IRA. This was an agent who would sometimes have to prepare other agents and informers for execution and, moreover, to play his part convincingly, pouring vitriol into their ears about the unconscionable betrayal of the republican cause, while still being able to look at himself in the mirror for doing exactly that.

To have succeeded in playing his part with total conviction must have required ice in Scappaticci's veins, an ability to switch off when playing psychological games with a fellow agent/informer quaking before him. His task was focused solely on securing the all-important confession the IRA rulebook required for a member of the Army Council to pass the death sentence. And secure it Scappaticci did, on several occasions, knowing he was sending his victim to their grave on a false promise. That promise of 'confess and you'll be allowed home', or 'we're taking you to a press conference' usually worked because, after many hours, and sometimes days, of gruelling interrogation, hope was the last thing that died. The offer also served the execution team's purpose by helping to keep the victim calm before they were shot. '[T]hey think they're going to go home,' as Scappaticci himself acknowledged, 'but they don't.'[22] A few victims were not allowed even that final delusion. 'Some execution people were very, very vindictive,' explained one former IRA member. 'They've told the victim, "You're not going to a fuckin' press conference; you're gettin' fuckin' shot."'[23]

As with Brian Nelson, it was Freddie Scappaticci who was in control – not his handlers. Agents are not automatons who simply report and react. They are human, with self-preservation at the core of every move they make. 'You never – never – get the full truth from an agent,' a former senior MI5 officer explained.[24] The agent is the one who determines how much of what they have discovered is fed back to their handlers; they also determine when that happens. Both gifts are entirely conditional upon the agent's assessment of how the content and timing might threaten their own existence. So, when Scappaticci did pass intelligence to his handlers that risked compromising his security, he must have trusted implicitly that they would use that information in a way and at a time that never led back to him, even if that sometimes meant not reacting at all, with the inevitable consequence that someone would die. While the ability of most agents to communicate with their handlers in the 1980s was limited to phone boxes, home telephones and meetings in safe houses or vans, in Scappaticci's case he had a microphone built into his car, which allowed for a detailed and near-contemporaneous record to be made, but it could only be shared with his handlers when they met up and the tapes retrieved. There was no mechanism in those days for electronic transmission.[25]

To have survived a decade leading a double life, one minute wholeheartedly preparing a living soul for death, the next covering your tracks in order to securely pass on the IRA's innermost secrets, required a steady nerve, instinctive guile and cunning, plus a great deal of resilience and self-confidence. Scappaticci had all those qualities in spades, as he demonstrated at the beginning of his IRA career serving as commander in the Markets area of Belfast in the early 1970s.

Born Frederick (not Alfredo as some reports have it),[26] Scappaticci was the son of an ice-cream parlour owner, whose parents had emigrated from Italy to Belfast in the late nineteenth century. His lifelong friend Sean Flynn recalls that he became a talented footballer known for his 'tough and ferocious tackling' in matches in the streets around Donegall Pass. As the stand-out player for Ormeau United Under-14s, he had a month's trial for Nottingham Forest, which was in what was then called the First Division. He was sent back to Belfast because Forest told him his short thickset frame needed to lose weight.[27] Scappaticci gave a slightly different version of this story. He told a neighbour in later years that he was in digs and just got homesick but had since regretted leaving.[28] At the time – around 1980 – the neighbour was a soccer-mad teenager and begged Scappaticci to be his team's manager, to which came the reply, '[T]he fucking IRA own my life. I don't have a minute to do anything …' By then, British military intelligence owned a good chunk of it too.

Short though the young Scappaticci was, his fearless muscular aggression and fierce temper characterised his whole life. Examples abound, and the fullest – and best sourced to date – are recounted in a biography by former IRA man Ricky O'Rawe. A 'vicious c***,' says O'Rawe of Scappaticci, recalling the time when he slapped his brother-in-law round the face for complaining when Scappaticci only half-finished a DIY task he'd undertaken to complete.[29]

O'Rawe first encountered 'Scap', as he was popularly known, in their respective cages of Long Kesh in the early 1970s. He describes how Scappaticci's first brush with the law was as an eighteen-year-old apprentice bricklayer, when he and a mate had a brawl with two Protestant youths and ended up chasing them until they were stopped by the police. Scappaticci landed in court and was fined £10.[30]

At the age of twenty, Scappaticci married Sheila Cunningham, who in many ways was his complete opposite: devoutly religious and gentle. She was the sister of the wife of Jim Davison, a leading local republican who became Scappaticci's IRA boss in the Markets area of Belfast. Davison told me how Scappaticci devoured James Bond films, with *Dr No* a favourite, especially the scene where at the press of a button 'a bomb goes off and someone says, "That's him back in the salt mines."' He recalled how Scappaticci kept repeating that phrase. 'He really liked it.' Due to his swarthy Mediterranean complexion, Scappaticci was routinely referred to as 'The Wop, as well as some other names.'[31] In late 1960s Belfast, racially insulting a fellow citizen of Italian descent doesn't appear to have raised eyebrows as it would today.

At the time, the Northern Ireland civil rights movement had just begun, but it had yet to explode into the violence out of which the Provisional IRA was born as the more militant off-shoot of the Marxist-leaning Official IRA. The PIRA grew out of the latter's perceived failure to defend Catholics from marauding loyalists burning them out in Belfast, captured by the slogan 'IRA – I Ran Away' scrawled derisively over the walls of Catholic ghettoes. Scappaticci was not in the first flush of recruits to the 'Provos', as they were known; he started out as a vigilante patrolling the streets to protect them from loyalist mobs.[32] His decision to join was no doubt encouraged by the fact that in 1969 he and his family were burned out when a petrol bomb was thrown through their living-room window. They moved to a new home half a mile away in the Markets, where Scappaticci would become a household name.[33]

Witnesses describe Scappaticci as having a brooding, authoritative presence, which helps explain why he soon became the PIRA's OC of the Markets area.[34] 'He wasn't a big drinker,' said one senior IRA man who knew him well and disliked him. 'My recollection is that he was the quiet one, always listening, taking in everything.'[35] Still, planting bombs under the noses of the British Army in Belfast city centre won the admiration of his loyal volunteers in the Markets. 'He had balls to burn,' said one.[36] At this stage, he appears to have been a diehard republican.

He also instilled fear. O'Rawe quotes one of his neighbours in the Markets saying that he was a 'fucking bully' who 'had the place terrorised … because they knew he was a top 'RA man'. The neighbour also says he 'regularly beat the crap' out of his wife, Sheila, who, unlike her husband, appears to have been extremely popular.[37] She was 'a lovely person,' said another resident, who also told O'Rawe that Scappaticci 'beat her black and blue'.[38] Nevertheless, they had six children and the marriage survived, even after he was outed as a spy,[39] although not, it seems, without reservations.

When Sheila fell seriously ill some years after he was outed as Stakeknife, she is said to have declined to take his money for treatment, presumably due to the fact that it had come from the British.[40]

When Scappaticci and his family moved to Twinbrook in the late 1970s, neighbours soon understood that 'you didn't want to be on the wrong side of Scap. He was a tough nut.' One made the fatal error of complaining to a friend in Ardoyne that he was fed up with living on 'Provie Hill', citing Scappaticci and a couple of his IRA-supporting friends as 'Provie gobshites'. Word got back to Scappaticci. Into Fat Harry's bar in Castle Street strode the brick-built Scappaticci, after the neighbour was spotted having a pint. With a half brick in his jumper sleeve, Scappaticci pounded into him, also threatening two doormen when they moved to intervene, warning them: 'This is IRA business.'[41]

The years did not seem to subdue Scappaticci's appetite for bull-like aggression. Some two decades later, after being outed as Stakeknife, a dishevelled Scappaticci emerged from his house in a dressing gown to threaten a BBC camera crew: 'Take no more photos of this house. Fucking scum youse are. Stories youse make up … Don't take any more photos of this house, I'm telling you now. Because if you do, I'll come out and I'll fucking do you.'[42] Of course the only stories being made up were by the ranting Scappaticci.

In 1971, Scappaticci was interned, having spectacularly failed to practice what he'd preached to the IRA volunteers under his command the night before internment was introduced. He warned them the move was imminent and to leave their homes immediately, yet when soldiers came to lift Scappaticci the following morning, they found him at home in bed.[43] A volunteer from Derry who shared the same Long Kesh cage with Scap, and played football with him, said that, unlike the 'big mouths' amongst them, Scap 'kept his mouth shut. I actually liked him. It seems he could be a nasty wee fucker, but he was never, ever nasty to me.'[44]

Others were not so partial. One inmate, also from the Markets, who sometimes walked around the cage yard with Scappaticci, came to dislike him intensely because he was so preoccupied with his status. 'The world was viewed exclusively through the prism of Scap's ego,' he said. Scappaticci was also openly critical of the IRA leadership, and he had a 'pornographic mind' and spoke crudely about women.[45] Within the IRA, stories about Scappaticci's sexual predilections were legend. A senior member of the Belfast Brigade from the 1980s told me he had a reputation for riffling through drawers for women's underwear and sniffing them at call houses whose owners put them at the IRA's disposal for secure meetings or to snipe at the security forces.[46] At IRA meetings in the leisure centre in the Lower Falls, he is said to have drilled through the wall so he could peek into the ladies dressing room.[47] 'Scappaticci would have fucked a cracked cup,' said Tommy Gorman, an IRA contemporary of Scappaticci in the 1970s.[48]

Following his release from internment in 1973, Scappaticci returned to Belfast and, like many of his fellow IRA volunteers, could be found on a Saturday night at the Jubilee Club in the Markets. It was there that as a sixteen-year-old who'd just joined the IRA, Anthony McIntyre encountered him and the 'Big Bossman' persona he'd cultivated. 'You could see he thought he was THE man. I think he loved that persona.'[49]

As McIntyre's senior in both age and rank, Scappaticci took an avuncular interest in the new recruit. He ordered him to hijack a car, for which McIntyre, still a juvenile, was arrested, charged with IRA membership and detained at a boys' home. Scappaticci sent someone to 'get me out', but McIntyre had already absconded. With Jim Davison, Scappaticci helped him escape south to Dundalk. 'I looked up to Scap then,' said McIntyre. 'I thought he was a good IRA man, someone I wanted to take orders from when he was organising an operation.'[50] McIntyre also found him 'serious and sombre. He was neither friendly nor unfriendly. What he had was a sense of self-importance.'[51]

For a brief period in the summer of 1974, Scappaticci was promoted OC, Belfast Brigade, the beneficiary of an attritional period from January of that year, during which one PIRA OC after another was arrested. Now high on the British Army's sighting list, he was spotted in mid-July.[52] A month later, on 16 August, he was caught and returned to Long Kesh. The *Belfast Telegraph*'s front page carried the headline: 'Troops capture top IRA officer' with 'an Italian-sounding name'. Scappaticci is reported to have swaggered back into his 'cage' brandishing the newspaper 'as if he was 7ft tall' (he was, in fact, 5ft 3ins), recalled one inmate. It was Scappaticci's way of saying, 'the Cage needs to respect me'.[53] When internment ended, he was one of the last to be released.

It was now December 1975. The IRA was expecting Scappaticci to report back for duty immediately. But he didn't, a decision that 'was viewed with a certain amount of disdain' by his comrades.[54] Two months later, Anthony McIntyre was arrested for murder after shooting a UVF man; he spent the next eighteen years in jail.[55] Meanwhile Scappaticci took a break from the IRA – at least for a while. Having spent the best part of three and a half years in Long Kesh, his immediate focus appears to have been on his family and making some money, a goal he soon achieved by getting himself into the heart of a VAT scam on building sites. This involved using tax certificates in the form of vouchers to falsely declare that subcontractors had paid tax on their weekly wages, while pocketing the tax. It was an extremely lucrative scam which, according to O'Rawe, saw Scappaticci reward himself with a series of lavish extensions to his family home at 45 Farnham Street off the Ormeau Road, where he moved in the late 1970s.[56] Florida became a particularly favoured destination for family holidays.[57]

Some of the gaps in the story of how Scappaticci transitioned from his release from Long Kesh in December 1975 to recruitment as a salaried military intelligence agent in the autumn of 1978 can now be filled in. He was sometimes seen with ex-internees at the Whitefort Bar on the Andersonstown Road, and O'Rawe quotes an ex-IRA leader who used the pseudonym 'Diarmuid O'Toole' as saying that by the end of 1976, Scappaticci was back with the IRA's Belfast Brigade operating in a security role. 'I'm not exactly sure who talent-spotted Scappaticci,' says 'O'Toole', 'but even then, he was recognised as a top man when it came to debriefing the volunteers who were being released from Castlereagh.'[58]

The British Army also seems to have had Scappaticci on its recruitment radar for some time. Operation Kenova referred to the 'Army's cultivation and recruitment of Stakeknife' as having begun in the late 1970s.[59] 'Everyone who was interned was a person of interest, and even more of a follow-up interest if they were coherent, smart,' a former senior FRU officer told me.[60] Scappaticci had shown himself to be both in prison. In 1973 the army had listed 'Fred Scappaticci, OC B Coy, 3BN, IRA' amongst candidates for release from internment because they had 'recanted' their involvement with the IRA, although they had declined to undertake not to rejoin.[61]

It has been popularly supposed that Scappaticci's main motivation for betraying his IRA comrades was to avenge a humiliating slight to his pride and status; it appears to be true that Scappaticci got a brutal hiding in a fight outside a bar with a cousin, which, unusually for a man handy with his fists, he lost.[62] One version goes that he was set upon by two fellow IRA men to settle a personal dispute (over a woman), and he vowed to get his revenge against the republican movement for being so publicly humbled. A former senior member of the IRA told me that one Saturday morning his wife bumped into Scappaticci's wife, Sheila. The women were friends and Sheila explained that 'Freddie got a beating. He says, "I'll pay them back for what they did to me."' She also said that he had gone to Dublin for a while to 'lick his wounds'.[63]

An ex-military intelligence officer told me he'd 'tried to turn Scappaticci' in the summer of 1976. This officer said he sensed a real willingness. 'I recall he was treated for a cut on the back of his hands after being involved in a fight', and that he'd 'gone away thinking things over'.[64] It would be a further two years before Scappaticci finally made the switch to the army, claiming the delay was because he had been unsure about how to make contact. In the autumn of 1978, an army patrol solved that problem by bringing him in for 'screening' to the Grand Central Hotel in Royal Avenue,[65] then serving as headquarters of 39 Brigade, which covered the Belfast area of operations.[66] There, Scappaticci met Sergeant Peter Jones of the Devonshire and Dorset Regiment. Jones was a member of the Brigade Research Office, the agent-running forerunner to the FRU that was established in 1982. He and Scappaticci hit it off from the start and Jones became his first handler.[67]

Several factors appear finally to have driven Scappaticci into the arms of the military. He'd begun his informer life as a police agent, the RUC having him over a barrel on his extremely lucrative VAT tax fraud, providing them with prosecutorial leads over the scam, which was widespread in Belfast. An RUC officer who became a member of the force's surveillance unit E4A recalled meeting Scappaticci off building sites in the late 1970s in a van with a sliding door.[68] His army file lists financial gain as one of his motives for changing his allegiance to the military,[69] as the army paid much better than the police. 'The army had a lot of money – more than us', a former Special Branch officer told me. 'You wouldn't live on what we paid you as an agent, and what we paid came from MI5.'[70] Other listed motivations included a desire for the conflict to end, dissatisfaction with the IRA leadership and a desire to protect his family.[71] Presumably he meant protecting them financially, since becoming a double agent at the heart of the IRA's security department was extremely high risk and threatened lifelong community ignominy for his family if he was caught.

The late General Sir John Wilsey, former GOC Northern Ireland, has a highly romanticised version of how Scappaticci was recruited. Due to its source, this ought to serve as the definitive version, but it contains some inherently incredible claims, which Kenova has also shown to be untrue. The account is set out in a book by Wilsey called *The Ulster Tales*, which captures the lives of ten individuals from Britain who found themselves caught up in the conflict, one of whom is Scappaticci's first handler, Sergeant Peter Jones. Wilsey does not refer to Scappaticci by name, giving him the fictitious codename 'Kerbstone' instead of 'Stakeknife', one of his authentic codenames, of which he had several.[72]

It seems Jones was a brave and resourceful soldier who won the Queen's Gallantry Medal and was later awarded the George Medal for 'acts of conspicuous gallantry, not in the presence of the enemy'. The last citation refers to Jones's three and a half years as a warrant officer commanding a covert military intelligence detachment close to the South Armagh border with the Irish Republic, branded 'bandit country' by the then Northern Ireland secretary, Merlyn Rees, because the IRA was so deeply embedded there thanks to the support of a community generally hostile to the British. Troops could often only move by helicopter to evade sniper and bomb ambushes, and they were regularly hit by small arms and heavy machine-gun fire. Running agents in this terrain, where almost every eyeball was on high alert for undercover soldiers, took a certain type of cold courage. Capture meant torture and certain death.

According to Wilsey, Jones' first citation was for running an agent successfully 'for longer than any other army handler in the Northern Ireland campaign and in particularly hazardous circumstances'. But it is the way that Wilsey described Jones as having 'hooked and landed his fish' that, to those of us who lived in Belfast in the 1970s, provokes an eyebrow-arching moment. Wilsey refers to Jones – a 'natural chatter upper' – as having been 'authorised' to don civilian clothes and grow his hair long, so he could cruise the 'clubs and bars of Belfast frequented by republicans' until he 'forged a drinking companionship with one of … many engaging characters', carefully nurturing this contact by 'sinking pints until the early hours', until 'over time their relationship matured into mutual friendship and trust. PJ's new republican friend was attracted by what he saw in PJ as a rebellious streak. There was no reason to suspect PJ was in the security forces, still less a soldier.'[73]

There are a number of problems with this account. First, it is hard to imagine any soldier other than an indigenous Irishman being authorised by the army to ingratiate himself in bars frequented by the IRA. As a former FRU officer and colleague of Jones told me, 'Peter is a very charismatic individual, one of those rare people who can recruit people,' but allowing him to spend his evening in republican-frequented bars 'was not a mainstream tactic at all. It would not have been endorsed.'[74] Second, Scappaticci was not much of a drinker. Third, he was noted for his reticence, a man of few words and distinctly not a social animal – a 'very tight man' as one of his former IRA comrades said.[75] Fourth, in the acutely paranoid climate that existed at that time, most especially in bars and clubs frequented by republicans, there would have been every reason in the world to suspect that a man with long hair and an English accent was an undercover soldier. And finally, if Scappaticci was contemplating defecting to the British, the last thing he would sensibly have done was risk being recognised by fellow republicans and asked what he was doing spending so much time with someone who so obviously was a Brit.

Wilsey quotes what he says was Jones' own guide to successful agent handling: 'In this secret world, the relationship between agent and handler is a marriage – but a one-sided one. The handler must know everything about his agent: his fears, his personal problems, his concerns about money, how often he has sex and with whom; his relationship with his wife, and who he hates within the IRA and who he likes.' This begs the question: did Jones know that the females Scappaticci most wanted to have sex with were underage girls?

Anthony McIntyre recalls an IRA friend telling him of a time when he and Scappaticci were watching some teenage girls playing in a park. Scappaticci's eyes fell on a girl aged about fifteen. The friend recalled Scappaticci 'almost frothing at the mouth. He says, "They're better when they're younger and when they're in a school uniform", rubbing his hands.'[76]

Years later, Scappaticci would be investigated by the police for molesting the child of a neighbour for whom he was babysitting.

His old IRA friend and boss, Jim Davison, also appears to have known of Scappaticci's taste for under-age sex. Four months after my meeting with Davison, I telephoned him to ask if we could meet again to check some facts. He was visiting a cemetery and there was a marked change in tone. He told me he was visiting the grave of his son Jock, himself a former senior IRA commander in Belfast who had been shot dead the previous year in a gang feud.[77] In any case, he said he was uncomfortable talking about Scappaticci anymore and hung up – or thought he had. I could hear him talking about my visit to a friend, how I was trying to understand what had motivated Scappaticci to defect to the British Army. Davison told his friend he was wary of going further. His friend concurred: 'These fellas come over here and in a couple of weeks they'll be sitting on the settee with the secret services ...'

At first, I resisted the temptation to listen, because it was so obviously a private moment of paying his respects to his murdered son. But then, between the muffled gusts of wind, I heard him talking about Scappaticci and women. His friend butted in, 'That bastard, a paedophile!', to which Davison responded, 'I've forgot about them things ... there are things that I know, and things that I don't know and things that I don't want to know.'

Did Peter Jones and the British Army know about Scappaticci's taste for young girls and sexual predilections that, decades later, would see him convicted of possessing extreme pornography involving 329 images of animals? Jones has maintained a monk-like silence over his agent-handling career. In any case, if military intelligence did know, it seems to have been of secondary importance. The army had bigger fish to fry.

Chapter Six

6126 – Three Shots in the Night

SATURDAY, 14 FEBRUARY 2004, METROPOLITAN Police interview suite, Teddington police station. For forty-five minutes, Detective Chief Superintendent Dave Cox and Detective Chief Inspector Phil James put a lengthy list of questions to Freddie Scappaticci under caution. Beyond telling them that the FRU CO Colonel Kerr had assured him he was 'bomb proof' and he was now feeling betrayed, he remained silent.[1] So, having exhausted their questions, the two officers left and Scappaticci was taken back to his cell.

Half an hour later, Scappaticci sent word that he was now ready to talk, provided he was no longer under caution. Eager with anticipation, Cox and James hurried to his cell, where they were greeted by a smiling Scappaticci. For the briefest of moments, they dared to wonder if their place in policing history was about to be assured; that they, through sheer force of personality, had cracked open the highest profile spy story in the Northern Ireland conflict. The moment came and went. 'Lads, I'm not the monster people think I am,' said Scappaticci. 'I'm not as bad as people say.' 'What exactly do you mean?' asked James. 'That's all I've got to say,' he replied.[2]

Cox and James were members of the team led by Metropolitan Police Commissioner Sir John Stevens investigating the FRU, which, in 1982, had taken charge of all army agent-running operations in Northern Ireland, where, previously, brigades and battalions had made their own arrangements. It was the closest the two detectives got to getting Scappaticci to open up about what had motivated him to become a spy back in 1978. The explanation in the files of military intelligence – that he was tired of gratuitous violence and thought the IRA campaign pointless[3] – didn't sit easily with the role he'd chosen to help bring the IRA's campaign of terrorism to an end. In 2024 Operation Kenova concluded that Scappaticci had helped prepare thirteen suspected agents for execution[4] and had participated in a further fifteen abductions of those suspected of informing.[5] A prosecution file about a fourteenth execution had been submitted to the Director of Public Prosecutions (DPP) in Belfast relating to the execution of twenty-three-year-old Joe Mulhern in July 1993. Kenova had become involved following well-publicised claims by Joe's late father, Frank, that Scappaticci had admitted being present at his son's execution. However, Kenova was satisfied that Frank was an unreliable witness whose statements were inconsistent.[6] In any case, by July 1993, Scappaticci was no longer active in the IRA, having been stood down from the ISU after himself falling under suspicion.[7]

His baptism into that dark world was summer 1979. The victim was Michael Kearney, a twenty-year-old IRA volunteer who had joined the PIRA less than a year earlier, despite the Provos having shot him in the right knee for having the effrontery to throw a couple of drunken IRA men out of a bar where he was working as a bouncer. Nonetheless, Michael joined up as an act of solidarity with his elder brother, Séamus, who was serving fourteen years in HMP Maze for conspiracy to murder a UDR soldier and was part of the 'Blanket Protest', in which republican prisoners wrapped themselves in blankets instead of wearing prison uniforms to support their demand for special political status in jail.

The story of what led up to young Michael Kearney's execution is unremittingly bleak. It is a vivid illustration of the depths to which both sides of the conflict could sometimes descend, involving on the one hand, an unsentimental case-hardened police force that cynically abandoned its first duty to protect human life – even the lives of its enemies – while on the other, an IRA, pitiless in its denial of civil and human rights even to one of their own, when it was that very denial by which its leaders justified its 'armed struggle'. Bleak though the experience was, however, it would not prove sufficiently bleak to deter Scappaticci from his decade-long role as an enforcer of the IRA's ultimate disciplinary penalty while doubling as a British spy. That said, on this particular occasion, it seems some of his fellow ISU interrogators considered the IRA Army Council's death penalty for Kearney as too harsh. Given the circumstances that have subsequently emerged, it is easy to see why. Perhaps when Scappaticci sought to persuade Messrs Cox and James that he wasn't a monster, he had the fate of young Michael Kearney in mind.

On 23 June 1979, Kearney had been released from the RUC's interrogation centre at Castlereagh after being questioned on ten occasions for over sixteen hours. While he was in custody, the security forces had recovered 6lb of (unusable) commercial explosives, along with IRA uniforms and masks, from a weapons hide behind a false wall in the Lenadoon estate, West Belfast.[8] Kearney knew its location because he had delivered the weapons there. Inevitably, the IRA put two and two together, which was not difficult: Kearney's early release without charge less than twenty-four hours after the weapons were seized indicated he had betrayed its location in exchange for his freedom.

Kearney had indeed given away the weapons hide. He also admitted to carrying out much more serious crimes – moving guns after the murder of a UDR soldier and ferrying a gun team from the scene of an attempted murder. According to one of his interrogators, Detective Sergeant Mervyn Bishop, Kearney also admitted to delivering forty-two cylinder bombs to a lock-up garage in Belfast's Short Strand the previous March, intended for an IRA bombing spectacular – to black out Belfast.[9] Confronted by the prospect of fifteen years in jail, Kearney agreed to 'gather information' for the police in exchange for his release.[10] As a result, the police released him without charge. The inference the IRA drew from his early release was that he'd agreed to this.[11]

The IRA rule book forbade arrested volunteers from responding to police questions, but Kearney had broken after three days. He told the IRA he had been 'slapped, punched in the stomach, clipped across the balls' and nearly suffocated while a fifteen-stone detective smoking a cigar sat on him, ordering him to do press-ups while blowing smoke in his face. He said he was then made to stand on his tiptoes with his arms up. Every time his arms fell down, he was slapped across the face. An IRA volunteer with whom Kearney had been arrested would later attest to hearing much thumping and shouting through the wall of an adjoining interrogation room.[12] Having spoken to some of Kearney's interrogators, Operation Kenova found it likely that he had indeed been 'subject to violent interrogation'.[13]

Detective Sergeant Bishop warned his RUC colleagues that by releasing Kearney without charge they were 'sending this lad out to die', because it would have been so obvious to the IRA that he'd done a deal. Insisting that Kearney would be 'much better off in prison', Bishop had urged them to charge him. His RUC colleagues, it seems, did not share this moral imperative. According to Bishop, Detective Chief Superintendent Bill Mooney, the head of Belfast CID no less, decided to resolve the issue by putting Kearney's fate to a vote amongst four CID officers, Bishop included, as if a life could be gambled with like a lottery. Bishop, a patently moral officer compared to his colleagues, lost 3–1.

So obvious was it that Kearney's swift release would mark him out as a newly turned informer that even Special Branch declined their CID colleagues' offer to run him as an agent.[14] In fact, the situation was worse than that. Senior members of the Belfast Brigade had already marked down Kearney as working for the branch. The forty-two cylinder bombs he'd moved to Short Strand the previous March had been seized after Kearney had dropped them off and, in the IRA's postmortem of what had gone wrong, he was being talked of as the likely traitor. That was completely untrue, as years later the IRA would acknowledge – but only a quarter of a century after murdering him.[15]

And so, at 2.50 p.m. on Saturday 23 June, Michael Kearney walked out of Castlereagh and into the arms of IRA Internal Security. What Detective Sergeant Bishop predicted would happen, happened. At 7 p.m., four days later, Kearney was driven to the car park of the Glenowen Bar in West Belfast under orders to report to the ISU for what he was euphemistically told would be a 'debrief'. At 6 p.m., his mother, Kathleen, had told him she was taking the dog out for a walk. Kearney was lying on the sofa and told her he planned to take a fortnight's break in the Irish Republic. That was the last time she saw her son, a possibility that Kearney himself appears to have contemplated. On the way to the Glenowen, he seemed full of foreboding. 'I don't think I'll be seeing you again,' were his parting words to the OC of his unit, who had driven him there.[16] How prescient they were. We now know that on that same day Special Branch was told by an informant that senior members of the Belfast Brigade wanted Kearney executed, even though he had yet to be interrogated, let alone court-martialled.[17]

Parked in the Glenowen were two vehicles waiting to take him to the 'debrief' – not in Belfast but in the Irish Republic. One was a scout car to check the road ahead was clear; in the car behind was Kearney, accompanied by the senior member of the Belfast Brigade whom Kearney had been told would be a familiar face. Kearney's elder brother, Séamus, believes that Freddie Scappaticci was also in the convoy, which seems quite possible, since Michael had been told at the Glenowen car park that he was to be handed over to the 'security team',[18] of which Scappaticci was a member. Years later, the IRA would admit to Séamus Kearney that, while Scappaticci had not played a 'central role' in his brother's execution, he had been present at his 'debrief', consistent with Scappaticci having accompanied Michael in the two-car convoy to his interrogation.[19]

The convoy's first stop was Crossmaglen in County Armagh, less than two miles from the border, where Kearney was taken to a house. He was then driven across the border to the home of a businessman in Ballinamore, Country Leitrim.[20] His bedroom there would effectively serve as his death-row cell as he awaited his court martial. Kearney had been taken to the Republic because the Belfast Brigade was unpersuaded by his insistence that he'd only feigned agreement to become an RUC informer, even though, on his release from RUC custody, he'd followed the IRA rule book to the letter by going straight to his unit commander and openly admitting he'd broken under interrogation and had given away the weapons hide in Lenadoon. He'd also emphasised to his OC that he had no intention of becoming an informer, and he repeated this assurance in a bar that Saturday evening to two senior members of the Belfast Brigade. One of them was the 'familiar face' now accompanying him to the Irish Republic for his 'debrief'.

Kearney was unaware that his fealty had already been under question for weeks within the brigade because the Short Strand operation to black out Belfast had been so obviously compromised by an informer.[21] It didn't seem to matter how inherently unlikely it was that he had been that informer. Based on what he told the Belfast Brigade immediately after his release from Castlereagh, it was obvious Kearney himself had been betrayed by the real informer, because his RUC interrogators had told him that they had followed him 'in your white transit. We saw you load up the cylinder bombs, and we saw you unload them in the lock up.'[22] They said they had been watching him ever since and had seized their moment to arrest him when they saw him driving a car that had been hijacked.[23] Someone had clearly informed on Kearney – not the other way around.

There was no logic to the brigade's allegation that Kearney had been the Short Strand informer, particularly since he'd been completely open about having betrayed, under physical duress, the Lenadoon weapons hide. So why wouldn't he be telling the truth about the Short Strand as well? That, anyway, appears to have been the rational assessment of one of his ISU interrogators after questioning Kearney for two to three days, as recorded in one of 'five separate source reports available to RUC SB' over the course of Kearney's fourteen-day incarceration in the Irish Republic.[24] The fact that both the FRU and the branch had received intelligence reports on Kearney's plight would suggest that, even in the infancy of the ISU, Scappaticci wasn't the only agent to have penetrated it. One report said that Kearney's ISU interrogator, who evidently believed his version of events, had concluded that his death sentence was 'excessive'.[25] That presumably would not have been his view had he found credible the Belfast Brigade's allegation that Kearney betrayed the bomb hide in Short Strand.

Yet Kearney's court martial found otherwise. On 6 July, he was told he'd been found guilty of breaching the IRA's General Army Orders by responding to the RUC's questions.[26] The verdict appears to have been officially based on Kearney's admission that he'd disclosed the Lenadoon weapons hide to the RUC, with no mitigation for the fact that he had done so under physical duress and owned up to it immediately on release, or that the small amount of explosive recovered was, in any case, unusable because it was waterlogged.[27] The intelligence reports reaching Special Branch indicate that the verdict was strongly influenced by the Belfast Brigade's desire to pin the loss of the Short Strand cylinder bombs on Kearney, with two senior members of the brigade, who were in County Leitrim for some of Kearney's incarceration, actively pushing for his execution.[28]

These intelligence reports also say that, although Kearney was to be allowed to appeal, his execution was a near certainty and would happen within a few days. In fact, they indicated that the Belfast Brigade had already started planning the logistics for the execution, at one stage suggesting that he should be brought back to Belfast to be shot, presumably because there was a shortage of available executioners within a sufficiently short travelling distance.[29]

Kearney was not told that he was to be executed, only that he had been found guilty of breaching IRA General Army Orders. His appeal relied on a twelve-page debrief he had written for the IRA within hours of his release. This, he pleaded, would exonerate him because it recorded exactly what he'd told his unit commander, his bosses in the Belfast Brigade and the court martial – that, far from him betraying the Short Strand, both he and the brigade had been betrayed by a person or persons unknown, as evident from the RUC's boasts during his interrogation about how he'd been followed from West Belfast, over Queen's Bridge, to the Errigal Inn in Ormeau Road, where he'd loaded up the forty-two cylinder bombs before ferrying them a couple of miles to the Short Strand hide in Kilmood Street. Unfortunately for Kearney, he hadn't brought his debrief with him to County Leitrim. Instead, he'd secreted it in a cornflake packet and entrusted it to his twin brother Seán to hide in their mother's house.

On 10 July, the senior Belfast Brigade officer known to Michael as the 'familiar face' called on Seán to retrieve the debrief from the cornflake packet, which he had hidden behind a dresser, but the packet was nowhere to be found. It had slipped down to the floor and was only discovered by Seán in 1982, when he was retiling the kitchen.[30] That one slip – quite literally – may well have sealed Michael Kearney's fate. In the absence of the debrief, it was assumed that Kearney had been lying about writing it, and this was enough for the Belfast Brigade to insist the death sentence now be carried out.

On the night of 11 July, the IRA invoked its usual procedure for keeping a condemned man calm through deception until the final moment of his rendezvous with eternity, in Michael's case now just hours away. He was told his ordeal was over and that he was going to be driven home to his mother and brother Seán in Belfast.[31] Sitting in the van as it trundled north in the early hours of 12 July, Kearney may well have experienced a sense of relief, for north was the right direction if he really was homeward bound. But any hope Michael might have been clinging to would finally have vanished when forty-five minutes later, at around 2 a.m., the van pulled into the car park of the Leggykelly Inn, County Cavan, a few yards south of the border with County Fermanagh. In the darkness, awaiting its arrival, was an ominously lone car from which two men emerged. The van driver was instructed to carry on and turn into a lane seventy-five yards across the border, conforming to normal IRA practice of carrying out executions just inside Northern Ireland. It was only then that Kearney was formally told he was not going home.

For a twenty-year-old, Michael appears to have accepted his fate with remarkable composure. His executioners noted that he emerged from the van not hooded or bound as the condemned usually were. Nor did he make a run for it. Instead, he asked if he could say a prayer, which was allowed, although his executioners would likely have told him to make it brief, since the lane, remote though it was, was used by the occasional motorist. 'He was brave,' the IRA told his elder brother Séamus. 'That would be typical of Michael,' said Séamus. Instead of kneeling, he appears to have prayed while standing, because when he'd finished, he was shot three times in the head and neck by the two executioners and fell back on a grass verge, face up.[32] A witness living on a nearby farm heard 'three or four shots' and the sound of a car driving away.[33] Some minutes later a motorist did in fact pass by and saw Michael's lifeless body with blood on his forehead. He telephoned the Garda Síochána.[34] As dawn broke an army helicopter did a visual check for booby traps on the body. By 5.45 a.m., the RUC had secured the crime scene, not that much effort seems to have been devoted to solving the crime, despite 'numerous intelligence reports' identifying the perpetrators thereafter.[35] Only a smattering of these were passed on to the CID by Special Branch under the 'no downward dissemination' rule, which prioritised the protection of their intelligence sources, from whom they'd been receiving regular reports of Kearney's impending fate, over arresting the perpetrators.[36] In common with all executions involving the ISU, which was by no means penetrated by Scappaticci alone, no one was ever charged or convicted.

At 3.30 p.m. on 12 July, Michael's twin brother Seán identified his sibling's body at Erne hospital mortuary, Enniskillen.[37] Publicly, the IRA justified Kearney's execution for having 'imparted information of vital importance to the British war machine' and for having agreed to become an agent. It wasn't disclosed that he'd made it clear that this was never his intention, merely a ruse to secure release from RUC custody, or that the RUC's recovery of a small, waterlogged pack of explosives hardly qualified as information of 'vital importance'. Following a demand from Séamus Kearney in 2001 that the IRA reopen his brother's case, in January 2003 the family was finally provided with a statement in which the IRA acknowledged that Michael was 'in no way' responsible for the Short Strand operation being compromised.[38] The statement notably lacked contrition: 'The army regrets that this execution of one of their own Volunteers had to take place under the circumstances at that time [i.e. Formal Standing Orders of the time] but stands by that decision.' In September 2003 the IRA agreed to issue a joint public statement with the Kearney family, emphasising that Michael had spoken 'freely and frankly to them about his situation' and adding, 'Unfortunately, at the time the IRA took a stance ...'[39] Again, there was no apology, a source of great anguish to Michael's mother.

Like all police forces, the RUC's first duty was the preservation of life – all life, irrespective of a person's antecedents. By releasing Kearney from custody just hours after recovering the Lenadoon weapons hide, the RUC might just as well have pinned a shirt on him saying, 'I've done a deal with the Police.' Moreover, fourteen days was ample opportunity for the security forces to have contacted the Garda Síochána and put together a rescue plan for Kearney. Scappaticci had provided 'very detailed information' to his handlers about Kearney's abduction and interrogation, and had given the name of one of those involved.[40] Special Branch had also been in receipt of intelligence reports on the day that Kearney was abducted, saying the young man's execution was preordained.[41]

However, that duty to preserve all life has only been enshrined in UK domestic law since Article 2 of the ECHR was incorporated in the Human Rights Act of 1998. And in 1979, the IRA was murdering members of the security forces as often as it could. In a contest between letting a young IRA man die or attempting to save him and, in doing so, risk blowing the cover of well-placed agents, the choice for many police officers at that time presented no moral dilemma. 'Personally, I didn't give a rat's arse if the IRA wanted to punish their own,' reflected one seasoned Special Branch detective when I put to him Michael Kearney's story. 'I didn't see myself as having a duty of care over someone like that, who would have been prepared to blow you to bits the day before.'[42]

Many will sympathise with that view. Yet it was also true that, during the counter-insurgency, source protection had become such a priority that it almost always overrode all other considerations. This was especially so in Scappaticci's case, since his position at the epicentre of the IRA war machine held such promise for years to come. It is also true that the thirteen executions and fifteen abductions in which Scappaticci was involved in his eleven years and three months as a member of the ISU were just one part of his duties, extensive though the planning and logistics were that went into arranging an in-depth interrogation that might last weeks and occasionally months. Other ISU duties included providing security at republican demonstrations and funerals, investigating missing funds, security leaks and operations that went wrong, as well as vetting new recruits and debriefing volunteers released from RUC custody. With each of these tasks providing access to almost every facet of the IRA, the potential for high-grade intelligence, including from the upper echelons of the IRA, was enormous.

And so the pressure was on Scappaticci to act like a model terrorist, which, in his case, even extended to sacrificing family friends – a bridge too far for most mortals to stomach, but not for Stakeknife.

Chapter Seven

6126 – Sacrificing Friends and 'unspeakable horrors'

IN 1984, A FARMER WAS walking his dog on land he'd been draining outside Knockbridge, just south of Dundalk, when the dog paused, sniffing something in the ground. It was the lower part of a skull; the rest of the skeleton was still submerged. A gaping hole in the skull marked where the victim had been shot. The remains belonged to Eugene Simons, a twenty-six-year-old father of three who, at around 1.30 p.m. on New Year's Day in 1981, had gone with trusted friends to buy some milk and bread in Castlewellan, County Down.[1] No one heard from him again.

Simons, an IRA quartermaster,[2] was one of seventeen Catholics formally designated as 'The Disappeared', whom the IRA abducted, executed and secretly buried in fields and bogs on suspicion of being informers, leaving their relatives with nowhere to mourn their loss.[3] For the Simons family a further indignity was the admission years later by the authorities in Dublin that they had lost his skull.[4] When his remains were unearthed, it was at least some comfort to his father, Walter, that found with his boy's remains was a small crucifix he'd carried with him. Walter held this tightly in his hand when he told his story to detectives from Operation Kenova three decades later.[5] The PIRA's merciless cruelty – signed off by its leaders it should be remembered – was not without precedent, however. During the 1919–21 War of Independence, dozens of disappeared bodies of enemies of the Irish

Republic's founding fathers – 'the good old IRA' – were left to decay in bogs and fields.[6]

Eugene's sister, Angela Donnelly, would later learn from Kenova that Simons' New Year's Eve 'friends' included suspects involved in his abduction. Some of these 'friends' had joined Simons and his second wife, pregnant with his fourth child, the previous night at the New Year's Eve celebrations in the Fountain Bar in Castlewellan.[7] Once Simons was abducted, he was taken to a farm near Bailieborough, County Cavan, where, over the course of eleven days, he is said to have confessed on tape that he had worked for Special Branch, including wearing a 'wire at a PIRA meeting'.[8] Freddie Scappaticci was involved in the court martial that authorised his execution.[9]

He had also been involved in Simons' abduction five months earlier,[10] when the IRA suspected he'd agreed to become a spy after being released by the RUC from questioning. On that occasion, he was held for four days at a barn near the County Monaghan village of Inniskeen and was brutally beaten.[11] In light of his earlier experience, it is likely that his taped 'confession' in January 1981 – if such existed – would have been extracted by brutal torture, quite possibly over many days.[12] 'They took him on January 1 [1981], they murdered him on January 11,' said another of his sisters, Moira Todd. 'So he had eleven days of probably unspeakable horror that the authorities knew about and totally ignored.'[13]

The FRU and Special Branch may well have known. When Simons was being held the previous August, the branch was in possession of intelligence which clearly indicated his life was in danger. That intelligence wasn't acted on because, to protect the source, it was graded 'Not for Downward Dissemination'.[14] Simons arrived home badly bruised and was so terrified that he slept with his father's legally held shotgun by his bed.[15] Scappaticci had warned his FRU handlers that the IRA suspected there was an informer in its South Down/Castlewellan Active Service Unit, following arrests after explosives dumps were found.[16] Because Simons had failed to make any admissions to the IRA that he was an informer during his first interrogation, when he was abducted again in January 1981, the IRA ruled he had 'no immunity' and would be 'buried in a hole with no publicity'.[17] Whether such 'immunity' would have been granted even had he confessed the first time around is surely questionable.

In Ireland, no greater shame exists than to have collaborated with the Crown. The classic iconic imagery that endured for half a century was of a 'tout's' sparsely attended funeral, the bereaved's front door closing, the police rarely, if ever, darkening it with information about the perpetrators of their shamed relative's fate. In this conflict's hierarchy of victimhood, as far as the authorities were concerned, the relatives of the executed dead were at the bottom of the pile. That only changed in 2017, when English detectives from Operation Kenova enlightened them with information that had never been shared with them, which gave them a voice, allowing them to take their rightful place in the memory of suffering. In 2025, Angela Donnelly captured the burden of the stigmatised bereaved in a moving interview with the BBC:

> … when we did speak to the Kenova team, we found out stuff we never knew … Kenova told us we have intelligence that he was still alive anywhere from twelve to fourteen days after his disappearance … it's one of those awful things, bittersweet … I think I prefer honesty, tough and all as it may be, than dishonesty and left not knowing … everybody else gets to speak, but we are all quiet because we're afraid, or there's just that sense of, can I speak? Are they [the IRA] going to bring any repercussions for speaking? … even as a family, we haven't really talked an awful lot about it … because I think it's all been just so painful … it's like dancing on eggshells around one another … keep it shut away somewhere, because it's too ugly, it's too, too awful to talk about … as a Catholic, to have a brother in the IRA and a brother who's an informer is like the worst thing that could happen to a family and the judgements that come with that … Just feeling gagged. Who do I talk to if I did talk to somebody? What could that possibly lead to, especially when my father was told: 'You, stop or you'll end up in the same place.' … And therefore, it was carry it like a lump of lead around and just go on living … [I] tried my best to leave anything that happened down around here in a box in some part of my mind that I didn't really want to visit … To hear that his [Scappaticci's] handlers let him be murdered was shocking. You just think, yes, he's a dead IRA man, but to us, he was our brother … What I used to say was – especially when he disappeared … where is he lying? It's always the

> memory of where was he lying for those years? … At the end of the day, he was my brother. What good does it do now to be told he's not an informant? He's still dead. It's the ones who knew he wasn't an informer …What were they doing with him all that time?[18]

After Eugene Simons was abducted, family members were spat at in the street. Adding to their torment today is the revelation by Kenova that even though Special Branch knew from multiple intelligence sources that he was dead, the RUC never informed the family. 'They [the RUC] knew he was dead,' said Moira Todd. 'They didn't tell us. My father hunted high and low, my brother walked the streets of Dundalk, of Dublin, hoping to bump into him, and all the while, the authorities knew that he wasn't coming back, he was gone.'[19]

Simons' execution in January 1981 was the first of four that year in which Scappaticci was involved. In February, the snow-flecked body of father of three Patrick Trainor (28) was found on waste ground off the Glen Road, Belfast. Hearing shots, a local resident had gone to the scene and was preparing to administer first aid but stopped when he realised the extent of the victim's injuries and prayed over the body instead. Trainor had been shot four times in the head, three at close range. He also appeared to have been beaten about the head with a blunt instrument while alive.[20] In a statement, the IRA said Trainor had been working for the British Army and Special Branch since being recruited in June 1976, after his arrest for a robbery.[21] The RUC told his inquest that was untrue, a statement which under today's strict regime of evading questions about legacy killings allegedly involving agents would be wholly impermissible, attracting instead an automatic NCND response in accordance with Cabinet Office protocol.

Scappaticci and his wife, Sheila, had previously socialised with Trainor's sister Eileen Hughes and her husband, and at one point Scappaticci had worked for his brother Bernard. None of these ties appear to have inhibited Scappaticci from reportedly having fired the shots into Trainor's head while – according to a former ISU member, Eamon Collins – finding it extremely funny. In his biography, *Killing Rage*, Collins gives an account of what is almost certainly the same incident as told to him by Scappaticci and the then reputed head of the ISU, John Joe Magee. As a new ISU recruit, Collins had inquired if there might come a time when he would have to shoot an informer. Scappaticci, his mouth full of food, replied that 'when the time arrived' he would have to do it. Collins says he then 'asked whether they always told people that they were going to be shot? Scap said it "depended on the circumstances."' Collins writes that Scappaticci turned to Magee and 'started joking about an informer' who'd been duped into confessing by being 'offered an amnesty'. Scappaticci recounted how he'd told the alleged informer that he would be taken home, reassuring him that he had nothing to worry about. As they walked away from the car that had dropped them off, Scappaticci told the man to keep the blindfold on for security reasons, adding, 'It was funny watching the bastard stumbling and falling, asking me as he felt his way along railings and walls: "Is this my house now?" and I'd say "No, not yet, walk on some more …"', whereupon Magee butted in: 'and then you shot the fucker in the back of the head!' According to Collins, both men then 'burst out laughing'.[22]

In his book, Collins didn't identify the victim by name, and the draft chapters, held by his co-author Mick McGovern and shown to Operation Kenova, make no mention of the name Trainor,[23] presumably because Collins didn't know it. The account, however, is highly likely to be a reference to Trainor for two reasons: first, Kenova recovered the account of the same killing that Collins gave to the RUC, which is entirely consistent with what was in his book;[24] second, it is also consistent with the version Trainor's brother Hugh (aka 'Buster') said Scappaticci gave to him two months after Patrick's murder. Hugh had also been in the IRA and said that Scappaticci told him his brother was a tout. Scappaticci explained that Patrick had been driven blindfolded to a location where he was told to get out, that he was told he was in the road where he lived and was instructed to walk on, using the railings and wall as a guide, and to keep going until he was told he was outside his front door. After walking a while Trainor asked if he was now home and was told to walk a little further. As in Collins' book, Scappaticci recounted to Hugh how Patrick had been told to use the railings and the wall as a guide,[25] which also matched the location where Trainor was shot.[26] Collins himself was murdered in January 1999 as he walked his dog; he was knifed and battered by someone with the savagery of a 'primitive caveman' commented one RUC officer. Collins had denounced the Real IRA the previous year and at one time had even agreed to act as a supergrass against the PIRA, before reconsidering and withdrawing the offer.[27]

A former senior IRA member who worked with Scappaticci in South Armagh – and distrusted him – told me it was inconceivable Scappaticci would have doubled as Trainor's interrogator and executioner. 'It's bullshit, just bravado, the execution team was always separate.'[28] That was indeed the standard procedure, but the evidence that an exception was sometimes made to that rule is compelling. When Scappaticci – using the alias 'Frank' – was asked by journalists from ITV in 1993 if he had ever killed anyone, he remained silent.[29] He did, however, recount the IRA's modus operandi in keeping the condemned man calm with a reference that uncannily resembles Trainor's last moments. 'They would have blindfolded him,' Scappaticci explained, referring to Frank Hegarty directly after Martin McGuinness had interrogated him in 1986. They would have 'assured him they were taking him home, then would have taken him from the car and told him to keep walking' and then put 'a bullet in the back of the head'.[30] Kenova found other compelling evidence that Scappaticci used guns. At lunchtime on 12 October 1987, he shot an IRA man eight times in his ankles, knees and elbows to avenge his 'insolence' for refusing to hand over his new car to the IRA for an operation. In a statement to Kenova, the victim said he was at home with his partner and their two children when he saw six men, one of whom was Scappaticci, outside his house. After they burst in, the victim recounted how Scappaticci stood over him firing the first shot into his ankle. He then heard Scappaticci say, 'Put one in the back of his head and save the rest of the bullets.'[31]

Was Scappaticci not just the leader of this punishment-shooting gang but also its instigator? The victim's evidence suggests he was very much in charge. If so, how many abductions leading to executions might Scappaticci have instigated as the insurance premium he felt compelled to pay to maintain his cover? Unfortunately, a definitive answer has been lost to history because the full record of the life and times of Agent 6126, as immortalised daily in the CFs by the FRU's special unit dedicated to running him, were destroyed by the army after the embarrassment over the FRU's other highly valued agent: 6137, Brian Nelson. What the surviving records do show is that the 9mm Parabellum pistol that Scappaticci had fired in October 1987 had also been used in four punishment shootings and six executions; two of the victims – Anthony McKiernan and Thomas Wilson[32] – were interrogated by Scappaticci before their execution.

IRA sources have confirmed that Scappaticci had a role in the IRA's so-called 'civil administration', its alternative to the RUC, which was responsible for punishment shootings.[33] It therefore seems likely that he would have been involved in beating local anti-social elements and criminals with clubs, iron bars and hammers, and shooting them in their legs, elbows or knees as a way of intimidating the community into subjugation. Eileen Hughes says that in 1984 she was summoned to a meeting at Connolly House, headquarters of this 'civil administration' and told by Scappaticci's ISU partner, John Joe Magee, that the next time he received a complaint about her son Tony dealing drugs, he would 'personally blow the head off him'.[34] Tony was indeed shot, execution-style, a decade later, although there is no evidence of Scappaticci's involvement because by then he had been stood down by the IRA.[35]

Kenova has made it clear that Eileen Hughes could at least have been spared the grief of the equally brutal loss of her brother Patrick in 1981 had the RUC responded to intelligence reports that his life was in danger. Its investigation recovered pre-murder intelligence reports indicating that he was under suspicion by the IRA, including one report from Scappaticci 'only a few days before' he was murdered, saying the IRA 'were investigating a suspected SB informant'.[36] The alleged informant does not appear to have been named, but it was known that Trainor was under suspicion.[37] Yet no attempt was made to forewarn him, nor does the RUC appear to have made any serious attempt to investigate his murder, despite Kenova having recovered no fewer than sixteen post-murder intelligence reports which, between them, identified eighteen suspects, as well as the location where Trainor had been interrogated. However, Kenova could find no evidence of the RUC investigating this latter 'significant line of inquiry'.[38] Although this intelligence was assessed as accurate – and was received soon after Trainor's execution – there is no record of the RUC having even searched the house.[39]

In keeping with his need to show himself to be a model enforcer of IRA discipline, Scappaticci stomached a similar sacrificial experience involving a family friend in June 1981. Once again, he cold-bloodedly put aside loyalty and sentimentality by playing his part in the execution of a former IRA comrade from his days in the Markets in the 1970s. Like Trainor, the victim, Vincent Robinson, was savagely beaten.

Robinson, a twenty-eight-year-old father of two was in the PIRA having defected from the Official IRA in the Markets area of Belfast in the 1970s, where his family and the Scappaticcis were on friendly terms.[40] On Wednesday, 17 June 1981, Robinson was arrested for an alleged offence under the Prevention of Terrorism Act, held overnight at Castlereagh interrogation centre and then released the following evening.[41] He was told to report for debriefing by the ISU to find out what he'd said – if anything – to the police. Debriefings by the ISU of republicans released without charge from RUC custody were standard, because Special Branch was known to routinely offer not to press charges in exchange for informing. Suspicion that Robinson might have accepted such an offer arose when he failed to present himself for interrogation at a house in Cleeve Walk on both the following Monday and Tuesday.[42]

On Wednesday 24 June, after going to the barber with his eight-year-old son, Robinson visited his mother-in-law at her home. There he was told that one of his grandmother's brothers-in-law wanted to see him, so he told his wife that he was going to meet him for a pint.[43] This appears to have been an ISU ruse to abduct him for interrogation, as the brother-in-law had not sent for him.[44] An elderly witness told the Robinson family that as Vincent walked along Glenveagh Drive on the Lenadoon estate, presumably on his way to the pub, a taxi pulled up. The driver was a man with whom Robinson had had a fight some three weeks earlier and an 'altercation' ensued.[45] This appears to have been the last time anyone not involved in his murder saw him alive.

Two days later, Robinson's body was found by three young girls in a large pool of blood in the darkened electric meter room in Divis flats, where he had been taken to be court-martialled after his interrogation.[46] The IRA claimed he had become a police informer,[47] but this was denied both by the RUC and the Dungannon priest, Father Denis Faul, who said it was 'patently false'.[48] As, indeed, it appears to have been. Following the murder, two IRA men knocked on the door of Vincent's widow, Eileen. One said, 'We're just here to let you know that Vincent's death was a mistaken identity. We're really sorry.'[49] So much for the IRA's public announcement within hours of Robinson's body being found that he'd supplied the police with the names and movements of IRA members.

Robinson appears to have been the innocent victim of an extensive 'tout' hunt by the ISU that month, in which Scappaticci had been 'peripherally involved'.[50] Several intelligence reports implicate Scappaticci in his murder.[51] One noted that the gun used to shoot Robinson in the forehead and temple from close range was a 0.22 calibre rifle with a discarded stock and shortened pistol grip that had been held by Scappaticci.[52] However, Kenova says there is 'nothing to suggest he was present during the interrogation' that led directly to his execution.[53]

Watching the evening news on the day of Robinson's murder, his younger sister recognised her brother's shoes protruding from a white sheet covering the body. That evening Scappaticci visited her, her husband and her brother to explain why he'd been shot. After Scappaticci had said his piece, she inquired plaintively, 'Was my brother tortured?' She'd heard his body was badly marked. 'No,' replied Scappaticci looking her straight in the eye,[54] but he had 'got one in the head' and 'wouldn't go down, so he was battered'.[55]

The full truth emerged at the inquest. Robinson had endured a hideous end. When his interrogation was concluded, he had been moved to the electricity service room to be court-martialled. Anticipating his fate, he had put up a struggle and was brutally kicked in the stomach and bludgeoned five times around the head with a rod-type implement while still alive, fracturing his skull. He was then shot twice in the head having endured a 'very severe beating before his death', Detective Inspector William Hawke told his inquest.[56] The version the IRA gave the family a decade later was that he was beaten about the head because the gun had jammed and that was the only way to kill him.[57]

Fifteen minutes before Robinson's body was found, a two-vehicle mobile police patrol had stopped three men in the vicinity of the Divis flats. When they saw the patrol approaching, the trio split up. One of them, Joe McKee, was seen to have blood on his trousers and a shoe,[58] but he was released after he explained this away by saying he'd been in a fight at the Pound Loney club (an IRA haunt). All three were members of the ISU,[59] two of whom – McKee and Paddy Monaghan – were expelled from the unit in 1986 by the overall head of IRA internal security, Brendan Hughes, who accused them of having tortured suspects.[60]

While Scappaticci is not believed to have participated in Robinson's interrogation, Kenova recovered intelligence and witness testimony showing that he likely 'initiated' the abduction, interrogation and murder of yet another family friend, forty-four-year-old Anthony McKiernan, on 18 January 1988.[61] He lured his friend from the security of his home into the arms of the ISU by exploiting their friendship, so that McKiernan could be abducted with minimal fuss, taken to a safe house for interrogation and then shot. Like Vincent Robinson, McKiernan had known Scappaticci since their days together in the Markets in the early 1970s. 'Monkey' McKiernan – as he was known – became OC of the Markets when Scappaticci was interned. Their friendship had endured to the extent that their children had enjoyed sleepovers together. So, when Scappaticci sent one of his sons to the McKiernan household to tell one of his children, 'My da says can your da call down to the Pound Loney Club?',[62] McKiernan would not have been unduly alarmed. The IRA claimed to have secured evidence that McKiernan was working for Special Branch – denied forcefully by his family. Operation Kenova is satisfied that McKiernan's abduction from the Pound Loney Club and subsequent murder could have been prevented, but that, once again, protecting Scappaticci as a key source seems to have taken precedence.

Scappaticci was in a tight spot himself at that time. In the months leading up to McKiernan's execution, he feared he was under suspicion from some IRA elements, amongst them Martin McGuinness.[63] Besides his ISU role, Operation Kenova found that he was also performing additional tasks for the IRA's Belfast Brigade;[64] they are believed to have included screening operations, which may help to explain why from 1987 the IRA in Belfast was finding that its bombing operations were increasingly being frustrated. 'By the end of the 1980s the IRA went for a period of two years without being able to detonate a single bomb in the city centre,' wrote the IRA veteran Gerry 'Whitey' Bradley,[65] who told author Brian Feeney: 'You've no idea how many times we tried to blow up the Europa. There were VCPs [vehicle checkpoints] every time we moved. There seemed to be so many leaks. The IRA was also losing bomb teams.'[66]

The FRU attempted to deflect any suspicion from Scappaticci by exploiting an execution in which he'd been involved. At 11.25 on the morning of 25 June 1987, witnesses close to an alleyway off Rodney Parade, West Belfast, heard several shots and found the bound and gagged body of Thomas Wilson (35) lying face up with his shoes removed. The father of four had been shot four times in the head after being held for fourteen hours. The IRA said he was a police agent with the codename 'Zero' and had been seen meeting his handlers every Tuesday night for the previous six weeks.[67] His family emphatically insisted he was not an informer, pointing out that he was a member of the Workers' Party, the political wing of the Official IRA, which was inactive. At the time his wife and sister also spoke of his 'abhorrence of political violence' and said that he was a 'devoted father'.[68] According to a 'sensitive RUC source', Scappaticci was 'directly implicated' in the interrogation of Wilson that led to his murder. Evidence of his involvement comes not only from the RUC source but also, says Kenova, from 'witness and ballistic evidence', which 'overwhelmingly points to [his] involvement'.[69] To deflect the suspicion in the IRA that Scappaticci believed was building up against him, his FRU handlers suggested to the RUC that he be arrested for Wilson's murder, along with six other suspects, but not charged.[70]

For whatever reason, the RUC didn't play ball, so it may be that Scappaticci felt it wise to demonstrate his loyalty to the IRA ultimately by showing no mercy to his friend Anthony McKiernan when, in October 1987, the IRA began to suspect McKiernan was an informer. In the subsequent two months, Scappaticci provided his handlers with 'numerous' reports that McKiernan was under suspicion, and the FRU dutifully passed these on to Special Branch, though the branch appears to have done nothing with them. By December the FRU seems to have decided they had given all the warnings they reasonably could without compromising their prized agent and told the branch there should be 'no downward dissemination' on any further intelligence the FRU might supply about McKiernan. This meant that they did not want information shared with anyone else without prior discussion with the FRU.[71]

Scappaticci continued to supply intelligence to his FRU handlers on McKiernan's impending fate, it seems, right up to the last moment. Three days before he dispatched his son to the McKiernan family home with his fateful 'my-da-wants-to-see-your-da' message, designed to lure the victim to the Pound Loney Club on the false prospect of joining a new PIRA intelligence cell, Scappaticci provided his handlers with the 'exact time, date and location' of McKiernan's abduction, together with the address of a well-known IRA sympathiser in Clonard Heights where he was due to be interrogated. Kenova found no evidence that the FRU shared this intelligence with Special Branch, until six days *after* the murder.[72] On the day of the abduction, Scappaticci also spoke to his handlers by telephone, though no record of what was said has survived.[73] Whatever it was, such was the bond of trust that Scappaticci had forged with the FRU over nearly a decade that we can safely assume he was confident that none of this would be passed to the RUC in advance of the murder lest it compromise him. Or, to put it another way, in a choice between the risk of blowing 6126's cover and stopping McKiernan's execution, 6126's survival took precedence.

Three days after McKiernan was murdered, Scappaticci gave his handlers a 'comprehensive account of the interrogation and alleged confession' made by McKiernan.[74] It included how he had 'actively sought an execution decision from members of the PIRA's Army Council',[75] the fact that the Army Council had insisted on a signed confession, which Scappaticci reported the ISU had secured, and how, on receipt of this, the Army Council finally confirmed the death sentence.[76] McKiernan is reported to have broken after two and a half hours, and IRA sources say his interrogation ended with him asking: 'How did you get me?'[77]

Having thus prepared the way for McKiernan's imminent execution, Scappaticci left the house in Clonard Heights, reporting two hours later that the 'execution detail' had arrived.[78] Although the Public Prosecution Service (PPS) in Belfast has reported that there was nothing in a recovered MISR to indicate that 'the Source [i.e. Scappaticci] returned to the address in the intervening period', Operation Kenova's reading of the intelligence is that he might well have done and handed the case directly over to the 'execution detail' – in this case, two 'young' IRA volunteers.[79] They bundled McKiernan into a car and drove him less than a mile to an alleyway in Beechmount Crescent, off the Falls Road.[80] There he was ejected from the car, with witnesses describing a familiar ritual: the sound of shots fired, car doors being slammed, a car racing away and men running from the scene. McKiernan's body was found at 7.38 p.m. with four gunshot wounds to the head, the first to the back of his head at close range.[81] Twenty minutes later, the murder was claimed by the IRA on Downtown Radio.

The high level of detail provided by Scappaticci to his FRU handlers and recovered by Operation Kenova left little doubt that he was 'an active participant in the murder' of Anthony McKiernan.[82] Indeed, Scappaticci freely admitted he had been involved and, according to Kenova, he was involved in 'numerous similar murders in the years before and after Anthony's murder'.[83] The surviving intelligence suggests, in fact, that Scappaticci had not just initiated events that night but also co-ordinated them.

McKiernan's inquest was told that he had 'consumed so much alcohol' – four times over the legal limit – that he would likely have died anyway.[84] When that was reported in the newspapers, it was interpreted as McKiernan's former IRA comrades easing his ordeal by making him oblivious to the fact that his life was about to end. This must have seemed a small mercy to his wife and children. Unfortunately, it turns out to have been untrue. On requesting McKiernan's postmortem records, Operation Kenova was told by the Coronial Service that the coroner had made an error. Although no explanation was offered, the assumption was that either the wrong blood sample had been given, or it had been wrongly interpreted at the time.[85] Forensic blunders were not uncommon during the conflict.

The detailed account Scappaticci had given his handlers of McKiernan's ordeal included the leading role he himself played and the names of the IRA members involved in the murder, including the role of the PIRA Army Council. And while all this was shared with the branch *after* his execution, there is no evidence that the branch shared any of it with the CID entrusted with the criminal investigation into McKiernan's murder.[86] So, far from making any serious attempt to bring the perpetrators to justice, there appears to have been a deliberate decision to prevent this happening, 'purely for source protection reasons'.[87] Nor is there any record of the RUC providing meaningful updates on their inquiries to McKiernan's family.[88] Yet the intelligence, had it been made available to the CID, would have provided an extremely rich seam of evidential leads.

By no means was this series of events unique to McKiernan's murder – Kenova found they were 'repeated numerous times'.[89] Responsibility for this failure of criminal justice ultimately lay at the door of the RUC. Although requests from the FRU and MI5 not to downward disseminate a particular piece of intelligence from their sources were almost always respected, since the RUC had police primacy, they had the authority to make an exception. As for the FRU, the five handlers and officers involved in the McKiernan case appear to have made certain there was no risk of the branch making an exception by ensuring that they did not receive any details in advance of where, when and how McKiernan's execution was to be carried out. All five FRU soldiers were questioned by Kenova under caution and all remained silent. Kenova found that they were all 'acutely aware' well in advance of the fate that lay in store for McKiernan.[90]

McKiernan had been something of a republican icon. If – as it appears – he was sober when he was shot, as a former member of the ISU,[91] as well as a revered bomb maker active in both the Markets and South Armagh, he would have had no illusions about the fate that awaited him. The IRA said he had betrayed weapons dumps and the IRA command structure to the security forces after being dismissed in 1987 for 'misconduct'. His family has long maintained that he was not an informer,[92] and the IRA has never provided them with proof that he was, despite their requests.[93]

Seven months after McKiernan's murder, his son, also called Anthony, called at Sinn Féin headquarters in Connolly House. He was shown into a room where two masked men entered, one with a gun. When the unarmed man began talking, Anthony, who was married to Scappaticci's niece, realised it was him. 'Freddie, I know it's you,' he said, whereupon Scappaticci took off his mask and threatened Anthony by 'telling him that his Dad was a tout and that if he didn't stop asking questions he would end up with a bullet in his head, the same as his Dad'.[94] Some years later, Anthony received the IRA's 'civil administration's' most extreme punishment short of death – a 'six pack' punishment shooting in the elbows, knees and ankles.[95]

If Scappaticci were alive today, he – like his handlers – would no doubt justify his involvement in the deaths of former family friends and acquaintances by explaining that spying inside a terrorist organisation necessarily involved enormous moral compromises, even if this meant occasionally sacrificing a friend. I venture that very few people could have comfortably lived with that, as Scappaticci clearly did for many years. IRA membership was not compulsory, so he could have left at any time. He always had a way out with resettlement permanently available. But he stayed and the question is: why?

Among the various motives for becoming a spy recorded in his military intelligence file was his claim that it was for the greater good – he said he wanted to play his part in bringing the conflict to an end. Scappaticci may well have believed the IRA's 'armed struggle' was ultimately futile, yet it is hard to believe altruism would have repressed the feelings of profound guilt and remorse that most people would experience in the face of such acute moral compromises as Scappaticci was so obviously willing to make. Besides, altruism is not usually what motivates people to become spies. The lead motivators are known within the intelligence community by the acronym MICE (money, ideology, coercion/compromise, ego). As a subset of ideology, altruism accounts for only 10–20 per cent of recruits. Those who knew Scappaticci well speak of his planet-sized ego as the main motivation and the impulse that kept him going. Like Brian Nelson, his sense of being at the epicentre of the conflict fortified the self-importance and power he had enjoyed in the 1970s as a revered IRA commander. 'He was principally focused on himself, and nobody else,' said PSNI Chief Constable Jon Boutcher. 'He exploited everyone around him.'[96]

Back in March 1982, Scappaticci had shown -himself to be a model IRA enforcer, and the FRU's discomfort at this – but also acceptance – was clear. He was south of the border preparing to interrogate Seamus Morgan, a twenty-four-year-old father of four. Suspected of having betrayed an IRA arms dump, Morgan had been abducted from a function at a hotel in Monaghan.[97] His execution a few days later would be the sixth in which Scappaticci played a role, this time a very central one. And while the FRU would insist that the principal purpose of recruiting an agent like Scappaticci was to save lives, the Morgan case vividly illustrates the pattern reflected in FRU's surviving records – that, when Scappaticci became involved, it often ended in death. As one source who has seen the surviving records put it, 'If you see it once, you think, "Okay"; but then when you see a constant explaining away of the inaction – always subtly done – you begin to look at it with a more suspicious eye.'[98]

In Morgan's case, Scappaticci provided a 'running commentary', from the IRA's plan to abduct him right up to a day or so before his execution.[99] He reported in advance that a safe house had been prepared for the arrival of a suspect for interrogation, whose name he claimed not to know because he hadn't yet arrived. He reported that masks and a gun had been brought to the safe house, which turned out to be the same two-storey barn at the farm near Bailieborough where Eugene Simons had been interrogated in January 1981 prior to his execution. Once again Scappaticci's hosts were the two elderly bachelor farmer brothers who owned the property and who seem to have been a few bricks shy of a load, as the saying goes. Referring to Simons, one of the brothers enquired, 'What happened to that other nice fella you brought here?'[100]

Scappaticci also notified the FRU that he was to be involved in the interrogation and that if the suspect tried to escape, he would be shot in his presence. Was that Scappaticci getting in his insurance, so that the FRU record would show he'd reported faithfully to his handler that he might have no choice but to get involved in murder, offloading responsibility to the FRU and presenting them with a dilemma: should they sanction Scappaticci's involvement or turn a blind eye? Or just order him to get out while he could? Of course, even if escape had been possible, it would have sealed Scappaticci's fate. Shorn of any serious options other than a plea from his handler to do his best not to get involved, when Scappaticci replied that even that might not be possible, the handler fell back on the only option left: 'Just don't tell us.'[101] Over the course of the conflict, scenes like this between handler and agent would have played out countless times.[102] Confronted with similar dilemmas, there was often no right answer, as Operation Kenova has acknowledged.[103]

Upon Scappaticci's return to Belfast, he faithfully reported the details of his direct involvement in Morgan's looming fate to his handlers: how he'd played a 'central role' in securing his confession and his participation in Morgan's court martial.[104] Presumably, to have endeavoured to pass on details of Morgan's fate in real time from the Irish republic would have been logistically difficult, as well as risky. Morgan had been interrogated, court-martialled and sentenced to death, but the sentence had yet to be carried out. It had been Scappaticci who had interrogated him, secured his confession and moved with him to another location for the court martial,[105] where he had presented the case for the prosecution. It was also Scappaticci who stayed with Morgan overnight before handing him over to those who would guard him until the arrival of the execution detail.[106] In the meantime, unlike McKiernan, the condemned man was reportedly fed whiskey and vodka, while crying over photos of his children.[107]

When he returned to Belfast, Scappaticci told his handlers that Morgan's days were numbered, but when this was passed to Special Branch, the latter took a more relaxed view.[108] The following day the branch rather optimistically assessed that Morgan might be reprieved, because the previous January the IRA had offered informers an amnesty.[109] The problem with this assessment was that the IRA had also made it clear that 'once the amnesty runs out' – which it did at noon on 13 February – they would be in a 'strong position to take stern and immediate action'.[110] The surviving paperwork registers no attempt to seek the co-operation of the Garda Síochána, just as no attempt was made to save Michael Kearney or Eugene Simons. Morgan's body duly turned up on a roadside close to the border at Forkhill, South Armagh, hands tied behind his back, eyes taped.[111] As with Trainor and Robinson, the police told the inquest that Morgan had not been an informer,[112] a breach of NCND by today's MI5 rules, but without, it seems, the sky falling in as a consequence.

Of course, Scappaticci was walking a tightrope: trying to avoid IRA suspicion that he too was an informer, while trying not to be caught red-handed by the CID or uniformed branch. In July 1981, he had the first of several close shaves. After interrogating Dermot Perry, who was also badly beaten up, Scappaticci and fellow ISU comrades left him tied up in a house in Belfast.[113] This was at a time when the hunger strikes by republican prisoners in the Maze H-Blocks were in full swing over their demands to be treated as political prisoners with special status, as opposed to criminals. Perry was left trussed up and alone, while Scappaticci and co. attended the funeral of the fifth prisoner to die, Joe McDonnell. As ageing ex-IRA Chief of Staff John Joe McGirl paid his graveside homage to McDonnell – 'not a criminal but a patriot' for whom the 'world stands in wonder and admiration'[114] – the RUC burst into the house where Perry was being held captive and rescued him. Their intelligence had come not from Scappaticci but from an anonymous tip. Scappaticci and others escaped arrest because Perry was too frightened to give evidence against them.[115]

Following a similar incident in 1983, Scappaticci had another close call after an abductee he was interrogating took his life in his hands and leapt from an upstairs window, managing to run to an RUC station. The couple who owned the house were arrested and Scappaticci fled south to the Irish Republic. Several other members of the ISU had also fled Belfast after the Belfast Brigade adjutant, Robert 'Beano' Lean, turned supergrass, naming dozens of senior IRA personnel.[116] This was a very uncertain time for Scappaticci, and MI5 explored the possibility of taking over running him, since neither the branch nor the FRU's remit extended south of the border.[117] In their desire to recruit Scappaticci, MI5 appears to have put to one side an earlier assessment from the RUC that Scappaticci was 'an unreliable, mercenary petty criminal', who, 'although well placed … frequently failed to give advance warnings of PIRA activities, and a very large proportion of plans on which he reported seemed to come to nothing'.[118]

Scappaticci remained with the FRU, however, providing valuable intelligence from the Republic about IRA operatives suspected of having gone to England. He returned to Belfast just in time for Christmas 1983, after the collapse, on 19 December, of the trial of the owners of the house where the abductee had been unlawfully held. On New Year's Eve, he was arrested at his home in Farnham Street in the Lower Ormeau Road and taken to Castlereagh. There he had his fingerprints taken.[119] This was one of two occasions when he was arrested and released by the RUC ostensibly, it seems, to afford Special Branch an opportunity to try to poach him from the FRU, their earlier assessment of Scappaticci as unreliable seemingly revised.[120] He declined, and fearing his refusal might be repaid with an arrest for real in the territorial feud that occasionally erupted between the rival agencies, he sought sanctuary in South Armagh for several months.

Scappaticci's many months there were not his happiest. The IRA's insular South Armagh Brigade regarded themselves as the ultimate fighting force against the British. Posters brazenly warned the public: 'Sniper at work', and it is true that the IRA's sniper and bomb teams turned this sparsely populated border region into a graveyard for soldiers and police officers. Culturally the place was as far from Britain, and in several respects even Belfast, as the North Pole. There, Scappaticci, often accompanied by the large bulk of John Joe Magee, conducted regular interrogations, with most of the individuals released from the two men's custody after they were satisfied with their answers.[121]

Like a handful of other senior PIRA figures, Magee is widely reported to have served in the British armed forces, in his case as a Royal Marine who then graduated to the elite Special Boat Service.[122] If this is true, his younger self must have cut a very different figure to the obese man in poor health that he had become in his fifties. According to Billy McKee, a former president of the IRA Army Council, Magee had run a brothel in the Lower Falls in the mid-1970s, staffed by girls from the Shankill.[123] A monumentally cavalier security risk, if true, which, McKee says, nearly got Magee executed, but somehow it didn't prevent him going on to head the ISU when it was established in 1978. Ever since, rumours had been rife within the IRA that Magee was an agent, fuelled by the failure of several city-centre bombs which it was suspected had been tampered with. The collapse of the IRA in North Armagh, which was Magee's area of control, only added to the mutterings, as did the fact that a flat he used in Distillery Street where he debriefed volunteers was never hit.[124] Yet nothing came of all these questions, suspicion presumably offset by the fact that many alleged agents and informers under his watch were executed.

Of the two ISU interrogators, Scappaticci was 'the quiet one, always taking everything in,' said an IRA veteran who worked closely with him and Magee during their spell in South Armagh.[125] Nonetheless, outsiders like Scappaticci were generally regarded with suspicion, and it was in this climate that the first mutterings within the IRA about his loyalty surfaced.

Sunset along the South Armagh border on 13 February 1984 was at 5.30 p.m., after which Scappaticci had warned his handlers that a forty-one-year-old IRA volunteer from Portaferry on the Ards peninsula was due to be executed. Months earlier, Scappaticci had warned his handlers that the ISU had suspicions about James 'Jas' Young, after IRA operations in County Down were abandoned and several IRA volunteers killed or captured.[126] Now Young had been lured to the Republic by the IRA on the pretext of a meeting, where he'd been interrogated and court-martialled.[127] The FRU had warned the branch this was going to happen, but the branch had made no attempt to warn Young.[128] Scappaticci had been involved in Young's interrogation[129] before he allegedly broke after several days of detention, admitting he had 'jarked' bombs to ensure they didn't explode. Young was also alleged to have brought a sub-machine gun to Belfast at the behest of his handlers, who had inserted a tracking device in it.[130] Like Michael Kearney, Young had been confronted by Special Branch with an unenviable choice: work for us or go back to jail to serve out the second half of an eight-year sentence for robbery in 1976, for which he'd earned 50 per cent remission. With four children to feed, this 'very quiet' and 'pleasant' man chose freedom.[131]

At what point should the law have intervened to save Young's life? This is the eternal moral-maze question in the contest between source protection and saving a life. Operation Kenova found that Scappaticci had told his handlers three days before Young was executed that he'd been sentenced to death. Surviving records do not show when precisely the FRU alerted the branch, except that the branch seems not to have sought the assistance of the Garda Síochána until the very last minute. In some other cases where Scappaticci was closely involved with the execution, and where fuller records have survived, the FRU does appear to have delayed passing on his intelligence to the branch. On the other hand, the fact that there is a record allowed the FRU to show that it eventually did the right thing,[132] or, as one source who has analysed the files cynically observed, the FRU needed 'something in the log to keep ourselves right, but let's not do anything that compromises Scap's security'.[133]

In the case of Jas Young, the alert was necessarily passed on late because Scappaticci had to be clear of the area before the gardaí intervened. But it was too late, with no room left for error. And there was an error. The location where Young was being held was rural. Scappaticci had told his handlers that the deadline was sundown, and it was only shortly before then that the gardaí arrived in force and cordoned off one of several cottages in a row, but it was the wrong cottage. Watching the garda cavalry arrive, from the vantage of the house higher up the hill where Young was being held, was the execution team, whose task had now been complicated.[134] Young was promptly extracted from the building and driven to an unknown location, where he was shot in the head. His body was then moved to Crossmaglen, presumably to try to confuse the authorities about the actual location of his interrogation, and he was left face down at the side of a road.[135]

Even though the request to the gardaí for assistance came very late in the day, the FRU was, it is fair to say, taking a risk with Scappaticci's cover this time. The evidence of an informer somewhere in the ranks could hardly have been clearer, and what pointed suspicion towards Scappaticci was the events connected to his interrogation of another prisoner at the same location about an IRA operation that had been compromised.[136] This man had been told to report to a car park in Dundalk; he had obediently obliged and had been collected by Scappaticci. After being blindfolded, he was taken to the house and questioned in a room adjoining Young's cell; he recalled later that he could hear Young 'was in trouble'. While it soon became apparent that he was in the clear because he wasn't hiding anything, Scappaticci persisted with questions about operations that had gone wrong, raising the blindfolded man's suspicions and ire. 'Why do you need to know that?' he asked, an unusually fearless response to one of the IRA's most feared interrogators. Affronted by his insubordination, Scappaticci called in his boss, John Joe Magee, complaining that his questions were going unanswered. Magee, however, took the prisoner's side, complimenting him on his discretion, and promptly ordered his release. Scappaticci was tasked with taking him back to Dundalk.[137]

At 6 a.m., the following morning the IRA man, who lived just north of the border, was arrested by the RUC and taken to Belfast for interrogation, where he got the distinct impression from the questions the branch asked him that they knew all about his experience the previous day.[138] It seemed clear to the IRA man that the branch had been talking to someone who had been in the company of a very small circle that included Scappaticci.

The South Armagh Brigade is reported to have shared its suspicions about Scappaticci with the Belfast Brigade. 'He was very definitely not trusted down here,' said an IRA veteran who worked closely with Scappaticci in South Armagh.[139] Belfast appears to have dismissed these fears as typical of South Armagh paranoia. Still, the onus was back on Scappaticci to perform as a model enforcer. This he appears to have achieved, assisted by his involvement in at least six further executions of suspected agents, where he performed the double act of dutifully providing his handlers with intelligence about someone's impending fate, while playing the part in full when the intelligence services chose not to act, which appears to have been more often than not.

By August 1986, the IRA had become intensely suspicious of Paddy Murray, a thirty-year-old IRA man who was also a bricklayer with a penchant for making 'brilliant dumps' – secreting ready-made bombs in the most unlikely places, the locations of which he'd shared with his Special Branch handlers since they recruited him in 1978. Scappaticci was involved in the ISU's investigation, preparing the prosecution case, and he gave details to his handlers of the date and time of Murray's abduction and the address where he was to be interrogated. The FRU told Stevens 3 that these details were passed to Special Branch and was 'adamant' that the branch knew Murray was going to be lifted and therefore had time to intervene and prevent his murder. The branch chose not to, however. It had decided not to forewarn Murray that he was at risk because, for some unfathomable reason, it didn't appear to consider that he was.[140] Nevertheless, having been told to report to the ISU for a debriefing at 8 p.m. on 13 August, Murray gave his handlers the address,[141] and the RUC told him the location would be put under surveillance.

Another suspected informant (Brendan 'Ruby' Davison) was told to report to the same location.[142] Accounts vary as to what happened next: according to IRA veteran Gerry Bradley, both suspects were tied up, blindfolded and held in separate rooms. Murray soon confessed by telling his captors that his handlers were outside.[143] That much at least has been corroborated by Operation Kenova.[144] 'Who did you tell you were coming here?' Murray is said to have been asked. 'I phoned my handler,' he replied.[145] One can only imagine Murray assumed that disclosing this bombshell was his way out. Kenova also confirmed intelligence reports from the time that say two members of the ISU were seen by the RUC surveillance team hurriedly leaving the property.[146] Bradley says Davison and Murray were then untied and the former was told to walk the latter to a new nearby location, yet – bizarrely – neither took the opportunity to escape.[147] Kenova's version – that Davison alone was taken to another address while Murray stayed behind and was later moved to a club – seems more plausible.[148] Murray's interrogation, in which Kenova reports Scappaticci was involved, continued at the new location. There, Murray made further admissions about his work as an agent, including that he had betrayed the IRA's 1979 Short Strand bomb operation,[149] for which young Michael Kearney had been executed in July that year. Presumably Murray was still relying on his handlers having his back, but they no longer had. They'd left after only two hours, having been 'stood down' and 'no intervention was planned or conducted'[150] – whether this was because the branch still thought Murray would come to no harm, or that he was assessed as expendable, is unclear.

Murray was held until shortly before 2 a.m. on 15 August, whereupon a black taxi that had been hijacked a few hours earlier was brought to take him to the corner of Dunmore Street and Clonard Street. With his feet bound, hands tied behind his back and eyes sellotaped shut, he was dragged out of the cab and shot twice in the head.[151] The CID found the address where he was first taken on a piece of paper in his breast pocket, but detectives were prevented from getting a search warrant by the branch. The CID was also instructed not to put any details of the address in the investigation logbook.[152] Other vital intelligence was withheld from the CID, 'severely hampering its pursuit of those involved'.[153] Again the obvious explanation is source protection, and perhaps this time more than one source, since it seems clear from Kenova's interim report that Scappaticci was not the only agent to have penetrated the ISU.[154]

While some in Northern Command were sceptical about Scappaticci, he kept suspicions within the Belfast Brigade at bay with the occasional bravura performance as the hardest nut in town. IRA man Gerard Hodgins recalls such an event in the summer of 1988, at a funeral in Milltown cemetery. One of his colleagues spotted a man with a large bulge under his jacket who closely resembled a prison officer he'd known in jail. Scappaticci told them to 'take the screw away'. Upon searching him, however, the bulge turned out to be a large tobacco pouch and the 'screw' was now a taxi driver who had just brought some photographers to the cemetery. 'So we let him go,' said Hodgins. 'But we knew what Scap meant by telling us to "take him away" – he wanted us to shoot him. He was quite casual about it.'[155]

As with any agent, the priority for Scappaticci was self-preservation. Taking a forceful proactive role like this was all money in the bank. Two months later, he would need all the credit he had when questions again surfaced about his loyalty to the IRA. Not for the first time, he and those running him would do whatever it took to make those questions go away, such was the iron-clad trust that a decade of surviving as a double agent in the most precarious of IRA positions had forged between Agent 6126 and his handlers.

Chapter Eight

6126 – The Executioners' Weekend Hosts

BARNAMS WORLD OF ICE CREAM is a much-loved café on Belfast's Lisburn Road, which has been family owned for the best part of its near four-decade history and, to this day, sells multiple ice-cream flavours. On 11 October 1988, the café was being minded by off-duty police officer John Larmour (42) on behalf of the owner, his brother George, who was on holiday with his family.[1] At 10 p.m., just as the café was closing, two men walked in. One strode to the counter and asked Larmour could he please have a chocolate ice-cream sandwich known colloquially as a slider. The other languished by the door. As Larmour turned towards his customer, the man whipped out a Ruger pistol and shot him several times. His fellow gunman also carelessly opened fire and wounded two customers, hitting one in the elbow and the other in the shoulder.[2]

The IRA tasked Scappaticci with finding out what had gone wrong, so he was entrusted with the names of the two perpetrators, which he passed to the FRU, who passed them to Special Branch. If this intelligence was passed on with the FRU's oft-used caveat that there should be no downward dissemination, on this occasion the request was ignored. Shortly afterwards, the two gunmen were arrested. The FRU was furious that the RUC had prioritised avenging the murder of one of its own over the protection of the source of the intelligence, and its mistrust of the branch arising from this incident lasted several months.[3] Serious damage appeared to have been done to Scappaticci's security. The circle of knowledge within the IRA over Larmour's murder was so tight that, this time, some in the IRA's Belfast leadership began to contemplate the possibility that Scappaticci was one of a small number of candidates who could have betrayed them.

Since early 1988, the Belfast Brigade had also been harbouring growing suspicion about the highly valued Special Branch informant Joe Fenton, a thirty-five-year-old wheeler-dealer estate agent and Belfast version of Arthur Daley, the affable, smooth-talking dodgy-dealing chancer from the TV series *Minder*. Unusually for an estate agent, Fenton was popular locally. 'People mattered to Joe,' said his father, Patrick. 'They always mattered to Joe. If he knew somebody that needed a house, that was unemployed, he might say, "Yeah, he's employed in such a thing, you know, to get his mortgage through."'[4]

A secret, darker side to the affable Fenton, however, had developed in recent years. It had a familiar genesis: caught shifting explosives for the IRA in 1981, the branch made him an 'offer' to work for them – or he could go to jail. Like so many before and after, it ultimately proved to be an offer Fenton felt he could not refuse, although at first that is exactly what he tried to do. He applied to the Australian embassy to emigrate, and he and his young family were granted visas. The Fentons were booked to leave on 4 January 1982, but, shortly before this, Joe got a message asking him to report to the Australian High Commission in London and to bring his visas with him. There he was told they were the wrong visas and that they were being cancelled. A crestfallen Fenton returned to Belfast, where Special Branch was waiting for him.[5] Since the alternative to refusing their 'offer' was ten years in jail, he succumbed – like so many others – to what in effect was state-sponsored blackmail.

Fenton was given the codename 'The Driver' because he had a sideline driving a minibus. The branch also gave him money to establish an estate agent business on the Falls Road, which he called 'Ideal Homes'.[6] For the branch, this arrangement was indeed ideal. Fenton provided the IRA with 'safe' houses and garages in empty properties that were on the market, where MI5 installed listening devices to monitor conversations. According to the IRA, Fenton also supplied 'clean' cars to them by hiring the cars out to be used to bring explosives across the border.[7] The money the branch paid Fenton was privately invested by them so as not to arouse suspicion, and it wasn't released to him, even when his business began to fail.[8]

Soon valuable intelligence began to flow in from both of these intelligence-gathering operations, leading to the interception of explosives consignments from the Irish Republic, recovery of weapons in Belfast and arrests. Inevitably, over time, these successes attracted the IRA's suspicion, a danger not lost on Fenton, whose counter-measures cast his affable persona in a rather more chilling light. According to a Special Branch report, by 1987 Fenton had told the IRA he suspected that a former IRA man – who was also a friend of Fenton's – was an informer.[9] The IRA investigated and in April 1987, the thirty-two-year-old father of two, Charles McIlmurray, was abducted to County Louth, where he was brutally interrogated with the IRA's version of waterboarding.[10] A confession was extracted in the form of a handwritten letter, which was then sent to his family. He was then shot and his body left in a van at Killeen, County Armagh, with a plastic bag over his head.[11] McIlmurray's execution was notable for spurring on Gerry Adams, then MP for Belfast West, to remind his constituents in a matter-of-fact way that 'anyone else living in West Belfast knows that the consequence for informing is death'. This reminder was issued by the Sinn Féin president a few hundred yards from the McIlmurray home.[12]

Scappaticci had been involved in the ISU's initial investigation into McIlmurray. He told his handlers why McIlmurray was suspected and gave them details of how the plan to abduct him would be carried out. These were passed onto Special Branch, but the RUC warned McIlmurray only 'in general terms',[13] which was clearly insufficient to alert him to the looming danger to his life. 'The threats were not acted upon appropriately by the RUC,' says Kenova.[14] One of McIlmurray's handlers has alleged that he was ordered by his branch superiors not to pass on further warnings.[15] The reason is unclear, but it is notable that the branch very much wanted to keep Fenton in play, raising the chilling possibility that McIlmurray had become expendable in order to enhance Fenton's standing. That anyway became the suspicion of some within the IRA Belfast Brigade, and in June 1988 Scappaticci was tasked with exploring exactly that theory.[16]

One thing is clear: Fenton was becoming trapped in a vortex of competing self-preservation pressures. The more his influence waned, the greater the pressure one of his two Special Branch handlers put on him to get results to justify that officer's substantial appetite for lucrative overtime, much to the disgust of the other handler.[17] Likewise, the more Scappaticci himself came under suspicion for the arrests for the murder of Constable Larmour, the more he was under pressure to prove his fealty to the cause by pursuing his fellow agent. If McIlmurray had indeed been sacrificed, it was only a matter of time before the one who sacrificed him would, in turn, be sacrificed. For the majority of soldiers and police officers who conducted themselves with integrity during this conflict, to suggest they were part of a 'Dirty War' is understandably deeply offensive. Yet not for nothing has that label stuck to the agent-running element of the counter-insurgency.

Fenton's misfortune was Scappaticci's fortune. The latter had been reporting regularly to his handlers that Fenton was being watched closely by the IRA.[18] Since Scappaticci himself was feeling the heat from the Larmour arrests, it was time for another bravura performance as a model enforcer to enhance *his* status with the IRA, at the expense of Fenton if necessary, despite the fact that, like Scappaticci's previous victims, Fenton had a family to support – four young children and a wife.

In June 1988, Scappaticci summoned Fenton to see him at Sinn Féin's office in Sevastopol Street in Belfast's Lower Falls. Fenton's wife, Michelle, drove him there, and it was a thoroughly humiliating experience for both of them, no doubt designed to be so in front of the Sinn Féin staffers who worked there. Michelle knew Scappaticci by sight because his children went to the same school as hers, and she also knew him by his fearsome repute. Winding down the car window, Fenton told Scappaticci: 'She's asking – am I going to be alright?' 'Yes,' replied Scappaticci, but his tone was dismissive, signalling that Michelle should make herself absent. An hour later she returned. Fenton had arrived dressed dapperly for the interrogation in a jacket and tie, as was his style. He returned to his wife white as a sheet, his tie askew. As Michelle drove him home, he said ominously, 'If I go missing, contact a priest.'[19]

Over the months that followed, Scappaticci sent word to his handlers that the net was closing on Fenton, that his life was increasingly at risk. Similar warnings were coming to Special Branch from their other agents. In all, some twenty separate sources warned the intelligence services that Fenton was highly likely to be shot.[20] Scappaticci even made suggestions to his handlers as to how Fenton might best counter the suspicions against him.[21]

Matters came to a head in January 1989. Brendan Hughes, head of IRA Internal Security on the General Headquarters (GHQ) staff in Dublin, confronted the Belfast Brigade's OC, 'Big Harry' Burns, about Fenton. Burns, who was on good terms with Fenton, swore by him. The two were friends, a relationship Burns later came to regret following the discovery of a bug in a light fitting in the front room of his house.[22] This might well have explained the RUC's successful interdiction of cross-border weapons movements, since Burns had been running them.[23] The extent to which MI5, on behalf of the branch, placed bugs in properties managed by Fenton presumably also helps explain the confidence the branch had that Fenton's days were numbered. Martin Dillon, in *The Dirty War*, quotes an unnamed 'senior IRA leader' referring to a bug having been discovered after Fenton's death in a house where 'IRA members discussed Fenton's fate and the evidence against him'.[24] That 'IRA leader' has been confirmed as Brendan Hughes, apparently authorised by the Army Council to talk to Dillon.[25]

Also in January, Scappaticci reported that Fenton was to be interrogated and that this time he would not survive.[26] This was to be his third interview with Fenton.[27] Neither the FRU nor Special Branch could have been in any doubt that Fenton's life was hanging by a thread. Early in February 1989, the FRU's CO, Colonel Gordon Kerr, made a decision that may have helped seal Fenton's fate. Kerr appears to have reached the limit of what he was prepared to share with the branch, lest the latter act precipitously on Scappaticci's intelligence, as no doubt Kerr feared they might, given that Fenton was so highly prized by the branch. The branch had, after all, risked Scappaticci's security in October by arresting the two suspects he'd identified as being responsible for the murder of Constable Larmour. In a letter to the branch, Kerr candidly explained: 'This HQ is unlikely to receive more specific prior warning of Fenton's abduction.'[28] What Kerr meant was that FRU Agent 6126 was unlikely to be providing even his own handlers with any more intelligence on Fenton for his own self-preservation. Not that 6126 would not have had any more intelligence on Fenton's impending fate to provide – he clearly would have known the details, since it was he who was scheduled to conduct Fenton's interrogation. And so it proved. Scappaticci had two days' warning in advance of Fenton's abduction.

Had Kerr made an uncompromising decision to put the protection of his agent ahead of Fenton's life? If so, bloodless as that may seem, the relationship between agent and handler depended on the agent trusting 100 per cent that the handler had his back. Absent that trust, Scappaticci was unlikely to continue to provide the flow of intelligence that he did, which by all accounts may have been more fulsome than has hitherto been speculated in the media.[29] It was precisely this degree of trust that had caused Scappaticci to believe his handlers would only share his product in a manner and a timing that always put his security first. The Larmour incident had fractured that trust.

Meanwhile, Fenton's friend Harry Burns had warned him that Brendan Hughes suspected him of being an informer, so Fenton took himself off to England and Scotland to reflect on his future, travelling around in the cab of the lorry driven by his brother. Hughes has speculated, as have others, that Fenton was told by his handlers to come back to Belfast 'because everything was alright'.[30] Martin Dillon quotes a 'senior member of the IRA … in a position to know about the Fenton case' as asserting 'British intelligence' told Fenton to return to Belfast 'to sacrifice him … to cover their tracks because they had someone equally important in place'.[31]

It is highly likely that the intelligence services had not one but several key sources they wanted to protect. Scappaticci, for example, was not the only informer/agent in the ISU, as Operation Kenova has made clear.[32] The available evidence, however, does not support the idea that Fenton was encouraged back to Belfast by his handlers as a sacrificial lamb for the protection of others. The reverse appears to be the case. Fenton returned to Belfast against the advice of the RUC.[33] Surviving records show he was repeatedly warned by police about the threat to him, but that he refused to heed the warnings.[34] The assessment by Operation Kenova is that there was a 'concerted effort by the police to look after Fenton'.[35] It seems likely that Fenton had decided himself that it was a reasonable bet to return because Burns had assured him he had his back, and Burns, in turn, had the ear of Gerry Adams.[36] As Fenton's widow, Michelle, told the RUC at the time: 'I don't think he was in fear of any danger to himself as if he was he had plenty of opportunity to stay away when he was in England.'[37] In any case, return home to Belfast Fenton did, at 5.30 a.m. on Friday 24 February; he spent the day indoors. At half past seven that evening two men arrived at 124 Carrigart Avenue, on the Lenadoon estate, bringing with them a bag of bandages, cotton wool and Sellotape. The householder, James Martin, welcomed them in as they took the bag up to a first-floor bedroom, where Fenton was to be interrogated. One of the men was Freddie Scappaticci; the other, according to Martin, was known only to him by his first name, Eddie.[38]

One of Scappaticci's FRU handlers claimed to have seen a record in his file that he'd 'pushed' the FRU to ensure Fenton was executed because he'd come to believe that Fenton suspected he too was a spy.[39] Kenova was unable to find such a document. However, the surviving intelligence reports do suggest the FRU went to exceptional lengths to ensure that Scappaticci was allowed to interrogate Fenton without the risk of the cavalry intervening, by generating a bogus 'out of bounds' order in an area of the Lenadoon estate where the interrogation was due to take place. Four days before his abduction, the branch received a FRU communication by way of an MISR emanating from Agent 6126 warning that a Control Wired Improvised Explosive Device (CWIED) had been planted in the area. Although the MISR made no reference to Fenton, a second CWIED warning was issued a day before the abduction identifying 'a specific street name', presumably in or around Carrigart Avenue. This was also the day Scappaticci had been told Fenton would be abducted.[40]

The warnings appear to have had the desired result, with the 'out of bounds order' reportedly served on the location.[41] The way was now clear for Fenton's interrogation and execution without risk of interference or rescue by the security forces. If these CWIED warnings were indeed phantom, the fact that the FRU so securely had Scappaticci's back would have reassured him about his position and that he was pretty much untouchable as far as the law was concerned.

The following day, sometime after 1 p.m., Fenton told Michelle he 'had a wee message to do and that he wouldn't be long', without saying where he was going.[42] The precise details of how he was lured to 124 Carrigart Avenue, just five minutes' drive away from his home, are unknown, save that he arrived there after dark. Scappaticci and at least one other man, Eddie, were waiting for him, and he was bustled up the stairs and into the bedroom, which had been prepared for his incarceration until he confessed.

That confession would not come easily. 'There was a lot of scuffling, it seemed to be hot and heavy and heavy verbal shouting … he seemed to be getting punched or something,' James Martin later told the RUC.[43] Not that this seems to have bothered Martin especially. Amid the sound of creaking floorboards, shouting, banging and the odd thump, he sat down to watch the world heavyweight boxing title fight between America's Mike Tyson and Britain's Frank Bruno in Las Vegas.[44] He and his wife, Veronica Ryan, also enjoyed a Chinese takeaway before retiring to bed, and, according to her, they managed to sleep peacefully until 10 a.m. the following morning while the interrogation continued in the adjoining room.[45] No. 124 Carrigart was not a spacious property. Far from it. The intimacy of the horror that was unfolding a matter of feet from where they slumbered peacefully does not seem to have perturbed the couple in the slightest.

The next morning, making tea and toast for Fenton's captors, Martin observed that there was 'still quite a bit of noise from upstairs. It seemed to be constant. The ceiling was vibrating.' Shouting continued into that Sunday afternoon. Fenton must by now have realised he was literally fighting – physically and psychologically – for his life.[46]

Ryan made Sunday lunch for Fenton's captors, after which she had a lie down and then a bath. She heard more shouting, as if 'somebody was trying to get a point across or something'. Perhaps, having confessed, Fenton was now begging for 'mercy', as his father later put it, 'and to be allowed to go home to his wife and kids'.[47] Ryan continued to relax in her bath and about half an hour later 'heard people moving about outside'.[48] This appears to have been Scappaticci leaving, his work done. At some stage, Fenton had confessed; the tape would later be played to his father, Patrick, the IRA's way of 'dignifying' an informer's execution. His executioners were scheduled to arrive after dark. James Martin was downstairs and Scappaticci told him they would all be leaving soon.

The time was shortly after 6.30 p.m. Scappaticci stood by the kitchen window looking out as if he was expecting an arrival. Soon a woman did arrive, later identified by Martin as Geraldine Crawford, an IRA sniper in the 1970s who survived being shot.[49] Scappaticci unlocked the front door to let her in, and both he and Crawford then stood staring out of the window,[50] as if awaiting the arrival of others – presumably the execution team. A further five to ten minutes passed before Scappaticci popped his head round the sitting-room door to tell Martin, 'We're away now.'[51] A car carrying Fenton's executioners had arrived. At about the same time, Martin 'heard some noises out on the stairs' – presumably Fenton being brought down – and heard them 'going out the front door'.[52]

Fenton was taken to the car that was to take him to a location where he could be safely disposed of. The evidence in James Martin's statement leaves little doubt that Scappaticci had waited to hand Fenton over to the execution detail. It is at this point that Fenton appears to have decided his only hope was to make a dash for it. With a bandage trailing loosely from his wrist, he took off at a sprint, pursued by two gunmen. Hoping to confuse his pursuers, after some 150 yards he turned sharply into a laneway at Bunbeg Park, but they were as fast as Fenton and, outside the fence facing onto No. 12 Bunbeg Park, they fired a shot that hit Fenton in the right shoulder. The shot was not fatal, but its proximity to his spine caused him to collapse.[53] As the two gunmen closed in, he was heard begging for his life and crying for his mother by a witness traced by Operation Kenova.[54] The gunmen showed no mercy and, at less than twelve inches from his face, three more bullets were fired into his head. Death came instantly.[55] This being a Sunday, people coming out of chapel had to walk past the body.[56] Fenton was so badly disfigured that, according to Scappaticci, he had to be identified by his jewellery.[57]

The few surviving military and branch files about this incident record that Scappaticci phoned his FRU handlers ten minutes before the shooting was reported to the police.[58] The record says he did this 'as soon as possible' after leaving 124 Carrigart Avenue. However, that ten-minute claim is inconsistent with the evidence of James Martin, whose account has Scappaticci, Crawford, Fenton and those guarding him all exiting the house at about the same time. 'I heard the door closing, and the house was quiet,' Martin told the police. 'I knew they were all gone. About two minutes later, I heard some cracks, what I knew were shots.'[59] In other words, as in the case of McKiernan, once again Scappaticci was handing over a victim from whom he'd extracted a confession directly to the team tasked with murdering him.

A uniformed police officer outside Lenadoon heard the shots and had to seek authority to enter the estate since it was still out of bounds to security forces because of the alleged CWIED threat.[60] That threat was lifted the following day, adding to suspicion that it was a calculated FRU invention to ensure the execution went ahead without disruption, once again prioritising Scappaticci as a prime source to be protected, whatever it took.[61] Put cynically, it might also suggest that both the FRU and Scappaticci needed Fenton dead following questions about the former's loyalty provoked by the Larmour incident. Whilst the FRU told the branch after Fenton's murder that he had been held at 124 Carrigart Avenue, to ensure against the RUC fomenting yet more questions by arresting the Martins, the MISR to the branch came with a 'no downward dissemination' restriction to the CID.[62]

None of this allayed the deepest suspicions about the overall integrity of the Belfast Brigade by the man in overall charge of the IRA security department. 'Belfast was rotten ... rotten,' Brendan Hughes recalled in 2002, in a series of seminal interviews with his close friend and former IRA man Dr Anthony McIntyre. Hughes had wanted Fenton brought across the border to be 'held for as long as possible', convinced there were 'other ... higher-ranking spies' in the brigade and that the ISU had colluded in sacrificing Fenton 'to protect someone bigger'.[63]

If true, this rather magnificent conspiracy theory would have required several key members to be acting in concert on behalf of the British. Had Hughes perhaps become lost in his own wilderness of distorting mirrors, similar to the frenzied paranoia counter-intelligence induced in the CIA and MI6 Cold War warriors of the 1950s, who saw Reds under the bed almost everywhere in the American and British governments? Quite possibly. Hughes had become deeply disillusioned at the constitutional direction in which his former close comrade Gerry Adams was taking Sinn Féin/the IRA.

However, there is, in fact, a more mundane explanation for the IRA's Belfast Brigade ensuring Fenton was dispensed with in Belfast, out of Hughes' orbit. Hughes himself alluded to it in his interview with McIntyre. Gerry Adams' minder, Terence 'Cleeky' Clarke, was a hero to many in the IRA with his stories of derring-do,[64] twice escaping from jail and disarming two corporals in 1988 at the funeral of IRA Volunteer Kevin Brady, who were then lynched and brutally beaten before being shot. Adams said he 'came to know and love [Clarke] as a brother',[65] and lauded his ability to 'scrounge doors, lights, intercoms, security grills, toughened glass, bullet-proof vests and anything else that he could get his hands on which undoubtedly saved lives'.[66] They might also have made Clarke a small fortune on the side. As Hughes recounts, 'Cleeky and other people were involved in dodgy jobs', and Fenton was Clarke's fence for stolen goods.[67] Knowing that Fenton could have exposed the extent of this dodgy dealing, it seems possible that this was one reason why the Belfast Brigade wanted him silenced in Belfast rather than elsewhere.

The question as to why Fenton was dealt with in Belfast and not taken south for a full 'debriefing' was raised at a postmortem about his execution during an IRA meeting or 'buster' in Donegal. It is reported to have been chaired by a senior Northern Command member, who railed at his subordinates for having ignored his order that Fenton was to be taken south. 'Who gave the order?' he demanded. One of those present pointed to a Belfast-based colleague, on whom the IRA leader then turned: 'You don't give the fucking orders, I give the orders!'[68]

For Hughes, though, there was far more to be untangled from the Fenton affair than some racketeering by Clarke and his mates on the side. According to Hughes, besides fingering McIlmurray as an informer, in his confession Fenton had also admitted to offering up the names of two more informers – Gerard and Catherine Mahon – to ingratiate himself with the IRA.[69] This couple had been storing weapons for the IRA, which they had allowed the branch to 'jark' with tracking devices. What exactly alerted Fenton to the Mahons is unclear: one report has it that it was their deposit for a mortgage through his estate agency without any obvious sign of an income, because neither of them worked.[70] Another was that Fenton got to know Gerard, who was a mechanic who serviced Fenton's car.[71] After the couple was seen meeting their handlers, in September 1985 they were abducted, interrogated and put in a black taxi at night to be taken to an alleyway in Turf Lodge. First to be executed was Gerard (28), witnessed by his twenty-seven-year-old wife, who saw her husband being shot in the head and face. She made a run for it, her hands bound behind her back, down an alleyway, but she was cut down by a burst of automatic fire. Like so many others, the couple had succumbed to Special Branch pressure to gamble with their lives by informing, in return for charges being dropped for unpaid fines and wages equivalent today to just £60 per week.[72]

Weighing up the costs and the benefits from the moral compromises that were made in the undercover side of this conflict is a near impossible task. The Fenton story was by no means unique: a man blackmailed with a choice of going to jail or spying for the state. Fenton chose the latter, and while this surely did lead to lifesaving intelligence and the recovery of IRA munitions, it also led to him getting in so deep that he had to make enormous moral compromises by sacrificing the lives of a former friend, Charlie McIlmurray, and, it would appear, a young couple, before he himself was quite cynically sacrificed by a branch of the state, leaving a widow and four children. Of course, had all of the state's warnings about Fenton from Stakeknife been passed on and immediately acted upon, Stakeknife would have had to be pulled out, and the state would have lost an asset who was delivering valuable intelligence. It follows that compromises had to be made, but when that involves questions about who lives and who dies – as it did here – the spymaster enters dangerous 'playing God' territory. Some, such as the current PSNI chief constable, have concluded that even were it possible to 'accurately and reliably' show that a particular agent did more good than harm, 'the morality and legality of agents doing any harm – with the knowledge of or on behalf of the state – is something that we would never ever allow today'.[73] One former home secretary speech writer is not alone in questioning the practical reality of this approach.[74]

Of course, few of the darker intrigues of agent running were known during the Diplock Courts era of the conflict. What some former police officers have referred to as 'satellite files' are said to have been regularly submitted to the DPP. Attempts by one law firm to establish how frequently have so far not borne fruit. Since the Good Friday Agreement, it has become increasingly clear that the 'sensitive' material often being protected was the existence of an agent or agents involved in serious criminality. How ironic that the courts – the very embodiment of the rule of law that the counter-insurgency strategy was aiming to re-establish – were also the shield behind which the lawlessness of that strategy was being concealed.

In fairness to the RUC leadership, this irony was not lost on them, strange as that might strike their adversaries. From the start of 1987, the senior command made a concerted effort to address the fact that they, MI5 and the FRU were operating well outside a regulatory or even legal framework governing agent running. The then head of Belfast Special Branch, Ray White, recalls raising the issue directly with Margaret Thatcher on a visit to

Belfast. 'Have you got everything you need, Mr White?' she asked, to which White replied, 'Well Prime Minister, I would welcome detailed guidance and regulation in relation to what we do.'[75] Thatcher appears to have had no idea this didn't exist. 'We are operating in a very grey area,' as White delphically put it to her.

Irony of ironies, this gaping legal lacuna also troubled the self-same MI5 officer whose report in 1981 had expanded it by recommending that decisions about criminal investigation and prosecution be subordinate to intelligence gathering by agents. Seven years later – in May 1988 to be precise – Sir Patrick Walker, then MI5's director general, was urging Thatcher to mitigate the impact of his review with the need for clear agent-running guidelines.[76] Nonetheless, at the Conservative party conference in October that year, Thatcher maintained the fiction that the security forces operated strictly within the rule of law, as indeed, the majority – but not all – did. Thanking the SAS soldiers who that March had shot dead three unarmed IRA terrorists in Gibraltar planning a car-bomb attack on British military personnel there, she said that 'unlike the terrorist who skulks in the shadows and shoots to kill', the SAS had 'acted at all times within the law and to save lives'.[77] By then Thatcher knew very well that the IRA weren't the only ones operating unlawfully in the shadows.

For the next four years, a variety of reports, internal reviews and gatherings of an NIO Working Group sat with metaphorical wet towels around their heads trying to produce a workable set of agent-running guidelines for Northern Ireland. In England, Wales and Scotland, if an agent involved in non-terrorist crime had been involved in murder but hadn't told his police handler, despite having the opportunity to do so, he could expect to be charged with murder. But this was Northern Ireland and a criminal context that was regarded as entirely different. One agent who'd been involved in murder, and who had also delivered an IRA man suspected of being an informer to the ISU for four days of the most brutal torture imaginable, after he was resettled in England lectured new agent handlers, in the course of which he freely admitted his involvement in serious crime.[78] Not surprisingly the Working Group failed in its 'mission impossible', for the obvious reason that there was no magic solution which would make legal actions by agents in terrorist organisations that were manifestly illegal.

Squaring this circle was impossible even for mere membership of an illegal organisation, never mind the more serious criminality in which Agents 6126 and 6137 had engaged: conspiracy to murder and actual murder.

As mentioned previously, the morality and legality of agents doing any harm with the knowledge of or on behalf of the state is something Boutcher says would never be tolerated today.[79] The state is, however, paying a price for a more purist, stricter rules-based regime. Covert Human Intelligence Sources (CHISs) are often the best source of intelligence for fighting crime and terrorism, yet there has been a significant decline in the number operated by, for example, the Metropolitan Police,[80] partly due to the evidence emerging from the long-running Undercover Policing Inquiry of systematic abuse by undercover officers who infiltrated allegedly subversive organisations and even engaged in long-term sexual relations with those they were spying on.[81] During the Northern Ireland conflict, the agencies avoided the legal challenges inherent in penetrating a terrorist organisation simply by doing their best not to get caught. That was the reluctant conclusion of Solicitor General Sir Derek Fatchett in 1992, after the Working Group finally produced its guidelines: 'the thrust of para[graph] 4 appears to be "Don't get caught"! This is unpromising territory for Ministerial approval,' minuted Sir Derek.[82] The outdated Home Office rulebook, originally drawn up for East End gangs, remained, in effect, window dressing: on the one hand it involved a pretence to the public that agents were governed by the rule of law, while simultaneously allowing the authorities to 'wash [their] hands of the consequences' when 'anything comes unhappily unstuck'.[83]

FRU Agent 6126 had been in place for ten years, surviving that long only because, in the absence of a legal framework governing his handling, his spymasters had turned a blind eye to his activities. Even so, many agents in Northern Ireland had a finite shelf life and, by the summer of 1989, FRU Agent 6137's was about to run its course. The lid that had been so tightly closed over the secret and unlawful world that licensed his rampant criminality was about to come off.

Chapter Nine

6137 – The Lid Comes Off

ON THE EVENING OF 24 August 1989, Brian Nelson was chairing a meeting of UDA intelligence officers and 'military commanders' from Belfast and Derry at a social club in the Taughmonagh estate, a staunchly loyalist neighbourhood in South Belfast. He was complaining that other than 'one or two brigades in the Belfast area, the others were doing nothing'. He meant, of course, doing nothing about killing 'legitimate' targets. Unless the UDA upped its game, he warned, 'it would end up going nowhere as a movement'.[1]

In response, the UDA's 'brigadier' for South Belfast told Nelson he had something for him. Thrusting an envelope containing fifty sheets of paper into Nelson's hand, Bobby Philpott said, 'I got this from an SB officer in Lisburn but some of it is mixed and if I were to target everyone in this, we'd end up shooting one another.' Philpott then left in a hurry.[2]

One of the targets listed on the top page was a twenty-eight-year-old father of four from Rathfriland in County Down, Loughlin 'Locky' Maginn. At approximately 12.45 a.m. the following day, two UDA gunmen in black balaclavas smashed through his living-room window with sledgehammers, as he and his wife tucked into a Chinese takeaway, and opened fire with Browning pistols. Wounded in the chest, Maginn made for the stairs but collapsed on the landing, where he bled out in front of his ten-year-old daughter Jenny, who had been woken by the noise. 'I could see the wounds on his body, you know … there was blood splattered just everywhere,' she told me thirteen years later. 'He started to fall asleep, and [a] neighbour had said to me … get a pillow for his head and he was telling him not to go to sleep … and daddy died … he died there.' It's an image that 'never seems to go away. I see it all the time.'[3]

What marked out Maginn's murder from the hundreds of other loyalist assassinations was the brazen way the UDA justified it. Maginn was an IRA foot soldier, it said, and, in an attempt to prove it, it showed the BBC a film of an RUC collators' bulletin listing IRA suspects in the southern half of County Down, which included Maginn. The UDA's West Belfast 'brigadier', Tommy 'Tucker' Lyttle, had first approached David McKittrick, *The Independent*'s Ireland correspondent, asking him to publish a still photograph of the bulletin. McKittrick was told that he would be shown the material at Lyttle's home but would have to say that he had been taken by the UDA to an unknown location in order to protect Lyttle from prosecution. McKittrick declined on those terms, as did Barney Rowan of BBC Northern Ireland when the offer was put to him. The material later appeared on the BBC in a report by Rowan's colleague, Chris Moore. In his jail journal, Nelson said Moore had been shown the video at UDA headquarters in Gawn Street, Belfast.[4]

The video had been shot the previous December by two UDR soldiers at the Ballykinler army base in County Down, after Nelson had supplied the UDA with a camera for precisely this purpose. Maginn had often been stopped by UDR patrols. 'I have a wee word of warning,' one soldier told him, according to a note he'd written, 'I'll stiff you when I get the chance.'[5] To the frustration of this UDR soldier and his mates, no one in the UDA had yet taken that chance, despite Nelson having warned the UDA in January 1989 that if 'no attacks resulted on any of those mentioned on the video tape, the UDR personnel who supplied it would not supply anymore [targets]'.[6] Now, Nelson was giving a similar message to the UDA bosses just hours before Maginn was shot, prompting Philpott to give him an envelope containing fifty targets, with Maginn among the top names.

What had especially annoyed the UDR soldiers about the UDA's failure to shoot any of the targets they had supplied was that they had told the UDA their hit team could hide in the Ballykinler base should they have difficulty escaping. As an MoD official later observed, this fact was 'potential dynamite'.

Should it become 'public knowledge, the security forces' credibility would be severely damaged'.[7]

It had been known well before Nelson supplied the camera, not just by the FRU but also by MI5 and Special Branch, that the UDA intended to gain access to intelligence from Ballykinler, yet no attempt had been made to prevent this happening because the branch had decided there was 'little to be gained ... since the UDA already had lots of this stuff anyway, and they would find nothing of value ...'[8] But now the UDA had found a target that they valued – Loughlin Maginn – and the question remains: did Nelson prompt the gun team into action after giving his pep talk to the UDA and Philpott passing him a target list with Maginn's name on it?

At the very least, Nelson seems to have known an attack was afoot. Some twenty minutes before the attack, he telephoned the FRU. Once again, he was drunk. He appeared to want to know if anything had happened. 'Receiving such a call only twenty minutes prior to a murder taking place in which certain personalities known to him were involved, is very worrying,' the FRU noted.[9] Twenty minutes after the attack, Nelson again phoned as if curious to know if anything had happened.[10]

The video of Maginn's name on an RUC collator's bulletin, shot with a camera inside an army barracks, supplied by FRU Agent 6137, was the spark that lit the fuse that, in the months and years ahead, blew lid after lid off the secret side of the Northern Ireland counter-insurgency. Here was the unvarnished evidence of what had long been suspected: that elements of the security forces were brazenly colluding with loyalist death squads. And the louder the public outrage, the more Tommy Lyttle ordered leaked montages of IRA suspects to be plastered across Belfast. They included material leaked by the police, for example photographs of suspects stolen from a display cabinet in Dunmurry RUC station.[11] There was certainly no shortage of the stuff. 'I was getting documents, day and daily. I was getting that many documents that I didn't know where to put them,' Bobby Philpott later recalled. These included 'intelligence reports, photos, what colour socks republicans was wearing ... what sort of cars they drive, where they lived ... their safe houses'.[12]

In bragging about the precision of the UDA's intelligence, Lyttle's purpose was to demonstrate to the public that the UDA was no longer the sectarian force that randomly killed Catholics just because they were Catholic. He sought to persuade the public that the organisation's targeting was now accurate; it was now 'professional', and 'professionalising' the UDA's targeting was, of course, the task that FRU Agent 6137 had been entrusted with by Colonel Gordon Kerr, albeit, he would insist, not in the way it had worked out.

A major Anglo-Irish row erupted. Dublin demanded an immediate inquiry, something the newly appointed RUC Chief Constable Hugh Annesley could scarcely refuse. The policeman chosen for this task was a tall, larger-than-life figure, John Stevens, who went on to become Metropolitan Police commissioner. He would lead three inquiries into 'collusion' in Northern Ireland. At the conclusion of the first (Stevens 1) in 1990, Stevens assessed that collusion was 'neither widespread nor institutionalised'.[13] By the time he'd completed his third investigation (Stevens 3) in 2003, he'd radically revised that assessment.

When the call came to lead Stevens 1, he was still unpacking boxes, having just moved to Cambridge to take up a new post as deputy chief constable. On the evening of Thursday 14 September, under assumed names, Stevens and the head of Cambridgeshire CID, Detective Superintendent Laurie Sherwood, flew to Belfast from Luton airport. Sherwood and Stevens were close friends, having both been detective sergeants in the Metropolitan Police's flying and robbery squad. They checked into the stately Culloden Hotel overlooking Belfast Lough, built in the nineteenth century as the official residence for the Lord Bishop of Down, Connor and Dromore. The next day, they met Annesley, who reassured them he didn't expect the job to take much more than a month,[14] which soon proved to be a spectacular underestimate, indicative of how even the newly appointed chief constable had yet to appreciate the depth of the hostile terrain into which he had invited Stevens. Stevens would spend much of the next thirteen years, in the course of three separate but connected inquiries, prising open a world that many in the intelligence services believed should remain closed forever. Taken together, the three inquiries would be the largest ever external investigation in Northern Ireland and the most extensive of their type ever undertaken in the United Kingdom.

That Annesley thought Stevens would be in and out of Belfast in a month begs the question of how much he'd been told by the FRU, Special

Branch and MI5 about the lawless rein given to state agents, and, in particular, how the murderous conduct of Agent 6137 threatened to expose this, undermining the covert side of the counter-insurgency. Stevens' terms of reference included the leak of security force material from Ballykinler Barracks 'associated with the murder of Mr John Anthony Loughlin Maginn' and 'any associated matters which come to light during the course of the enquiry'. It was that reference to 'any associated matters' that threatened to open a Pandora's box.

The FRU's immediate priority was to conceal from the criminal investigation the fact that a salaried state agent was at the very heart of the Maginn murder conspiracy – and much, much more. The evidence shows that Special Branch was an accomplice in this cover-up, at least initially. And not only did the branch cover for the FRU, but it was also determined to protect the reputation of the RUC, knowing it was significantly involved in leaking information to loyalist paramilitaries. MI5 was also fully in the picture but was powerless to dictate to either the FRU or the branch what to disclose to Stevens about what they knew, both about Nelson's role and the sheer scale of security-force leaks to the UDA. MI5's role was purely advisory. Four years earlier, MI5 had assessed that 85 per cent of the UDA's 'intelligence' emanated from the police and the army,[15] including senior ranks in both: 'Reliable and repeated reports covered comparatively senior officers in the RUC through to senior officers in the UDR ...'[16]

Anticipating that Annesley would have no choice but to initiate an outside criminal inquiry following the outcry over Loughlin Maginn's murder, a fortnight before Stevens' arrival, FRU records show it 'briefed' Nelson 'on resistance to interrogation ... should he be arrested during the next reporting period. The need for utmost secrecy regarding work for this office was pointed out and speedily digested.' Nelson was clearly rattled. After Maginn's murder, he'd missed his handler meeting and arrived 'visibly shaken and worried' when it was rearranged. However, his handlers reported that after reassuring him about the 'importance of his work for this office' and that he was the 'last person' with 'anything to worry about, he chirped up'.[17] Events would prove the opposite, despite criminal levels of obstruction by the FRU, who ordered Nelson to say 'absolutely nothing to any interrogators no matter what the threat'. Agent 6137 was instructed 'never to mention his work for this office. Even if a Special Branch or CID officer may state that they knew he was an agent, he was to deny all knowledge and say nothing.'[18]

Martin Callan, who'd handled Nelson for much of 1987, his first year after returning from Germany, was also worried. Callan asked his OC if he was likely to be interviewed in the event of a criminal inquiry. 'I knew Nelson had been involved in targeting and that I had reported such activity to my superiors,' Callan would later tell Stevens. 'I knew he had been involved in criminal activity.' But at the time, Callan says he was reassured by the FRU that if anyone was to be interviewed it wouldn't be him but his superiors, the FRU officers.[19]

Stevens and Sherwood meanwhile had gone home for the weekend, returning to Belfast on the morning of Monday 18 September having selected a thirty-strong handpicked team of detectives. The four-week stint Annesley had suggested was already looking optimistic. ACC Wilfie Monahan – one of several RUC officers Stevens would come to trust – told Stevens, 'John, you really do need to know that you've come into a can of worms.'[20]

He certainly had. At the end of their first week, Stevens and his team attended a briefing at army headquarters in Thiepval Barracks, Lisburn, by a colonel who was chief of the army's G2 Intelligence Section. Out of the blue, Detective Constable Sarah Bynum asked the colonel if the army ran informants. According to Bynum, he 'categorically denied running agents'. Only the RUC 'had the role of intelligence gathering', said the colonel, not the army.[21]

This was a lie of epic proportions, since the colonel himself was responsible for the field intelligence fund that financed the FRU.[22] Thirteen months later – having discovered the lie – Stevens was told by the army that the colonel had been 'under instructions based upon special branch advice' not to disclose that military intelligence had been engaged in covert intelligence gathering.[23] Exactly who was giving the instructions about what should and should not be disclosed to Stevens remains wreathed in confusion to this day. The answer depends on whose version of the disclosure protocol to Stevens, agreed between the army, the RUC and the chief constable, appears most credible.

The GOC Northern Ireland, General Sir John 'Muddy' Waters, claimed that the deputy head of Special Branch, Detective Chief Superintendent

Brian Fitzsimons, told the army Annesley had instructed him that no intelligence was to be disclosed to Stevens without clearance by him.[24] FRU CO Colonel Kerr said that was also his understanding.[25] A document presented in September 1990 to the chief of the general staff and the defence secretary records that even before Stevens had arrived in Belfast, Annesley had told General Waters that Stevens 'would have no access to intelligence documents or information, nor the units supplying them'.[26] Annesley emphatically denied he'd instructed the army to deny Stevens access to any intelligence material.[27] He insisted he'd given the order for Stevens to have access to whatever intelligence he needed to do his job, except that which was clearly irrelevant, precisely because he didn't want a recurrence of the fiasco caused by the 1982 series of 'shoot to kill' incidents investigated by deputy Chief Constable of Manchester John Stalker. Just about the only thing all parties agreed on was that Annesley had instructed that his deputy head of the branch, Fitzsimons, should be the disclosure conduit.[28] But that seems to have been the proximate cause of the disclosure problem. In practice, Fitzsimons seems to have become a strict gatekeeper, although whether he was obeying a much stricter letter of Annesley's law, or his own, is unclear.

The result was that within three weeks of Stevens' arrival, any intelligence that might have led back to Brian Nelson, or which damaged the RUC's reputation or showed the sheer scale of security force leaks, was withheld. So, while Fitzsimons gave Stevens a list of names and addresses where he was told he might find leaked security force documents held by loyalists,[29] the one address that was conspicuously withheld from him was 2J Forthriver Crescent, which contained the mass of leaked intelligence files used for targeting and which was protected by a Special Branch-ordained 'do not search property without reference to FRU' notice.[30]

On 22 September – four days after Stevens arrived in Belfast – Colonel Kerr had the dump transferred to army headquarters.[31] Fitzsimons would later 'categorically' insist he'd never been made aware either of the dump's existence or that it had been seized.[32] The evidence is clear, however, that the RUC Source Unit, run by Special Branch, *was* aware of both.[33] Whether Fitzsimons was told by his own people is disputed; certainly he insisted to me that he had not been.[34]

As to the scale of security force leaks to the UDA and other loyalist paramilitaries by rogue soldiers and police officers, both the FRU and MI5 drew up their own separate lists showing how extensive the problem was. In the FRU's case, Colonel Kerr said he created a file from CFs and MISRs listing forty-two instances of army and RUC intelligence leaks because he wanted the GOC, General Waters, to be aware of the problem so that he could bring it to the chief constable's attention. He said the GOC then instructed him to take this file personally to Brian Fitzsimons who, in turn, had told him that Annesley had asked to look at it.[35] Stevens never got a look in.

The scale of leaks was supremely relevant to this, the first of the Stevens inquiries. Yet Fitzsimons decided not to disclose the file to Stevens because of the 'sensitivity' of the information in it,[36] despite Kerr acknowledging the relevance of 'Nelson's reporting' because it showed 'security force collusion'.[37] Fitzsimons also failed to disclose to Stevens the fact that a Special Branch officer had given the list of targets including Maginn to the UDA's Bobby Philpott, who had passed this on to Nelson at the Taughmonagh social club several hours before Maginn's murder.[38] Likewise, a 'highly sensitive' compendium of security force leaks drawn up by MI5 was not disclosed to Stevens,[39] despite MI5 having cleared its disclosure to his inquiry.[40]

Fitzsimons also withheld from Stevens all information about Nelson, as did the FRU, while beefing up its lessons on how he should resist interrogation, should he be arrested.[41] His handlers noted: '6137 was once again reminded, at some length. He must make absolutely no mention of his work for this office no matter what tack is used by his interrogators or what consequences with which he may be faced.'[42]

Instead, to the limited extent that the branch did assist Stevens, it was to put the focus on the UDR as being principally responsible for leaks, which was probably true, except that the RUC was not far behind.[43] Indeed, when it came to tipping off impending security force operations, according to MI5 'the RUC predominates'.[44]

It would seem, therefore, that all disclosure roadblocks led to Special Branch and its deputy head Brian Fitzsimons, despite his having acknowledged privately to MI5 that Nelson had been 'badly handled and poorly exploited'.[45] Yet, while Fitzsimons may have been the proximate cause of the obstruction in this first critical phase of Stevens 1, it is not at all clear that he was its root cause. I had several dealings with Fitzsimons over a decade, and he struck me as an honest man, as indeed the Stevens team concluded when later in their inquiry Fitzsimons was regarded as having been helpful to them. Their assessment of Fitzsimons was that he was under intense pressure to limit disclosure from Annesley, a new chief constable as yet unblooded in the visceral turf war between the three spy agencies, and that Annesley himself was torn between his need for a trusting relationship with the army top brass and his obligations to full disclosure to the criminal inquiry he himself had commissioned. Fitzsimons was also under fierce pressure from some of his subordinates not to assist Stevens, to the point where on one occasion his loyalty to the RUC was questioned so forcefully by colleagues that he was momentarily reduced to tears.[46] As for Annesley, who'd been in post just two months when the collusion crisis hit, it had begun to look to Stevens 'as if Hugh was wondering if he'd done the right thing calling us in'.[47]

Stevens was wondering about that too, but for a different reason. At forty-six, he was an experienced detective and had a reputation as a facilitator – finding ways around obstacles, especially the bureaucratic ones, and getting things done. Nonetheless, he admitted to feeling professionally challenged by the scale of the task confronting him. Hostility from some sections of the RUC was also palpable. Senior officers like ACC Monahan were mostly welcoming, as was Stevens' driver and bodyguard, the 'splendidly calm, laconic' Detective Sergeant Grahame Foote. Others, not so much. 'What a monumental waste of time and money,' was the view from the Belfast head of CID, Detective Chief Superintendent George Caskey.[48] Most of the opposition came from Special Branch. 'If we spent half the money we spent on you, we'd be able to fight terrorism,' one officer told Stevens' SIO, Detective Chief Superintendent Vince McFadden.[49] 'Suddenly we could feel the heat all around us,' said Stevens.[50]

The antipathy from Stevens' officers towards those RUC officers who took Caskey's view was mutual. McFadden recalls being invited to lunch by ACC Monahan at his golf club. Caskey joined them. Either Monahan or Caskey was club captain (my note from the time is unclear). McFadden recalls that, whoever it was, at the lunch the other referred to him as 'Captain' rather than by his first name, even though they were close police colleagues of similar senior rank. 'I nearly vomited at the obsequiousness,' recalled McFadden.[51]

Stevens' team of detectives were all hand-picked from the Metropolitan

Police and a handful of other constabularies, including Surrey, Hampshire, and Dorset, but they'd yet to get a feel for that elusive phenomenon sometimes referred to as the 'Ulster psyche', a parochial suspicion that no Englishman could possibly understand how the place ticked unless they'd lived there for half a century. Few of these officers had set foot in Northern Ireland during the conflict; it was just a place they'd read about in the papers. That also went for 'Mr Stevens', as his officers referred to him, for he most assuredly was the 'guv'nor', a man with an occasional fierce temper if crossed but with a gift for cutting through what, to others, seemed like impenetrable bureaucratic walls. Eventually, I and my BBC colleague Geoff Seed would get to know his mellower side and his prodigious taste for good champagne. For the moment, however, 'Mr Stevens' and his team were completely closed to the media. The closest he'd come to doing an interview was on his arrival at Aldergrove airport. With a clipped 'hello' to the waiting press, followed by a 'if you'll excuse me, we've got work to do', his team fell in behind him, and we, the media, heard nothing more for weeks.

Stevens set up shop in a suite of offices at the back of Seapark, a giant building in Carrickfergus on the Antrim coast where the RUC's central stores were housed. Visitors were funnelled along an entrance of high concrete blast walls to a checkpoint. Over the coming months, Geoff and I made a number of visits to Seapark, the policemen peering at our ID all chins and noses, their eyes obscured by angled peaks to their caps like military policemen, cradling their Second World War sterling sub-machine guns. Seapark was vast, mysterious and forbidding, and the security lights dotted around its barbed-wire perimeter were so bright they blotted out all contours and looked as if they were suspended in a black void. Geoff called Seapark the 'Edge of Darkness' because it reminded him of a haunting BBC TV series of that name about the death of a young environmentalist in mysterious circumstances.

Geoff and I had arrived in Belfast planning to make a programme for BBC *Panorama* on the 'collusion' crisis. One of my first calls was to a prim terraced house in the warren of streets behind the Protestant Shankill Road, in the heart of working-class loyalist West Belfast. Painted in shades of grey and white, with solid brick walls, these houses looked as if they would last forever. Inside one of them lived Tommy Lyttle, the UDA's boss in West

Belfast, a thick-set man who listened more than he talked; when he did talk, he came across as measured, with a dry wit.

You couldn't help liking Lyttle – at least I did. He had a gentle manner for one who presided over an organisation that dealt in death, racketeering and unspeakably brutal punishments meted out to those who offended the organisation's raw political sensibilities or became too greedy. That was the side of Lyttle you never saw but you knew was there. I had known him since the 1970s, when bombings, shootings and constant checkpoints were all part of the daily routine in the early years of the Troubles. On Friday nights, Lyttle was a regular at the 'Whip & Saddle' bar of the Europa, which revelled then in the distinction of being the world's most bombed hotel. There he would sit, nursing a pint, his mistress, Maisie, by his side, nodding to almost everyone in the bar, because almost everyone was a journalist and everyone knew Tommy. Some journalists, me included, had taken up semi-permanent residence there.

In the autumn of 1989, Lyttle exuded a new confidence. It was he who'd been trying to give the UDA a makeover to shake off its reputation as an organisation engaged in random sectarian killings to one which targeted IRA members based on leaked security force intelligence as, so he claimed, had been demonstrated by the murder of Loughlin Maginn. The previous year the UDA had also taken possession of a sizeable number of assault rifles and pistols shipped to Northern Ireland from Lebanon. Lyttle talked about at last being able to take the war to the IRA. 'Is this really true, there's no shortage of this leaked intelligence material?' I asked him. He told me it was true.

Personally, I never witnessed in Lyttle the crude sectarianism so evident in some of his fellow UDA members. He recognised that Catholics had legitimate grievances and he was not averse to talking to the IRA if it would achieve peace. He spoke of 'lazy bloodshed'[52] and would insist violence was not gratuitous, yet the West Belfast Brigade had within its ranks some of the conflict's most murderous individuals. 'Could you show me the extent of the intelligence you're getting from sympathisers in the security forces?' I asked. Lyttle told me to meet him at his UDA headquarters in the Shankill the next day and he would show me what he meant.

The men who typically guarded the entrance to the West Belfast UDA headquarters were disinclined to give outsiders the benefit of the doubt. Waved through the door by two men with harsh, lined faces, heavily tattooed limbs, thick necks, chunky gold bracelets, beer bellies and vast arm muscles that had no doubt broken ribs in romper rooms, I climbed the stairs. 'John, this is Brian,' said Lyttle, pointing to a wiry, bespectacled man, aged about forty, absorbed in a copy of *An Phoblacht*, the IRA's weekly propaganda newspaper, his feet on a table. Also on the table was packet of Players No. 6, which Nelson was getting through one by one. 'Brian, show this man some of your stuff,' said Lyttle. Nelson looked up, quizzical – with good reason.

What I didn't know then was that Nelson and Lyttle had had a furious row over the latter's demand to up the ante by boasting about the leaked intelligence the UDA was getting. Two days after Nelson had delivered a leaked sightings list of the PIRA's South Armagh Brigade, it had appeared on the BBC *Nine O'Clock News*. Nelson protested that if Lyttle kept doing this, he risked compromising the UDA's sources, whereupon Lyttle flew into a rage: 'If you don't want to f**ing do it, I'll employ someone who does!'[53]

Now Lyttle was ordering Nelson to let me see for myself the scale of security force leaks by taking me to see his entire intelligence dump. Nelson was non-committal. He didn't exactly say yes, but he didn't say no; he just said that it wasn't something he could arrange at short notice, which was an understatement because, of course, unknown to me or to Lyttle was not only the fact that Nelson was an army agent but also the fact that by now the FRU had moved his intelligence dump to army headquarters at Thiepval Barracks. If Lyttle's demand had caused him to panic, I can't say I noticed it. Nelson calmly gave me his phone number and agreed to meet six days later at 7 p.m.

FRU records show that Nelson reported this conversation to his handlers, who told him not to attend, but that if, under pressure from Lyttle, he felt he had no choice, he should 'change the venue' of our meeting 'at short notice' without prior notice to me of the new venue. The FRU noted:

> The source seemed oblivious to the type of trickery the media can get up to. It was pointed out to the source that there would be many dangers exposing himself to a pre-arranged meeting in a public place. He was reminded of body-fitting microphones and secret cameras, all

> of which BBC TV news teams have at their disposal in the interest of 'good journalism' and keeping the public rightly informed.

Nelson was encouraged by his handlers to appeal to the head of the UDA's 'military wing', Eric McKee, to try to persuade the UDA boss Tommy Lyttle to 'steer opinion away from the present course of action' and to 'use his influence to bring the present "affair" with the media to a close as discreetly as possible'.[54] The problem was that Lyttle didn't want the media 'affair' to be brought to a close. Far from it. He wanted to highlight the full extent of the UDA's access to security force intelligence on a prime-time BBC *Panorama* episode as part of his campaign to show that the UDA was targeting only Catholics actively supporting the IRA.

Days were turning into weeks, with Nelson making elaborate excuses as to why it was too risky to show me his intelligence dump in the current febrile climate with Stevens on the ground. On the few occasions when he did agree to meet, in his smoky Citroën car or in a bar, he was always strung so tight you could almost twang the sinews in his neck. He tried to persuade me that not even Lyttle fully appreciated the security risks for the UDA in showing me the full range of material, samples of which had been flaunted in posters across Belfast.

A weary ritual ensued. I would get back to Lyttle and he would put pressure on Nelson, to the point where the latter would put pressure on his handlers to return his files. On 2 November, the FRU emphatically refused: 'Handler tried to convince 6137 that denying his stores was not a permanent arrangement but at the moment it was in 6137's own best interest that the office retained them.'[55] As the pressure mounted, Nelson pleaded with them again six days later: 'Yet again the source was reassured that though he would be returned his stores presently held by this office, the time was not right yet.'[56]

The reassurance that Nelson would eventually get his files back was based on the assumption that Stevens might soon give up and go home, and they could all get back to business as usual. But Stevens had no intention of leaving because, by then, he'd had a breakthrough. Searches of several properties, including ones that were derelict and uninhabited, had turned up piles of documents and photographs. Common to the finds at four sites were photocopied 'P' (personality) cards of potential targets written in distinctive spidery handwriting.[57] Stevens sent the documents to Scotland Yard for fingerprint testing, where their advanced systems were capable of yielding evidence inaccessible to the RUC.[58] The results identified Brian Nelson. His reckless habit of copying his 'P' cards for other loyalist killer gangs was coming home to roost. After three years of impunity, the legal net was closing.

Stevens now had a name to work with of someone who was clearly central to his terms of reference. In his biography he says that when he spoke to his RUC link man, ACC Monahan, about 'this man Nelson', he was referred to Brian Fitzsimons, who became 'evasive' and said, 'We can't help you with this man. He told me we don't know where he is.' Fitzsimons had just been promoted to the rank of assistant chief constable and head of Special Branch.

At the same time, I was putting pressure on Nelson to deliver the access to his intelligence dump that his boss Lyttle had instructed him to give me. Transmission was looming for the programme that Geoff Seed and I were working on for *Panorama* about the UDR, which, it was clear, was responsible for a sizeable chunk of security force leaks to loyalist murder gangs.

Despite the rising tension created by Lyttle's demands for more exposure of information from Nelson's intelligence dump and his handlers' strict instructions to resist this, the FRU observed that the crisis was forging closer bonds between Nelson and his handlers: 'Though under a great deal of pressure … 6137 has developed an increased loyalty to his handlers.'[59] Meanwhile, no rest was being given to the man whose murder Nelson had helped bring about and which was about to blow the lid off the agent-running regime in Northern Ireland. Loughlin Maginn's freshly dug grave had been vandalised and his coffin damaged, with Sinn Féin blaming the Parachute Regiment.[60]

Although Fitzsimons was still withholding from Stevens the fact that his prime suspect was a state agent, the discovery of Nelson's prints all over the targeting files recovered by Stevens meant that it was only a matter of time before he was arrested for possession of material useful to a person committing or preparing an act of terrorism. At the same time, Lyttle was still vigorously demanding that Nelson show me the full extent of this self-same material. A vice-like grip was tightening on Nelson, with Lyttle on one side and the FRU on the other. On 5 December, Nelson came up with a ploy that he calculated would loosen it. In fact, it simply showed how reckless he was.

My notebook records that on that day, Nelson asked me to meet him at a UDA social club in Mayo Street at 3 p.m. From there he drove me to his home. In his living room he lifted up a coal scuttle, under which was a pile of photographs, mostly of republican parades, bearing the stamp 'Pacemaker Press' – a well-established Belfast agency – on the reverse. According to Nelson, the UDA's store of photographs 'concerning Republican funerals and ceremonies' was regularly passed to them 'by an employee of [the] Belfast *News Letter*.'[61] Nelson pointed to a man in several photographs, including one outside Crumlin Road Gaol and another of a wreath-laying parade at Milltown cemetery. There was also a republican news report of this man allegedly having been beaten up by the RUC in Leeson Street and of security force observation of his house.[62]

'Who is he?' I asked.

'Hugh Malone – he's next.'

'You mean ...?'

Nelson nodded, then beckoned me to a bedroom upstairs. From an Amstrad computer, he printed off samples of his 'P' cards on individuals about whom he'd been gathering targeting information before handing them to the UDA for shooting. I can only assume he thought this would so impress me that it would ease the pressure from me on Lyttle to show me his entire dump. FRU records would show that the notorious UDA gunman, Winkie Dodds, was indeed targeting Malone,[63] but he was stopped from locating his house by the presence of an army patrol.[64] The FRU also noted that the Pacemaker photographs of Malone had been acquired by Sam Duddy, reputedly one of MI5's three agents in the UDA.[65]

Following this meeting with Nelson, my immediate priority was to find Malone – whom I'd never heard of – to warn him his life was in danger. Unlike Dodds, I did manage to find him after a couple of days. Grateful for my warning as he was, Malone appears not to have been too surprised, since the front door he opened to me was heavily reinforced with solid steel. The BBC agreed that I should also report the threat to Malone to Stevens himself, to ensure his protection. This was easier said than done.

Stevens had made himself inaccessible to the media, refusing all requests for interviews. He'd given only one brief introductory press conference outside RUC headquarters and allowed himself to be filmed reading documents at his desk. 'Why should Mr Stevens see you?' was the response to my request to meet him. 'Because it may be a matter of life and death,' I replied. Reluctantly, I was told to report to Seapark that evening, where I met Stevens and his SIO, Detective Chief Superintendent McFadden. 'What's the source of your information about Malone?' McFadden asked. I explained I couldn't divulge that, but he needed to take it seriously. My recollection is that McFadden and Stevens made several references to my legal obligation under Section 18 of the Prevention of Terrorism Act to disclose information about acts of terrorism or individuals involved in terrorism, but when it became clear there were no circumstances in which I would identify my source, they sensibly dropped it and the mood lightened. The tight-lipped face Stevens presented to the public was replaced by a smiling enthusiast. 'Come over here and see what progress we're making,' he said, beckoning me to a large whiteboard giving statistics of searches and arrests to date.

Nelson doesn't appear to have disclosed my meeting at his house to the FRU, which had its own ideas about how to remove me from the picture. I was next due to meet Nelson at the Europa hotel, and I'd told him that I wanted to film any material he brought with him, a 'situation which could be exploited,' reported the FRU. What it meant was to get me off the pitch by having me arrested: 'Conspiring to receive material of use to a terrorist organisation is a criminal offence,' noted the FRU. 'Ware is leaving himself open to criminal charges.'[66]

This was pretty rich, bearing in mind that, for several years, not only had the FRU themselves been conspiring to ensure that Nelson was supplied with 'material of use to a terrorist organisation', but they'd also encouraged him to use it to help make UDA targeting more 'professional'. Not only that, but in the run-up to Christmas, Nelson had sent typewritten letters to the directors of two of Northern Ireland's largest construction companies and their relatives, threatening death if they gave evidence against four UDA leaders who had extorted substantial sums of money from them. He also sent Christmas cards, addressed in his handwriting, to the two directors, threatening them that Christmas 1989 would be their last. '6137's security awareness has dropped again,' reported the FRU in something of an understatement. The FRU's response was to order Nelson to chuck his typewriter in the river, a blatant perversion of the course of justice given that the directors had reported the threats to the RUC, which was now conducting a criminal investigation into UDA extortion. Instead, Nelson told his handlers that he'd wiped his prints from the typewriter with a sock, smashed it with a hammer and chucked it in a skip. 'Only an Irishman could consider this to be inconspicuous action,' his despairing handler observed.[67] More pertinently, the fact that this 'Irishman' had handwritten the cards had totally defeated the point of getting rid of the typewriter.

In the event, the FRU dropped the idea of setting me up for arrest. Instead, '6137 was … warned not to have any more dealings with Ware'.[68] It was reported that Nelson's 'motivation has been tested over the last few days over the John Ware incident and to his credit he has done exactly as his handlers have instructed. A high degree of trust has been developed over the last few months which has increased 6137's loyalty both to the handling team and ultimately the office.' Nelson was instructed to finally bring the 'affair to a close' by lying and telling me that 'the targeting material has been posted' to me at the BBC in London. '6137 was also to tell Tommy "Tucker" Lyttle that he had passed on the details to John Ware in this manner.'[69]

This would not, however, mark the end of the cat and mouse game that Nelson and his handlers were playing. Far from it.

On the morning of Saturday, 6 January 1990, Lyttle called me to come to his home. There he told me what he said he'd just been told: that he, Nelson and several other senior UDA men were going to be arrested by Stevens at dawn on Monday. Unknown to any of us, Nelson had moved to the top of Stevens' arrest list when he was alerted to the fact that there appeared to be a particular sensitivity whenever Nelson's name was mentioned. At Grosvenor Road RUC station, one of Stevens' officers had found a card bearing Nelson's details, describing him as the UDA's chief intelligence officer. When the officer asked for a copy, it was 'whipped away' and he was told he couldn't have it. The officer informed Detective Chief Superintendent McFadden, who went straight to Grosvenor Road and eventually secured a copy.[70] I asked Lyttle how reliable his tip-off about Nelson's arrest was. 'Very,' he replied.

He was correct. Bobby Philpott, the UDA's South Belfast 'brigadier' had been tipped off by his source in Special Branch, who had advanced knowledge of Stevens' plans, codenamed 'Operation Wheel'.[71]

In fact, for the FRU, that first weekend of the new decade and its immediate aftermath would prove to be much more serious than the loss of one agent. Agent 6126's double life – the spy the army called their 'golden egg' – was also about to run its course, triggering a whole new world of pain for the FRU, Special Branch, MI5 and the entire security and intelligence establishment.

Chapter Ten

6126 – 'The cops, they're coming here'

AT AROUND 2.30 P.M. ON Thursday, 4 January 1990, James Martin got a knock on the door of his home at 124 Carrigart Avenue from a neighbour in Belfast's Lenadoon estate. Tony Clarke had recently returned from England, having been jailed in 1977 in Liverpool for causing an explosion and conspiracy to cause explosions.[1] He was reported to have led the 1983 riot at the top security Albany jail on the Isle of Wight, in which some fifty prisoners, including IRA inmates wielding wooden staves, metal bars and broken glass, wrecked an entire cell block.[2]

Martin stepped out of his house and the two men chatted on the pavement. Could the IRA use his home for the upcoming weekend, Clarke inquired?[3] Based on his previous IRA house guests, who'd left with Joe Fenton and then shot him, Martin knew exactly what that meant, although he would later try to persuade the police that he believed it would be 'just a young hood for a couple of slaps or something'.[4]

This new request to host the IRA appears to have been anticipated by Martin, since he'd taken the trouble to carefully pack away in his bathroom airing cupboard the cotton-wool pads used to blindfold Fenton eleven months earlier. He'd also retained, in a large cupboard drawer in the sitting room, the bandages used for binding Fenton's hands. So, he readily agreed to Clarke's request, and that evening he unpacked the pads and bandages, laying them out in the same bedroom where Scappaticci had wrung the confession from Fenton that sealed his fate.

The bedroom was directly above Martin's sitting room, where he'd nonchalantly watched Frank Bruno and Mike Tyson on TV bashing lumps out of each other in Las Vegas while, above him, Fenton had been getting 'a lot of thumping and banging', as Martin would later admit to the police.[5] One of those administering the thumping was either Scappaticci, 'Eddie' or perhaps both. The coming weekend would once again see Martin watching TV while above him the ISU's latest victim was left to contemplate his imminent death. There was a slight complication, in that Martin had arranged for a special aerial to be fixed to the roof on Saturday to pick up Scottish TV programmes, and he didn't want to cancel the job. So, to prevent the TV engineer spotting a bound and blindfolded man from his ladder, Martin put up some curtains his wife, Veronica, had obligingly washed. He also brought a chair into the room, on which Scappaticci's victim would sit for hours facing the wall.

Thus began one of the most consequential weekends in the unravelling of Northern Ireland's so-called 'Dirty War'. While the investigation by John Stevens into collusion between the security forces and loyalist murder gangs prepared for the arrest and interrogation of army spy Brian Nelson, another army spy was preparing for his interrogation of a police spy. What Freddie Scappaticci didn't know was that this interrogation would be his last, just as Nelson's career as a spy was about to end. In Scappaticci's case, that weekend also marked the start of decades of attempts to hide the full extent of his murderous criminality, in which the intelligence services would acquiesce with the blanket application of the Cabinet Office's NCND protocol.

The suspected police agent to be interviewed was thirty-two-year-old Sandy Lynch. He'd been a police spy for seven years, first as a member of the dissident INLA, recruited on his release from a twelve-year sentence for multiple firearms and explosives offences.[6] Encouraged by his handlers, he later defected from the INLA to join the PIRA and was now a member of an intelligence-gathering unit in Ardoyne, North Belfast, while working as a taxi driver. Colleagues found him to be a 'happy-go-lucky bloke' addicted to drinking Coke, whose 'big aim in life was to get a girl and have a few children'.[7] He was in the process of trying to achieve that, having recently married a girl from Magherafelt, who suffered a miscarriage not long afterwards.

Lynch certainly seems to have put on a convincing act as a committed PIRA intelligence gatherer, a model terrorist whose lawbreaking was justified by his spymasters as acting in the public interest for the greater good. He'd been involved in bomb attacks on the Belfast-based aerospace company Short Brothers, two army observation posts and Girdwood Army Barracks, in which four police officers were injured, one seriously. Lynch had driven the getaway car for the bomb planter. He'd also proposed kidnapping a taxi driver and torturing him for information about the movements of one of his regular clients, a notorious UVF leader, after which, Lynch suggested, the taxi driver should be shot and buried in quicklime. As well as this, he'd urged a gun team to shoot an RUC officer he'd been tracking.[8] 'Sandy was always saying people should snipe against the Brits,' recalled an IRA man who had become friends with Lynch after meeting him in jail. 'When we were out in the car, he kept saying this or that target would be a good one.'[9] The fact that Lynch was also regularly harassed by the security forces added to his cover.

Yet he'd also made mistakes. While working for a taxi firm in Ardoyne called 'Wheels', he was spotted in a phone box, having said he needed to slip out of the office for ten minutes, despite the owner allowing the staff to use the phone. Two days later the security forces came looking for the owner.[10] That and the fact that he regularly seemed to succeed in getting into Belfast from Magherafelt without being detained at vehicle checkpoints evidently raised the suspicions of someone in the IRA, leading to an ISU investigation. Scappaticci had already collared Lynch for a preliminary chat about security measures shortly before Christmas.[11] Lynch told detectives from Operation Kenova that he was not unduly alarmed by this incident since the ISU conducted regular security debriefs.[12] He also emphatically denied claims, notably in Ingram and Harkin's book *Stakeknife*, that his handlers had given him three days advanced warning that he was about to be 'picked up' by the ISU but told him that he had nothing to worry about as long as he didn't admit to anything.[13] The evidence, which I address in Chapter 16, suggests Lynch was right.

The ISU's preferred *modus operandi* for abducting suspects was deception rather than physical force. On Wednesday 3 January, Lynch was told to come that Friday to a house in Ardoyne at 6.30 p.m. The house was familiar to him because it was used as a drop-off point for IRA messages. He duly complied, and there met Kevin Mulgrew, OC of his intelligence unit, and his second-in-command, Seán Maguire. According to Lynch, Mulgrew told him he had a potential target for him and Maguire to gather intelligence on. Although Lynch had parked his car nearby, Maguire told him to use a different vehicle, a blue Cortina, which Lynch noted had a lot of rust on it.[14]

The assignment to track a target appears to have been part of the IRA's attempt to distract Lynch from becoming suspicious that he was being abducted. Intelligence gathering on potential targets was, after all, his bread-and-butter IRA job. Maguire directed Lynch to drive him close to a house off Upper Dunmurry Lane, which Maguire said was the hideout for three criminals, one of whom was dealing drugs. Lynch says Maguire told him the IRA wanted them 'wiped out'.[15]

It was true that three criminals were linked to that address. Eight days later, on Saturday 13 January, all three would be shot dead by undercover soldiers during a robbery of Sean Graham's bookies at the junction of the Falls and Whiterock roads. Peter Thompson (23) and Eddie Hale (25) died in a hail of bullets from undercover soldiers of 14 Intelligence Company. Thompson was unarmed but Hale was carrying an imitation firearm. The unarmed driver of their getaway car, John McNeil (43), was shot execution-style as he sat at the wheel. Through a 'fence', the men had come into possession of a stolen coded security force map of West Belfast, a Heckler and Koch, and a 9mm pistol with ammunition clips, taken by joyriders from the boot of a vehicle belonging to 14 Intelligence Company in the car park of a bar near Thiepval Barracks. By Friday evening, the weapons had been retrieved but not the map, and Thompson, Hale and McNeil were still at large. IRA sources from the time have insisted they were not targeting the trio.[16] One imagines, however, that every available agent had been tasked with keeping their eyes and ears peeled for their whereabouts, so how Mulgrew and Maguire came to hear about this trio at a time when the intelligence services were also looking for them is certainly intriguing.

In any case, since Dunmurry Lane was part of the IRA's plan to ensure an unsuspecting Lynch was delivered to Freddie Scappaticci at 124 Carrigart Avenue, Maguire directed Lynch to drive the rusting Cortina to Lenadoon on the pretext of securing the approval of the Belfast Brigade's operations officer, Anto Murray, to get these 'hoods … out of the road', as Maguire is said to have put it.[17] Murray, he said, was currently at a safe house on the estate. It seems that Maguire had told Lynch to use the rusty Cortina because the latter wasn't registered in his name, so if the security forces came looking for him after he was abducted, the vehicle's final parking space wouldn't betray the area where he was being held.

The following account of his ordeal over the forty-six hours that he was incarcerated comes from his own testimony in a lengthy witness statement to the police and his subsequent deposition to the Belfast High Court.

Having parked the Cortina in Lenadoon, to further defuse any possible suspicion, Maguire carried on small talk as the two walked to the front door of 124 Carrigart Avenue. The outer front door was open and Lynch saw there were no lights on inside. As his eyes adjusted to the darkness, he says he saw a man at the bottom of the stairs who gestured to them to carry on up. Continuing the friendly patter – and the deception – Maguire commented, 'He must be up the stairs,' referring to Murray. But the man in the shadows at the foot of the stairs was probably Lynch's first hint that all was not as Maguire's relaxed demeanour sought to make it seem. He realised it was a person he'd sometimes seen in Fat Harry's bar in Castle Street: Scappaticci.[18]

As Lynch neared the top of the stairs, he saw two figures dart into a bedroom and abruptly close the door. His anxiety levels rising rapidly, he was led by Maguire into another bedroom, whereupon Scappaticci and the others he'd seen piled in behind and closed the door. 'IRA Security,' snapped one of them and Lynch knew he was under arrest.

For the next several hours, the IRA adopted their standard procedure for disorientating captives, deploying three of the five techniques used in 1972 during internment by the British Army against fourteen suspects known as 'the Hooded Men' – techniques the IRA had themselves condemned, as did the UK Supreme Court in 2021, as torture, judged by today's standards.[19] Lynch was blindfolded; the cotton-wool pads were bound round his head by a bandage; he was deprived of sleep, food and water; and he had inflicted upon him, a form of torment that Scappaticci himself later acknowledged was 'mental violence'.[20] This should surprise no one, for in the matter of human rights breaches by Britain, IRA double standards were shamelessly unconstrained.

The start of Lynch's ordeal was marked by pure farce. As he was being strip-searched, a battery powered device used by Scappaticci to detect electronic bugs screeched out a warning. 'This coat is wired to fuck!' howled one of Lynch's interrogators, believed by Lynch to have been Scappaticci. 'This machine is going haywire, the cunt's wired!'[21] Of course, Lynch's coat was not wired and no bug was found. Was someone other than Scappaticci and Lynch wearing a listening device – in other words, was there a third agent in the room? Or, had the room itself been wired by MI5, which was responsible for installing listening devices on behalf of the FRU and Special Branch? That Scappaticci was not the only agent in the ISU is not in doubt, Operation Kenova having 'established that some [of its members (plural)] were agents when they committed acts of torture, including shootings'.[22] The question is, besides Scappaticci, were 'some' of them present in the bedroom with Sandy Lynch?

Seán Maguire, for example, was publicly accused in 2003 of being an agent, though he categorically denied it.[23] The IRA subsequently conducted its own investigation into him,[24] the outcome of which is unknown, save that he was later allowed to oversee Sinn Féin's northern communications operation,[25] which would suggest he was cleared. The other two ISU members in the room were the man James Martin called 'Eddie', last name unknown, and John Joe Magee,[26] reportedly identified in 2003 by the Garda Síochána as an agent for both the British and Irish special branches – but, like Maguire, not proved.[27] Within the IRA, Magee and Scappaticci were notorious for operating as a double act, as they were now with Lynch.[28]

Whatever it was that triggered the bug detector's alarm, Scappaticci appears to have successfully defused the situation, the most obvious innocent explanation being that his detector had given a false positive due to the nylon of Lynch's underwear generating static electricity. So far as James Martin's wife, Veronica, was concerned, however, there was only one explanation. Over that weekend 'our house was a house full of spies, but only one of them is being tied up' she would tell a friend years later.[29]

Hands bound behind his back, blindfolded and stripped to his underwear, Lynch was sat on the chair that Martin had brought in for this purpose. 'Do you know who I am, Sandy?' asked a voice. 'Do you know why you are here?' Lynch responded that he'd thought it was 'just another security briefing', like the one he'd had before Christmas. No, he was told, the ISU had done its homework and, with the information they had on him, the only way he was going to leave this house was to be taken out and shot, just like Joe Fenton before him. He was told that two ISU teams would take it in shifts until he broke, and for as long as held out, he would get no sleep, nothing to eat or drink, and he would be refused permission to go to the toilet.[30]

After a while, another voice said, 'Do you know who I am, Sandy?' signalling the second interrogation team taking over. This time, Lynch replied that he did. 'You should, because we had talks just before Christmas,' continued Scappaticci. 'You know me, but I don't give two fucks because where you are going, you'll not be telling no one.'[31] It was Scappaticci's job to find Lynch's breaking point, an art he'd developed over a decade of experience. '[E]verybody being what they are, everybody has a breaking point, you know,' he later explained.[32] Scappaticci told Lynch he was taking a personal interest in breaking him.[33]

As he spoke, Scappaticci rested his chin on the back of Lynch's head, digging his two elbows into his victim's shoulders. According to Lynch, he was very aggressive and swore a lot. He told Lynch that if he had his way, he'd 'get a jab in the arse and waken up in God's country [South Armagh]. He said that I would waken up hung upside down in a cow shed and he would talk to me the way he wanted to talk to me, that he would skin me alive and that no one would hear me squealing.'[34]

Scappaticci then focused his mental violence on talk of Lynch's wife, who'd miscarried just before Christmas. Was she depressed, he enquired? When Lynch replied that she was, Scappaticci said she'd be 'a lot more depressed' when she came down to identify him, because he'd have no face for her to see. Tapping Lynch two or three times on the back of his head, he threatened, 'You'll get it right there … like that bastard Fenton.' Lynch recalls Scappaticci saying that he was the one who shot Fenton so many times in the face that he had no face left.[35] Scappaticci did not, in fact, shoot Fenton, but he handed Fenton over to the men who did.

By then, Lynch had been interrogated solidly for some six hours and was tired and extremely frightened. Sometime around 1.30 a.m. on the Saturday morning, the first team took over the interrogation again from Scappaticci, adopting a softer approach, offering Lynch an amnesty in return for a confession if he was judged to have been forced to tout for the police under duress. Making all kinds of promises was standard ISU procedure, but, having himself been in the INLA's Security Department, Lynch knew it was almost always just a ruse to get a confession to satisfy the IRA rulebook and justify a death sentence, which the IRA leadership would sanction without being too fussed about how that confession had been obtained. By contrast, the IRA's *Green Book* for volunteers was replete with accusations about the RUC using 'subtle psychological torture' and 'humiliation', as well as 'physical torture', thus highlighting the IRA's limitless gall.[36]

Lynch was told his only way out was to admit he'd been a tout and that the first words were always the hardest, but if he got them out his interrogator would see what 'he could do for me' and that the IRA wasn't as 'hard hearted as people paint them'. The interrogator then resurrected the topic of Lynch's wife – sometimes using her first name, causing Lynch to get 'all choked up' – a weakness his interrogator exploited because Lynch was becoming more upset every time her name was mentioned.

Sensing he was about to break, Lynch was offered a drink by his interrogators, but he said he was unable to swallow because he'd become 'quite hysterical, nervous and could hardly speak'.[37] At the same time, he was warned the amnesty would expire in five minutes unless he confessed, so he did. To everything Lynch was accused of, he meekly responded, 'Yes' – even though 'much of it was rubbish and false' – because whenever he said no he was threatened with the amnesty being withdrawn.[38] He heard someone mutter that 'he didn't do bad – nine hours', meaning Lynch had held out for nine hours before the IRA had broken him. He was told he'd have to put his confession down in writing, but that he shouldn't worry, since Scappaticci's 'recommendation' to the IRA leadership 'was fair and the other boy's was very good'. The blindfold came off and others in the room also assured him 'things should be ok',[39] a sure sign, as Scappaticci would acknowledge three years later, that 'you're getting double-crossed'.[40]

Scappaticci had now resumed control of the interrogation, directing Lynch how to word his written confession, and to go ahead and plead for leniency as to why he shouldn't be shot. He was also instructed to say he had not been abused or ill-treated in any way. As part of Scappaticci's reassurance that all would probably be well, Lynch was told he 'would be going home soon', another IRA ploy aimed at keeping everything under control by subduing the accused's rising panic. And it often worked. Yet as Scappaticci himself would later acknowledge, they don't usually go home.[41] And judging by his evidence, Lynch knew this too. 'I knew I was as good as dead,' he said.[42]

After some whispering, Scappaticci told Lynch that the 'cunts across the road' – meaning the IRA leadership – weren't happy with his statement and 'they want you to make a tape'. This was presumably another ploy to ensure his continued compliance by wearing him down. Clearly, no one was going to wake up a member of the IRA leadership at 3 a.m. or 4 a.m. to get approval for an execution. Lynch was ordered to dictate his confession into a microphone, but, on playback, the tape didn't work. This provoked a foul-mouthed eruption from Scappaticci directed at his colleague operating the machine, calling him a 'stupid wee bastard. Can you do fuck all right?'[43]

It was well into Saturday before the tape was finished. Lynch was told that he could expect a visit later from someone in the leadership to ask him if he had written both the statement and dictated it to the tape recorder of his own free will.[44] Lynch could smell cooking, and soon his captors were being offered stew cooked by Veronica Ryan, who'd been given money by Scappaticci to buy the ingredients. When the stew was brought up Scappaticci asked Lynch if he wanted a drop, saying it was 'great stuff, but he said it sarcastically' not expecting Lynch to answer, so he didn't.[45] Lynch meanwhile could only think about his wife and the 'street entry I was going to be shot in'. His captors said he would probably be going to a press conference, but Lynch 'knew' this was all part of 'keep[ing] me sweet' and that he would be shot 'whenever it was sanctioned'.[46]

That Saturday evening Scappaticci and the other interrogators left and were replaced by three guards, none of whom spoke a word to him. Lynch said he never left the bedroom or went to the toilet because he was 'scared to ask'.[47] He spent Sunday lying on the bed, still blindfolded but his hands were now untied. Cups of tea were brought up to his captors but not to him.[48] The Martins also fed their IRA guests handsomely. Sunday morning saw a fried breakfast for them, but no food appears to have been given to Lynch during the entire forty-six hours he was held captive.

Sunset that January Sunday afternoon was at 4.16 p.m., and so it was dark when, shortly after 5 p.m., a 'leadership' person whom Scappaticci had told Lynch to expect arrived at 124 Carrigart Avenue. Danny Morrison, Sinn

Féin's Director of Publicity, was accompanied by Anto Murray, the IRA's operations officer for Belfast. Just as he and Morrison were entering, they heard the distinctive sound of approaching 3.5-litre V8 engines that powered the RUC's Land Rovers. Murray stood in the hall for a few seconds, then ran upstairs. Peering out of the window, he yelled: 'It's the fucking Brits! They're coming here!'[49]

Lying on the bed, Lynch heard the front door being thumped and the words, 'Police! Open up!'[50] Outside, Constable Ivan McKelvey was banging on the door, which was locked. Although there were no lights on, he could just make out a person moving about but not responding. So he radioed his inspector for permission to kick the door in.[51]

In a panic, Morrison fled through the back door. He said a 'soldier lying in wait called upon me to halt or he'd shoot'.[52] He appears to have been referring to Private Simon Flower, except that Flower wasn't lying in wait. He was still scrambling into position, trying to get into the back garden of 124 Carrigart Avenue to try to stop anyone escaping. Flower and Private Cairns saw Morrison walk through the open back door of number 126.[53] Flower later went into 126 to get a clear look at Morrison who, he says, told him in a 'threatening way' that 'you better watch yourself'.[54]

Meanwhile, alongside Constable McKelvey was Constable Keith Nugent, his gun drawn, as they entered number 124, having kicked in the door. The sight that greeted Nugent was of Murray in a shirt, tie and trench coat running down the stairs. In the living room were six others talking and watching a soccer match on the TV: householders James Martin and Veronica Ryan, and the three IRA men who'd been guarding Lynch in the upstairs bedroom – Daniel Caldwell, Gerard Hodgins and James O'Carroll.[55] Sitting alone was Sandy Lynch, silent, barefoot, shaking and very pale, his clothes and hair dishevelled, his eyes still watering from the irritation of the cotton-wool pads. Asked to identify himself by Sergeant Edwin Potter, Lynch gave his name, to which Potter replied, 'You're coming with me.'[56] En route to the RUC's Castlereagh interrogation centre, Lynch appeared to be 'in a state of total shock,' observed Sergeant Adam McKinley.[57]

In the minute or two between the first knock on the door and securing authorisation from Woodbourne RUC station to kick it in, there had been sheer panic inside 124 Carrigart. Two men had run into Lynch's room desperately trying to remove any evidence of his captivity. 'Where's the handcuffs?' one asked urgently. 'There, there!' replied the other. Lynch was ordered to remove the blindfold from his face and the bandage from his wrist. Walking unsteadily onto the landing, he'd seen Murray frantically pulling tape from the recorder containing the confession in which he'd begged the IRA to see if there was 'any way to let me live', if only for the sake of 'my family, my wife'.[58] A panic-stricken Murray told Lynch they'd come to take him to a press conference, as he desperately tried to get rid of the tape containing Lynch's confession, ordering Lynch to get himself downstairs fast to join the others watching TV and to keep his mouth shut.

The search of 124 Carrigart Avenue had been hastily authorised from Woodbourne RUC station by Chief Inspector William Brown. Earlier that afternoon Brown had been alerted to a 'serious security situation developing', so he had decided to keep his early shift officers on past their usual 4 p.m. clocking-off time in case reinforcements were needed.[59] At 4.30 p.m., Brown was informed that 'armed terrorists were believed to be detaining a person against his will'. He was provided with three addresses to be searched, two of them in Lenadoon, including 124 Carrigart Avenue; the third address was in a neighbouring estate.[60] This seems to have been an attempt to create uncertainty within the IRA that the intelligence was as precise as it obviously was, in order to protect the source who had provided it. But, of course, the intelligence was very precise, because the name of the person being unlawfully detained – Sandy Lynch – had been divulged to Inspector Brown as evidenced by Sergeant Potter's response when Lynch gave him his name.

Operation Kenova established that the source of this life-saving intelligence was Scappaticci. He had told his handlers he had been contacted that Sunday by a senior member of the IRA to say that the leadership had decided Lynch's fate and that he would be executed after dark.[61] The FRU dispatched an urgent MISR to Special Branch warning them of what was to come.

Although the prosecution was unaware of this intelligence at Morrison's trial, Special Branch having deliberately withheld from the DPP the fact that Scappaticci was a state agent, the prosecution argued that, as a representative of the IRA leadership, Morrison's purpose in going to 124 Carrigart Avenue together with Murray was to satisfy himself that the correct procedures for a case involving the death penalty had been carried out and that the prisoner had not been physically abused. This echoed what Lynch said Scappaticci had told him – that somebody would come to ask him if he'd made the statement 'of my own free will and if I had been abused in any way,'[62] although Scappaticci had not said this was a prerequisite for his execution. On the other hand, the IRA was said to have implemented new rules following the frequent use of violence and sensory deprivation against suspects, including the IRA equivalent of waterboarding, by a couple of ISU members notorious for sadistic interrogations.[63] One IRA man – wrongly suspected of being an informer – had been lured to the Irish Republic on a false pretext, held for four days 'bollock naked' – as he put it – hung upside down in a sleeping bag, with scalding hot mugs of tea held to his back, his head held under water in a sink, and told to lie on the floor while he was walked on. Eventually persuaded that only an innocent man could have withstood such prolonged brutal treatment, his captors conceded that he was probably innocent and freed him.[64] The fact that suspects like Lynch had been subjected to extreme mental violence, by threats and coercion, didn't seem to count.

Morrison has always insisted that he was asked to go to 124 Carrigart Avenue only to see if Lynch was a credible enough character to put in front of a press conference, because he'd allegedly confessed that his Special Branch handlers had wanted him to set up two IRA men – Kevin Mulgrew and Seán Maguire – for assassination to avenge the death of a police officer. Morrison had seen this as further proof of an RUC policy of shoot-to-kill, [65] and he'd been told that Lynch was prepared to name his handlers at a press conference. 'I smelt a good story,' said Morrison.[66]

At Morrison's trial, Lord Justice Hutton gave him the benefit of the doubt, and one can see why: from Sinn Féin's point of view, and that of Morrison, their head of publicity, Lynch's story was indeed potent material. Lynch himself had also said he'd been told after he confessed that he might have to go to a press conference. Hutton therefore agreed that there was a 'reasonable possibility' that was what Morrison had intended by going to 124 Carrigart Avenue.[67]

If the new plan was for Lynch to go to a press conference, the IRA would appear to have had a change of heart a matter of hours after Scappaticci was told he was going to be executed after dark. Morrison insists that when Murray appeared at his door that Sunday afternoon asking him to accompany him to Carrigart Avenue, it was to arrange the press conference. Twenty-six years later, Morrison would go even further, saying that 'it was Freddie Scappaticci who had specified that I should come to Lenadoon and meet Lynch'.[68]

Danny Morrison declined to respond to any of my questions about Scappaticci's intelligence warning that Lynch was due to be executed, save that his lawyer claimed the original conspiracy to murder charge had been withdrawn by the prosecution before trial. The transcript of Lord Justice Hutton's judgment shows that to be untrue. Morrison was tried and acquitted on that charge after Hutton gave him the benefit of the doubt. I am not suggesting that Morrison should not still benefit from that doubt, for it is not impossible that by early evening a stay of execution had been agreed pending Morrison's assessment of Lynch's propaganda value at a press conference.

Some IRA members still believe it was likely Lynch was to be executed. 'I have no doubt at all that he [Lynch] was going for his tea,' said one. 'None at all.'[69] That is also Kenova's assessment, and the detective in charge of the Lynch abduction investigation shares that view. 'Do you think the IRA did intend to shoot Lynch?' I asked Detective Chief Inspector Tim McGregor. 'I've absolutely no doubt about that,' he replied.[70] Sandy Lynch had no doubt about his expected fate either. 'I don't mind saying that I shat myself,' he later confided to a trusted source. 'I started crying, I started shaking uncontrollably. I was sure I was going to die.'[71]

Scappaticci and the FRU had been here many times before: the calculus of what to pass onto Special Branch and with what restrictions on the dissemination of his intelligence, contingent on the extent to which a rescue might compromise his cover. Risks had occasionally been taken previously, most notably in the case of James Young back in 1984, albeit at the last minute and too late (see Chapter 7). But this weekend would see the agencies taking risks as never before with Scappaticci's cover. This was not business as usual. The rescue of Sandy Lynch was how the system was meant to operate, prioritising the saving of life over source protection.

Scappaticci had promptly relayed his intelligence about Lynch's impending execution to the FRU and the FRU had promptly passed this to Special Branch with an MISR, the sense of which was: 'You need to do something about this – now'.[72] The branch needed no persuasion, perhaps mindful of the fact that Scappaticci had robbed them of several of their agents, most recently

Joe Fenton. Reflecting a long-held frustration within the branch,[73] one officer involved in Lynch's rescue described the mood that Sunday as: 'Those fuckers [the FRU] are not taking out any more of our agents.'[74]

But was Lynch's life actually being prioritised? Or were other factors in play? After all, the FRU was acutely concerned about John Stevens breathing down its neck with the imminent arrest of Nelson. The risk of Stevens discovering that Lynch had been executed as a consequence of a confession extracted by another FRU agent must have concentrated minds. A possible third factor was that Scappaticci had told them Morrison would be at 124 Carrigart Avenue that evening, offering the prospect of arresting one of Adams' most senior and high-profile lieutenants – a triumph to flaunt before Stevens about the value of the FRU, and evidence that Nelson was the exception to how the FRU and their agents played it by the book.

Whatever the explanation, for Scappaticci that weekend marked the beginning of the end. He had also been extremely careless, leaving behind his bug detector, which was bagged and removed by RUC forensics. They would shortly match a print on it to one taken from Scappaticci when he'd been arrested on 31 December 1983,[75] after being named by another ISU victim who'd managed to escape the unit's clutches. So not only had the branch's decision to rescue Lynch revived lurking suspicion within the IRA about his loyalty to the republican cause; now the CID – still ignorant of his spy status – was after him again.

Not for the first time, Scappaticci fled south to the Irish Republic, along with John Joe Magee, who had also carelessly left behind his medicinal cream for his chronic psoriasis. Also fleeing south was Seán Maguire, who had abducted Lynch. Meanwhile, Morrison, Murray, Daniel Caldwell, Gerard Hodgins, James O'Carroll, Veronica Ryan and James Martin were in Castlereagh, where, two days later, a couple of singing detectives, revelling in having bagged so many republicans, serenaded Morrison with 'Happy Birthday' for his thirty-seventh.[76]

For the FRU, there was nothing happy about that first weekend of the 1990s. It was a total disaster. A decade of what they regarded as unavoidable lawbreaking for the greater good was about to run its course, with English police officers, committed to the rule of law, closing in. And that was only the start of it.

Chapter Eleven

6137 – The Fire

ON THE EVENING OF SUNDAY, 7 January 1990, at about the time that Danny Morrison and others were being lined up for questioning at Castlereagh interrogation centre, I was boarding the last flight of the day from Heathrow to Belfast when I spotted John Stevens sitting near the front. As I walked past with BBC assistant producer Amanda Farnsworth, I nodded to him before taking my seat a few rows behind.

In his biography Stevens cites this event as the explanation for scuppering 'Operation Wheel' – Monday's planned dawn arrests of Brian Nelson and several UDA leaders, including Tommy Lyttle, his son Tommy Jnr, Eric McKee and William 'Winkie' Dodds.[1] 'Lo and behold,' writes Stevens, 'on the plane were two journalists saying: "We've come for the arrests." "What arrests?" we [i.e. Stevens] said. "What are you talking about?" And sure enough, because of their presence, there weren't any raids on Monday morning, because we cancelled them.'[2]

Recollections may vary, as the saying goes. My own recollection is that Amanda and I deliberately avoided talking to Stevens on the aeroplane precisely because we didn't want him to know of our own filming plans for dawn on Monday. We knew about Operation Wheel because Lyttle knew he was going to be arrested and had tipped me off about it on Saturday morning before I flew home for the weekend. Lyttle himself had been tipped off by the Special Branch officer leaking secrets to Bobby Philpott.[3] Amanda and I were hurrying back to Belfast because we planned to film

Lyttle's arrest, by parking within sight of his front door.

Dawn outside Lyttle's house in the quiet back streets of the Shankill came and went with no sign of the cavalry. 'It was all very eerie,' Geoff Seed recalled, 'shadows occasionally drifted across our view through the windscreen. Quite tense.' Stevens had indeed postponed Operation Wheel after learning that the UDA had been tipped off, not from me but from a colleague, David McKittrick of *The Independent*, who had also been briefed by Lyttle. David had called Stevens' team on the Sunday for confirmation that arrests were about to be made. That was why they were rescheduled for dawn on Thursday.

The next morning, Tuesday, I got a call from Nelson asking to meet me at noon at the York Hotel, in Botanic Avenue in the university area of the city. In a final attempt to get Nelson to show me his intelligence dump as Lyttle had been promising he would for several weeks, Lyttle had ordered him to arrange the meeting before he and Nelson were arrested. Nelson had told Lyttle he didn't want to meet me but instead would drop off a sample of the UDA's best leaked material. Lyttle, though, had insisted the meeting go ahead, demanding that Nelson also do a silhouette interview for *Panorama*. I later learned from the FRU records that all this was reported faithfully by Nelson to his handlers at 10.10 p.m. that Monday night.[4] The upshot was that not only did Nelson go ahead with Lyttle's instructions to meet me the following day but, unknown to me at the time, his handlers came along too.

I found Nelson sitting at a table in the York Hotel bar by the window, his leg shaking, chain-smoking as usual and drinking vodka. He looked thin and pale. This would be our last meeting, he said. There was no package; instead, he said it would be delivered to the BBC in Belfast by 1 p.m. the following day. Thereafter, I was not to contact him ever again. He said he expected shortly to be arrested and that it was 'getting very hot', nodding to two large fellows standing at the bar; he said they had been following him. Both wore Barbour-type jackets, and I seem to recall that one was wearing cavalry twills; they didn't look much like policemen to me. I remember thinking they looked like soldiers – and how odd it was if plain-clothes soldiers were following a member of the UDA. Then Nelson left, and, odder still, they left too. I learned later they were FRU soldiers apparently wheeled out in an effort to give authenticity to Nelson's story that he was being followed, presumably to engender sympathy so that I would finally leave him alone.

The next day, Wednesday, 1 p.m. came and went, and there was no package. That evening I called on Tommy Lyttle at his home. He showed me into his pristine dining room where we sat at a highly polished table. The 'Big Evil' himself, 'Winkie' Dodds, was at one end, his bulk spilling onto the tabletop. I told Lyttle that Nelson had led me a merry dance with his promises to show me the full scope of his intelligence dump since we'd first met the previous October, and that I could no longer spend any more of the BBC's money on a project that was evidently unlikely to happen. Dodds sat there silent, brooding. 'Brian has gone AWOL,' Lyttle told me. He sounded genuinely dejected. No one could find Nelson, he said, and his wife thought he'd had some kind of breakdown. Dodds looked on – uncomfortable, as it seemed to me – at the fact that Lyttle was confiding internal UDA matters about Nelson to a journalist. Ignoring Dodds, Lyttle continued, 'I've stood Brian down', explaining that his absence was a crisis because now the UDA couldn't get access to Nelson's targeting material, never mind show it to me. Of course, what neither Lyttle nor I knew then was that Nelson's intelligence dump was long gone, spirited away by the FRU to army headquarters at Thiepval Barracks within the first week of Stevens' arrival in Belfast. Nelson would later tell the Stevens 1 Inquiry that the FRU had not returned his files to prevent Lyttle '"pressurising" him to hand the intelligence dump over to him to show to the *Panorama* programme reporter John Ware.'[5]

I left Lyttle's house and walked back to the hotel to pack my bags. *Bang goes my story*, I thought, though I was relieved to be free of Dodds' intimidating presence. 'Dodds is very mistrustful of you,' Lyttle told me later. 'If I'd told him to go and shoot you down the road after you left, he would have done – you know that?' He was only half joking, so I thanked him for his consideration.

As for Nelson, he was now at crush depth. 'He would shake, literally shake,' said his sister Carole, who had witnessed his decline in recent days. 'He was very much under stress.'[6] Relations with his handlers were also fraying. Their promise that he had nothing to worry about with the arrival of Stevens, and that they would protect him whatever happened, looked increasingly thin. 'Despite the camaraderie,' said a FRU entry for that Wednesday, 'source is extremely annoyed at the situation in which he feels this office put him. He said that this office brought him back from a good life in Germany to do this job but now the office was "stitching him up."'[7] In desperation, Nelson made a bolt for it. That night he slipped out of Belfast Harbour on board a ferry for Liverpool.

Sympathetic though his handlers were, his flight appears to have been against their advice. 'Source is in such a tight corner at present,' recorded FRU. 'His options are very limited. He is a very frightened man.' Implicit in this report was a belief that even if Nelson was arrested, he would be released, because his handler optimistically referred to their next scheduled meeting on 16 January.[8]

That night, at the Magheramorne Hotel overlooking Larne Lough, John Stevens had retired to bed earlier than usual in preparation for the delayed 5.30 a.m. launch of Operation Wheel. Sometime after 11 p.m. there was an urgent knock on his door from his special senior assistant, Detective Superintendent Laurie Sherwood. 'Guv, the incident room's on fire!' The full force of this news took a few seconds to sink in. '*What?* You're joking!' exclaimed Stevens.[9]

Sherwood wasn't joking. The alarm had been raised by Detective Constable Sarah Bynum, who had returned from Castlereagh interrogation centre at 11.05 p.m. with colleagues to see their offices going up in flames. At first, Stevens' response was 'just utter disbelief and incredulity.' Colleagues later told her that after Stevens ended a call with Bynum, he was incredulous: 'Sarah's been on the phone and she's saying the offices have been burnt down. What nonsense!'[10] A second call convinced Stevens this was real, and he, Sherwood and Detective Chief Superintendent Vince McFadden were soon on their way speeding south to Seapark. Others in the team followed.

As Bynum walked up two flights of stairs with two male colleagues to their office on the second floor, they smelled burning. The officers ahead of her yelled, 'It's our offices!' The suite of offices comprised five rooms, the largest of which was office number 2, the main investigation room where papers were kept. Through the high corridor windows, flames could be seen flickering there and licking under the corridor door.[11] The fire hoses were one floor below.

While Bynum's colleagues frantically pulled the fire hose away from the stand and up the stairs, she took off one of her high heels and smashed the fire alarm. Nothing happened. She ran to the second floor, smashed the fire alarm panel and pressed the button – again nothing. She then sprinted to the guardroom, where she saw a lone reserve constable. She asked him to call the fire brigade and recalls feeling 'very exasperated' because, instead of snatching up his radio immediately and getting on to the control room, he 'just sort of stood there and said, "Well, the phones are down," as if there wasn't any other course of action available to him.' His reaction was one of 'almost disinterest, as if to say: "Well, what do you expect me to do about it?"'[12] The officer counters that he did, in fact, 'radio to Belfast regional Control requesting for fire services.'[13] By then barefoot, Bynum 'ran like hell' back up to the first floor where she found an empty office with a phone and dialled 999; this time she was connected to the emergency operator. 'Fire Seapark, Carrickfergus,' she said twice, hung up and ran back to the second floor to help her colleagues.

They were fighting a losing battle, struggling to get water on the flames because the door to the investigation room was blocked by heavy metal cupboards. Detective Constable Stephen Lodge lifted Detective Sergeant Richard Harrison onto his shoulders to direct water through the broken windows. He managed to open the door about eighteen inches, playing water on the flames, but the smoke was so intense they had to retreat and ended up in hospital being treated for smoke inhalation.[14]

Bynum then ran back to the guardroom to tell the reserve constable to start a log of events. Only then was she able to go back to the only office where the phone was working to call Stevens.[15]

The two fire alarms and the phone in the guardroom weren't the only alert systems that hadn't worked that night. In Stevens' offices, a heat-sensitive intruder alarm system had been installed connected to RUC Belfast Regional Control. That hadn't gone off either.

The blaze was so intense that all the computers in the main investigation room were melting like Dali paintings; steel filing cabinets were becoming twisted beyond recognition. A vast amount of paperwork was also destroyed. Luckily, because Stevens had been warned on the 'second or third day' of the inquiry that there might be attempts to disrupt it, he'd taken the precaution of duplicating all documents and statements by sending them electronically at the end of every working day to Cambridgeshire Constabulary.[16] In his biography, Stevens plays down the fire's impact on the inquiry, saying that the only original document they lost was a typed version of a statement obtained that day.[17] In fact, while all the inquiry's statements and documents had been duplicated, all nonetheless required repeat proofreading and re-signing by the witnesses, a process which set the inquiry back by many weeks.[18]

The problem Bynum had had raising the alarm and getting a call through to the fire brigade raises an obvious question: was the fire an attempt by forces unknown to sabotage the inquiry or was it accidental? Weary cynics should never discount the phenomenon referred to by an army officer I knew – who, like me, shared a deep affection for Belfast – as the 'Northern Ireland Embuggerment Factor' (NIEF), meaning that in Northern Ireland if things could go wrong, they had a habit of doing so. Yet, if NIEF was responsible, this was a very bad case of it: fire alarms not working, phones not working, intruder detector systems not working in what was supposed to be one of the most secure buildings in the country, all on the eve of the arrest of an FRU agent.

John Stevens' RUC linkman, ACC Wilf Monahan, arrived on the scene. Surveying the smouldering embers of his office with Monahan, Stevens says he recalls him muttering: 'We think we know who did this.' According to Stevens, Monahan then mentioned the FRU. This was the first Stevens had heard of the existence of the agent-running unit, since a military intelligence colonel had flatly lied back in September at the army's introductory briefing to Stevens when Sarah Bynum had casually enquired if the military ran agents.[19]

The RUC carried out an investigation, led by Detective Superintendent Alan Simpson. He established that the fire had broken out a short time after six of Stevens' officers had locked up for the night at 9.55 p.m. Bynum and her three male colleagues arrived at around 11.05 p.m. to find the main investigation room well alight.[20] The Northern Ireland Forensic Science Laboratory said that 'nothing was found to suggest that an electrical fault had caused the fire'.[21] Those are about the only facts that Stevens and Simpson agree on. The detective superintendent's report concluded that 'in all probability the fire had been caused accidentally, perhaps even by the careless disposal of a lighted cigarette end'.[22]

The RUC's announcement on 9 February that Simpson had concluded the fire was accidental put Stevens in an acutely awkward spot. To have aired his suspicion that it was arson risked fatally fracturing his relationship with Chief Constable Hugh Annesley, already strained due to so much obstruction by the branch and the army. Asked for his response, Stevens said through gritted teeth that there was 'no direct evidence the fire was maliciously started' – a statement of fact, but one which was wrongly interpreted as him conceding that a member of his team had behaved recklessly.[23] A painful baiting session followed in the police canteen at Castlereagh when some of the team went there for lunch. From the canteen's jukebox came Billy Joel's 'We Didn't Start the Fire'. 'We just sat there, resigned,' said Bynum. 'It was a reflection of the generally hostile attitude towards our inquiry.'[24] McFadden remarked that he and his colleagues sometimes felt their 'only friend was the cleaner on the Belfast ferry'.[25]

In the summary report of Stevens 1, published three months later, Stevens referred to the 'severe accidental fire' at Seapark.[26] This was a gift to those in the RUC who resented Stevens' arrival. 'Silly bitch' was the summary judgement made by the ex-head of Belfast CID, George Caskey, of Constable Pat Tosney, one of the few smokers in Stevens' team who, without any evidence at all, was being gossiped about as the cause of the blaze.[27] Statements and notes purportedly written or handled by the Stevens team were also reported to have been found in a hotel where they'd stayed[28] and in a locker in a police station where they'd been interrogating suspects.[29] 'There was just this constant drip to show that we were a ham-fisted bunch of amateurs who couldn't be trusted with sensitive information,' said Sherwood.[30]

Stevens says that he always suspected arson and that has remained his firm position to this day. He is convinced that the fire was deliberately started in an attempt to destroy his inquiry beyond recovery; many of his officers on this, the first of his three inquiries into the intelligence services in Northern Ireland, are also convinced of this. The fact that it happened on the eve of his revised plan to arrest FRU agent Brian Nelson compounded that suspicion. Some officers who joined the third Stevens inquiry in 1999 are more sceptical and believe that it was probably accidental.[31]

For his part, Simpson insists there was no evidence of foul play. Instead, he has suggested that, as a matter of professional pride, Stevens had little choice but to insist the fire was arson, not accidental: 'When asked, "What did you do in Northern Ireland?", what was he going to say?' chided

Simpson. '"My Incident Room got burned down because one of my officers was careless?" I don't think so!'[32] In September 2001, Stevens, McFadden (who was by now retired but seconded to Stevens 3), Hugh Orde, the S3 operational commander, and his SIO, Detective Chief Inspector Phil James, met Simpson at his retirement home in France. No amount of questioning by McFadden would change Simpson's mind. When I met Simpson in France six months later, he was still adamant the fire was an accident.[33]

To be clear, Simpson was a very experienced detective, having attended some hundred murder scenes and confronted some of Northern Ireland's most notorious killers on both sides of the sectarian divide.[34] He was also openly critical of Special Branch for their 'over obsession with source protection', which he said became a 'sort of religion, source protection at all costs'.[35] So this was not an officer in the business of hiding uncomfortable truths as a paid-up member of the 'securocracy'. Far from it. In this particular case, however, he was clear that any suggestion of 'treachery afoot' was 'without regard to the objective evidence'.[36]

And yet, the question as to whether the fire was indeed arson has assumed symbolic status in the contested narrative about how dirty the so-called 'dirty war' had become. To this day, it remains unresolved, so it's worth objectively setting out the evidence in its essential detail.

The Smokers

Amongst the six Stevens officers who had been present in the office immediately before it was locked up at 9.55 p.m., all alarms set, were two smokers. Simpson told me he thought one – a detective sergeant whose name he couldn't recall – had admitted grinding a cigarette into a wastepaper bin. 'That was pretty honest of the officer,' he said. 'I might not have been so open about it if I had been in his shoes.'[37] Simpson can only have been referring to Detective Sergeant Nicky Benwell, since he was the only detective sergeant in the office at 9.55 p.m. who smoked. Benwell died in an accident at his home some years later, so it isn't possible to put this charge to him, but it seems unlikely. In his statement to the RUC, Benwell said he couldn't recall if he'd smoked in the office that night but thought it 'unlikely' since he was only present for two minutes, having arrived with colleagues to deposit some documents and a briefcase; anyway, he said, he did 'not normally smoke whilst walking about'.[38] But the key point is that had Benwell made any kind of admission, it would surely have been reflected in his statement. None is recorded there.

The other smoker, Police Constable Pat Tosney, had been inputting data to the computer system called HOLMES (Home Office Large Major Enquiry System) used for major complex criminal inquiries. In her statement to the RUC, she said she smoked 'two possibly three cigarettes' and kept an ashtray to the right of her computer next to the window 'at all times'.[39]

Of Benwell, Tosney and three of the four other officers with them, none said they'd smelled smoke or had seen anyone smoking when they locked up the office and set the alarms.[40] Had anyone, or anything, been smoking, the non-smokers are likely to have smelled this, said Detective Superintendent Arthur Mandry.[41] The fourth officer, Police Constable Alan Jackson, does not appear to have been asked by the RUC whether he saw anyone smoking or if he smelled smoke: there is no mention of this in his statement.[42]

Although Simpson suggested that one of two smokers was likely to blame, his report is inconclusive. It merely states that 'all the ingredients for an accidental fire were present and I believe that cannot be overlooked'.[43]

The Seat of the Fire

Simpson says the seat of the fire was close to the locked and alarmed corridor door to the main investigation room. Directly behind this was a large quantity of paper and plastic sacks. He implies – but doesn't say straight out – that the fire started in a buckled wastepaper bin near this paper stack. He also says one unnamed female officer had 'helpfully told us she deposited a number of used tissues during the day'. The bin 'would also have contained trimmings from computer print outs'.[44]

Newspapers appear to have been briefed by the RUC that the fire had started in the bin, no ifs or buts: 'It is understood that the cigarette was dropped into a wastepaper basket by one of the 14 British detectives recruited to the team …' reported the *News Letter* in Belfast.[45] 'The mystery blaze at the Stevens Inquiry offices was started by a cigarette end dropped into a wastepaper bin,' said the *Daily Mirror*.[46]

However, this conclusion contradicts the professional view of the fire officer in charge of the scene. In his statement to the RUC, Deputy Fire

Divisional Commander Cecil Mallon said he did 'not form the view that the fire started' in the bin.[47] In Vince McFadden's view, that's because a half-burnt packet of cigarettes was found inside the bin, but on top of the bin was a plastic square that had fallen from the ceiling directly onto the bin, thereby cutting off the oxygen supply, which would explain why the cigarette packet was only half-burnt.[48] Moreover, underneath the bin was pristine unburnt carpet, proving that it had not moved and is unlikely to have been the seat of the fire because otherwise the carpet would surely have been scorched.

However, the forensic scientist at the scene, K.J. Arnold, described the bin as 'crushed and burnt' containing 'fire debris which included at least one burnt cigarette packet'. The bin 'had been positioned immediately adjacent to paper stacks which were stored below the [exhibits] table', and 'the burning pattern on the veneered walls and metal cupboard was consistent with the fire having started below this table'. This led Arnold to conclude, like Simpson, that the fire was 'most probably caused by the careless disposal of smoking materials'.[49] That said, Simpson admitted to me that Arnold was in something of a dilemma before he committed himself to this view. 'Ken ummed and ahhed about the fire,' Simpson told me. 'I said to him: "You must commit yourself and give me a report."'[50]

If the seat of the fire was likely not the bin, but underneath the exhibits table, where exactly might a cigarette from either Benwell or Tosney have been 'carelessly' disposed? Was a lighted cigarette just recklessly tossed onto a stack of paper? Is it really likely that a police officer in a major inquiry room surrounded by paper and valuable documents would behave in that way? That seems highly unlikely. I got to know Benwell quite well and he struck me as a professional individual. According to several Stevens officers, since Benwell was only in the office for two minutes, the RUC focused its suspicion on Tosney, who was also an experienced major crimes officer. 'To suggest that Pat would suddenly go from being a careful experienced officer, to carelessly disregarding a burning cigarette I think is absurd,' said Bynum. 'Nobody in our team thought Pat did this. She had too much pride in what she was doing to make a silly mistake like that.'[51] Benwell, who had once been engaged to Tosney, said that the RUC had given both of them a 'hard time'. They were 'desperate to hang it on an accident'.[52]

Phones Not Working

Simpson agreed it 'initially seemed odd' that the telephones in the Seapark control room hadn't worked, but a 'check' had 'revealed that this has occurred on a number of recent occasions'.[53] His report does not say why the phones had not worked before. Nor does it offer an explanation as to why at 11.35 p.m. the telephone in the control room manned by the reserve constable was found to be working, whereas during the fire, at approximately 11.15 p.m., it had been stone dead, as Sarah Bynum had discovered.[54] No telephone engineer's report appears to have been commissioned to address this question.

No Sign of Forced Entry

Four of the five corridor doors to the Stevens suite of offices were alarmed through a key-operated system with thirty seconds to activate or deactivate the alarm. Simpson said, 'all sets of keys had been accounted for', so unauthorised entry seems 'a highly improbable chain of events'.[55] His report doesn't say who fitted the alarms. It has been suggested that they were fitted by the RUC's Technical Support Unit, which provided assistance to covert RUC units.[56] If so, presumably a duplicate set of keys would have existed. Were they accounted for as well?

Failure of the PIR Alarms Linked to RUC

Besides the door alarms, Rooms 2, 3, 4 and 5 were also fitted with passive infra-red sensors (PIR), which splayed a beam across each room diagonally and were designed to detect body heat. The PIR and door alarms were linked to the RUC's Belfast Regional Control.[57] However, the system was not examined by the Northern Ireland Forensic Science Laboratory (NIFSL) until twelve days after the fire, by which time the damaged rooms were undergoing extensive repairs.[58] One of the four PIRs was missing, believed 'discarded with other fire-damaged material'.[59] The NIFSL report does not say which of the four rooms the missing PIR was from, but it seems likely to have been Room 2, where the fire broke out. Another PIR was slightly damaged, but again the NIFSL was unable to test this one in situ because 'much of its wiring was missing and believed to be discarded by workmen working in the area'.

Simpson seemed to not regard this as particularly relevant because he said it was 'felt that heavy smoke obscured the infrared sensors'.[60] Who 'felt' this, though? Simpson doesn't say. Neither of the two NIFSL reports refer to smoke preventing the sensors from triggering an alarm. In 2001, for *Panorama*, I and my BBC colleague Sarah Mole consulted five PIR and fire experts. Their evidence was quite technical and not easily accommodated in a television programme, so it was never published, but it's worth setting out here.

Two experts were confident PIR sensors would not have been obscured by smoke and that flames would have triggered the alarm. One said that 'once visible flame has occurred within the field of view of a PIR, the device would create an alarm condition within one or two seconds of seeing the flame'.[61] He would have 'expected' the destroyed and damaged PIRs to 'have alarmed in response to naked flame' and would not have expected the smoke to have been 'dense enough to have obscured the infra-red detection'.[62] Another said he would be 'surprised if a PIR did not respond to a fire'.[63] The other three consultants were not so certain. However, what all five did agree on was that the fire damage to the PIR system should have triggered an alert to the RUC's Belfast Regional Control. The NIFSL had found that the 'fuse in the control unit supplying common power to the PIRs was ruptured',[64] consistent with fire-damaged cables causing a short circuit and blowing the fuse. Interrupting the power supply in this way should have sent a tamper signal to Regional Control that the PIR system wasn't working properly. One consultant pointed out that there were therefore five potential sources of alarm when power was lost to them (the blown fuse, the two defunct PIRs and two working in other rooms).[65] Neither the NIFSL nor Simpson addressed this point in their reports.

Accelerants

Simpson says the NIFSL took seventeen samples of material from around the seat of the fire but 'no evidence of an accelerant has been found'.[66] According to a senior divisional fire officer we consulted, if only a small amount of common accelerant – for example two tablespoons of petrol, paraffin, white spirit – had been used and was consumed by the fire, then 'it probably won't be found'.[67]

Seapark Security Guards

Simpson said the only people with an opportunity to commit arson were seven security guards, four of whom were reserve RUC officers, the others being civilians. Five could alibi each other, and the other two 'whose precise whereabouts cannot be confirmed by someone else' were 'carrying out a patrol of the grounds of the complex with one at the rear and the other at the front'. Simpson rules them out because to get to the Stevens offices they would have had to pass 'two of the civilian guards on duty in the entrance hall and there is no suggestion whatsoever that this occurred'.[68]

Outside Intruder

Simpson ruled out the possibility of an outside intruder, saying that he would have to have 'defeat[ed] the CCTV cameras' by scaling the perimeter fence. A search of 'the entire perimeter fence was carried out … but no evidence of an intrusion was found'.[69]

Stevens' officers countered that the fence was only about seven-foot high, a relatively easy height to scale by one man leaping off the joined hands of another. Also, with the complex itself covering some 35,000 square metres, the perimeter is vast.[70] Simpson does not say if its entire length was covered by CCTV, or even if the cameras were recording or merely observing. Electrical rewiring work is said to have been going on at the time in the roof space above the suspended ceiling, the suggestion being that an intruder could have lifted polystyrene tiles off the metal grid, dropped something into the room and set fire to the abundant stacks of paper.[71]

In 2003, at the conclusion of Stevens 3, Sir John said, 'This incident, in my opinion, has never been adequately investigated and I believe it was a deliberate act of arson.'[72] He is right that not all possibilities were exhaustively investigated. In response, the FRU CO, Colonel Gordon Kerr, was also correct when he said it was an 'accusation made without evidence', although Kerr's further claim that this accusation was made 'deliberately to create suspicion against us' is devoid of any evidence.[73] In summary, unsatisfactory though aspects of Simpson's report may have been, there remains as yet, no evidence to connect the FRU, or indeed any individual or organisation, to the fire in Stevens' office. It remains unexplained, albeit a striking coincidence.

On the night of the fire, Stevens, Sherwood and McFadden went back to their hotel in the early hours of Thursday morning but were back up at 5 a.m. for Operation Wheel, the revived arrest plan postponed from Monday. Several top UDA men were arrested but not Brian Nelson, who was stepping off his overnight ferry to Britain as his former UDA comrades were being rounded up. He'd fled without telling his handlers of his intention at their meeting the previous day. Although they had optimistically scheduled their next meeting with Agent 6137 for the following Tuesday, Nelson wasn't buying their reassurances of his safety, as suggested by the handwringing in this report entry by one of his handlers: 'Source is fully aware that the handlers have done all they possibly can to help him out of his current situation … Source realises that the handlers' hands are tied and that the advice he is given is well thought out by all those concerned, and it is for the best … source is in such a tight corner at present …'[74] Indeed he was, which was why he was now heading down the M6, en route to the south coast to catch a ferry across the channel, eyes fixed on escaping back to Germany, thoroughly 'fed up' that his 'time was up' because he was 'threatened' with arrest.[75]

'All hell's broken loose over these bloody documents,' Nelson told his sister Carole on the telephone from England. 'His voice was breathless,' she said as he explained that unless he got them back from his handlers his 'life was on the line' from the UDA.[76] The combination of his imminent arrest and UDA pressure to provide them with targets from his intelligence dump, which the FRU had removed after Stevens arrived, had pushed him to breaking point. And yet something caused him to make a final call to his handlers, who, according to Carole, somehow persuaded him to 'come back', that his intelligence dump would be returned to him and that it would be back to 'business as usual'. His handlers said they would meet him at 'something like 7 p.m.' the following day, Friday.[77]

So, Nelson turned around, caught the ferry back to Northern Ireland and went home. He never got to meet his handlers because at 6 p.m. he was arrested at home and taken to Castlereagh interrogation centre.[78] At first, he resisted – 'I don't want to say anything,' he told Detective Sergeant Lynn Evans – but then he thought twice about it and gave him the telephone number of his handler.[79] After that, there was no stopping him. 'Right, I'd like to tell you now that I work for military intelligence,' he told Evans, who found him quite personable. 'He talked virtually non-stop from Monday to Friday for weeks.' In fact, Nelson talked so much that the interrogation had to continue after he was remanded from Castlereagh to Crumlin Road Gaol, extending to several months.[80] 'I don't think he ever thought he would end up in court,' said Evans, assuming instead that he'd 'be protected because he'd worked for military intelligence.'[81]

Colonel Kerr, who had brought him back from Germany in the first place, made a final bid to save Nelson. Asked by Detective Chief Superintendent McFadden what he thought should happen to him, Kerr replied that 'Nelson should be released within the normal time frame' to pre-empt any UDA suspicion that he was a spy. In return, Kerr promised to help the Stevens team with their inquiries. Unfortunately for the FRU, business as usual was no longer on offer, and, to Kerr's regret and anger, McFadden applied for an extension in custody, thereby, complained Kerr, 'automatically compromising him in the eyes of the UDA who presumed that he was still co-operating with the enquiry'.[82]

Thereafter, Nelson's statements would run from ten to twenty pages daily, without ever showing an ounce of remorse, said Evans. 'He obviously enjoyed his role in the military intelligence set-up; he was just very keen on what he was doing.' Nonetheless, while his statement ran to 900 pages, 'Brian Nelson told us what he wanted to tell us and stopped short where he wanted to stop short.'[83] It was especially noticed by his interrogators that when it came to the killing of the Belfast solicitor Pat Finucane, he seemed 'always to button up on that'.[84]

Did he ever feel they had got to the bottom of it all, I asked Evans? 'If I'm honest, I would say not.'[85] That much was certainly true.

Chapter Twelve

6137 – The Trial

BURNED OUT OF THEIR OFFICES in Seapark, the Stevens team decamped to the heavily fortified RUC police station on the Antrim Road. They swapped the relative comfort of the Magheramorne Hotel for the cramped living conditions in the station. 'Our existence was highly claustrophobic,' wrote Stevens. 'There was no question of going out for a meal or even a drink or in a pub. Occasionally, we would bring in a Chinese meal ... the decor was abysmal, and the heavy windows of armoured glass would hardly open.'[1]

Still, given that Agent 6137 was at the heart of the issue for which John Stevens had been brought over to Belfast – the intelligence leak to the UDA that had led to Loughlin Maginn's murder – Nelson's arrest was a major breakthrough. Just how major, Stevens was yet to discover, but he was on the right road. 'Where is your intelligence based?' Nelson was asked. In a suitcase at army headquarters, Thiepval Barracks, was his reply. Naturally, Stevens demanded access and told Chief Constable Annesley that this was 'now a murder enquiry. We must have this material.'[2] But the obstructionist forces that for four months had known all about the centrality of Nelson's role to Stevens were not done yet. Opposed to the army giving Stevens access to Nelson's intelligence dump was the officer Annesley had appointed as disclosure gatekeeper: the recently promoted head of Special Branch, ACC Brian Fitzsimons.[3]

That was no longer the army's position, however. ACOS G2 told Fitzsimons that if he continued to object, their legal advice was to overrule him: they would probably have no choice but to hand the dump over to Stevens.[4] The 'say nothing' alliance between the branch, the FRU and MI5 – all of whom had known about Nelson's role – was starting to fracture.

As mentioned in Chapter 9, Fitzsimons would claim that he hadn't known that Nelson's intelligence dump had been seized by the FRU and taken to HQNI only days after Stevens arrived in Belfast, or even that the dump existed.[5] Even if that were true, the record shows that the FRU *had* informed officers in Special Branch's Source Unit of the dump's existence from at least as early as October 1987;[6] it also showed that in February 1988, the FRU had provided the address where it was being secretly held and stated that the information in it came from Agent 6137.[7] Whether anyone in the Source Unit had informed Fitzsimons of these facts is unclear, but the record showing that the Source Unit had been informed must cast doubt on the veracity of the denials from two successive heads of the Source Unit in their statements to Stevens – a detective sergeant and the then Belfast head of Special Branch – who insisted they knew nothing about the dump.[8] As for Colonel Kerr, he insisted that he'd phoned Fitzsimons shortly after Stevens arrived to say that the FRU intended to retrieve the dump.[9] Fitzsimons, however, 'categorically' denied that Kerr had ever made him aware of the dump's existence, though he later caveated that denial with 'as it has been described'; nor, he said, had he ever been aware of, or signed off on, a plan for the army to squirrel it away in HQNI.[10]

Kerr's and Fitzsimons' positions could not be reconciled. But because the law was now intruding into the most secret affairs of the state, the stakes were rising and so was the sophistry of language. To paraphrase a former British trade minister's justification during an Old Bailey trial in 1992 that a statement had only been partially true, it was hard to know which one of them – Kerr or Fitzsimons – was being economical with the *actualité*.[11] Fitzsimons later acknowledged to me that while he'd been aware of *a* dump, Kerr had omitted to say it was *Brian Nelson*'s dump, which is presumably what he meant when eighteen months later he told Stevens he'd never been made aware of the dump's existence 'as it ha[d] been described' to him by Kerr. Fitzsimons also told me he'd warned Kerr that if the dump was linked to an FRU source, that source would be arrested.[12]

Kerr and Fitzsimons also could not agree on whose idea it was to draw up the MISR list of army and RUC leaks mentioned in Chapter 9: Kerr said it was the GOC's idea, as did General Waters himself, whilst Fitzsimons said it was his.[13] Whichever was the case, MI5 described it as a 'fairly formidable folio on … [Nelson's] reporting on collusion'.[14] Yet this was withheld from Stevens for an entire year.[15] When Fitzsimons saw the FRU's list of the forty-two MISRs, he objected strongly to its disclosure, protesting that both the 'sensitivity of the information' and the risk to 'source protection' were 'major grounds for concern', despite the fact that neither MI5, nor the FRU whose source Nelson was, shared those concerns.[16] In October, MI5 produced their own compendium of leaks, which MI5's legal adviser cleared for sharing with Stevens.[17] That never got to Stevens at any stage, nor was he ever briefed on its contents.[18] The result was that, in the first four months of his inquiry, all Stevens got from Special Branch was a general briefing about UDR leaks, with all the information about leaks from rogue RUC officers, Nelson's existence and his intelligence dump completely withheld.

In apportioning blame for having 'seriously obstructed' Stevens, the then Northern Ireland DPP Sir Alasdair Fraser laid it squarely at the door of both the army and Special Branch: 'It cannot be satisfactory that the Chief Constable of the Royal Ulster Constabulary having initiated an Inquiry to investigate collusion between Loyalist paramilitary organisations and the security forces, the Army and the RUC Special Branch withhold important evidence from that Inquiry', said Fraser.[19] However, he ignored the elephant who'd been in the room for the previous four months, namely Chief Constable Annesley, who had called in Stevens in the first place. It was Annesley who had the power and overall responsibility to ensure that Stevens got all the information he needed to conduct an effective criminal inquiry. Yet Fraser made no reference to Annesley's decision to delegate the job of disclosure gatekeeper to Special Branch in the person of Brian Fitzsimons, perhaps because the extent to which Fitzsimons had been acting on the orders of the chief constable was never satisfactorily resolved.

The army was about to break ranks, overriding Fitzsimons' objections to giving Stevens access to Nelson's intelligence dump and finally permitting Stevens to retrieve it on 16 January. Fitzsimons dispatched one of his officers to accompany Stevens' SIO, Detective Chief Superintendent McFadden, to Thiepval Barracks. Fitzsimons told me his colleague was stunned at the sheer size of the dump. 'His jaw literally dropped in horror', Fitzsimons said. 'He'd never seen anything like it in his life.' The way Fitzsimons expressed this gave me the impression it was a surprise to him too.[20]

In May 1990, Stevens published his report on the conclusions of the first inquiry. It revealed that charges under the Prevention of Terrorism or Official Secrets or Firearms Acts had been made against thirty-two members of the UDA and eleven UDR soldiers. Two further UDR soldiers were charged with Loughlin Maginn's murder. Given that intelligence collusion by the RUC was about equal to that of the UDR,[21] having accelerated as a response to the 1985 Anglo-Irish Agreement,[22] the report was notable for the absence of any charges against police officers, 213 of whom had been interviewed.[23] That may have been partly a consequence of Fitzsimons withholding from Stevens the list of both police and army leaks that had been compiled separately by the FRU and MI5 , which showed the source of the leaks, whereas the suitcase showed what had been leaked, not necessarily who had leaked it. Accordingly, Stevens concluded that leaking of security force intelligence was 'neither widespread nor institutionalised'.[24] His view would change significantly with time.

Not for the first time, or the last, there were to be no prosecutions against the branch – in this case, those officers in the Source Unit whom Stevens believed had lied to him when they'd protested ignorance about Nelson's intelligence dump. The DPP ruled that the conflicting evidence between members of the army and the RUC undermined realistic prospects of a successful case against them for perverting the course of justice.[25]

One of Stevens' eighty-three recommendations in his first report was a proper set of bespoke guidelines for running agents. This was ignored,[26] despite echoing the recommendations of two previous reports, one by Charles McLachlan of Her Majesty's Inspectorate of Constabulary in 1988 and the other by John Stalker, deputy chief constable of Manchester, in 1985. 'In this country,' intoned a distinguished jurist in the Second World War, 'amid the clash of arms the laws are not silent.'[27] Except that for thirty years in Northern Ireland, the law was largely silent when it came to the criminal conduct of state agents. As I explained in Chapter 7, hard as they tried, NIO officials were never able to square the magic circle by making acts lawful which were so clearly unlawful, especially murder. To this day, both the Stevens 1 and Stevens 2 reports remain classified as 'Top Secret', as ordained by MI5, which today determines these matters on behalf of the state.[28] PSNI Chief Constable Jon Boutcher, who has read the reports, says it's time they were declassified and that to classify them as 'top secret' is outdated and simply feeds conspiracy theories, another obstacle to reconciliation.[29] He is surely right.

Although John Stevens had published his first report, the Pandora's box that Nelson's arrest had opened meant there was much more work to be done. Stevens now sought access to the classified CF reports that Nelson's FRU handlers had written arising from their regular weekly meetings. Granting Stevens access to Nelson's dump was one thing; granting him access to the evidential crown jewels of how Nelson had been run was quite another. At first this was refused, so Stevens had to settle for interviewing Nelson's handlers at army headquarters in far from ideal conditions. Several handlers were interviewed simultaneously at desks in a row. Each was questioned by two Stevens officers. Silent but ever-present in the shadows were representatives of military intelligence. Whenever a Stevens detective wanted an answer checked in the CFs, the checks were made not by the detective but by the handler being interviewed, because only they were allowed access. 'One had the definite impression that you weren't getting everything,' said Detective Sergeant Benwell.[30] When Stevens' SIO, Detective Chief Superintendent McFadden, finally got his hands on the several hundred CFs, Benwell's impression was born out. They found significant contradictions between what Nelson had told Stevens in his lengthy statement about particular incidents and what he had told his handlers, as recorded in the CFs.[31]

McFadden had only succeeded in gaining access to the CFs after months of prevarication by the MoD, which led him to issue a series of escalating threats, at which point the army lawyers intervened.[32] By September 1990 it was made clear to the army that, if necessary, the GOC himself would be held responsible and arrested on his return from his summer holiday. When Annesley heard about this, he telephoned McFadden: 'What's this I hear about you arresting the GOC? I promised the General I'd got a handle on this inquiry!'[33] The threat worked. On 21 September, Stevens' officers gained access to the FRU archives containing a record of all their contacts with Nelson.[34]

As the full gamut of Nelson's criminality, to which the FRU had turned a blind eye, emerged from the CFs, Special Branch was asked what it had known about this, given that under the policy of 'Police Primacy' the RUC was in the lead on counter-insurgency. 'Well, we certainly didn't authorise that,' replied Fitzsimons, when specific operations were put to him.[35]

More 'Not-me-Guv' responses came from MI5. The director and co-ordinator of intelligence, the late John Deverell, protested, 'I was interested in the intelligence product of the case rather than the actual handling details and I was certainly not "au fait" with day-to-day details.'[36] Despite the fact that two other MI5 officers, the assistant secretary political (ASP) and his deputy, were assigned to army headquarters, the former told Stevens that he 'had nothing whatsoever to do with the agent handling, frequency of meets or [Nelson's] direction and control. All I saw was the MISR. I did not see the de-briefing notes, nor did I ever ask to see them ...'[37] His deputy said that while she saw most MISRs, she couldn't remember if she saw the CFs.[38]

It's true that in July 1988 Colonel Kerr had removed FRU agent case files from the ASP's office as part of his version of 'Perestroika', by reorganising the FRU into what he called an 'independent unit' within military intelligence.[39] But until then, the files had been in the ASP's office. It's also true that MI5 did not have the authority to dictate to the FRU how Nelson should be run, and anyway Kerr was not the kind of man to have taken kindly to that approach. Yet the Security Service regarded itself 'by a stretch' as the 'most ethical' of all three intelligence services in Northern Ireland,[40] so it could – and many like de Silva have argued should – have played an important co-ordinating and advisory role, which it doesn't appear to have done. MI5 had been well aware both of Nelson's enthusiasm for going after targets *he* considered 'legitimate' and the FRU's flawed handling of him, yet somewhat bureaucratically defended its lack of intervention on the basis that the 'executive direction of the FRU' lay with Kerr 'within the normal military chain of command'.[41]

In July 1990, based on Nelson's own admissions in his 900-page statement taken under caution (though not evidence from the CFs to which Stevens had yet to be given access),[42] Detective Chief Superintendent McFadden forwarded to the DPP in Belfast files relating to eight murders, eight attempted murders, fourteen conspiracies to murder, one kidnapping and torture, one conspiracy to pervert the course of justice, and one conspiracy to import weapons.[43] While the DPP assessed the evidence, I wrote to Nelson while he was on remand in Crumlin Road Gaol and was surprised to hear back that he would be happy to meet. Between March and July 1991, I visited him on six occasions.

The jail was a forbidding place, and I distinctly recall encountering the same pile of rotting detritus in the courtyard on two successive visits to the remand wing. Nelson, though, seemed in good spirits. He had access to a day room, where he could catch up on the news, and also a gym for exercise. He said he spent his time reading and was also writing a book, which he suggested I might help him with when he was released. 'You're confident you will be?' I asked. 'Yes,' he said, based on what the army had told him.[44] By my fourth visit, his confidence was ebbing. The army had told him that the Attorney General Sir Patrick Mayhew QC was pressing ahead with two charges of murder, namely of Terry McDaid (mistakenly shot for his brother Declan) and Gerard Slane, and four charges of conspiracy to murder. Nonetheless, Nelson said he remained hopeful he'd be acquitted. He was going to plead not guilty, his defence being that he was 'just doing my job as an agent'. He expected the trial to last about a month.[45] I'm not sure how hopeful he actually was. He looked visibly paler than on my previous visit and smoked two cigarettes in the thirty minutes we were together.

My last visit was three weeks after he'd appeared in court on 15 June for his preliminary examination of thirty-four charges, including the six murder and conspiracy to murder charges. 'When I saw the crowd assembled in court, my legs gave way,' he told me. What had particularly unnerved him was a statement from one of his handlers, who said that although he'd been recruited to control UDA intelligence, he'd rendered that useless by disseminating his targeting files to the rest of the UDA and several other murderous loyalist groups. 'What was I supposed to do,' complained Nelson, 'tell the UDA that although I had collated our intelligence into a system, they couldn't have it back?'

He talked about how he had begun to feel he was 'the meat in the sandwich' and that he was contemplating 'cashing in my insurance', by which he meant disclosing several incidents he hadn't yet mentioned in his marathon statement to Stevens. He alleged, for example, that the army captain who commanded the East Det FRU – to whom Nelson referred as 'the boss' –

had encouraged him to get the UDA to bomb targets in the Irish Republic as a way of pressuring them to 'rethink their extradition policy', citing the example of an oil refinery outside Cork.[46] He'd also previously mentioned that his handlers had assisted him in targeting Declan McDaid and Belfast IRA leader Brian Gillen[47] – all allegations that both the det captain and his handlers categorically denied when put to them by Stevens in 1993.

The evidential decision to prosecute Nelson for the murders of McDaid and Slane, four charges of conspiracy to murder, one charge of attempted murder, a charge of aiding and abetting the possession of a document used in Patrick Finucane's murder, and various lesser charges – was taken by the Northern Ireland DPP Sir Alasdair Fraser. However, since the case involved national security, it was left to Attorney General Sir Patrick Mayhew QC to decide whether, even if there was sufficient evidence, prosecution was in the public interest. The so-called Shawcross Convention encouraged – although did not require – the attorney general to consult with Cabinet colleagues in such cases.[48] It also limited the response from colleagues with objections to 'relevant facts'. Bare pressure was not permitted. In this case, the Convention seems to have been breached, since the mitigating 'facts' that the attorney general was getting from the MoD, via Secretary of State for Defence Tom King, were irrelevant because they were eventually shown to be misleading.

King had, of course, been getting these 'facts' from his own officials in the MoD, who in turn were getting them from the FRU, which was reporting that Nelson had been 'regularly reminded' not to become involved in criminal acts, whereas the record showed he extensively targeted individuals for murder without criticism from his handlers, other than when he got so close to the targets that he put his own security at risk. It was standard policy for the FRU MISRs to disguise from the police the extent of Nelson's criminality by not identifying him as the source of the intelligence when it 'would implicate him in criminal activity, or even put at risk his identity'.[49] The MoD argued that Nelson's intelligence had been used to save the lives of fifteen named individuals he'd targeted,[50] whereas the record showed that claim could only factually be applied to possibly three lives. (These were Gerry Adams, Harry Maynes and one unnamed other. In the case of Adams and Maynes, it seems this was only as an expedient: Adams because he was a parliamentary candidate for Belfast West, and Maynes because Nelson risked being caught red-handed as the trigger man signalling to the gunmen when the coast was clear to shoot him; the third was someone who had helped the police.)[51] The remaining twelve had been extensively targeted for murder by the UDA, several of them with Nelson's active support. So much for King telling Mayhew that 'many people in Northern Ireland owe their lives to Brian Nelson'.[52]

To the head of the General Staff Secretariat in the MoD, the fact that Stevens had even pursued Nelson in the first place was seen as unworldly, because police officers from England found it 'difficult to come to grips with either the role of the FRU or the terrorist environment in which it works'.[53] In other words, they were 'Policeman Plod' over from the sticks, out of their depth, lost in a world of Big Boys' rules, i.e. no rules. Advice to King said prosecuting Nelson would only 'feed the speculations of those who believe that the security forces are involved in a "dirty tricks campaign" and are in collusion with loyalist paramilitary groups'.[54] But some members of the security forces *were* colluding, including a small number of senior police officers.[55] Furthermore, MI5, FRU and Special Branch records had all used precisely that word – collusion – to describe the leaks from rogue soldiers and police officers to the UDA.[56] Still, King was adamant: Nelson 'should not go near the courts'.[57]

The defence secretary was supported by Northern Ireland Secretary of State Peter Brooke, Home Secretary David Waddington, Cabinet Secretary Sir Robin Butler, MI5's Director General Sir Patrick Walker and Prime Minister John Major's principal private secretary – all of them essentially prioritising the reputation of the intelligence services over the administration of justice.[58]

The RUC's position was less coherent. While ACC Monahan told the DPP that Nelson should be prosecuted because he'd become an 'agent provocateur' by recommending targets for assassination,[59] Chief Constable Annesley was opposed on the basis of objections from his head of Special Branch, Brian Fitzsimons. In July 1990, Fitzsimons had said Nelson had 'provided a mass of intelligence' that had been 'suitably actioned to frustrate the terrorists' intentions both North and South of the border'.[60] This directly contradicted Fitzsimons' assessment shortly after Stevens arrived, when he told MI5 that Nelson had been 'badly handled and poorly exploited'.[61] By

January 1991 Fitzsimons had reverted to his original position by retracting his July 1990 assessment, saying that Nelson's involvement with the UDA 'could not be ascribed wholly to an altruistic desire ... to assist the authorities', a change of heart that apparently came after seeing additional information from Stevens.[62] Nonetheless, he believed that prosecuting Nelson would not be in the public interest because 'unscrupulous propagandists ... would give credence to claims of police collusion with terrorists'.[63] It was surely the other way around. Too much was becoming publicly known and talked about for claims of collusion *not* to be given credence, a matter that needed to be resolved by trial.

The only member of the Cabinet who supported Mayhew was Foreign Secretary Douglas Hurd. As for John Major, he seemed to sympathise with both sides of the argument,[64] but Mayhew seemed resolute. 'No case which I have seen as a Law Officer has caused me more concern,' he told King in a letter, reminding the defence secretary of Lord Justice Lowry's reference in 1983 to the 'vital legal principle' underpinning the Rule of Law: that even during war, the law must be upheld.[65] Mayhew, himself a former soldier, having been a national service subaltern in the 4th/7th Royal Dragoon Guards, told King that Nelson was 'precisely' the 'sort of case' where that rhetoric should be 'put to the test'.[66]

Perhaps Mayhew was making up for his failure to put it to the test three years earlier, when he had decided it was not in the public interest to prosecute anyone in MI5 or Special Branch for perverting the course of justice after they destroyed a tape from a bug installed by MI5 that proved RUC officers had lied, as instructed by their superiors, when they claimed to have given a warning before shooting dead seventeen-year-old Michael Tighe and wounding nineteen-year old Martin McCauley in one of the notorious 1982 'shoot-to-kill' cases. The then DPP in Northern Ireland, Barry Shaw, told Mayhew there was sufficient evidence for a conviction. However, in the dock would have been a senior member of MI5, as well as Special Branch officers; to Mayhew, this appears to have been an unthinkable vista.[67] His 'no prosecution' decision in January 1988 had angered Hurd, who is said to have told Mayhew at the time, 'I want a process to weed these people out.'[68] Perhaps that's why Hurd supported him on Nelson in 1991.

On 22 January 1992, a handcuffed Brian Nelson was led into the dock at Crumlin Road court. Watching him forlornly was Terry McDaid's young widow, Maura, sitting on the same bench as Carole Creighton, sister of the man whose botched targeting had led to the murder of Maura's innocent husband, the father of her two young girls.

Nelson originally stood indicted on thirty-four counts, including four of conspiracy to murder Alex Maskey, James Morgan, Patrick Monaghan and Brian Gillen, and two counts of aiding and abetting, counselling and procuring the murders of Gerard Slane and Terence McDaid. Crown Counsel John Creaney QC added a thirty-fifth charge – conspiracy to murder Declan McDaid – and then requested that Nelson be rearraigned on all counts. Nelson was invited to resubmit his formal plea to a reduced number of charges on which the Crown was now going to proceed.

The net result was that what had been billed as a trial that would last several weeks, in which the intelligence services' dirty washing risked being aired because Nelson was contesting the two murder charges, was going to be a simple hearing with nothing contested and just the bare minimum of facts presented. The two murder charges were dropped in exchange for guilty pleas to five charges of conspiracy to murder. Nelson also pleaded guilty to a further fifteen counts of possessing documents likely to be useful to terrorists, three counts of collecting information (useful to terrorists) and one count of collecting a homemade sub-machine gun to be used to assassinate Brian Gillen.[69] The remaining thirteen counts to which Nelson pleaded not guilty, most of which were relatively minor, remained 'on the books', meaning that although the charges were not being pursued to trial, they were not being formally dismissed either and could be revived depending on Nelson's future conduct.

With the only matters before the court those to which Nelson pleaded guilty, Crown Counsel Brian Kerr QC, representing the attorney general, gave the briefest outline of the evidence. No longer was there any need to prove the facts on murder or each of the remaining counts. Gone was the spectre that had haunted the securocracy of Nelson calling his handlers as witnesses for his defence to be cross-examined by his formidable counsel, Desmond Boal QC, and pressed as to why they weren't in the dock, having turned blind eyes to Nelson's criminality.

In a handwritten note to Prime Minister John Major, his principal private secretary expressed the hope that when the judge realised the prosecution was relying on Nelson's debriefing by his handlers, effectively treating the CFs as 'confessions', the defence would 'object … that this is not a proper statement taken under [the] Police and Criminal Evidence Act' (i.e. under caution), and that if that objection was sustained, the case could 'collapse at the start – a very good outcome'.[70]

A trepidatious MoD thought it might not be that simple and that the hearing could descend into a full-blown airing of the conflict's lawless agent-running world. Officials referred to the 'complicated public interest issues [that would] arise from disclosures that might arise if Nelson were to appear as a witness or to be prosecuted',[71] not the least of which was the question of 'why they [Special Branch] ignored threat warnings and reports of leaks'.[72]

A long and deep sigh of relief must, therefore, have been audible across Whitehall and the NIO when it became apparent that there would be minimal scrutiny of how Nelson had been run – in effect a hearing, not a trial – thanks to the disputed murder charges being dropped in exchange for guilty conspiracy to murder pleas. This last-minute re-arraignment also provoked suspicion that for all his steely resolve to Cabinet colleagues and high-minded rhetoric about the law not being silent 'amid the clash of arms', at the final furlong the attorney general had blinked by agreeing to a deal that would minimise the court's intrusion into the murkier aspects of the undercover war. After all, Mayhew had known that in his defence Nelson would 'say that he kept the Army very fully informed about his activities and assert that they encouraged the conduct, which is now alleged to be criminal or, at the least, acquiesced in it'.[73]

In February 2015, I asked Mayhew if he had sanctioned a deal. He was by then quite unwell, suffering from Parkinson's and cancer, so it was not an easy conversation. Mayhew emphasised that Nelson's decision to plead guilty to the conspiracy to murder charges in exchange for the two murder charges being dropped was 'nothing to do with me. I had no discussions about whether he should or should not plead guilty.' That, said Mayhew, was 'entirely a matter between Nelson and the prosecution; a man called Creaney was involved in that'.[74]

With all due respect to the late attorney general, he does not appear to have told me the truth. I was in court during the Nelson trial, and John

Creaney QC, who normally led for the prosecution, played a very minor role indeed. Dominating the proceedings was Brian Kerr QC (who became lord chief justice in Northern Ireland), who led for the Crown as Mayhew's representative and had therefore been instructed by Sir Patrick himself. On matters of national security, the DPP usually exercises its authority subject to the superintendence and direction of the attorney general, which means the DPP must at the very least consult the attorney general on all matters pertaining to national security. In this case, the attorney general had done much more than merely 'consult'. Mayhew had put in place his own counsel to ensure his view of the national interest was fully protected in the proceedings, with no deviation from the deal that had been agreed. This had never happened before, nor has it since, in any conflict-related trial in Northern Ireland, despite the fact that the Belfast courts dealt with scores of trials on national security-related issues. As senior counsel to the attorney general in Northern Ireland, Kerr normally had nothing to do with prosecutions. 'It was unheard of for the Attorney General to appoint his own counsel in a prosecution that had been mounted by the DPP,' said a senior KC in Belfast.[75]

The reason I'd telephoned Mayhew was because I'd been told that at the last moment Desmond Boal QC had approached not Creaney but Kerr, threatening to cause mayhem if he didn't agree to the terms of a deal. In that event, said Boal, Nelson would contest all thirty-four charges and had arguable grounds for doing so. That is consistent with what the MoD is reported to have been told, having 'heard rumours' that a plea bargain was under way.[76] It is also consistent with Boal's plea in mitigation on behalf of Nelson to the judge, Lord Justice Kelly.

Boal submitted that, save for Nelson's conspiracy to murder Alex Maskey while he was having his Sunday lunch (in which Nelson was clearly a willing participant), Nelson had 'very plainly a working defence' to the remaining four conspiracy to murder charges, which he had 'not availed himself of'. Quoting Lord Bridge in an appeal to the Law Lords in 1985,[77] Nelson's 'working defence', argued Boal, was based on the principle that those 'concerned with law enforcement, may enter into agreements that a course of conduct shall be pursued which will involve commission of a crime without the least intention of playing any part in the furtherance of the ostensibly agreed criminal objective, but rather with the purpose of exposing and frustrating the criminal purpose of the other parties to the agreement …' In other words, the essential element of conspiracy was not just the agreement to commit a crime but required the intention to actually participate in executing it. Boal argued that in those four cases, Nelson had no intention of participating.[78] He made a similar claim in respect of Nelson's guilty plea to three counts of collecting information useful to terrorists. These are the arguments that Boal would have made on the eve of trial directly to Brian Kerr and the client who had instructed him (Sir Patrick Mayhew), in effect telling Mayhew: 'If you prosecute my client for the two murders, we'll blow the lid off this case.' Boal would undoubtedly have followed through, and – characteristically – to deadly effect.

Perhaps conscious of the suspicion that the attorney general had too readily grasped Boal's proffered hand, in court Brian Kerr sugar-coated the Crown's climbdown by emphasising that the murder charges in respect of Terry McDaid and Gerard Slane had been dropped 'solely on an evaluation of the factors likely to affect the outcome of the case and the demands of justice'. This, he said, had followed a 'scrupulous assessment of possible evidential difficulties for the prosecution and a rigorous examination of the requirements of justice'.[79]

In short, Kerr was saying the Crown was no longer confident it would prevail on either of the two murder charges. That may have been the case with Gerard Slane, since Nelson had given his handlers a lot of information in advance about the planning for the murder and had no idea it was imminent. But in respect of Terry McDaid's case, while it was clear that Nelson had, at first, been horrified the UDA had got the wrong man, the fact that Nelson had conspired to kill Declan did not lessen his liability for Terry's murder. Furthermore, Kerr omitted the important fact that the CF record showed Nelson had perked up after his handler, Sergeant Margaret Jones, had reassured him there was a PIRA trace against Terry's name,[80] despite the fact that Terry had nothing to do with the IRA.

With Brian Kerr having outlined the bare facts of the prosecution, the court adjourned for a week to hear a lengthy plea in mitigation on behalf of Nelson from Colonel Gordon Kerr, who had re-recruited him in 1987. The jaws of the Stevens team – sitting opposite us on the packed press bench –

visibly dropped as the colonel claimed that Nelson's 'primary motivation' had been 'to save lives'. Nelson had wished to do that, said Kerr, to 'make up for his past misdemeanours' – the lynching of the half-blind Gerry Higgins in 1973.

In support of this claim, Kerr said Nelson had 'provided his handlers with more than 700 threat warnings against a total of some 217 individuals ... All these warnings were passed to the RUC Special Branch's Source Unit to prevent any harm coming to the intended victims, either by warning them, if time and circumstances permitted, or by flooding the target area with forces to prevent the attack taking place.'[81]

Kerr's statistics were subsequently ridiculed by Stevens, Justice Cory[82] and many others, including myself over the years. In fairness to Kerr, however – and as a matter of public record – that criticism merits revisiting. Unlike Stevens, in 2012 Sir Desmond de Silva found that in most of those 730 MISRs, the FRU did, in fact, pass 'significant and exploitable intelligence' to the RUC.[83] Furthermore, de Silva found that Kerr's reference to 730 threats to life was a 'conservative estimate'.[84] Kerr did not say 217 lives had actually been saved as a consequence of Nelson's 730 MISRs; rather he emphasised their life-saving potential. Had the RUC acted upon them, more lives might well have been saved. Of course, Kerr's careful phrasing – 'more than 700 threat warnings against a total of some 217 individuals' – suggests he was well aware of this. Where Stevens' criticism survives is in the gloss that Boal put on Kerr's carefully worded statistics. 'There is an enormous number of people who have got reason to be grateful to the man standing in the dock,' Boal told Lord Justice Kelly, 'some of them grateful to the point of their lives.' 'Some' being the operative word. As mentioned, in his review de Silva concluded that just three lives were likely saved as a result of Nelson's reporting.[85]

Stevens was also right to criticise the FRU's apparent failure to press Special Branch for answers as to why they weren't exploiting Nelson's MISRs. 'Somewhere along the line you'd think questions would have been asked,' reflected Detective Chief Superintendent McFadden. 'But nobody seemed to be doing anything at the end of the day.'[86] So far as I am aware, the FRU has never addressed this point, and de Silva finds that the likely explanation is that the branch's inaction 'suited their aim of protecting a source'.[87]

Lord Justice Kelly got to the heart of the matter by posing this question – one he said he'd been 'asking myself really, all morning': What had Nelson 'really achieve[d] at the end of the day?' Had he, as Colonel Kerr said, intended to 'bring down' the UDA? Were any UDA members actually prosecuted for 'conspiracy to murder or attempted murder?' 'Not that I know of my Lord,' the normally bullish Boal sheepishly acknowledged.

The judge jailed Nelson for ten years, having taken into account 'much of the mitigating material given forcefully' by Colonel Kerr, including the fact that Nelson had passed on what was 'possibly lifesaving information in respect of 217 threatened individuals'. In the meantime, Colonel Kerr was awarded an OBE (Military), Captain Geoffrey Gillion, OC of East Det FRU (which ran Nelson), was awarded the MBE (Military), and one of his handlers, Sergeant Margaret Jones, was awarded the BEM (Military) and promoted to staff sergeant.[88]

After the trial, General Sir John Wilsey, the army GOC who had replaced General Waters, gave a rare interview to the BBC. Did the army feel shame, asked Barney Rowan? 'Certainly not ashamed,' replied the general.[89] A few days later, Wilsey wrote to Kerr congratulating him 'most warmly' on his court performance. To John Creaney QC, Kerr's impassioned performance in the witness box had felt more like 'he was on a crusade'.[90] In particular, Wilsey commended Kerr for having promoted 'a long and overdue focus upon the constraints and contradictions inherent in the agent-running system'.[91] This was a reference to Kerr's observation – fully endorsed by the intelligence services – that it was nigh on impossible for any agent to successfully penetrate a terrorist organisation by sticking strictly to the Home Office's outdated guidelines governing the handling of informers in cases concerning what the RUC would drolly refer to as 'ordinary decent criminal' gangs compared to the IRA.

In that, Kerr was echoing the memorable maxim of former PSNI ACC Ray White that exploitable intelligence against terrorists doesn't come from milkmaids, and if ordered to, say, deliver a bomb, 'the agent can't say: "Sorry, I don't do bomb runs. But I'll make the tea."'[92] And yet, in another breath, Kerr had said the FRU had not wanted Nelson to 'get involved in murder gangs', a wholly unrealistic aspiration on his own admission.

In his sentencing, Lord Justice Kelly had made it clear that the criminal justice system could never tolerate such a dispensation as Kerr considered Nelson deserved: 'there is no refuge or halfway house in criminal culpability … our system does not create for the agent an in-between category that lies somewhere between guilt and innocence'.

An 'in-between category' was effectively what Kerr and the army top brass were asking for – and expected. An MoD postmortem on the trial blamed the 'formal and independent nature of the Stevens inquiry (and the relative lack of familiarity of its members with law-and-order practices in Northern Ireland)',[93] which was a polite way of saying that, unlike the RUC, a bunch of coppers from England had foolishly had the temerity to apply the Rule of Law to the situation – never mind that this was the eternal ministerial mantra as the only way to bring stability and peace to Northern Ireland. Prior to Nelson's trial, Attorney General Mayhew had rebuked Secretary of State for Defence King, saying he was 'much troubled by the relationship between the Army and Nelson'.[94] Yet, having commissioned his own inquiry into the FRU after the trial, General Wilsey declared himself very much untroubled by the relationship, saying he was satisfied with the FRU's conduct,[95] despite the fact that Nelson pleaded guilty to five counts of conspiracy to murder. So satisfied was he, in fact, that the army is reported to have awarded Nelson the standard campaign service medal for Northern Ireland, even though he didn't serve there as a soldier.[96]

Three months into Nelson's sentence, he had a visit from Colonel Kerr, who asked him why he'd talked himself into a prison cell. Had he taken his handlers repeated advice to keep schtum in the event of his arrest, he wouldn't be here now, Kerr gently chided him. Nelson replied that Stevens had given him the impression he was helping them to 'clean up the UDA'. Even though every page of his 900-page statement had been taken under caution, asked Kerr? As he rightly observed, this was 'not a very convincing excuse' but rather indicated how Nelson had 'collapsed under the weight of his situation and once he started talking, he could not stop'.[97]

I was responsible for some of that weight, given the pressure that Tucker Lyttle, at my behest, had repeatedly imposed on Nelson to show me the scale of his leaked intelligence dump for *Panorama*. The fact is that Nelson had run out of excuses about why he couldn't get access to the dump because only he knew the FRU had seized it to stop it falling into Stevens' hands.

For the Stevens team, at least, their work was done. By then the burned-out Seapark offices had been restored, so John Stevens' close aide and friend, Detective Superintendent Laurie Sherwood, arranged for everything in them to be loaded onto two Ford transit vans, which the RAF flew to Transport Command's base in Lyneham, Wiltshire; from there they were driven to Cambridge.

According to Stevens, some of his officers found the two-year experience to be extremely stressful, with several having phantom heart attacks, dropping in the street, while others came out in boils.[98] Still, they had shone a light into a dark place. The trouble was, there were many more dark places. In just over a year, Stevens would be back.

Chapter Thirteen

6126 – Decline and Fall

JOHN JOE MAGEE WAS NOT a happy man. Sitting in a Belfast bar with a friend on the evening of Sunday, 7 January 1990, it wasn't just his vast girth that was weighing heavily on him. News was filtering through that Sandy Lynch, the man he'd interrogated the previous day with his deputy Freddie Scappaticci at 124 Carrigart Avenue, had been rescued by the RUC. Magee was well aware that he too could have been sitting in a police cell along with Danny Morrison contemplating the next decade of his life behind prison walls. Worse, Magee also knew he might soon join them unless he made a run for it. He'd carelessly left behind a tub of ointment for his psoriasis, his prints all over it. 'I've no choice,' he told his friend. 'I'm going south.'[1]

Confronting a similar predicament, Scappaticci and Seán Maguire – who'd abducted Lynch – were also packing their bags and about to disappear from view across the border. Of the two, Scappaticci was the more vulnerable to arrest because he too had been careless, having left behind the electronic bug detector he'd used to check Lynch for a listening device. Since he'd put the battery in it, he could reliably count on his prints being found by the RUC forensic team.

The trio also knew that as the inevitable postmortem by the IRA's Belfast Brigade got under way, their comrades would be wanting answers to a question of their own: which one was the tout? One of them, two of them, all three? Maybe the whole house, as Veronica Ryan would speculate – only half-jokingly?[2] Years of angst and confusion at the scale of British penetration had induced severe paranoia, provoking tension within the ranks, with many not knowing what to believe. As Danny Morrison acknowledged, 'for years we had suspicions about one or two other IRA people who had interrogated Lynch'.[3]

Ever since his release from prison in 1986, the brigade's former legendary OC, Brendan Hughes, had harboured deep misgivings about the high level of British penetration within the IRA, including the ISU. Following the Lynch debacle, the suspicion within some at brigade level was that all three – Magee, Scappaticci and Maguire – were likely informers. In 2003, Maguire was accused of being an agent by another British agent – a claim he has always strenuously denied.[4]

Morrison has said that while on remand in Crumlin Road Gaol, he was told 'inter alia by the IRA that Scappaticci, after my arrest, was "stood down" along with others involved in the Lynch affair ...'[5] This has been disputed by Gerard Hodgins, convicted along with Morrison and three others on charges linked to Lynch's false imprisonment. 'There was never any word sent into the prison that Scap had been stood down,' he said in 2016. Nor was there 'any suggestion he'd been the informer in our case'.[6] One thing has since become clear, however: Scappaticci was by no means the only British spy to have penetrated the IRA's ISU. Without naming them, implicit in Operation Kenova's interim report is that they were amongst the IRA members who were interviewed, but instead of showing remorse, were 'defiant, dismissive and unrepentant about how they mistreated alleged agents'. PSNI Chief Constable Jon Boutcher commented that they had 'no grounds' to be unrepentant, 'particularly when some covertly assisted the security forces.'[7]

In the case of Scappaticci, there is credible evidence that doubts were being publicly expressed by senior members of the IRA within months of him going on the run to Dublin after the Lynch affair. Padraic Wilson, the alleged head of the IRA's 'civil administration', which policed areas dominated by the IRA,[8] was seen outside Sinn Féin's headquarters at Connolly House, pointing his arm at the imagined figure of Scappaticci, somewhere out there in the far distance, shouting: 'That man is worth watching. He's an informer!' As one witness recalls, there was an audible 'Holy f***!' response from the crowd who heard the outburst.[9]

Anthony McIntyre also recalls senior IRA members in HMP Maze speculating about Scappaticci's allegiance. McIntyre was nearing the end of his life sentence for shooting dead a UVF member in 1976, and from 1991 he was eligible for home leave. Alex Murphy, a friend and fellow inmate – also serving life for what his trial judge described as the 'savage and vicious' killings of two young British corporals whose car had strayed into an IRA funeral cortege in 1988[10] – was openly branding Scappaticci a 'fuckin' tout'. Murphy asked McIntyre on his next home leave to check if Scappaticci's family was still living in the Ormeau Road area. Murphy explained that the IRA had learned that a member from that area had a code name 'Rolls Royce' and it was thought there might be a connection with the name of the street where Scappaticci had lived.[11]

McIntyre obliged and concluded that there wasn't a connection, but the story serves to further demonstrate that while Scappaticci was lying low in Dublin, the IRA leadership was having serious doubts about him. Curiously, no attempt appears to have been made by the IRA to interrogate either Scappaticci during the almost three years he spent as a fugitive in the South, or Magee, who went to live in Dundalk because his health was failing, or Maguire, who busied himself by working for the *Republican News* in its Dublin office.[12]

Consistent with the intelligence services prioritising source protection of their agents over the rule of law, Scappaticci's status as an agent had been deliberately and unlawfully withheld from the DPP in Belfast, Sir Alasdair Fraser, as he prepared the prosecution case on a series of serious charges against Danny Morrison, Anto Murray, Gerard Hodgins, Daniel Caldwell, James O'Carroll, James Martin and his English-born wife Veronica Ryan for conspiracy to murder Sandy Lynch and false imprisonment, and, in the case of the Martins, making 124 Carrigart Avenue available for terrorism. Their twenty-six-year-old son, Liam, was also charged with falsely imprisoning Lynch. James Martin was also charged with Joe Fenton's murder in February 1989, and he and his wife were further charged with falsely imprisoning Fenton and again for making 124 Carrigart Avenue available for terrorism.[13]

The fact that at least one state agent, Scappaticci, had been involved in Lynch's abduction and interrogation was a highly relevant and material fact, which by law the police were duty-bound to disclose to the DPP. The fact that this information was deliberately withheld prevented Sir Alasdair from exercising his option of not prosecuting on the grounds that it would not have been in the public interest to disclose that the ISU had been penetrated by a state agent. That was a choice which the DPP would normally make in consultation with the attorney general in London, who would ultimately have the whip hand since it involved a matter of national security. In the probably unlikely event of the attorney general having sanctioned a decision by Sir Alasdair to prosecute, he would have been obliged to disclose Scappaticci's status to the defence, which was entitled to know about any material not relied upon by the prosecution which might assist their defence. And in this case, the knowledge that the state, through Scappaticci, had been aware of Lynch's kidnapping in advance, yet had allowed it to happen, was an argument that the defence would almost certainly have wanted to make. Depending on the facts, it would likely have assisted Morrison and his co-defendants.

So, one way or another, disclosure of Scappaticci's secret status would have posed a very serious risk of undermining the prosecution case – as it proved when all eight convictions relating to Lynch were eventually quashed in October 2008 after Scappaticci's spy status was exposed. A few years later, so too were the convictions of Veronica Ryan and James Martin in respect of Joe Fenton's murder.[14]

Although Scappaticci had been recruited and run by military intelligence, responsibility for the decision not to disclose this to the DPP lay squarely with Special Branch. Since the army was operating in support of the RUC, which had primacy over policing, the disclosure buck stopped firmly with the RUC. The branch's decision to deceive was all the more egregious given that Scappaticci's name surfaced several times during the trial.[15]

On 8 May 1991, Lord Chief Justice of Northern Ireland Sir Brian Hutton handed down his ninety-two-page judgment. Morrison and six of his co-defendants, who were charged with conspiracy to murder, were acquitted of that charge, but he and Murray were convicted of aiding and abetting Sandy Lynch's false imprisonment, as were James Martin, Veronica Ryan and their son Liam. Hodgins, O'Carroll and Caldwell were also all convicted of false imprisonment. In respect of Joe Fenton's interrogation and murder a year earlier, James Martin and Veronica Ryan were convicted of aiding and abetting his false of imprisonment, and Martin was additionally convicted of making his home available for terrorism. Sentences of between twelve years and six months suspended were handed out. Hutton referred to Martin as 'deeply evil' and his wife as 'wicked' for having twice made their home available for what they must have known might end in murder.[16]

As Morrison and the others languished in jail, nursing a deep sense of betrayal by IRA men unknown, Scappaticci was becoming homesick and severely despondent as he whiled away his days in the suburban village of Clondalkin, on the outskirts of Dublin. He continued to report to his handlers at meetings along the border (FRU reports say they always took place on the northern side), despite there being a warrant out for his arrest for conspiracy to murder and false imprisonment.[17] His intelligence was limited to whatever fragments he was picking up about the different departments in the PIRA's GHQ operations based in Dublin city, the priority being the quartermaster's department, which was responsible for the supply of weapons.[18] He also provided intelligence about IRA fugitives from the North.[19] To keep his spirits up, with MI5's knowledge, the FRU took him for a couple of R&R breaks in Britain, resting up at hotels where he is reported to have got together 'with hookers', conceivably all at taxpayers' expense.[20] He was clandestinely removed from Northern Ireland via RAF Aldergrove, where he was given a military identity.[21] As with Brian Nelson, the FRU had promised him he was bomb-proof, yet here he was on the run with an RUC warrant for his arrest hanging over him on charges for which, potentially, he faced life imprisonment.

The repeated harbouring of a wanted offender is a serious crime. That, of course, is not how the FRU saw it, and his spymasters had not been idle. With the apparent approval of the then head of the Belfast CID, Detective Chief Superintendent George Caskey, senior officers had hatched a plan to get Scappaticci back to operational life as an agent. The FRU appears to have secured Caskey's agreement to improperly interfere with the CID's investigation into Scappaticci's role in the abduction and interrogation of Sandy Lynch by ensuring that, upon his return to Belfast, he would not stand trial. Or, to put it more bluntly, by flagrantly conspiring to pervert the course of justice.

The plot also meant that the suspicions of those Scappaticci had helped put in prison as a consequence of tipping off the FRU about Sandy Lynch's imminent execution needed to be assuaged. That opportunity came at Sinn Féin's eighty-sixth annual conference – or Ard-Fheis – in February 1992 in Ballyfermot, Dublin, where Scappaticci bumped into Veronica Ryan. She'd been paroled the previous autumn from her three-and-a-half-year sentence. 'Veronica, I'm sorry about what happened,' Scappaticci told her, adding with a straight face, 'it had nothing to do with me.' He said he was desperate to get back to Belfast and that he was missing his wife and children.[22] It appears that Ryan gave Scappaticci the benefit of the doubt, for she would become a willing accomplice in the plot cooked up between the FRU and Caskey that succeeded in preventing him from being charged when he finally crossed back over the border into Belfast eight months later, in October 1992.

The details of the FRU–Caskey plot were laid out in a FRU document dated 19 November 1990, which minuted a meeting between several FRU operatives and Caskey. It was unearthed in early March 2004 by the ever-diligent Detective Sergeant Andy Ansell, a member of the Stevens 3 Inquiry, as he leafed through an army file. So brazen was the plot as outlined in the document that it left Ansell trying to catch his breath. 'Governor, come here!' he called to Detective Chief Inspector Phil James. 'Take a look at this!'[23]

The officer now leading Stevens 3, Commander Dave Cox, did not mince his words. At one of his regular meetings with the DPP, he told Sir Alasdair Fraser that the FRU and Caskey had engaged in an 'overt official operation to pervert the course of justice' aimed at 'deceiving your office by concealing or falsely representing facts, ensuring a direction of no prosecution against the agent'.[24] It involved Scappaticci being given a false alibi for the thumbprint that the CID had found on the bug detector battery. Fraser is understood to have been aghast at the betrayal of trust by a senior police officer, particularly by one he regarded as a friend and knew not just professionally but also socially as they were members of the same golf club.

Caskey had enjoyed a reputation as a diligent detective, a bit 'pompous, but a good boss', as one of his colleagues put it,[25] and an officer with integrity. In 1990, he had, for example, valiantly encouraged BBC reporter Chris Moore to expose MI5's obstruction of his 1980s investigation into sexual abuse at the Kincora boys' home, where at least one member of staff – the paedophilic housemaster William McGrath – was also an MI5 asset. McGrath, the so-called 'Beast of Kincora' was the leader of the far-right loyalist quasi-paramilitary group Tara, and he had presumably provided MI5 with insights into its 'doomsday' plan to help prevent Northern Ireland from being taken over by republican forces and also, as Moore says, to find out if his fellow loyalists 'shared his sexual predilections'. Caskey told Moore how, time and again, a senior MI5 officer had avoided his attempts to interview him.[26]

Yet while Caskey was admirably pursuing MI5 for obstructing his investigation into Kincora, he appears simultaneously to have been colluding in a criminal conspiracy to assist another branch of the intelligence services to pervert the course of justice. It seems Caskey saw no contradiction in this. Presumably in his moral universe, he regarded both as serving the greater good: on the one hand exposing MI5's unconscionable obstruction of a criminal inquiry into vile sexual abuse of boys, while on the other fighting the IRA by helping the army to keep in play a valuable agent, albeit one whom Caskey must have suspected was involved in the murder of fellow agents. Yet if 'noble cause corruption' was indeed what had persuaded Caskey to assist in ensuring that the charge against Scappaticci went away, it is unlikely to have been the first time this senior and very seasoned detective had crossed the line.

Horrified by Dave Cox's revelations about his golfing friend, Sir Alasdair Fraser promptly recused himself from any further dealings in the case, handing it over to other officials in the PPS while emphasising his commitment to the Stevens 3 Inquiry and any prosecutions that arose from it.[27]

As set out in the documents discovered by Detective Sergeant Ansell, the FRU–Caskey plot to ensure that Scappaticci evaded prosecution involved four elements: 1) to keep Scappaticci out of Northern Ireland until the trial and any appeal by Danny Morrison *et al.* was concluded; 2) to manage the timing and circumstances of his arrest when he returned to Belfast; 3) to coach him on the false alibi to explain away his thumbprint on the bug detector battery; 4) to ensure that Sandy Lynch did not give evidence against him.[28]

The false alibi required the assistance of Veronica Ryan, who, in the autumn of 1992, was approached by the daughter of the IRA's former OC in Lenadoon, Con McHugh.[29] Known as 'The Bald Eagle', McHugh was a close friend of Scappaticci. 'My daddy wants to speak to you,' Ryan was told.[30]

When they met, McHugh told her that 'Scap was looking to come back' but needed an alibi for his thumbprint. Could she 'alibi' Scappaticci by saying he'd been doing some 'electrical work' at 124 Carrigart Avenue?[31] It would at least carry a ring of truth, since Scappaticci was a builder by trade.

In the meantime, Kevin Winters, just three years out of law school, had been asked to act for Scappaticci, the latter's importance in the IRA, far less his value to the intelligence services, completely unknown to him. Winters had also represented James Martin during his trial for holding Lynch and Fenton captive. 'They've sent me a boy!' Martin had complained when he set eyes on the fresh-faced lawyer. Scappaticci showed Winters more deference. They met twice on Dublin's O'Connell Street, first for Big Macs and fries at McDonalds, then later on a public bench. 'As a client, I actually found him pretty easy to deal with,' recalls Winters. 'He was friendly, engaging – ebullient, even.' No doubt Scappaticci had perked up since offloading his woes to Veronica Ryan several months earlier at Sinn Féin's Ard-Fheis, because by now he had the prospect of a false alibi, though the fact that it was a pack of lies was concealed from Winters. 'I heard nothing for a while, then – bang – he's arrested' on his return to Northern Ireland.[32]

With the appeal of Morrison and others having concluded in failure in July 1992, the way was now clear for Scappaticci to make his return to Belfast, which he did on 6 October with very deliberate visibility. That day Detective Chief Inspector Tim McGregor was told by his boss, George Caskey, that word had reached him that Scappaticci was back in town, working on a building site in the centre of Belfast. McGregor had been the SIO in the case against Morrison and the others, so Scappaticci was on his wanted list. McGregor says that at no stage was he ever told by Special Branch or by Caskey that Scappaticci was an agent, nor had Caskey confided in him the plot to get him off the hook.[33] Having been directed by Caskey to put an arrest package together, McGregor dispatched uniformed officers to the building site. The officers found Scappaticci with a bag containing two spare pairs of underpants and 'toiletries', clear evidence that he'd been tipped off to expect an arrest that day and to be prepared for a few days in custody.[34] That was not the only intimation of a secret pre-planned deal between Caskey and the FRU. Events would show that what the FRU documents discovered by Detective Sergeant Ansell said would happen, happened almost to the letter.[35]

McGregor's police diary shows that on 6 October he and a detective sergeant interviewed Scappaticci at Castlereagh. Scappaticci refused to answer any questions except those relating to his thumbprint on the bug detector battery. He explained that the battery had been in the TV remote, which he said Veronica Ryan had asked him to fix on a different day from when Lynch was being held captive at her home. By speaking at all, he was breaking the IRA's strict rules; as a senior member of the ISU, he had previously enforced these rules against others and on at least two occasions – with Michael Kearney and Anthony Braniff – this had led to their executions. But Scappaticci had no choice. Had he not accounted for the thumbprint with his bogus alibi, he would have been charged there and then. In that eventuality, Caskey is understood to have made it clear to the FRU that his officers would have no choice.[36]

On 7 October, McGregor rang the bell at 124 Carrigart Avenue to check Scappaticci's alibi with Ryan. Receiving no answer, he left a note asking her to call him at Woodbourne RUC station. The note said he wanted to talk to her about a person in custody, without naming Scappaticci. The FRU would later comment that her absence had been 'unforeseen' – intimating that the arrangement had required her to be available to confirm Scappaticci's alibi. Since Ryan was not at home, McGregor extended Scappaticci's time in custody to allow further time to investigate his alibi.[37]

Operation Kenova saw this as unusually generous to an IRA fugitive high up the wanted list, who'd been on the run for almost three years. Giving a wanted IRA man as senior as Scappaticci the benefit of the doubt in the face of compelling forensic evidence of his involvement in abduction and false imprisonment by the ISU was not how other IRA suspects would have been treated, they reasoned. The RUC's normal approach would have been to charge Scappaticci and to leave it to his trial to test the credibility of any alibi witness he wished to call.[38] McGregor disputes this. He says checking Scappaticci's alibi allowed him to determine whether there was a viable evidential case against him, particularly since Lynch had mistakenly described Scappaticci in one of his statements as having grey hair instead of black. It is true that sometimes Lynch appeared to muddle up Scappaticci with Magee, although there was no dispute that both had taken turns to interrogate him.[39]

On 8 October, McGregor says he got a call from the solicitor Oliver Kelly to say he was representing Veronica Ryan and to ask what he wanted by calling at her house. McGregor replied that he wanted to talk to her about a man he had in custody called Freddie Scappaticci. Being deeply mistrustful of the RUC, obliging them would not have been Kelly's natural disposition, but on this occasion he did. 'Mrs Martin does want to meet you and is happy to meet you,' he told McGregor.[40]

McGregor and his detective sergeant took Ryan's statement in Kelly's office. In it, she corroborated Scappaticci's alibi that he'd done 'some electrical work' at her home, which involved a battery, and that he had not been there when Lynch was held captive. McGregor says he made it clear to Ryan that he didn't believe her and warned her that if her alibi was disproved, she would be prosecuted for perjury.[41] On 9 October, McGregor released Scappaticci from custody.[42]

Following this, McGregor and his RUC colleagues had a 'wrap up meeting' to discuss what other lines of inquiry they might pursue.[43] McGregor says he enquired about the possibility of getting Sandy Lynch to make a statement but was told by Caskey that 'Lynch was being seen by psychiatrists, and that he was in no fit state to go through the rigours of another trial'.[44] That information was based on a visit Caskey had made to Lynch in England where, for the time being, he'd been resettled. Caskey told the DPP that Lynch was unwilling to give evidence and that he was unwell.[45] This does not square with Lynch's evidence to Operation Kenova.

When Kenova officers interviewed Lynch, he said he had no clear recollection of what Caskey had said to him, but it could not have included a request to return to Belfast to give evidence against Scappaticci because he would certainly have agreed to testify against him.[46] 'I'd done it before at the trial of Morrison, so why wouldn't I have done it again?' he told Kenova.[47] Lynch explained that in the hours immediately following his rescue by the RUC on Sunday, 7 January 1990, he'd made a vow to himself. Lying in a cell where he'd been put for his own safety while the RUC collected his belongings and his wife from their home in Magherafelt, he'd decided that although he was a police agent, he wouldn't 'grass up' anyone except those who'd so severely traumatised him that weekend. Against them, explained Lynch, he'd always been willing and able to give evidence, and he had never wavered in that.[48] McGregor said, 'Maybe Caskey lied to me then. When he told me Lynch wasn't fit to give evidence, I obviously believed him.'[49] The criminal investigation into the FRU–Caskey plot was conducted jointly by Operation Kenova and the Police Ombudsman's Office. Kenova found further evidence that they believe would have undermined Scappaticci's false alibi. The RUC had retrieved an eyelash from a glove on the floor by the front-room sofa. DNA testing, which had been unavailable to the RUC at the time, showed it was Scappaticci's.[50] Had the eyelash been tested in 1990, it would have indicated that Scappaticci was likely to have been in the house during Lynch's confinement, because the glove is unlikely to have lain where it was, undetected, for days.

In October 1992, McGregor sent a prosecution file to the DPP, but in March 1993 the decision was made not to prosecute Scappaticci. Following the imbroglio over Brian Nelson, the FRU underwent a makeover and was reorganised into a reformed covert intelligence-gathering unit called the Joint Support Group (JSG), though it appears that it was still on something of a learning curve about its relationship to the rule of law. Greeting the DPP's decision, the JSG praised the way the case had been handled, even though the FRU–Caskey plot amounted to a blatant act of perverting the course of justice. The JSG sent the RUC a note thanking Caskey and McGregor, saying they now had '9001 [Scappaticci's new agent number] released with his security not only intact but enhanced. This is the best outcome JSG could have hoped for.'[51] McGregor says the first he had heard of such a note was when I told him about it. 'It must have just gone to Caskey,' he said. 'Caskey never mentioned this to me.'[52] McGregor did, however, say that he had been aware of some 'army people' checking on the case at Woodbourne RUC Barracks where he was based, but he hadn't associated them with the intelligence services.[53] In the meantime, one of Scappaticci's key handlers was awarded a gallantry medal.[54] As for Scappaticci's fellow fugitive, Seán Maguire, he returned from his exile in the Irish Republic a few weeks after Scappaticci, was arrested in McDonalds in Belfast city centre and released after several days' interrogation, during which he is reported to have said nothing.[55]

When Operation Kenova reviewed the case, they were suspicious that although McGregor had not been involved in the discussions between Caskey and the FRU, he had implemented 'aspects of the alleged conspiracy',[56] on the basis that, since there had been sufficient evidence to charge Scappaticci on his arrest, his alibi could have been checked later, whereas his period in custody was unusually extended in order to accommodate checks into his alibi. 'When you've got an IRA fellow bang to rights to be charged, in what other circumstances would a senior RUC officer be tear-arsing around Belfast looking for somebody to give him an alibi to get him out?' asked one Kenova officer. 'Not very usual, I would suggest.'[57] McGregor had long since retired and lived in France. Kenova detectives flew there to search his house, and he was questioned under caution on his return to London.

In October 2019, amongst the first of Kenova's prosecution files submitted to the PPS in Belfast was one on McGregor and Caskey.[58] Confronted by the masterplan of the conspiracy unearthed by Stevens 3, Caskey was 'quite dismissive', telling his interrogator that he 'didn't really know what he was talking about'.[59] Caskey died twenty-eight months later, without the PPS having made a decision on his case,[60] again demonstrating how under-resourced the Northern Ireland PPS had become in dealing with legacy cases. A further twenty months passed before the PPS announced its decision that McGregor had no case to answer, saying it was satisfied he'd 'provided an explanation and justification for his actions'.[61] As for Scappaticci, he showed his gratitude to Veronica Ryan by surprising her on her return from work one day to personally thank her. She found him ensconced in her living room wearing a pair of sunglasses.[62]

While the JSG thought Scappaticci's security had been 'enhanced' on his return from the Irish Republic, the IRA leadership had other ideas. Deeply suspicious that he'd betrayed Morrison and others in the Sandy Lynch disaster, Sean 'Spike' Murray, a senior Belfast-based member of Northern Command made it clear to Scappaticci that his time in the ISU was over and that he was to depart the IRA stage quietly but decisively.[63] Lesser suspects would not have been given the benefit of the doubt and by then would have been lying stone cold in a Belfast alleyway or on the side of a road a few yards inside Northern Ireland's trackless border. The assassination of Denis Donaldson in 2006, a spy who did far less damage to the IRA than Scappaticci, is a case in point. While claimed by dissident republicans, suspicion survives that it may have been the PIRA.[64] But Scappaticci was no ordinary IRA volunteer.

Not only would his murder be an admission of his treachery, which would have shaken the IRA rank and file to its core, but it would have raised the question: if someone at his level was working for the Brits, then who else?

To the British Army, Scappaticci was their 'golden egg' – a sobriquet awarded by the former Northern Ireland GOC, the late General Sir John Wilsey, to 'that Fred chap, whatever his name is …'[65] It was an accolade widely agreed on by his FRU handlers and those who dealt with his intelligence product. 'He saved a number of lives including my own actually and another colleague directly, so I have more than a vested interest,' a senior military intelligence officer told me. 'I dealt with his product on an almost daily basis, and I know he did fantastic work.'[66]

Having reviewed approximately 90 per cent of the summary written intelligence reports attributable to Scappaticci, PSNI Chief Constable Jon Boutcher is less impressed. 'Any serious security and intelligence professional hearing an agent being likened to "the goose that laid the golden eggs" … should be on the alert because the comparison is rooted in fables and fairy tales,' concluded Boutcher, although he has acknowledged that Scappaticci was 'undoubtedly a valuable asset who provided high quality intelligence about PIRA at considerable risk to himself'.[67] Kenova recovered a total of 3,517 separate intelligence reports attributed to Scappaticci – and that's only the number that survived destruction. Inevitably, much was mundane – 'sightings of individuals in the street, individuals seen talking in various drinking establishments or snatches of overheard conversation'.[68] But much was valuable, both strategic – in terms of the IRA's direction – and tactical, although in general there was more of the former.[69] Whether this translated into a net gain of lives over those lost is impossible to say, as Sir Iain Livingstone, who succeeded Boutcher as the officer in overall charge of Operation Kenova, has emphasised.[70]

In the aftermath of Scappaticci's return to Belfast, his sense of self seems to have taken a knock. Shunned by the IRA leadership, Agent 9001 was worried that one day he might share the fate of his FRU contemporary, Agent 6137. Concerned that Stevens might soon be breathing down his neck, he sought assurance from the army's top brass about the value of his work for them. Wilsey willingly gave it in person at a meeting in South Belfast.[71]

Occasionally, Scappaticci would visit Veronica Ryan while her husband,

James, was still serving out his longer sentence. He would leave money on the mantelpiece, telling her, 'You're getting it hard. Nobody from the republican movement is helping you.' It may also have been because he was attracted to her. 'Veronica's a good-looking woman,' a friend heard him comment. She apparently told him she didn't want his money.[72]

Friends and acquaintances of Scappaticci noted that his aggressive swagger had given way to a bitter open hostility to the IRA. An ex-neighbour who bumped into him in Belfast in 1993 recalled

> Scap looking at me, asking, 'So what are you doing?' And I looked at him and I says, 'What do you mean, what am I doing?' He says, 'I hope you're not in any fucking nonsense.' I says, 'What do you mean?' He says, 'You know what I fucking mean … I hope you're not in any auld nonsense … youse keep your nose clean.' And I was laughing. I says, 'I'm doing political work.'[73]

Scappaticci had a similar message for another friend, who, unlike the neighbour, had been active in the IRA. 'He said to me, "Are you still fucking active? It's a waste of time. Do yourself a favour. Get the fuck out of it. It's a waste of time." Coming from him, I couldn't believe it!'[74]

In August 1993, Scappaticci drifted even further off message. In a supremely reckless act, he telephoned the investigative ITV programme *The Cook Report*, after he had heard they were investigating Martin McGuinness. Unwisely, he agreed to meet the programme makers at the Culloden Hotel outside Belfast, without ensuring that he wasn't being covertly recorded, an opportunity which was far too tempting for the journalists to forego. Either Scappaticci's native cunning and caution had deserted him, or maybe he no longer much cared, but the conversation that ensued would seal his fate a decade later when it was broadcast, finally demolishing his long string of denials that he was the agent known as Stakeknife.

In that tape, his chutzpah is world-beating. To the question of why he had left the IRA, from the man who'd taken so active a role in the IRA's chilling execution process came this reply: 'Well, there's more to life than killing.' When it came to household republican names, he pulled no punches: he said Danny Morrison was a 'pen pusher' who had 'no balls'; as for McGuinness:

> There is something quite wrong with his head. He talks to you very quietly, very softly, but he would think nothing about putting us [him and the two journalists in the car] down. He would be praying in chapel one minute, go outside and think nothing about ordering a shooting … He gets a kick out of it, out of killing … He is a cold person. One minute he would be in church and next he would say 'stiff him'.

Coming from a man who primed many souls for execution and may himself occasionally have pulled the trigger, this was rich. Richer still was his contempt for the way ISU interrogators (like him) made false promises of freedom to their victims provided they confessed: 'See if someone in the IRA says, "I swear to God," or, "I swear on my mother's life," then you know you are getting double-crossed. That's the code word. You say, right – "bolt. Bolt."' When asked how many executions there had been, he replied, 'I can't keep a score of them. Forty? Fifty? Sixty? A hundred?'[75]

Alarmed though his JSG handlers were at his reckless departure from some fifteen years of strict discipline, Scappaticci remained on their payroll, his handlers attempting to buoy up his spirits with assurances that his work was unfinished and that his loss would be 'felt throughout the intelligence world'.[76] This was no longer true. With limited access to the IRA's innermost secrets, the value of his product was diminishing. The JSG kept him on because he kept his ear to the ground and occasionally got access to Sinn Féin headquarters at Connolly House by assisting with electioneering.[77] His insights into the emerging political picture were also valued as Gerry Adams inched the IRA towards the 1994 ceasefire.

March 1995 saw a major strain in his marriage to his loyal wife, Sheila, who had forborne so much. Scappaticci's former ISU colleague Eamon Collins broke ranks and appeared in the ITV documentary *Confession*.[78] In it, he named Scappaticci as second-in-command of the 'Nutting Squad' and a senior member of Northern Command, who had an 'amazing mine of information' and a 'lot of experience' because of his 'expertise'. The programme quoted at length Sandy Lynch's graphic account of Scappaticci's menacing threat that unless he confessed, by the time he'd finished with him he would have no face and his widow would have a job identifying him.

Sheila is reported to have been repulsed. She had known her husband was in the IRA but apparently not his role as a brutal ISU enforcer responsible for torture and executions.[79] As Agent 9001 grew increasingly disgruntled, the JSG asked MI5's Central Resettlement Unit (CRU) to come up with a plan for his resettlement outside of Northern Ireland.

When the JSG finally pulled the plug in August 1995 by taking Scappaticci off their payroll, there was talk of arranging a farewell dinner, although it's unclear if it actually took place.[80] Scappaticci was then resettled in Britain, but this was 'short-lived and an abject failure'.[81] He was homesick, missed his family and was putting his own life as well as his handlers' lives at risk with what they described as 'cavalier' behaviour. Then one day, out of the blue, without telling his handlers, he returned to Belfast; it was only when he was spotted driving a car in the city that the CRU learned he had returned.[82] To provide for his future, the JSG considered 'five and six figure financial incentives to cover a pension or annual salary' and offered him money to buy a property in a safer part of Northern Ireland than Belfast.[83] He declined the offer, presumably having reassured himself the IRA couldn't – or wouldn't – touch him.

As the decade wore on, a curious power play between Scappaticci and the IRA leadership ensued. Aware that Scappaticci had been making no secret of his disenchantment with the leadership of the PIRA, whilst giving the impression he was untouchable, the IRA staged an incident that had all the appearance of a reminder of who – quite literally – called the shots.

It began with a game of soccer at Andersonstown Leisure Centre in 1997, when Scappaticci approached Tommy Braniff, whose older brother Anthony (27) had been executed by the IRA in September 1981, having been accused falsely of being an informer. 'What happened to your Anthony was wrong,' Scappaticci said. Somewhat startled, Braniff pressed him for details. 'I'm just telling you what happened was wrong,' Scappaticci replied.[84] Tommy, who, unlike Anthony, had not joined the IRA, says he remembers the occasion vividly because he was struck by Scappaticci's apparent sincerity; he also recalls that Scappaticci was wearing bright red socks.

As a member of the ISU at the time of Anthony Braniff's murder, Scappaticci would certainly have been in a position to know what had happened to him, particularly since he had initiated the chain of events that had led to the young man's execution. Following Braniff's release from interrogation by the RUC, Scappaticci had conducted the ISU's customary debrief, during which Braniff admitted he'd broken IRA standing orders by not remaining silent, albeit insisting he'd given nothing away. Scappaticci told him he was suspended and reported him to senior IRA members, which led to his 'abduction, interrogation and murder'.[85] A hastily convened court martial rejected Braniff's insistence that, despite having responded to some RUC questions, he hadn't betrayed information of any value.[86] Two of his interrogators – one of whom was later resettled in England after being unmasked as an agent[87] – accused Braniff of having given away the location of a rifle and the movement of IRA volunteers, and said that he'd met his 'Special Branch contacts regularly'.[88] However, Scappaticci believed Braniff was being truthful, since the weapons dump the rifle had been taken from was known only at brigade level, not by Anthony's local unit.

When Scappaticci became aware that the IRA intended to shoot Braniff, FRU records show he attempted to identify where he was being held and told his handlers, who informed the RUC. They in turn attempted – unsuccessfully – to disrupt the execution.[89] The fact that hundreds of mourners attended Anthony's funeral indicates the level of community scepticism about the IRA's claim.

Scappaticci's post-soccer match comments to Tommy Braniff in 1997 eventually led to a series of IRA inquiries culminating in vindication for Anthony in September 2003, when the IRA acknowledged there was no evidence that he had betrayed them.[90] The Braniff family were told that the inquiry would be led by 'Spike' Murray, who'd stood Scappaticci down after his return in October 1992 from being on the run in the Irish Republic. When Scappaticci learned of Murray's role, he withdrew his offer to give evidence. Murray however, insisted Scappaticci should appear. It soon became clear that the purpose of this was as much to do with putting Scappaticci publicly in his place as hearing his evidence about Anthony's innocence.

A hearing was scheduled at the home of a Braniff family relative. A number of local residents were also present. For ten minutes Scappaticci gave his evidence with a notetaker present. Suddenly, Murray entered the room and began questioning Scappaticci aggressively, accusing him of making an unsubstantiated accusation against a fellow ISU member. At this Scappaticci withdrew, saying, 'I'm taking the fifth', a reference to the US Constitution's Fifth Amendment, which allows a person to refuse to answer questions that might incriminate them.[91] To the Braniff family, this very public humiliation of Scappaticci must have been utterly baffling; to Scappaticci, though, the message must have been clear: 'You were told to stay out of IRA business after you returned from Dublin. So, stay out of it.'

Unlike Murray's orchestrated put-down of Scappaticci, their next encounter was quite by chance. Finding himself in a crowded shopping centre, Murray turned around only to come face to face with his nemesis. A source close to Murray said the colour seemed to drain from Scappaticci's face.[92] In terms of IRA authority, there was no dispute in this encounter as to who held the highest rank.

Chapter Fourteen

6137 – Stevens 2

THE CALL CAME TO MEET a man in a layby. It was early 1992, some weeks after Brian Nelson's trial. A car drew up, the driver got out, handed me and my BBC colleague Geoff Seed an envelope, and drove off. Inside were some 171 pages of spidery handwriting – what has become known as 'Nelson's journal/diary'. More accurately, it was, as Nelson himself later acknowledged, a series of 'defence submissions' penned while on remand in Crumlin Road Gaol in support of his intention to contest the charges against him.[1] Since, on the eve of his trial, the Crown had dropped the two most serious charges – the murders of Terry McDaid and Gerard Slane – he'd had no call for the journal.

Nelson's writings contained some extremely serious allegations that took the gloss off the courtroom attempt by the FRU's CO Colonel Gordon Kerr to mitigate his ten-year sentence; they also contradicted some of what Nelson told me in our half dozen conversations when I visited him on remand. Notably, Kerr had told the court that Nelson had handed a 'bulk transfer' of targeting documents amassed by the UDA to the FRU. He had indeed handed over the contents of a bin liner stuffed into a large suitcase and cardboard box with over 1,000 police and army intelligence reports on IRA suspects, photographs and maps. What Kerr didn't say was that, according to Nelson, his handler had helped refine his targeting files by removing leaked intelligence data on republicans who were either dead or in jail.[2]

Kerr had also said Nelson made it 'quite clear' to the gunmen who had kicked in the door at 4 Newington Street and murdered Terry McDaid that the intended target, Declan McDaid, wasn't actually staying at that address. It was, in fact, far from clear that Nelson had done any such thing. Nelson told me that he'd begun his surveillance on Declan at 22 Oceanic Avenue, because that was where the electoral register said he was living. Concerned that he was exposing himself in a hard-line republican area, about a week before Terry was shot, his handler had suggested he look in Newington Avenue.[3]

In his journal Nelson said his handlers had also assisted him with his targeting of two other republicans. One was Belfast Brigade Operations Officer Anto Murray, whose house the army photographed at his handler's request because surveillance by Nelson was too risky. The handler copied the photograph for Nelson on tracing paper, who then gave it to the UDA. Nelson acknowledged he had 'totally omitted' any mention of this to Stevens.[4] The other was David Clinton of the INLA. Nelson thought he lived in Rutland Street in Belfast but said his handler told him Clinton had moved to Downpatrick.[5] Nelson also told me that one of his handlers had helped him locate Brian Gillen, the Belfast Brigade's OC.[6] Gillen had been Nelson's favourite subject.[7]

Kerr had told the court that Nelson was 'not loyal to the UDA, Brian Nelson was loyal to the army … he wished to help the army in its attempts to counter terrorism and to save life … that was his prime motivation'. Yet it was clear from both my conversations with Nelson and from FRU records that the only lives Nelson wanted to save were Catholics he deemed innocent; what really motivated him was the prospect of using his position as UDA chief intelligence officer to target and kill not just active members of the IRA but also their supporters.

Finally, Kerr had said that when Nelson sometimes became 'too involved' with UDA assassins and 'forgot temporarily his true role' by 'trying to find out' where targets lived, 'in all cases … he was taken to task by his handlers'. That was often true, but it wasn't because Nelson was breaking the law – his handlers feared he was putting himself at risk of being killed by the IRA or arrested by the security forces. Nor did Kerr's claim sit easily with Nelson's allegation in his journal that the FRU had encouraged him to bomb certain targets in the Irish Republic. Specifically, Nelson alleged that a FRU officer he referred to as 'the Boss' had encouraged him to blow up a fuel dump in Cork to pressurise Dublin into relaxing its ban on extraditing IRA fugitives. He'd written, 'The Boss asked me if the UDA could carry out such a campaign? I said, "I'm sure they could." The Boss said "Good". He then told me that the oil terminal outside Cork would be well worth a look at. I said that I would have to talk to the right people, but I didn't see any problems. The Boss replied "I'll leave it with you then."'[8]

Nelson said he proposed this to John McMichael, the UDA's South Belfast leader, 'who was totally taken with the idea'. When, at his next FRU meeting, Nelson told his handlers that McMichael was on board, 'no comment was made'.[9] Nelson claimed to have noted that one of his handlers, Sergeant Margaret Jones, had given 'the impression she didn't know what I was talking about and I had to recount … the conversation I had had with McMichael'. He wrote that he believed Jones had 'feigned ignorance' because there was another handler present who was 'unaware of the conversation that the Boss had had with me'.[10] FRU records recount that McMichael did dispatch someone to the Republic to take photographs of the refinery, and a roll of film was handed to Nelson.[11] He took this to a one-hour processing shop in Belfast and had an extra set of prints run off, presumably for handing to the FRU.[12] The FRU noted that after McMichael asked Nelson if he knew of a demolition expert capable of training the UDA to blow up an oil terminal, one of Nelson's handlers noted Nelson would suggest to McMichael that the UDA use the same person who'd built the limpet mine intended to kill Gerry Adams.[13]

In court, Colonel Kerr also sought to exculpate Nelson from having any role in the murder of solicitor Pat Finucane by insisting that Nelson had been 'misled' by the UDA into believing they were going to kill one of his clients – the IRA man Pat McGeown – not Finucane himself. This had happened five days before Finucane was assassinated, when Nelson said UDA military commander Eric McKee had duped him into believing the target was McGeown by requesting from him a photograph of McGeown leaving court with Finucane. Kerr said that when Nelson was debriefed two days after Finucane was murdered, 'we had every reason to believe, as he did, that [McGeown] was the target'. None of that made sense. Nelson had many photographs of McGeown alone and he'd also produced two 'P' cards on McGeown.[14] If McGeown was the intended target, why was Nelson being asked for a photograph of both him *and* Finucane?

Nelson had already said in his statement to Stevens that McKee had asked him to start targeting Finucane six to eight weeks earlier, after McKee told him, 'I would really love to get that bastard Finucane' because 'he is the brains behind P.I.R.A.'[15] The FRU knew that Nelson had been 'participating willingly' in the UDA's attempt to murder high-profile republicans.[16] Given all this, was it really credible that Nelson could have been tricked into thinking McGeown – not Finucane – was the target? Not according to MI5, which had a source it assessed as reliable who reported that Nelson had carried out a recce of Finucane's home,[17] consistent with what the UDA's Tucker Lyttle (and others) told me.[18] All the evidence points to Nelson having consciously handed over the photograph of McGeown and Finucane knowing full well the intended target was the latter.

The conflicts between Kerr's evidence and Nelson's journal encouraged Geoff and me to investigate further for *Panorama*. Army Headquarters Northern Ireland appears to have got wind of this and was not at all happy. Some weeks after the trial we met John Stevens in a London wine bar. 'The army want me to arrest you,' he told me. 'What's the charge?' I asked. 'God knows,' said Stevens with a mischievous grin. 'Delving into matters they don't seem to think you should be delving into.' It later became clear this related to Nelson reporting back to his handlers on the pressure Tucker Lyttle had put on him at my behest to show me the scale of the intelligence dump, which of course I knew nothing about at the time. I reminded Stevens of this incident recently. 'We all certainly took the threat seriously,' he told me. 'I can assure you that there was absolutely no chance of me or any of my team agreeing to arrest you.'[19]

The title of our *Panorama* was 'Dirty War' and it was transmitted on 8 June 1992. The programme made headline news and understandably caused Nelson to regret ever having talked to me. He was especially troubled about how we had acquired a copy of his diary and at the prospect of his case being re-opened. The DPP in Belfast said they were reviewing the programme and there was talk of Colonel Kerr being in the frame, so when the FRU's former operations officer visited Nelson four days after transmission, he found him 'very agitated and concerned'.[20] For a while it looked as if the

Treasury solicitor was also trying to put me in the frame. A hand-addressed letter arrived at the BBC, warning me that revealing further contents of Nelson's journal might 'constitute an offence under Section 5 of the 1989 Official Secrets Act' by causing 'damage to the work of the security forces'.[21] A further warning came seven months later, after I referred to the content of the journal in a BBC interview.[22] Both warnings were ignored. No harm was being done to national security, only national embarrassment.

The real damage, both to the reputation of the army and rather more importantly, to people's lives, had been done by Nelson and by the failure of the FRU to exercise sufficient control over him – easier said than done with a maverick like Nelson, but those experienced in agent handling insist more could have been done to rein him in. That was why the DPP was reviewing the programme and had requested a transcript. In May 1993, Northumbria Police, of which John Stevens was now chief constable, announced that he was 'continuing with his inquiry in Northern Ireland which involves allegations made by the *Panorama* programme'.[23] Eleven months had passed since transmission, but one of the allegations that seems to have tipped the balance in favour of a second Stevens inquiry was a disclosure to the DPP on 3 March 1993 by the Crown Solicitor's Office in Belfast. They reported that Nelson's solicitor had informed them that Nelson's journal said it was his handler who 'supplied him with the McDaid address in Newington Street'.[24] This was very similar to the allegation that Nelson had made to me in 1991 when I visited him while he was on remand in Crumlin Road Gaol. Intriguingly, this claim did not feature in the version of the journal that had been leaked to me, so I assume there were at least two iterations. Nelson's solicitor had also told the Crown solicitor that his handler had updated the information in Nelson's intelligence dump and added some information.[25]

Nelson's solicitor had raised these points with the Crown Solicitor's Office as the prospect loomed of not just another criminal case but also of a civil case against him and the MoD for damages. Eight days after Nelson had been sentenced, Patrick Finucane's widow, Geraldine, had begun civil proceedings.[26] The Crown Solicitor's Office had warned the DPP that in the event of the civil case going to trial, Nelson might feel compelled to defend himself by giving evidence, 'including a number of serious allegations', against his handlers.[27] For the so-called securocracy, the dreaded spectre of the intelligence services being forced to wash their soiled linen in public – a threat that on the eve of Nelson's criminal trial had been removed by the deal he'd done with the Crown – had reared its head again.

Whereas Stevens 1 had focused on Nelson, the principal focus for Stevens 2 was the extent to which Nelson's FRU handlers were implicated in murder and other unlawful acts. In the first flush of interviews with Nelson's handlers in Stevens 1, only they had access to the CFs, not the detectives, and since the handlers had been allowed to refresh their memories in between questions, the atmosphere had generally been cordial. Having now had time to immerse themselves in the detail of those CFs, Detective Sergeant Benwell and his colleagues reinterviewed several handlers during Stevens 2, with the questions now much more targeted and most aimed at the handlers not Nelson.[28] What, for example, had the FRU known about Nelson's intentions in the attempted murder of Alex Maskey, the murders of Terry McDaid and Patrick Finucane? And what had they done to try and constrain him? Also – as Nelson alleged in his journal – had the FRU encouraged a UDA bombing campaign in the Irish Republic? And had they helped Nelson update his targeting files?

On 8 August 1993, Benwell interviewed Sergeant Margaret Jones, Nelson's handler during both the murder of Terry McDaid and the attempted murder of Alex Maskey. Sitting with her army lawyer, Jones was asked why she had confirmed to Nelson (as evidenced by the transcript of a telephone CF) that the vehicle registration number of a car outside a Belfast hotel where Maskey was having Sunday lunch was probably used by him? Nelson had been trying to muster a gun team to shoot Maskey when he emerged. Jones made no reply to that question or to another concerning the registration numbers of vehicles she was alleged to have checked for Nelson while he was targeting another republican, Harry Maynes, for assassination. Jones made no reply, not even to confirm that she had read the telephone CFs evidencing her conversations with Nelson that Benwell put in front of her.

Benwell then asked Jones a series of questions about the murder of Terry McDaid: had she supplied Nelson with the 4 Newington Street address – as Nelson's solicitor said his client alleged in his journal – in the mistaken belief that his brother Declan lived there? What had caused Nelson to direct the murder gang there instead of to Declan's registered address 350 yards away at 22 Oceanic Avenue? Why were there no transcripts of three of the four panic-stricken calls Nelson had made soon after the killing, when he realised the wrong man had been shot? Did she have any knowledge of the FRU officer whom Nelson described in his journal as 'the Boss', alleging he'd encouraged him to blow up a fuel dump in Cork?

To each of these questions, Jones made no reply, speaking only at the end of the interview to say that she'd declined to answer on legal advice, adding that she 'absolutely' denied 'any suggestion or allegation that I deliberately or inadvertently assisted or conspired with Brian Nelson to conduct murder or any other crime'.[29] Soldier C, Jones' co-handler, told Benwell that he could 'categorically state' that she had not 'at any meeting' given Nelson the Newington Street address.[30]

The FRU captain to whom Nelson referred as 'the Boss' emphatically denied encouraging him to blow up the fuel dump in Cork, insisting he had 'never discussed explosives with Brian Nelson and under no circumstances would I give such instruction'.[31] One of the two handlers running Nelson when Finucane was shot said Nelson had never informed them that Finucane was being targeted and had only mentioned the lawyer's name after he was shot.[32] Every handler interviewed denied ever having passed any targeting information to Nelson. Five of them did admit there were times when Nelson sought information from them, like vehicle registration numbers, but they insisted they never gave him any. FRU handler Soldier C admitted that he 'did, on occasions, tell Nelson if he had wrong information, 'but I never corrected such information'.[33] And handler Martin Callan emphatically denied Nelson's suggestion in his journal that he had assisted him in 'weeding out' the UDA intelligence dump.[34]

In all of the above cases, it was Nelson's word against his handlers and, therefore, the evidence was inconclusive. Where the FRU was more evidentially culpable was in their loss of control over Nelson's targeting files, which they allowed him to proliferate widely within the UDA and other loyalist murder gangs after Nelson said the FRU had updated them on 14 October 1987. The FRU had then asked Nelson to 'copy all UDA targeting files and computer floppy discs'; presumably these were the updated files which the FRU knew Nelson had promised, on 15 October, to disseminate shortly to the UDA. On 20 October, he passed them to three notorious assassins and two other senior UDA leaders.[35] The reason for distributing the files? 'To increase the targeting capacity of the UDA,' said the FRU.[36]

Benwell and his fellow officers soon discovered that just as they thought they'd resolved one question, like Russian dolls, another one appeared. For example, was Nelson lying when he told Stevens that, contrary to his handlers' denial, he had warned them Finucane was being targeted? Was he lying when he said he only found out by chance that Finucane had been shot because he just happened to be eavesdropping on the RUC radio net when Finucane was actually shot?[37]

In the hope of resolving some of these issues, in February 1993, three months before John Stevens officially announced he'd begun a second inquiry, he and a detective inspector visited Nelson in HMP Bristol, where he had been moved. Stevens found him an utterly changed man. The free-flowing conversant who had cheerfully engaged with Detective Sergeant Lynn Evans' questions immediately after his arrest in 1990 was now unforthcoming and monosyllabic. He refused to confirm or deny what he'd written in his journal about handler assistance with locating IRA targets; he even refused to confirm or deny he was the author of the journal. He did, however, deny that he was in any way involved in the murder of Patrick Finucane.[38] After the formal interview, Nelson asked to 'have a chat off the record'. When Stevens suggested to him that he'd only ever told 'about two thirds of the truth', Nelson nodded in assent.[39]

Why did Nelson backtrack in the formal part of the interview on what he'd told Stevens and written in his journal? The answer appears to be fear that the MoD might review their generous welfare payments to him and his family because they suspected that he'd leaked his journal to me. The MoD was certainly very angry that he'd talked to me while on remand and extremely frustrated that he'd talked to Stevens in the first place. The day after transmission of the 'Dirty War' *Panorama* broadcast, the JSG's new CO assured the MoD that Nelson was 'fully conscious of his need to honour our requirement for his co-operation in silence'. This, the CO tellingly acknowledged, was a 'quid pro quo' for the 'care and custody of his wife and family during his prison sentence and his own ultimate resettlement'.[40]

Interviewed again in April 1993, this time by Detective Sergeant Benwell, Nelson continued to insist he hadn't written a journal, saying he'd written only 'thirty or forty' pages of notes for his solicitor.[41] The journal leaked to me and Geoff Seed was 176 pages long. Also, contrary to what he had written in his journal, he now denied that his handlers had updated the intelligence files in his dump; he was also dismissing as 'absolute nonsense' any suggestion that 'the Boss' had encouraged him to blow up the oil refinery in Cork or that his handler had assisted with Declan McDaid's address, or even that his handlers had ever fed him information.[42] He continued to categorically deny any involvement in Finucane's murder, despite the wealth of evidence to the contrary,[43] including Tommy Lyttle's evidence to me that he'd driven McKee to reconnoitre Finucane's home,[44] corroborated independently by an MI5 informant.[45]

Nelson was now trying to square the circle between the absence in FRU records of any warning from him that Finucane was being actively targeted and his insistence in his original statement to Stevens that he had informed his handlers of this. With a straight face, Nelson was now saying that when he'd told Detective Sergeant Evans in January 1990 that McKee had told him 'I would really like to get that bastard', Nelson hadn't known the name of the solicitor McKee wanted to 'get' because McKee hadn't identified him by name.[46] Nelson seemed to have forgotten that when quoting McKee in his 1990 statement to Evans, he'd given 'that bastard' a name – Patrick Finucane.[47] He also seemed to have forgotten that in his journal he'd written that McKee had named Finucane when he'd asked Nelson to 'see what I could dig up on Finnucane [*sic*]'.[48] He even denied that he'd drawn up a 'P' card on Finucane, despite the fact that after Finucane was shot, FRU records showed Nelson had admitted making a 'P' card for him.[49]

In his journal, Nelson also claimed that 'all such [targeting] information was duly photocopied by my handlers and returned to me. This also included the blue index ['P'] cards that I had put together myself.'[50] If so, this would suggest that at some stage the FRU may well have been aware that Nelson had Finucane down as a potential target, without Nelson having disclosed to the FRU when the targeting was under way. At the very least, it made a nonsense of the claim that Colonel Kerr had made in court, and which Nelson was now making to Benwell, that when he'd handed McKee a photograph of Pat McGeown leaving court with Finucane five days before Finucane was shot, he hadn't realised Finucane was the real target. As Brian Fitzsimons, head of

Special Branch, told me, Nelson must have known Finucane was the target when McKee asked him for the photograph.[51]

On the third and last attempt to get more out of Nelson, in June 1993, Benwell asked him to elaborate on a reference in his journal to his handler, Sergeant Jones, having provided him with 4 Newington Street as Declan McDaid's address, whereas he actually lived 350 yards away at 22 Oceanic Avenue. His reply, which was inconsistent with his interview on the subject the previous April, was, 'You are nearly there, but not quite.' When it was put to Nelson that Jones had 'given him help', he said that she 'was involved, but you'll never get a statement from me about it'. Although Benwell continued to press him about McDaid, he repeated that 'we were almost there but it was not up to him to tell us'.[52] He continued to insist that it was his own month-long surveillance in the area that led him to pinpoint 4 Newington Street as the right address for McDaid. How Nelson had achieved that in a nationalist/republican area acutely alert to strangers and what he meant by his handler having been 'involved' remain a mystery to this day, as does the content of three of the four panicked telephone calls Nelson made to his handlers between 12.41 a.m. and 1.27 a.m. shortly after the shooting, when he realised Terry McDaid had been shot instead of his brother Declan. Benwell discovered that those transcripts no longer existed. 'This was the only occasion I can recall where there were no [surviving] transcripts of telephone calls,' he said.[53]

Also unknown is the basis on which Sergeant Jones had reassured a 'depressed' Nelson that Terry McDaid had a PIRA trace on him, after which Nelson was 'quite content'.[54] Yet Nelson was easily satisfied, as had become clear at our first meeting back in October 1989, when I first discussed the murder of McDaid with him. 'You always know from the police if you've got the right guy,' he told me, meaning if the victim was IRA-linked. 'They never say anything. Take McDaid. We got the wrong guy, but the police said nothing.' This was nonsense. Just the previous month, at Terry's inquest, the RUC had made it clear that he had no involvement with the IRA.[55]

Nelson's provocative hints that Sergeant Jones was in some way partly to blame for Terry McDaid's mistaken murder came in another casual conversation after his formal interview under caution, in which Nelson clammed up completely: 'on the advice of my solicitor I have nothing to say'.[56]

It seems that the army had 'consciously and comprehensively' bought his silence, even to the point of preventing him from co-operating any further with a criminal inquiry.[57]

One of the more incendiary revelations in our 'Dirty War' *Panorama* was the fact that besides targeting Patrick Finucane, Nelson also had some involvement in targeting another solicitor, the doyen of Belfast's criminal lawyers, Paddy McGrory, who'd represented the families of the three IRA members shot dead in March 1988 by the SAS in Gibraltar. The SAS opened fire without warning after being told the IRA was planning a car-bomb attack on a military parade. After the shootings, Spanish police found a car with bomb-making equipment just across the border and, in another rented car in Marbella, 140lbs of Semtex and 200 rounds of Kalashnikov ammunition.[58]

The UDA was also targeting a third solicitor, Oliver Kelly. The threats to all three men, weeks in advance of Finucane's murder, were registered by both MI5 and the RUC. To this day, neither organisation has satisfactorily explained its failure to respond adequately to the escalating threats to the lives of the three solicitors. Stories implying active allegiance to the republican cause over and above their duty as lawyers to their clients, many of whom were IRA members held on terrorism charges, had appeared in loyalist publications. This seems to have been a consequence of MI5's so-called 'propaganda initiatives',[59] which disseminated information through its agents in loyalist organisations principally directed at undermining PIRA figures assessed as either 'unrecruitable as agents or who had been approached and had refused'.[60] It was also extended to targeting prominent figures in the broader nationalist and republican communities,[61] including Finucane, McGrory and Kelly, by overtly identifying them with their clients, despite knowing that all three lawyers were under threat from loyalist paramilitaries.[62]

In December 1988 – two months before Finucane was shot – the UDA spoof *An Phobcrapt* had been published. The caption on one image read: 'IRA volunteer Patrick McGeown, along with IRA solicitor Pat O'Cocaine, walks free from Belfast's Crumlin Road courthouse after miraculously beating the rap due to "lack of evidence".' McGeown had been charged with helping to lynch two army corporals.[63] This recklessly inflammatory propaganda strategy was terminated only after MI5 acknowledged they risked legitimising the named individuals for assassination by loyalist murder gangs, a danger that must have been as obvious to the initiative's midwives as the nose on their faces. Yet it appears to have taken the murder of Patrick Finucane for this reality to sink in.

The precise details of MI5's propaganda initiatives remain classified to this day; they are included in the material withheld from the three inquiries by Sir John Stevens and also kept from Mr Justice Cory. The programme's existence was only disclosed to Sir Desmond de Silva QC for his 2012 Review of Finucane's murder. Sir Desmond gave few details as to precisely who the 'initiatives' had targeted, save that they 'included the dissemination of rumours' against both Kelly and McGrory, which 'added to and reinforced a variety of other conversations taking place within UDA circles at the time with regard to the supposed allegiances of these solicitors'.[64]

One of those 'conversations' was reported back to MI5 by one of its agents in the UDA. On 19 December 1988, there had been a UDA meeting to discuss killing McGrory, Kelly and '"the shoot to kill" solicitor'. A telegram was sent to MI5's Assessments Group, which reported to those in charge of MI5 Irish operations.[65] MI5 told the Cory Review it hadn't acted on this threat because it was 'by no means clear' who the '"shoot to kill" solicitor' was.[66] This claim was barely tenable, since an inquest in which Finucane was involved had been the subject of widespread media coverage and had looked into one of three notorious 'shoot to kill' incidents, in this particular case involving the RUC shooting dead three unarmed IRA men in a hail of 109 bullets. Finucane, on behalf of the family of the one of the dead IRA men, Gervaise McKerr, had just won a Court of Appeal judgment ruling that the officers were compellable witnesses at the inquest.[67]

By the time Finucane was shot, it was known by at least one journalist and the Irish ambassador to the UK that, the previous December, three prominent UDA gunmen being held in Castlereagh had been encouraged by their RUC interrogators to kill all three lawyers.[68] Only after Finucane's murder did the RUC respond to the threat to McGrory, despite MI5 having been alerted to this two months earlier, and only, it seems at the prompting of the Irish government, following a senior Irish government official's visit to McGrory at home on the day after Finucane was shot.[69] That evening the Irish ambassador in London made representations to the British Cabinet secretary, Sir Robin Butler.[70] The RUC offered McGrory an armed escort – which he declined. He did, however, apply for a personal protection weapon, but that took seven weeks to be approved, despite pleas by the Irish government to speed it up.[71] Kelly also declined an offer of RUC protection, apparently believing that moving home would be a safer bet. 'I wouldn't have wanted them to know about the detail of my personal security,' he said. 'They were not to be trusted.'[72] In fact, the threats to the lives of McGrory and Kelly were considerably more serious than ever they were made aware of.

On 16 February, four days after Finucane was shot, a Special Branch source reported that three UDA men – Matt Kincaid, Jim Spence and Eric McKee – were overheard in a bar saying that McGrory and Kelly were 'next on the list'. The report was marked 'Limited Dissemination'.[73] Handwritten notes on Special Branch forms recorded the acronym 'PIRA' next to Kelly's name and 'PIRA/INLA Solicitor' next to McGrory's name, indicative of the fact that some branch officers had yet to fully appreciate the peril of associating lawyers so squarely with their clients in a society as divided as Northern Ireland.[74]

On 17 February, MI5's assessment of the threat to McGrory and Kelly said that 'the possibility of attacks against them remains'.[75] Yet neither McGrory nor Kelly was informed of these escalating threats because of the constraints on the dissemination of the intelligence. Referring to McGrory, MI5 acknowledged that the October 1988 edition of the *Ulster Magazine* had 'clearly identified' him as 'being of the same stuff as those killed by SAS and it was implied he deserved the same fate', while making no mention of the real possibility that one of the reasons McGrory had been so identified in the first place was thanks to MI5's propaganda campaign aimed at 'unnerving' lawyers whose clients included high-profile republicans on terrorism charges.[76]

Yet if MI5 had by then cottoned on to the risk facing McGrory and Kelly, the FRU seems not to have been particularly perturbed. On 10 July – five months after Finucane's murder – came a second threat to McGrory's life. Nelson reported that a UDA contact had given him a piece of paper referring to 'P.J. McGrory [who] spends a lot of time in the "'Chester" [bar and restaurant] late afternoon in company with Pascal O'Hare, (Sos) [solicitor] and 'every Sunday … visites [*sic*] the Kitchen Bar … the car (merc) out of the road i.e. unproted [*sic*], he is always with is [*sic*] son (also Sos).'[77]

Yet the FRU did not pass this on to Special Branch, depriving the RUC of the option of warning McGrory or taking further protective measures. The FRU later justified their failure by saying Nelson hadn't regarded McGrory as a target, though this completely ignored Nelson's reckless habit of proliferating targets to other murder gangs as he saw fit without notifying his handlers. There was yet a further threat to McGrory's life in October 1989, this time from the UVF, which again the RUC failed to warn him about. The then deputy head of Special Branch, Brian Fitzsimons, asked that Chief Constable Sir Jack Hermon's morning briefing be notified of the threat. Whether Hermon was consulted is unclear, but the outcome is not: a note in the Threat Book recorded, 'NFA [No Further Action] on Fitzsimons' instructions'. Despite all the threats to McGrory's life, the Special Branch Threat Book contained only one reference to him being targeted and this didn't appear until October 1989, some eight months after the first warning was received.[78]

McGrory survived the threats to his life only to die prematurely three days before Christmas 1994, a considerable loss to the law and to the search for peace, with his efforts behind the scenes to persuade the IRA to end violence. The Taoiseach Albert Reynolds flew by private helicopter to attend his funeral on Christmas Eve. The following month, Stevens submitted the final report of his second inquiry to the DPP in Belfast. In February 1995, the DPP issued a direction of no prosecutions,[79] a supersonically swift response compared to the more glacial pace of its cash-strapped replacement, renamed the Public Prosecution Service in 2005. Stevens later remarked to me that a potential prosecution had come 'within that much' (holding up his thumb and forefinger close together) of happening.[80]

As with Stevens 1, the public was to be told none of the details. The report of Stevens 2 was classified 'Top Secret' and remains so to this day, despite much of its content being relatively mundane. In his March 2024 interim Kenova report, Jon Boutcher argued that, 'at the very least', Stevens 2's principal conclusions and recommendations could be declassified and made public without damaging national security.[81] MI5's tendency to over-classification highlights how embedded deploying NCND has become in closing down the uglier side of the conflict's legacy, thus evading embarrassment.

One thing the public is certainly entitled to know is exactly who in the military chain of command was ultimately responsible for Nelson being retained as an agent year after year, knowing that he was motivated by wanting to kill republicans and having materially increased the UDA's capacity to do so. The answer is that no one has ever accepted responsibility – neither Nelson's handlers at the bottom of the rung, nor the officers at the very top, nor any of the ranks in between. In overall charge for most of the relevant period as GOC in Northern Ireland was General Sir John 'Muddy' Waters. He was receiving reports from the CLF, also a general, who in turn was receiving reports from another general, ACOS G2, who was being briefed by both the FRU operations officer and its CO, Colonel Kerr, who himself was being briefed by the FRU operations officer and the OC of the East Det FRU, who was being briefed in detail by Nelson's handlers.[82] Save for a small number of handlers, none of them appears to have raised concerns about the degree of criminality in which Nelson had become involved.[83]

The MoD considered the question of command and control three days after our 'Dirty War' *Panorama* was broadcast in June 1992 – and dismissed it with a shrug. Secretary of State for Defence Tom King was told that because of Nelson's senior position in the UDA, he was 'bound to be involved with major crime', which inevitably involved 'difficult judgments' in handling him.[84] That was certainly true. Yet set to one side had been the CLF's July 1986 FRU Directive, which had required Kerr to inform ACOS G2 if 'there is any possibility of a source becoming involved in criminality'.[85] Also apparently ignored was the rule that no operation that didn't conform to this directive or to the instructions for source handling was to be carried out without the CLF's prior authority.[86] This was a classic example of the chasm separating the theoretical from the practical in getting reliable actionable intelligence from within the heart of a terrorist organisation.

Questioned during Stevens 1 and 2, it became apparent that probably neither ACOS G2 nor the CLF knew exactly what Nelson had been up to because, they said, neither of them had received the CFs setting out the extent of his criminality. Nor, on the admission of Kerr and his operations officer, had they sought authorisation for Nelson's involvement in criminality.[87] None of this appears to have troubled General Sir John Wilsey, Waters' successor as GOC Northern Ireland, however. After considering the allegations against the FRU, Wilsey said he was satisfied with their conduct.[88] This was despite Attorney General Sir Patrick Mayhew having told Waters' boss, Defence Secretary King, the previous year that he'd been 'much troubled by the relationship between the Army and Nelson'.[89] As Sir Desmond de Silva QC concluded, the 'Army and the MoD appeared to be in denial about the implications of the Nelson case'.[90]

As for MI5, besides having access to FRU files – and said to be technically their owner – it also had an officer embedded in the army's All-Source Intelligence Cell in HQNI.[91] However, MI5 claimed to have only very limited knowledge of Nelson's activities from perusing only the FRU MISRs summarising Nelson's CFs, almost never the CFs themselves, and to have had no involvement in how the FRU ran the agent.[92] Colonel Kerr, by contrast, said MI5 supervised the handling of Nelson and also 'knew of my approach to the application of the [CLF's] Directive and Instructions and they never suggested it was wrong'.[93]

Kerr is correct, in as much as MI5 knew at the outset of Nelson's second stint with the FRU that he had been targeting republicans with an 'inappropriate degree of enthusiasm for carrying out "justifiable" UDA targeting'.[94] So it is hard to believe the service was unaware that he and the FRU were sometimes breaking the law.[95] De Silva concluded that, at a minimum, MI5 'failed to carry out its advisory and co-ordinating duties adequately in the Nelson case'.[96]

Although Stevens submitted his final report on Stevens 2 to the DPP in Belfast in January 1995, it brought no end to the Russian dolls to which Detective Sergeant Benwell had likened the investigation, particularly in the case of Patrick Finucane's murder. The more Stevens had plotted out, the more it became clear there were more questions than answers, particularly in relation to the role of Special Branch: what they knew, when they knew it, and what they did or didn't do about it. Of particular interest was the fact that McKee had tasked Nelson with gathering targeting information on Finucane in January 1989, after police officers had encouraged a UDA gunman they were interrogating to kill Finucane because he was 'the brains behind the PIRA'; also that the branch knew, through one of their many agents – Billy Stobie, a UDA quartermaster – that an attack against a 'top PIRA man' was imminent using a 9mm Browning pistol that Stobie had been asked to hand over to the hit team.[97]

With so many ends yet to be tied up, Geoff Seed and I set to work again, in an attempt to put together a second *Panorama* programme. We secured access to a substantial amount of new information, much of it too sensitive at the time for the authors of the documents to talk about openly on TV. So, we turned to newspapers, and in March 1998, the *Sunday Telegraph* published our report containing extracts of the classified FRU records of Nelson's meetings with his handlers. We disclosed for the first time how Nelson had been recruited to professionalise the UDA's targeting, so that – as one CF put it – 'sectarian killings are not carried out, but that proper targeting of Provisional IRA members takes place prior to any shooting'.[98] Even for a newspaper normally loyal to the security forces, the British Army in cahoots with an ex-soldier jailed for murderous sectarian bigotry was too serious to be ignored. 'This is the first time that there has been any substantial evidence to support the extremely serious allegation that the army helped loyalist paramilitaries decide whom to kill,' said the *Sunday Telegraph*'s editorial, headlined 'Not above the law'.

By now the Irish government was taking a keen interest in developments, as was Jane Winter, the unfaltering director of the British Irish Rights Watch (BIRW) NGO. Much of the detail that Geoff and I had amassed was extremely complex, but Jane had both the appetite for detail and a scrupulous regard for facts. I came to trust her implicitly and so I shared our material with her. On 12 February 1999, the tenth anniversary of Finucane's murder, based largely on our material, Jane delivered a sixty-four-page confidential report to the British and Irish governments and to the United Nations' Special Rapporteur on the Independence of Judges and Lawyers. Called 'Deadly Intelligence: State Involvement in Loyalist Murder in Northern Ireland', it set out in forensic detail what only a written report can do, focusing in depth on Nelson's role in and his handlers' response to the murder of three innocent victims: Patrick Finucane, Terence McDaid and Gerard Slane.[99] In a letter to new Secretary of State for Northern Ireland Mo Mowlam, Irish Minister for Foreign Affairs Liz O'Donnell enclosed her officials' own assessment of the BIRW report, saying that 'the case for a public inquiry' into Finucane's murder was 'compelling'.[100]

Tasked by the NIO with reviewing 'Deadly Intelligence', Anthony Langdon, a former senior Home Office official, presented a report to Mowlam that appears to have contributed to John Stevens being called back to Belfast for the third time,[101] as announced by the RUC on 18 March.[102] The British government told the Irish government that the decision had been the RUC chief constable's and his alone. The Finucane family would have preferred a public inquiry because, like many relatives of the conflict's murdered dead, Geraldine Finucane wanted the truth delivered through full disclosure and compellable witnesses, rather than 'justice' delivered through yet another criminal inquiry with a narrower remit. Neither option was palatable to the securocracy, though if there had to be an inquiry, better it was criminal, because disclosure would be so much more limited. Geraldine was supported by the Irish government, which suspected the securocracy had taken control and were playing for time.[103] 'It's a delaying tactic,' said one senior official in the Department of Foreign Affairs. 'They don't want an inquiry. The Brits are squirming over Finucane.'[104] The British responded that they weren't ruling out a public inquiry, but the criminal inquiry had to be completed first.

There was some confusion over the remit Flanagan had given Stevens, which was to conduct a criminal investigation into the murder of Finucane, whereas Stevens had said at the end of his second inquiry that the killing had been 'fully investigated'.[105] A junior defence minister, Doug Henderson, also told Parliament that Finucane's murder had indeed been investigated.[106] Stevens' terms of reference were later clarified: he was to investigate the contents of Jane Winter's report and review 'in its entirety' his and the RUC's previous investigations into Finucane's murder.[107]

Judging by the authorities' initial response to Geraldine Finucane's ongoing civil action against the MoD and Brian Nelson, the omens for the disclosure of all the information held in Special Branch, FRU and MI5 files on the murder were unpromising. Her lawyer, the late Eamon McMenamin, told me the MoD had disclosed a mere five documents that were considered relevant and material to the proceedings. Furthermore, the Crown Solicitor's Office had intimated there was really nothing in the files that the MoD had reviewed that pointed to collusion. I knew that to be untrue, having myself been aware of many of the documents. I informed McMenamin of this and gave him a list of suggested topics on which he might seek further discovery. His application succeeded. On 25 March, Master Wilson, in the High Court of Northern Ireland, ordered the MoD to make further disclosures based on my list and for the MoD permanent secretary to verify that 'all relevant documents which are or have been at any time in the possession, custody or power of the ministry' were disclosed. On 20 May, thirty-six extracts from CFs and MISRs, and twenty-three handler statements were disclosed to McMenamin.[108]

Within five weeks, Stevens himself was revisited by the attritional war that had dogged him since he'd set foot in Belfast a decade earlier. Ken Barrett, a member of the three-man gang that murdered Finucane, had proudly confessed to CID Detective Sergeant Jonty Brown on the evening of 3 October 1991. With Brown in the car was his namesake from Special Branch, Detective Constable Ian Brown. On behalf of the CID, Jonty Brown was investigating the Finucane murder; on behalf of the branch, Ian Brown was trying to recruit Barrett as an agent. The winner was never seriously in doubt. Consistent with the Walker Directive of 1981, priority was given to intelligence gathering over locking up one of Finucane's killers and Jonty Brown was ordered to cease investigating Barrett for the murder. 'Move away from it [the CID investigation]', Jonty Brown was told,[109] in a decision made at Special Branch superintendent level.[110]

Fast forward to 27 April 1999, when the branch (at a level senior to Detective Constable Ian Brown) made a desperate but crass attempt to cover this up. Jonty Brown arrived for interview by Stevens at his office in Seapark. Having signed a statement to say he was sure of his recollection that Barrett had confessed on 3 October 1991 while he was in the car with Detective Constable Ian Brown, Jonty Brown was then played a tape the branch had given Stevens, claiming it was a recording of the 3 October meeting. Jonty Brown was astonished to hear it contained no confession from Barrett, yet it showed him talking in the car to Jonty as if it was 3 October. Unbeknownst to both Jonty Brown and Stevens, the branch had switched the tape of 3 October with the tape of Jonty Brown's second meeting with Barrett on 10 October. The switch appears to have been a ploy to persuade Stevens that Jonty Brown was a liar who had invented Barrett's confession. But for the fact that Jonty Brown noticed Barrett referring to two murders that had happened just hours before the meeting on 10 October, he would never have spotted the switch and would have been charged by Stevens with attempting to pervert the course of justice.[111] The 3 October tape has never been found, its disappearance yet further evidence of how the Walker doctrine had been corrupted to ensure that the CID never investigated Barrett.[112]

Two years later, over the course of twelve meetings with Barrett, he boasted to me and my *Panorama* colleague Eamon Hardy in another car, this time fitted with a secret microphone: '… the hit went down. I wasn't arrested.' Barrett also disclosed that loyalists being questioned by the RUC were encouraged to kill Finucane. 'See to be honest, Finucane would have been alive today if the Peelers hadn't interfered,' he said. 'They know who killed Pat Finucane … They orchestrated it from the start … The Peelers wanted him whacked, we whacked him and that is the end of the story.' Barrett, a psychotic killer who, when I asked him how many people he'd killed, held up both hands showing all fingers and thumbs, also explained how Nelson had been up to his neck in targeting Finucane.[113] Our evidence contributed significantly to Barrett's conviction for Finucane's murder in 2004.[114]

Nelson will forever be associated with the murder of Pat Finucane, yet his legacy is much wider. While the way he was run as an agent was a disaster, the quality of his intelligence was high, yet it was never properly exploited by Special Branch to save lives, and the FRU seemed strangely indifferent to that. Had his intelligence been more fully exploited, several of the murders in which Nelson was involved could have been prevented and their perpetrators taken off the streets. But Walker had prioritised source protection and 'building pictures' over disruption and criminal justice, and so the murderous West Belfast UDA was left alone while Nelson was in place.

Was this because some of the murderers with whom Nelson colluded were, like him, state agents? That appears to have been the case. 'We came to realise that almost everyone Nelson was reporting on was an agent working for a different agency,' said a source who had access to classified files.[115]

Chapter Fifteen

6126 – A Legal Charade

ACCORDING TO THE CABINET OFFICE, the policy of successive governments of giving evasive answers to questions about the intelligence services by 'neither confirming nor denying' is invoked only when it's in the public interest to protect sensitive information.[1] And it is obviously right that information which genuinely undermines national security needs to be protected; also that what passes between state agents and their handlers needs to remain secret while they are operational and, in some cases, long after that. But should this apply to every case, irrespective of the extent to which the state allowed them to engage in serious criminality, including murder?

PSNI Chief Constable Jon Boutcher and his successor as head of Operation Kenova, Sir Iain Livingstone, have themselves often relied upon NCND in their policing careers and are firm supporters of the principle behind the policy. This is all the more reason why their opposition to the blanket way MI5 has applied NCND to all cases of unsolved murders involving agents in the Northern Ireland conflict should be taken seriously. NCND has morphed into an 'implacable dogma or mantra with the qualities of a stone wall,' says Boutcher,[2] nowhere more so than in the case of Stakeknife, which he says demonstrates just how 'untenable' the policy has become, bordering on 'farce ... a pantomime'. For, as Livingstone says, 'Neither Jon nor I are constitutional vandals. We are part of the infrastructure.'[3]

For the last quarter of a century, ever since Stakeknife was exposed as Freddie Scappaticci, successive secretaries of state have been beguiled by

MI5's insistence that to confirm his identity would pose a threat to national security. Throughout that period the state has doggedly continued to neither confirm nor deny that Stakeknife is Freddie Scappaticci, even though the world and its wife have known that he is, and even though he's dead and was involved in the multiple murders and sometimes torture of fellow agents. Nonetheless, 'the agent known as Stakeknife' has been the only form of words which ministers have permitted Boutcher, Livingstone and government officials to use when referring to Scappaticci. Under pressure from both police chiefs and the MPs on the Northern Ireland Affairs Committee, the government now says it is reviewing the position. but as this book goes to press, the status quo remains. Even if it is finally lifted in Scappaticci's case, there is no expectation the lid won't stay firmly closed on legacy cases yet to be resolved even as they fade into history.

In emphasising the importance of applying NCND consistently, Cabinet Office 'guidance' argues that 'to depart from the NCND principle in one case … would create a clear risk of serious harm to essential UK national security interests. It could, furthermore, potentially put lives at risk.'[4] The case law most often cited by government in support of this 'principle' is Lord Justice Carswell's 2003 judgment arising from Scappaticci's bogus application to disapply the use of NCND in his case in his attempt to convince the public that he was not Stakeknife.

Prior to that judgment, there were many examples of the principle being dispensed with when officials considered it appropriate, including in Northern Ireland, when the RUC had both denied and occasionally even confirmed claims, including by the IRA, that an individual was an agent.[5] MI5's argument in favour of consistency appears to be that, however seriously an agent may have broken the law, the greater public interest lies in neither confirming nor denying whether that agent has been involved in murder, lest this should discourage the recruitment of agents or stop those already in place from freely supplying valuable intelligence, particularly in the fight against terrorism. That is the essence of the Carswell judgment on which MI5 and ministers have relied. 'The breaking of promises of anonymity given to agents would also be likely to make existing and prospective agents unwilling to cooperate with us,' says MI5.[6]

With his long experience of covert policing, and running agents during investigations into Islamist terrorism and serious crime, Boutcher insists there is no empirical evidence demonstrating a link between the recruitment and retention of agents and NCND.[7] He argues that MI5's unyielding application of NCND in the case of Stakeknife, and other cases involving state agents in some of Northern Ireland's 1,200 unsolved killings, has become not only futile but also counterproductive. Secrecy, he says, feeds suspicion that NCND is being abused to hide criminality, including murder, by the security forces,[8] deepening mistrust in both the government and the PSNI, and running completely counter to 'lots of warm words about legacy' and the importance of reconciliation.[9]

Arguing before the Supreme Court in June 2025 for the preservation of NCND at the long delayed inquest into the brutal murder in 1994 of Liam Thompson (25), in which a state agent (or agents) are suspected of having been involved, Sir James Eadie KC, for the secretary of state, acknowledged that NCND was 'not an absolute' and that there were times when national security may be 'better protected by limited disclosure'. This concession has not been applied in Thompson's case, nor any case that has come before the Northern Ireland courts in recent years. Sir James said a 'gist' or summary of an intelligence report approved by Boutcher should never have been disclosed by the coroner, despite the fact that neither Boutcher nor the coroner were arguing for identifying by name any agent (or agents) involved in Thompson's murder, but merely for confirmation of the fact of state involvement without any further details.

To most reasonable people, this might seem to be an entirely reasonable proposition. Not to Sir James, however, who spent the best part of the morning session using his silken advocacy to develop a defence of NCND as not just 'some separate thing' limited to protecting agents, but as part of the more multifaceted concept of protecting 'national security', which required 'expert assessment by those with experience, day in, day out'. It was all rather vague, although one imagines the chief constable was just such a person. Not in the eyes of Sir James, it seems. He forcefully argued that what is in the public interest to disclose should always rest with the Northern Ireland secretary, never with the chief constable, not even in the case of intelligence generated decades ago by his police force and therefore inherited and owned by him.[10] Sitting silently by Eadie's side, occasionally nodding in assent, was

Tony McGleenan KC, who has steadfastly held the disclosure line on behalf of the Crown Solicitor's Office in Belfast, instructed by the state, typically the NIO, the secretary of state or MI5, depending on the issue at hand.

The strict imposition of NCND on Operation Kenova has meant that Sir Iain Livingstone is not only forbidden from telling relatives of victims of Stakeknife that he was Freddie Scappaticci, but also whether any of his twenty-nine murdered and abducted victims were also agents. This stance deprives those victims who weren't agents of the relief from the stigma their families have borne for decades. It is as if their loss and decades-long community isolation are not grief enough. Take, for example, David McVeigh, a forty-one-year-old father of three, whose bound and gagged body was found on the Flagstaff Road near Carlingford, 200 yards north of the County Louth border, on 9 September 1986. He'd been shot in the head with a high velocity weapon, and the IRA sent a message to his family claiming he'd confessed to being an informer. His body showed signs of cigarette burns to his thighs, legs and right buttock, suggesting his confession was forced under severe duress.[11] According to Kenova, Stakeknife was involved in McVeigh's murder, including being present at the beginning of his interrogation.[12] NCND has prevented Kenova from telling families like McVeigh's whether their murdered relative was or was not an informer.[13] All that Kenova has been permitted to say is that confessions under duress are unreliable and that not all of Stakeknife's victims were agents. In McVeigh's case, Scappaticci is reported to have told the family bluntly that he had been shot because he had confessed to being an informer.[14] Kenova told McVeigh's family that they believe the reason there was no attempt to bring the perpetrators to justice was 'in order to protect an informant' – presumably Scappaticci – despite the branch knowing which ISU members were involved in his interrogation within days of his murder.[15]

NCND appears to have its origins in the Central Intelligence Agency (CIA), whose own application of the principle has sometimes been as bizarre as it has been in Northern Ireland.[16] The song 'Wind of Change' by the Scorpions, which celebrates the fall of the Berlin Wall and the end of the Cold War, has long been rumoured to be a CIA creation to persuade young Russians of the liberating impact of capitalism and democracy. When a journalist put that question to the CIA, hoping that America's robust Freedom of Information Act would entitle him to a clear answer, the one he got was anything but: 'We can neither confirm nor deny,' said the CIA.[17] Still, in the CIA's case, at least it recognises how applying NCND can sometimes come across as farcical. In 2014, when at 6.49 p.m. on 6 June the CIA joined Twitter, its first tweet was a drole: 'We can neither confirm nor deny that this is our first tweet.'[18]

During the Northern Ireland conflict, NCND was applied many times in the criminal courts in the form of Public Interest Immunity (PII) certificates signed by ministers to prevent information from being disclosed during proceedings, not just to conceal the involvement of an agent but also to protect spy tradecraft and every aspect of intelligence, however mundane. As mentioned, there was the occasional departure from NCND. Today, however, in legacy proceedings in Northern Ireland, NCND has been applied with a 'much heavier hand' than in any other part of the UK, to the extent that it has become a proxy 'for preventing national embarrassment, rather than protecting national security,' says Sir Iain Livingstone.[19]

That embarrassment is the slow but inexorable unravelling of the counter-insurgency policy upon which the fight against terrorism was reorganised in 1981 following the intervention of MI5's Patrick Walker, who was not a police officer, but whose recommendations were enthusiastically adopted by the RUC and supported by MI5 and the FRU. The singular importance of intelligence in the fight against terrorism became an RUC mantra chanted time and again by successive chief constables. By prioritising intelligence gathering and protection of sources over the pursuit of criminal justice, the Walker doctrine has come to be seen by Boutcher, de Silva, Cory, Stevens and many others as having got its priorities back to front.

The way Walker was applied in 1981 to the first of three loyalist conspiracies to murder Patrick Finucane is just one of many examples of the intelligence services consciously choosing not to warn the intended victim or to arrest the perpetrator(s) for fear of compromising a valued source. In Finucane's case, it was a decision taken by all three intelligence services prioritising the protection of an MI5 source. 'For all concerned the balance of advantage lay with preserving [the agent] as a source for as long as possible,' recorded an MI5 note. 'Everyone present agreed …'[20] Nor was a warning given or interdiction actioned on receipt of intelligence of another UDA assassination plot against the solicitor four years later.[21]

In Scappaticci's case, the attritional war to prevent disclosure over decisions to protect him at the expense of the lives of lesser-valued agents goes back to August 1999, when the late Liam Clarke, Northern Ireland editor of *The Sunday Times* identified the existence of an agent codenamed 'Stakeknife'. In fact, Clarke had first heard the name 'Stakeknife' in the early 1980s, when a loose-tongued military intelligence officer on the G2 staff at a boozy press reception hosted by the GOC told him he was 'the army's top agent within the IRA'.[22]

In his 1999 article, Clarke described Stakeknife as 'the crown jewel of British intelligence in Ulster, a man at the heart of the IRA's war effort who had to be kept happy at all costs'.[23] Since being outed in 2003, various hypotheses have emerged within West Belfast that the code name was a media invention or, alternatively, that Stakeknife was a generic name to cover several agents. Neither is true. In the FRU files, the code name began with the spelling 'Steaknife' and morphed into 'Stakeknife',[24] although Scappaticci was also allocated a variety of other code names.[25] As to his importance as an agent, credible evidence has subsequently emerged of agents even better-placed than him, although there can be no doubt about his high value. Often referred to as having been head of the ISU, the surviving intelligence files do not record Scappaticci holding that position; while he may have been the ISU's foremost interrogator,[26] he remained deputy to John Joe Magee, both effectively departing the ISU stage in January 1990 after Sandy Lynch was rescued.

As speculation grew about the identity of Stakeknife – and what he was alleged to have done – the MoD sought assurances from Special Branch that he 'would not be vulnerable to the allegations being made'. MI5's resettlement unit said that while it couldn't prevent him being interviewed were there to be a criminal investigation, he would be provided with a lawyer who would advise him to exercise his right of silence.[27]

The authorities clearly regarded it as inevitable that sooner or later Clarke's source would name Scappaticci, since they knew it was an ex-FRU handler going under the name of Martin Ingram; the intelligence services soon identified that the pseudonym belonged to Ian Hurst. He alleges they 'burgled' his home in the Irish Republic, taking an early draft of a book he later co-authored about Stakeknife.[28] The first of a series of injunctions to delay the inevitable, against Hurst, Clarke and the *Sunday People* newspaper, which also took up the Stakeknife story, soon followed.[29]

Stevens 3, meanwhile, quietly absorbed Stakeknife into their remit under their terms of reference for the Finucane investigation, which allowed them to include 'any matter elicited during its progress which appears … to be linked or otherwise connected to it'.[30] That 'link' was the fact that both Brian Nelson and Freddie Scappaticci had been recruited and run by the FRU, not that the latter had breathed a word of Scappaticci's existence to Stevens 1 when detectives had uncovered the rampant criminality of Nelson a decade earlier.

The expansion of Stevens 3 led to an abrupt end to a weekend's leave for several officers, including the inquiry's operational commander, Hugh Orde, then a Metropolitan Police deputy assistant commissioner, and another Met officer, Detective Chief Inspector Phil James. On arrival at Heathrow early one Saturday morning, Orde was called by Stevens and told to about-turn back to Belfast. Stevens had just learned that some hitherto undisclosed FRU files had been located at Army HQNI in Northern Ireland.

Orde recalls that, on arrival at Thiepval Barracks, his search party faced 'what can only be described as organised obstruction'. A 'middle ranking officer in his pyjamas and dressing gown, accompanied by two Labradors' made Orde and his officers 'go through every security check, photograph, etc. that you can be made to do'.[31] The search party did recover some documents, including a file on Scappaticci, but they were mostly MISRs that the FRU had sent to Special Branch, instead of the vastly more detailed CFs, which had comprehensively recorded what passed between Scappaticci and his handlers.[32] The army maintained that the CFs had been destroyed,[33] in accordance with a five-year non-retention directive. Given that one MoD assessment of Stakeknife was that he was 'one of the most productive long-term agents run by any agency in Northern Ireland', it seems extraordinary that the army did not retain a record of his reporting.[34] But the army had learned its lesson from the Nelson debacle, when Stevens 1 gained access to the full archive of CFs, which had done so much damage.

Not for the first (or last) time, Gordon Kerr, FRU CO for the last three years of Scappaticci's time as Agent 6126, became a key focus for Stevens. By now promoted to brigadier as military attaché in Beijing, Kerr fulminated at being called back for interview for the umpteenth time. The interview in the latter half of 2002 at Kensington police station lasted several days. 'He was an angry man,' recalls Phil James,[35] much of his ire provoked by repeating what he had told the previous two Stevens inquiries, that running both Nelson and Scappaticci as agents had been done with the knowledge and authority of MI5. In effect, Kerr was saying that he was the 'collector of intelligence' for the Security Service. 'I collect for MI5, and they take it away. There was political authority for what we did. They are the people you need to talk to.'[36] MI5 has consistently rejected Kerr's version of history, but Kenova would find that there was more than a grain of truth in it.[37]

By now, Commander Dave Cox had replaced Orde as Stevens 3 operational chief, the latter having been appointed chief constable of the fledgling PSNI. In his new role, Orde was horrified by the sheer numbers of agents on Special Branch's books, and one of his first acts was to address the legacy of Walker by removing 40 per cent of them. 'Are you guys running murderers?' Orde asked his senior branch officers. 'Well, we're not running boy scouts,' came the reply.[38] It had 'become the norm to disrupt rather than arrest,' says Orde. 'It became culturally the way forward and we had to change that.'[39] In the specific case of the UDA, so prolific had been agent penetration, one senior officer mused, that the police could be accused of actually running the organisation.[40]

Cox had been assured by the army that there were no more papers to be disclosed. However, in December 2002, he told the DPP in Belfast that this wasn't the case because Stevens 3 had learned that Stakeknife-related documents had been copied to MI5. Due to a 'lack of clarity' about the extent to which MI5 had been involved with FRU's agent running, John Stevens had written to MI5 seeking their co-operation.[41] Although MI5 had issued a directive to its staff to co-operate, in practice that wasn't how things were working out, as Stevens himself acknowledged.[42] The three intelligence agencies 'appeared to be positioning themselves,' said a source familiar with the discussions.[43] That was certainly Phil James' experience when he channelled questions through one of MI5's lawyers, the late Andrew Slade, who had joined the Security Service from the Metropolitan Police Special Branch. 'I once asked him: "Andrew, how do I know I've got everything from you?" to which Slade replied, "Phil, you don't!"'[44] So frustrated were the detectives at being drip fed, that at one stage there was talk of getting a warrant to search MI5.[45] Had they done so, they would have found two lever arch files running to some 800 pages which had been prepared for the purposes of dealing with Stevens, but for some reason were never disclosed.[46]

Parallel to Stevens 3 was a judge-led paper review of whether the material Stevens had gathered over Patrick Finucane's murder merited a public inquiry. If the judge found that it did, Prime Minister Tony Blair had pledged in August 2001 to the Irish government and to Parliament that he would grant one. MI5 wasn't happy about that. The judge heading the review was an eminent member of the Canadian Supreme Court, the Honourable Peter deCarteret Cory.[47] Blair's undertaking, however, had been reluctantly given, a last-ditch quid pro quo to gain nationalist support for policing reforms, the peace process having reached one of its many critical junctures.

We now know that Blair very much hoped Mr Justice Cory's conclusion would *not* lead to a 'full-scale' public inquiry, because days before Blair had given his undertaking to Dublin and to Parliament, MI5 had raised what Blair's chief of staff, Jonathan Powell, described as an 'awkward security dimension', which Blair had discussed with MI5's Director General, Stephen Lander.[48] What exactly that 'dimension' was is not revealed in the declassified papers. Both Blair and his successor, Gordon Brown, duly backtracked on the promise of a public inquiry, despite Cory having recommended in 2004 that there should be one, having satisfied himself there was 'strong evidence' that the FRU, Special Branch and MI5 had committed 'collusive acts' in Finucane's murder.[49]

In 2011, Prime Minister David Cameron was similarly reluctant when he invited the Finucane family to No. 10 and offered a substitute to a public inquiry: yet another review of Finucane's assassination, this time by Sir Desmond de Silva QC, a distinguished criminal barrister who had also served as the United Nations chief war crimes prosecutor and had brought Charles Taylor, the former president of Liberia, to justice.[50] There were 'people in buildings all around here [10 Downing Street] who won't let it [a public inquiry] happen', witnesses to the meeting recall Cameron saying with a sweep of his arm.[51] Precisely what the 'awkward security dimension' raised by 'people all around' No. 10 was will presumably be one of the issues at the public inquiry into Finucane's murder, to which the current Northern Ireland secretary, Hilary Benn, has finally agreed. Benn candidly acknowledged the 'plain fact' that Blair's commitment to hold an inquiry remained 'unfulfilled'.[52]

From all that happened, one thing seems clear: MI5 was extremely apprehensive about the prospect of the review by Justice Cory and his co-counsel, Renee Pomerance. Both Canadians had been warned they might be 'followed, listened to, and subject to harassment'.[53] The warning seems prescient. According to Pomerance, 'watchers' stared intently as they read through documents at secure locations or walked to the bathroom. Cory himself told me on one occasion that he'd actually been 'escorted to the "John", the first time it happened since I was a kid'. He made a joke about it to his escort, who hadn't seen the funny side.[54] One agency extended a chilly reception, quite literally, when it sat them in a room so cold Pomerance had to wear gloves to type on her laptop.

The first time Pomerance and Cory left their London office in Brook Street, Mayfair, to visit army headquarters in Northern Ireland, MI5 representatives are alleged to have descended unannounced on Brook Street, demanding Cory's staff turn over their hard drives 'in the interests of national security'.[55] That alerted MI5 to what was coming from Cory because his review was in draft. The drives were wiped clean and returned minus their content. MI5 has denied removing anything, insisting it was NIO officials who made the unannounced visit; apparently all MI5 did, it says, was occasionally advise Cory and his staff about 'protective security measures'. MI5 claims the hard drive content was merely transferred onto 'encrypted laptops' with the approval of Cory's secretariat.[56] The Honourable Renee Pomerance, today a youthful sixty-something with her faculties solidly intact, remains perfectly clear in her recollection that on their return from Northern Ireland, she and Cory were told by their staff that the officials who had removed the drives had announced themselves as being from MI5 and that the hard drives were returned without their content.[57]

I also recall John Stevens, then the Metropolitan Police commissioner, telling me that, at the time, Cory had complained furiously to him about the incident. Fortunately, Cory had taken Stevens' advice to duplicate his material and store it off-site. The commissioner was no more a man given to idle conspiratorial musings than Pomerance or Cory, the latter having distinguished himself not only in the Canadian Supreme Court but also as one of the Second World War's youngest bomber pilots. The fact that MI5 has form for a tenuous relationship with the truth, having recently been found to have lied to three different courts over its use of NCND (see Chapter 18),[58] must lend some credence to Cory and Pomerance's version of events.

Renee Pomerance had a particularly disconcerting experience arising from the theft of her handbag while she was working on the review. This could, of course, have been simple bad luck, save for the fact that it took her several weeks to get a replacement key to her mailbox at the apartment the government had rented for her, and, when she did, she found that several weeks' worth of mail had been opened.[59] When it came to security vetting Cory's report, MI5 demanded that the ten full pages worth of redactions they required should be disguised in the published report as just a single line. Cory dug his heels in on that and won.[60]

While MI5 was making life difficult for Cory, in Belfast the DPP, Sir Alasdair Fraser and his staff were being briefed about MI5's lack of co-operation over Stevens 3's inquiries into Scappaticci. Progress was so slow, and there were so many murders Scappaticci had potentially been involved in, that Phil James warned that the investigation should realistically be 'quantified in terms of years not months'.[61] Three days later, all hell broke loose.

At 8.10 on the evening of Saturday, 10 May 2003, a Belfast-based reporter, Greg Harkin, knocked on Scappaticci's door. Casually dressed in shorts, socks and a football T-shirt, Harkin says Scappaticci bid him welcome. 'Come on in, Greg,' he said, before Harkin had even identified himself as a reporter from the *Sunday People*, which might suggest that the visit was no surprise. Harkin showed Scappaticci a copy of the front page the paper was about to publish naming him as Stakeknife. Shaking his head, Scappaticci calmly insisted, 'I'm not the same Freddie Scappaticci that all these claims are being made about … I don't even know what this person Stakeknife was supposed to have done. I've never heard of it. What is he supposed to have done?'[62] Given that several newspapers, including Harkin's, had been running stories about the agent known as Stakeknife for almost four years, this was unconvincing. Scappaticci's unflappable demeanour was explained by the fact that earlier that week, Special Branch had warned him his cover was about to be blown, and he had resolved to bluff it out, confident that he could and utterly determined to stay in Belfast with his family for as long as possible.[63]

The branch had been alerted by the MoD, who'd been alerted by Neil Mackay of the Glasgow based *Sunday Herald*, whose lawyers had found an ingenious way around the various injunctions preventing disclosure of Stakeknife's identity. Three Sunday newspapers, normally rivals, had agreed on a carefully choreographed injunction-busting plan. Mackay would write the front-page story for the *Sunday Tribune* in Dublin, it being the sister paper to the *Sunday Herald*. The *Tribune* would name Stakeknife as Freddie Scappaticci, freeing up publication by the *Herald* in Glasgow and the *Sunday People* in London, because the *Tribune* publishing in a foreign jurisdiction was not bound by UK injunctions. This allowed UK-based newspapers to report what the *Tribune* reported, and the *Sunday World* in Belfast then followed suit. Publication by the UK papers was only a matter of minutes behind the *Tribune* because they all had their stories written, set and ready to go. This time, the Treasury solicitor had to concede defeat, so much so that there was an unusually co-operative tenor to communications between Mackay and the MoD, with the former being assured by the latter that Scappaticci had been taken safely out of Belfast. Mackay explained his, quite proper, concern: 'I didn't want to wake up in the morning and find the guy was dead. No story is worth that.'[64]

In fact, it would take the branch several more hours to persuade a highly resistant Scappaticci that he needed to get out of Belfast. Had his wife, Sheila, not been away on a pilgrimage, he would have had some explaining to do, for, while she knew about his role in the IRA, she was completely unaware of his secret life as a British spy. Finally, the branch prevailed and sometime on Sunday morning he was 'exfiltrated' in an operation designed to leave no trace of his departure. Typically, an agent being removed in this way would be required to walk or drive somewhere via his usual route, then jump into a windowless van at an opportune moment. Scappaticci was taken to the RAF section at Aldergrove International Airport and flown to RAF Lyneham in Wiltshire, where he was met by personnel from MI5's CRU. The tenor of MI5's advice was clear: the game was up and there was no going back.

Not for the first time, Scappaticci ignored MI5's advice, confident that the political climate was conducive to him bluffing it out. He was fretting about needing time to break the news to his wife, as well as the fact that his daughter was about to sit her A-levels. In any case, he correctly calculated that if he was shot, it would be obvious the IRA did it and was admitting that the man widely regarded as the head of its security had been a tout. To the street-smart, politically savvy Scappaticci, that prospect seemed remote, at least in the short term, because killing him while the IRA was under growing pressure to help restore the collapsed power-sharing executive risked fatally undermining its public commitment to work towards decommissioning its weapons and abandoning its military structure. In vain did MI5 try to tempt Scappaticci to stay with the offer of a holiday. The soccer-mad spy did, though, seek one favour: could they get him a ticket to the Champion's League?

By Tuesday 13 May Scappaticci had been stealthily 'infiltrated' back into Northern Ireland, where his immediate task was to rebut the BBC's evening bulletin forty-eight hours earlier by their well-informed security correspondent Barney Rowan stating that he'd left Northern Ireland. Sinn Féin, seemingly as anxious as Scappaticci to preserve the fiction that he was not Stakeknife, had also quoted his family as saying, 'contrary to media reports', Scappaticci had 'not left Belfast'.[65] This was nonsense.

All eyes – the branch, the IRA and the media – were now on Scappaticci, but it was the IRA that was conducting the orchestra, acutely aware of the lethal damage any hint of an admission that Scappaticci had been one of its biggest traitors posed to the leadership's authority and to continued support for the peace process from IRA rank-and-file volunteers. Immediately on his return, Scappaticci had arranged a meeting with senior IRA members Padraic Wilson and Martin 'Duckster' Lynch, assuring them he would do whatever was necessary to 'deflect the public and the press away from this horror show'.[66] He also readily accepted Gerry Kelly's advice to 'go to a solicitor and make a public statement'.[67] 'My client … is not "Stake Knife" [*sic*],' said solicitor Michael Flanigan, instructed by his newest customer. 'He has never been an informer, has never contacted the intelligence services …'[68]

Before lunch the next day, 14 May, at a meeting with a senior republican, Barney Rowan was asked if he could assemble a TV crew for a press conference that afternoon. He was also asked to 'pool it', meaning Rowan was the only journalist to be invited with a camera on condition he share the footage with other media outlets. Special Branch was also watching, because Rowan then got a call from the PSNI's Director of Communications, Austin Hunter, to say 'your man is going to appear'.[69] As Rowan arrived at Flanigan's office, Bobby Storey, head of IRA intelligence, was seen by two other BBC journalists to be watching.[70] At 3 p.m. Scappaticci sat down with Rowan and freelance journalist Anne Cadwallader. He put on a daring performance – tightly policed by his solicitor:

> Rowan: Why do you think this label Stakeknife has been attached to you?
>
> Scappaticci: I don't know. I'm sitting here today with my solicitor ... I am telling you I am not guilty of any of these allegations.
>
> Rowan: Just one final question – were you at any stage involved and a member of the IRA and involved in the Republican Movement?
>
> Scappaticci: [five second pause] I was involved in the Republican Movement thirteen years ago, but I have had no involvement these past thirteen years.
>
> Rowan: And what about the allegation?
>
> Flanigan: That's us finished ... that's us finished ... You got three questions in.[71]

Scappaticci's admission that he'd had no involvement with the IRA for thirteen years was confirmation that he'd been told to stand down after the Sandy Lynch debacle. That afternoon, a short distance away, Gerry Kelly held his own press conference demanding 'full disclosure of these faceless and unaccountable agencies' that had spread the stories about Scappaticci. He accused 'securocrats' of extensively briefing British and Irish journalists about Scappaticci and of making 'a raft of serious and unsubstantiated allegations'. This had been 'accepted and repeated as fact by a large section of the Media without question and without criticism.'[72] The following day, further signs of an acutely embarrassed IRA closing ranks came from Gerry Adams and Martin McGuinness, who also accused 'faceless securocrats in British intelligence' of being behind the media stories in an effort to discredit the republican movement. Danny Morrison lavished praise on Scappaticci as 'the only person with the courage to go before the cameras ... to issue a statement in his own name', unlike the 'nameless and faceless securocrats in British intelligence'.[73] This was the same Danny Morrison who, thirteen years later, would admit to having known since 1990 that the IRA had 'stood down' Scappaticci, presumably because they strongly suspected he'd betrayed Morrison and his seven co-defendants over the false imprisonment of Sandy Lynch.[74]

If the IRA's chutzpah knew no bounds, neither did Scappaticci's. That Wednesday morning in Parliament, Northern Ireland Minister of State Jane Kennedy gave a 'blanket refusal' to either confirm or deny that Scappaticci was Stakeknife.[75] Scappaticci responded by instructing Flanigan to judicially review her use of NCND in his particular case, demanding that the government deny he was Stakeknife – a demand he must have known would be nigh on impossible as it would mean ministers authorising officials to tell a barefaced lie.

Scappaticci argued that Kennedy's refusal to deny he was Stakeknife was putting his life at risk from the IRA and that the government had a duty under Article 2 of the Human Rights Act to make an exception in his case to its otherwise strict NCND policy. Two days earlier, he had signed an MI5 waiver acknowledging that it was his choice to return to Belfast, not something he would have done had he genuinely feared his life was at imminent risk.[76] MI5's then director for Northern Ireland Terrorism, Andrew Parker (later to become director general), had also advised the NIO permanent secretary, Sir Joseph Pilling, that there was no immediate risk to his life.[77]

On 21 May 2003, in the presence of another solicitor, Scappaticci falsely swore on oath that he was not a security force agent, whether known as Stakeknife or by any other name.[78] It's unclear whether MI5 had cautioned Scappaticci against committing perjury (a serious offence), but what is clear is that when he did so, MI5 fell in fully behind him to help ensure that he did *not* win his judicial review. Winning was, of course, the very last thing either he or MI5 wanted, because ministers would then have been under a court order to state his status truthfully – which was that he was Stakeknife. Indeed, Scappaticci openly admitted to MI5 that he never expected to win but was quite cynically exploiting the court process purely to try to convince the wider public that he hadn't been a 'tout'.[79]

From the chrysalis of this legal charade, an unspoken Faustian pact between Scappaticci, the British government and the IRA was flowering. For Scappaticci, the optics of using the courts to clear his name would assist his determination to continue living in Belfast for as long as possible, because, as he correctly and cynically told MI5, judicially reviewing the government's refusal to comment on his status was the 'natural' response that an innocent man would be expected to make,[80] never mind that it was a flat lie. For the British government, at stake was the very survival of NCND policy, which, over decades, had been such a useful mechanism for avoiding awkward and unwelcome intelligence-related questions. Victory for Scappaticci would have driven a horse and coaches through that.

Also at stake, for both the British and the IRA, was the survival of the fragile peace process in which they and the Adams–McGuinness leadership had invested everything. To MI5's alarm, however, by mid-June 2003 it looked as if Scappaticci might very well win his judicial review. In granting Scappaticci leave to bring it to a full hearing, Mr Justice Kerr said he had raised 'an arguable case that it is reasonable to require the minister to make the statement that he seeks'.[81]

An 'arguable case'? Enter Philip Sales, the government 'Treasury Devil' – the title given to the hotshot barrister chosen to advise the Crown on key cases. He told MI5 there was a real risk of Scappaticci getting the win that neither Scappaticci nor they wanted, if the judge assumed that by bringing the case he was not Stakeknife. Anxious officials observed that that seemed to be exactly what Mr Justice Kerr had assumed. At a crisis meeting in July 2003 attended by MI5, Sales and officials from the MoD, the Attorney General's Office and the NIO, it was agreed that Kerr's favourable comments did not bode well for the full hearing scheduled before another judge, Mr Justice Sheil.[82]

The government appeared to be determined to protect Stakeknife's cover and to preserve NCND policy at all costs. In that case, advised Sales, the court should be put fully in the picture: that the applicant in the case, Freddie Scappaticci was, in fact, Stakeknife, contrary to his perjured affidavit. 'Has he not brought this on himself?' enquired Attorney General Lord Goldsmith. He had a valid point. After all, Scappaticci had rejected MI5's resettlement offer. 'Should we not hear from Mr Scappaticci himself in an affidavit?' Goldsmith quite reasonably enquired. For reasons which are not entirely clear, MI5 said this would not be possible, and eventually Goldsmith concurred with Sales' advice by agreeing that the lord chief justice of Northern Ireland at that time, Lord Robert Carswell, should be informed.[83]

In other words, contrary to the victory Scappaticci's affidavit supposedly sought, Carswell should be told the plaintiff about to go to court did not want what he said he wanted, namely that the court should order ministers to depart from their strict NCND policy. That, after all, would require the government to name him as the agent Stakeknife. As government lawyers, both Goldsmith and Sales will no doubt have been rightly concerned to ensure the court was not misled by Scappaticci, and there is no suggestion that either of them acted unlawfully. It's also true, of course, that giving the judiciary the full picture happened to serve the government's purpose perfectly.

Once again, a PII certificate would be the legal instrument by which Sales was to put Carswell in the picture. MI5 even consulted Scappaticci and got his approval for the government's approach to the acute legal and constitutional dilemma the rogue agent had imposed on them but with which they had chosen to collaborate.[84] The government, of course, had an alternative. Scappaticci could have been told that if he persisted with his charade, he was on his own. But the survival of NCND took precedence. In effect, the Respondent (the Crown) was co-operating with the Applicant (Scappaticci) to achieve an outcome they both wanted, even though the Applicant had proclaimed to the wider public that he vehemently opposed that outcome.

The PII certificate was signed by Jane Kennedy. A fundamental requirement of a PII certificate is that it should provide the judge with the fullest possible picture and must not be misleading in any way. However, the certificate Kennedy was invited to sign was manifestly misleading. It stated only that Scappaticci had provided 'lifesaving intelligence', making no reference to the fact that he was also under investigation by Metropolitan Police Commissioner Sir John Stevens for his involvement in multiple executions, torture and abductions of fellow British agents.[85]

Information included in a PII certificate for the minister's signature would normally be provided by MI5, so Kennedy was entirely reliant on their candour. There is no suggestion she was party to a deception. She would have assumed, quite reasonably, that she was being given the objective truth. The same cannot be said of MI5. They had known since 2002 that Scappaticci was suspected by Stevens of having participated in executions, not least since DCI James had been trying to get more information out of them on precisely that matter. The Attorney General's Office is also said to have been informed of the position by the DPP's office in Belfast.

The first approach to Carswell for permission for Sales to have a secret, or *in camera*, audience with him was made by the NIO. It was promptly rebuffed by Carswell's office, which questioned the propriety of this approach. Sales acknowledged that the circumstances leading to his PII application were 'exceptional'.[86] Today, as Lord Sales, he sits as a justice of the Supreme Court. 'Philip would not have been in his comfort zone,' observed a senior barrister who knows him.[87] When asked, Lord Sales' office said that because of his position today, it would be inappropriate to comment.[88] Spurned by Carswell's office, Lord Goldsmith then approached Lord Chief Justice for England and Wales Lord Harry Woolf, who appears to have succeeded in persuading his Northern Ireland counterpart to see Sales. Like Sales, Goldsmith also declined to comment on these events, the Attorney General's Office citing on his behalf the ministerial code that protects any advice given to government from being disclosed outside government.[89] Lord Woolf did not respond to my written questions.[90]

On 4 August 2003, Sales flew to Belfast, meeting Lord Carswell at his home close to the Stormont Estate in East Belfast, where, in 1984, the IRA had tried to kill him by putting a bomb under his car on the same day he was due to be sworn in as a High Court judge. There Sales presented Carswell with the PII certificate, seeking his approval not to disclose to anyone who was party to the proceedings that Scappaticci was Stakeknife – neither to Scappaticci's solicitor Michael Flanigan, nor even the Crown's own counsel, Declan Morgan QC.

As for Scappaticci, his chutzpah typically knew no bounds. Two days later, he swore a second affidavit linked to the allegation that he was Stakeknife, again in the presence of a solicitor.[91]

Although Mr Justice Sheil was scheduled to hear Scappaticci's challenge to NCND, following Philip Sales' visit, Carswell decided to take the case himself. At the hearing on 8 August, neither the public nor the press, nor even the lawyers for both parties, had the faintest idea of what had been going on behind the scenes. There were only two people in the court who did know: Carswell and Scappaticci.[92] Both knew Scappaticci had lied on oath and both knew he didn't remotely want the verdict he was publicly seeking.

On 18 August, Carswell's judgment was released. As expected, he rejected Scappaticci's bogus demand, fully buying into the government's 'slippery slope' argument for maintaining the strict NCND policy, with no exceptions: '[O]nce the Government confirms in the case of one person that he is not an agent, a refusal to comment on the case of another person would then give rise to an immediate suspicion that the latter was in fact an agent, so possibly placing his life in grave danger …' he ruled.[93] Carswell presumably knew that Scappaticci's sham case was being funded by the public purse, despite having received substantial payments from the MoD. He presumably also knew that besides preserving the NCND policy, his 'elaborate legal charade' – as one senior barrister privy to the details described it[94] – had been aimed at facilitating Scappaticci's goal of continuing to live in Belfast rather than accepting MI5's offer of resettlement. Following the verdict, Scappaticci continued to play games by making an application to appeal Carswell's judgment, despite having promised MI5 that when, as expected, he lost, he would not do this.[95]

In the event, the time in Belfast that Scappaticci's charade bought him was limited. The previous month, I had revealed on *Panorama* that the anonymous IRA man calling himself 'Jack', who had told ITV journalists in 1993 that Martin McGuinness was 'evil', was one Freddie Scappaticci. According to 'Jack', McGuinness had been 'ultimately responsible' for all IRA killings in Northern Ireland.[96] 'Jack' had been covertly recorded by the now defunct ITV *Cook Report* saying that McGuinness was one of the IRA leaders who usually signed off on executions on behalf of the Army Council.[97] Following *Panorama*, Sylvia Jones from *The Cook Report* confirmed publicly that 'Jack' was Scappaticci and revealed that, at the time, the RUC had urged her and her fellow *Cook Report* colleagues not to disclose his identity because he was a valued intelligence source.[98]

The strain on Scappaticci was showing. 'Get yourselves off,' a dressing-gowned and sandal-clad Scappaticci yelled at a BBC TV crew outside his house, advancing on them menacingly. 'Get yourselves off. Go on. Fuck off! Youse [*sic*] causing enough problems in this house. Take yourself off.' In the nearly minute-long tirade that followed, the world glimpsed the pulverising aggression in both his voice and his body language that would have confronted his victims, who, unlike the BBC crew, had nowhere to run. Squaring up to the crew and threatening violence, he bellowed: 'And take no more photos of this house ... Fucking sick of my family being tortured here over youse. Fucking scum youse are. Stories youse make up. Don't be holding your hand and saying it's nothing to do with you. Don't take any more photos of this house, I'm telling you now. Because if you do I'll come out and I'll fucking do you.'[99]

Over the months that followed Sylvia Jones' revelation, there were occasional reported sightings of Scappaticci, but they grew rarer, until by late 2003 he had left Belfast altogether, having finally accepted MI5's offer of resettlement. By then, he seemed reconciled to the fact that while he may have been safe during the ongoing peace process, in the longer run he was at serious risk. He subsequently had to relocate at short notice several times over the years as a result of death threats.[100] Any remaining doubts that he was Stakeknife had been definitively removed by a UTV programme broadcast in March 2004, when the *Cook Report* tapes were played with Scappaticci's instantly recognisable voice.[101]

Meanwhile, Phil James and his fellow detectives on Stevens 3 had identified Scappaticci's involvement in up to seventeen murders and abductions. In July 2004, the DPP in Belfast, Sir Alasdair Fraser, told Commander Cox that he considered it 'vital' that the investigation was 'as complete and thorough as possible'.[102] Two months later Cox launched Operation Waresley – in effect Stevens 4, dedicated solely to Stakeknife. Hugh Orde, as then PSNI chief constable, had other ideas for Cox, however. He wanted Cox to run his novel solution for dealing with what were then an estimated 2,000 unsolved conflict-related killings, the one legacy issue that the Good Friday Agreement hadn't catered for.[103] Popularly known by the acronym HET, the Historical Enquiries Team recruited some hundred ex-detectives to prepare family reports for relatives of the dead on the evidence available in police, army and intelligence files. In practice, the HET became a hybrid of investigators, reviewer-analysts and, for some families, welfare workers, a unique development in post-conflict policing. Cox agreed to take on the role, and James went with him as his deputy and the HET's director of intelligence and investigations. It was later established by Operation Kenova that 'in many cases significant intelligence which should have been passed to the HET was missing'.[104]

On Operation Waresley, Cox and James were replaced by a new cadre of detectives, who had to navigate from scratch the complex vicissitudes of investigating legacy cases in a jurisdiction in which they had not previously worked. The operation soon lost momentum, despite encouragement from the DPP for the investigation to continue.[105] But Sir Alasdair Fraser was also ailing, struck down by throat cancer. Evidential prospects were also assessed as poor, partly because of the dearth of original documents. Besides, Waresley was also burning a sizeable hole in Orde's budget.[106]

In March 2006, Orde closed down Operation Waresley. Five years' worth of evidence was packed into thirty-two boxes[107] and shipped over to the HET at Sprucefield, near Hillsborough, County Down, where they remained for the next decade. The plan was to review the evidence for reports to the families of victims of Scappaticci and his IRA nutting squad, instead of pursuing the case against Scappaticci himself to a criminal standard.[108] The HET's policy was to work through legacy cases in date order, so the Scappaticci files took their place in a lengthy queue going back to 1969. That said, a 'White Team' was established to prioritise the review of informer killings under 'Operation Chiggerhill'.[109]

In 2014 the HET was closed down after a critical report by Her Majesty's Inspector of Constabulary, regarded by many as deeply flawed. Orde was furious. The HET was 'the only original idea I've had in policing,' he reflected ruefully. His successor, Matt Baggott, 'should have chucked it [the report] in the bin'. Many families regretted the HET's passing.[110] Yet Orde had not been appointed PSNI chief constable to focus on the past but to build a police force for the future.

As for Scappaticci, MI5 would do its level best to protect the secrets of his past by continuing with the strict application of NCND, a commitment that would soon be put to the test. A month after Operation Waresley ended, a new threat emerged to the survival of the policy, which to date had done so much to prevent the history of the counter-insurgency from being set straight, through a growing appetite for truth that this secrecy had generated amongst lawyers and NGOs and especially the relatives of Stakeknife's victims.

Chapter Sixteen

6126 – Perjury, Scappaticci and the Law

FREDDIE SCAPPATICCI WAS NOTHING IF not a chancer. Surviving the perilous rapids of a double life simultaneously at the epicentre of both the IRA and British intelligence was a testament to that. Determined to maintain for as long as possible the fiction that he had not led a double life, on 3 February 2004, he swore on oath a third affidavit repeating the lie that he was not the agent known as Stakeknife. In this latest gamble with the Perjury Act of 1911, Scappaticci again 'strenuously denied' that he was Stakeknife, emphasising that he had 'already attempted to clear my name of this allegation through the courts'.[1]

The trigger for this latest wager with the rule of law was the imminent serialisation by the Belfast-based *Sunday Life* newspaper of a book by the ex-FRU handler Ian Hurst and journalist Greg Harkin about Scappaticci's time in the IRA's nutting squad. Not all of the book was accurate by any means, but it left no doubt whatsoever that he was Stakeknife.

This third affidavit was desperate stuff. Inviting the court to compel Hurst's former employer, the MoD, to injunct the *Sunday Life*, Scappaticci argued that by publishing confidential material, Hurst was in breach of his contractual obligations to the MoD. Concern for confidentiality undertakings within the British intelligence establishment was a novel argument for someone presenting themselves as a committed West Belfast republican.

Mr Justice Weatherup dismissed the ploy, which also backfired on Scappaticci, because Hurst responded by urging the PSNI to investigate him for perjury. The initial response from ACC Sam Kinkaid was to fall back on NCND. He said the matter was 'not capable of police investigation' because it would infringe the government NCND policy.[2] By April 2006, however, Kinkaid's successor, ACC Peter Sheridan, had reluctantly agreed to an investigation, albeit only after Police Ombudsman Nuala O'Loan had intervened.[3]

By now Scappaticci was in exile in England, and he was determined to close down media inquiries into him so he could live in relative peace. On 26 June 2006, almost three months after the PSNI opened their perjury investigation, he swore yet another affidavit – the fourth. Each affidavit was grounded in the lie that he was not Stakeknife.[4]

Unlike his attempt to stop Hurst's book being serialised in the *Sunday Life*, this fourth affidavit succeeded in persuading the court to issue an injunction, one of the most draconian ever against the media in peacetime. Journalists were prohibited from publishing or even soliciting any new name Scappaticci was using; any description of his address or information that could lead to it, or even the nature of his accommodation; any information about his care or treatment, or the name of his doctor; any picture, painting or drawing of him after 11 May 2003 when he was outed as Stakeknife, which included a ban on the footage of him ranting, cursing and threatening to 'do' a BBC crew. Finally, any reference to the nature and location of his employment was also prohibited.[5] It worked. Media outlets pretty much gave up looking for him.

It would be an understatement to say that the PSNI's decision to investigate Scappaticci for perjury was not welcomed by MI5. The reason was quite simple: a decision to prosecute Scappaticci for perjury would have been tantamount to the state admitting he was indeed Stakeknife, fatally undermining the NCND policy that it had worked so hard to sustain by participating in Scappaticci's bogus 2003 challenge to the policy.

It is also hard to avoid the suspicion that the PSNI wasn't too enthusiastic about a perjury investigation either. As one detective pithily put it, the PSNI's attitude was: 'This is a pile of s*** which we'd like to go away.'[6] From the outset, MI5 had sought to limit the scope of the PSNI investigation. MI5 knew that, in Scappaticci's attempt to persuade the public that he was not Stakeknife and to limit media scrutiny of his secret role, he had sworn four affidavits between 2003 and 2006, yet had only told the officer heading the PSNI investigation, Detective Chief Superintendent Philip Wright, about the first one he'd sworn in May 2003, despite the case having been referred to the PSNI on the basis of the third affidavit sworn in February 2004, in which Scappaticci repeated his 'strenuous' denial that he was Stakeknife.

'Defenders of the Realm' MI5 may be, but it is not its job to decide what is or is not relevant to a criminal inquiry conducted by the police. The Security Service is no more above the law than everyone else and PSNI Chief Constable Jon Boutcher says all four affidavits sworn by Scappaticci should have been disclosed to Detective Chief Superintendent Wright.[7] When interviewed by Kenova under caution as to why all four were not disclosed, the response from one of the two MI5 officers was that Wright had 'never asked'. That officer was a lawyer in the service's legal department.[8] Even though MI5 has a law-enforcement role, to Kenova, the lawyer's failure to disclose all four affidavits to Wright suggested that in this particular matter, the officer felt the Security Service was above the law. By way of example, could a police officer finding two dead bodies in a house justify revealing the existence of only one because they weren't asked if there might be another? Hardly.

The PSNI has questions to answer too. Why, in establishing the inquiry, had it not provided Wright with all four affidavits in 2006, when they were all in the public domain? To this day, the PSNI has been unable to provide a satisfactory answer.[9] Did it perhaps fear that to have disclosed all four affidavits risked making any defence by Scappaticci against the perjury charge harder to sustain, because the prosecution could have presented his perjury not as a one-off event in May 2003 but as a campaign? Just as baffling is why a detective with Wright's considerable experience does not appear to have discovered the existence of all four affidavits for himself.[10] As Belfast's most senior detective, in 2002 Wright had headed the investigation into the IRA's break-in to the locked vaults of Special Branch at Castlereagh police station, where so many secrets were stolen that a hundred officers had to be relocated or have their homes fortified.[11]

Besides withholding all the affidavits from Wright, MI5 also seems to have tried to set the ground rules for his investigation. They told the PPS's senior lawyer reviewing the case, Pamela Atchison, that work on it would have to be restricted to a laptop provided by them. Nor would she be permitted to retain copies of documents.[12] Former prosecutors have expressed surprise that the PPS acquiesced to these terms.[13] When I asked Atchison if MI5 had tried to dictate the conduct of the inquiry, her reply was emphatic, 'If you mean whether the Security Service sought to dictate the prosecutorial process, the answer is no, they did not and would not be allowed to do so under any circumstances.'[14]

In any case, Detective Chief Superintendent Wright appears quite quickly to have concluded that there was no case to answer against Scappaticci. In December 2006, he recommended to Atchison that the police take no further action.[15] When asked by the PSNI in 2015 why he had come to that conclusion, Wright – who by then had moved to Canada – is reported to have replied to the effect that 'This was the only way it could be done,' which sounds more like a compromise than a proper decision.[16] I put this to Wright, who is now a practising barrister in Canada, but he declined to respond.[17]

The reason Wright gave in writing to the PPS for not continuing the investigation was that he considered Scappaticci could avail himself of a rarely used legal defence known as 'defence of necessity/duress of circumstance'.[18] Wright is understood to have concluded that because of the risk to his life from the IRA, Scappaticci had little alternative but to perjure himself. This defence is normally restricted to defendants who, metaphorically speaking, have a knife to their throat. In other words, so fearful are they of imminent death or serious injury that they have no choice but to commit a crime[19] – in Scappaticci's case, perjury. Yet, just five days before Scappaticci swore the first false oath on 21 May 2003 insisting that he wasn't Stakeknife and that he was in fear of his life, MI5 had advised the NIO's Permanent Secretary Sir Joe Pilling that the IRA posed no immediate risk to him.[20] Furthermore, MI5 had offered Scappaticci a secure alternative to committing perjury: resettlement for him and his family – an offer he'd roundly rejected, choosing to return to Belfast just thirty-six hours after being named in newspapers as Stakeknife, confident that he was at minimal risk.

Atchison quite properly did not accept at face value Wright's recommendation in December 2006 to discontinue the investigation and in February 2007 directed him to interview Scappaticci under caution. Wright passed this straightforward instruction on to MI5, but the wheels ground exceedingly slowly. It was not until August that Atchison was told that MI5 had had Scappaticci psychiatrically assessed and that he'd been treated for depression. The assessment said that although he was capable of giving evidence, were he subjected to further criminal investigation, his depression would likely be triggered to such an extent that he would become unfit for interview, causing him psychological and physical harm. The assessment also said that Scappaticci had warned that were he to face criminal proceedings, he would commit suicide.[21]

Scappaticci had been fit for interview by the Stevens detectives three years earlier. Perhaps with that in mind, Atchison asked Wright to revert to MI5 'to determine if they considered that an interview was possible'. Three more months passed before Wright told her that the PSNI was 'unable to interview the individual and requested that a decision as to prosecution be taken'.[22] Both the PSNI and PPS appear to have accepted this without getting an independent psychiatric report of their own – as I am told would ordinarily be the case. 'Otherwise, no one would ever get interviewed,' as one detective put it.[23]

The following month, as recommended by Wright, Atchison accepted that Scappaticci had a defence of necessity/duress and, therefore, that he should not be prosecuted, the evidential test for prosecution, in her view, having failed. This decision was reached without having heard directly from Scappaticci about how he had felt about the immediacy of the threat to his life, for which the only available evidence appeared to be hearsay from the MI5 officer in charge of his resettlement.[24]

How viable was that defence? Even Scappaticci himself seems to have calculated he was in no immediate danger after he was outed in May 2003. Given the wily political animal that he was, he knew that if he ended up in a cross-border ditch with a bullet in his head, the peace process would be in mortal danger, which he also knew was very much not what the IRA leadership wanted, to say nothing of the disenchantment the IRA rank and file would feel at confirmation that the man they'd entrusted to protect them from penetration by British agents was himself an agent. Scappaticci seems to have correctly calculated that he was like a global-sized bank: too big to fail, at least in the immediate future.

In principle, a defence of necessity/duress depends significantly upon the accused being able to demonstrate he had no choice but to lie in the face of *imminent* peril. The fact that this defence hinges on the imminence of the threat, as well as the absence of an available alternative to lying on oath, explains why 'running it as a defence to perjury is near impossible,' explained a senior King's Counsel who has also sat as a judge. It's not about what a defendant might 'prefer'[25] – in Scappaticci's case it was simply his preference to live openly in Belfast, against MI5's alternative of resettlement. Atchison, however, concluded that a court was more likely than not to acquit Scappaticci of perjury, despite the strength of such a defence not having been tested on the man himself by questioning him under caution.

At the same time, the PPS appears to have been reluctant to disclose that the specific reason for the decision not to prosecute Scappaticci for perjury was lack of evidence. A brief letter dated 9 January 2008 to Jane Winter of British Irish Rights Watch, who had lobbied the PSNI to investigate him for perjury in 2006, stated only that the 'Test for Prosecution' hadn't been met.[26] It failed to make any mention of the case specifically having failed the 'evidentiary test' for prosecution, despite the PPS having recently adopted a new policy of giving 'reasons in the most general terms' for a decision not to prosecute,[27] which in this case would have meant disclosing whether the decision had been taken on evidential or public interest grounds. The letter conspicuously avoided saying that it considered Scappaticci had a viable defence of necessity/duress. Was that because the PPS calculated that public opinion would not find that credible? 'I certainly would not have found that credible,' Winter says.[28] A lawyer familiar with the details commented, 'The letter seems to have been deliberately vague.'[29] Atchison said she couldn't recall the letter.[30]

Still, as in 2008, so today the PPS insists that the decision was the correct one, taken on its merits. The DPP, Stephen Herron, has explained that because the case failed the evidentiary test, there was no need to consider the next stage in the prosecutorial decision-making process, which was whether prosecution would have been in the public interest. Or, to put it another way: Atchison's 'no-pros' recommendation spared the PPS from having to decide whether to prosecute or whether to apply NCND, when either choice would have sent the same barely coded message to the public: Scappaticci was the agent Stakeknife. Atchison, though, insists that kind of calculation never entered into her thinking. The case had fallen at the first hurdle through lack of evidence. 'I can categorically state that I have not taken nor seen taken decisions as to prosecution which were improperly influenced by NCND policy considerations,' Atchison told me. 'In my experience decisions as to prosecution were only taken after careful consideration of the available evidence and in accordance with the relevant law,' never 'out of expediency or otherwise'.[31]

Some lawyers familiar with the details of the case have argued that there was insufficient evidence at the time for Atchison to have decided there was no reasonable prospect of disproving the defence of necessity/duress,[32] and therefore the question of whether to prosecute Scappaticci should have been determined on whether it was considered to be in the public interest. Whichever view in law is right, what does seem clear is that the decision not to prosecute Scappaticci in 2007 prevented the risk of a veritable Pandora's box being opened up which would have severely embarrassed MI5, the attorney general and the NIO. Had it become known how collaborative MI5 and government law officers had been in Scappaticci's bogus legal charade in 2003 over his judicial review of NCND, confidence in the integrity of the legal system might well have been undermined. Damaging suggestions that the government had persuaded the lord chief justice to deliver a predetermined ruling on a judicial review of NCND would likely have invited questions about the independence of the judiciary from the executive. A month before the hearing, MI5 had kept Scappaticci abreast of how the government intended to argue the case against lifting NCND and he expressed his approval.[33] Right-minded people would no doubt have found it distasteful that a government agent, suspected of involvement in multiple murders and torture, had been allowed to exploit the judicial system for his own convenience, and moreover in consultation with MI5 in order to achieve that.

The discovery that Scappaticci was suspected of multiple murders would likely have provoked questions about the misleading PII certificate that the Northern Ireland security minister Jane Kennedy had been asked to sign by MI5, which referred only to Scappaticci having provided 'lifesaving intelligence', making no reference to his role in torture or murder.[34]

Inevitably, that would have invited questions about whether and to what extent the PII system had been misused for the duration of the conflict, when many certificates were issued. The PII procedure is entirely dependent on the state being trusted with providing a balanced, factual account of the national security issue it seeks to protect from public disclosure. The fact that the system had been abused in Scappaticci's case for the pre-eminent purpose of protecting NCND may have provoked a review of every PII certificate issued during the entire conflict.

Prosecution might also have provoked questions about the DPP's failure to alert the legal representatives of Danny Morrison and his seven co-defendants when the prosecution service learned, no later than 2002, that Scappaticci, named by Sandy Lynch as one of his interrogators, was a state agent. The fact that this had been deliberately withheld from the DPP in 1990, when the decision was made to prosecute Morrison and the others, was solid grounds for their appeal, since the defence could rightly argue they'd been deprived of the opportunity to invite the court to throw out the charges on the basis that to proceed to trial would have been an abuse of process – grounds which eventually led to the court of appeal quashing the convictions in October 2008.[35] Yet, despite learning from Stevens 3 about such a fundamental defect in the prosecutorial process six years earlier, at no stage had the prosecution service voluntarily alerted the defence lawyers to this.[36] I should emphasise there is no suggestion here that Atchison was responsible for that failing. The fact is, though, the defence lawyers only learned about the non-disclosure after Scappaticci's agent status had been unmasked by journalists in May 2003, not from the DPP. And the only reason the case got to the Court of Appeal was because the Criminal Cases Review Commission (CCRC) was alerted to this in 2004 by Morrison's legal team, following publication of the book *Stakeknife*.[37] While NCND prevented the DPP from confirming that Scappaticci was Stakeknife, his office did at least confirm to Morrison's lawyers that the information had not been disclosed to him in advance of his trial.[38]

The CCRC investigation was conducted by Phil James, by now a detective superintendent, who provided the commission with the information that it then included in secret annexures disclosed to the Court of Appeal: that Stakeknife had been a state agent. Crown Counsel Gerry Simpson QC 'nearly had a heart attack'[39] when, in quashing the convictions of Morrison and his seven co-defendants in October 2008, Lord Chief Justice Sir Brian Kerr said he saw 'nothing about the content of the annexures which on its face' couldn't be disclosed.[40] Once again, the sanctity of NCND was on the line, this time because of the most senior judge in the land. A shaken Simpson rose to his feet to say the Crown's objections related to a 'number of matters', which 'I'm afraid I cannot explain any further' because to do so would not be 'in the interests of justice and national security'.[41] This brought to mind Michael Mansfield QC's ridiculing of the British state's obsession with secrecy in the 1984 trial of the MI5 double agent Michael Bettaney, when the bench asked where the attorney general had gone, having momentarily left the court, and Mansfield quipped, 'It's so secret that not even the Attorney knows!'

After the lord chief justice and his fellow justices agreed to hear Simpson's submissions in closed session, they relented. Once again, NCND had held sway. Simpson had presumably regurgitated the judgment of Kerr's predecessor, Lord Chief Justice Carswell, upholding NCND in response to Scappaticci's bogus challenge. Carswell has been the defining judicial authority the government has relied on ever since.

In quashing his conviction for falsely imprisoning Sandy Lynch, Morrison has claimed that the Court of Appeal vindicated his long-held belief that he was 'set up for arrest by British Intelligence through their agent, "Stakeknife", who is Freddie Scappaticci',[42] using Lynch as bait.[43] For this, Morrison relied on Ian Hurst and Greg Harkin's *Stakeknife* book, which claimed that three days before Lynch's abduction, he'd colluded in a plot to entrap Morrison. The authors had written that Lynch was told by his Special Branch handlers that he was going to be 'picked up' for questioning by the IRA, but told 'not to worry; as long as he didn't admit anything, the IRA would stick to their rules and he would be released'.[44]

Is that really likely? To have acquiesced in this plot would have meant Lynch taking the most monumental gamble with his life. As one lawyer close to the case put it, 'From a human instinct survival point of view, the idea that Lynch would have agreed to take the chance seems inherently implausible.'[45] Lynch told Operation Kenova that it is emphatically untrue that his handlers told him he was about to be lifted by the ISU and to just wing it. Had his handlers asked him to do this, he said, he would never have taken the risk, and one can well understand why.[46] Once in the hands of the ISU, there was no guarantee of where he would be taken and held, what coercive measures they might use, and no certainty of a rescue. Indeed, Operation Kenova says it identified occasions when agents were under surveillance by the security forces and the surveillance team was actually withdrawn, leaving the victim exposed to torture and murder.[47] There were absolutely no guarantees for Sandy Lynch.

In his judgment on Morrison and his co-defendants, Sir Brian Hutton said Lynch was a man 'fully prepared to lie on oath to advance his own interest, a man of no moral worth whatever', that nothing he said should be believed unless corroborated.[48] But on this occasion, Lynch's evidence to Kenova is corroborated by the last-minute nature of his rescue. If Morrison was indeed the victim of an elaborate entrapment conspiracy from the outset, as he claimed, it was an extremely amateurish one. As explained in Chapter 10, the agencies only learned on Sunday 7 January that Morrison was due at 124 Carrigart Avenue that evening. Had his arrest been part of a pre-planned plot hatched days before Lynch was abducted, one might have expected the security forces to have surrounded the house, sealing off escape routes at the back before the two police officers knocked on the door. Yet two paratroopers were still scrambling into position when Morrison fled through the back door, into the garden and across the fence into 126 Carrigart Avenue.

Detective Superintendent James did not get to speak to Lynch during his investigation on behalf of the CCRC because, when he sought the assistance of MI5's resettlement unit to put him in contact, they said they were unable to help.[49] Hearing that Lynch was now living in the United States, James turned to the FBI liaison at the American embassy in London, and they appear to have communicated with Lynch. However, Phil James recalls that the message the FBI relayed was that Lynch didn't want to talk to him.[50] Kenova's request to MI5 a decade later was – at first – no more fruitful. 'Leave it with us,' they told Kenova's SIO Keith Surtees. 'We'll see if he wants to talk to you.' Surtees made it clear he would not be leaving it with MI5 because he didn't entirely trust they would do their best to get Lynch to talk to him. 'Either you put me in front of Lynch or I'll find him myself,' he told them. It was as well that Surtees gave the service this ultimatum. When one of

Surtees' officers, Detective Chief Inspector Jim Redmond, finally got in front of Lynch, he told him that, had he been asked if he had been party to a pre-planned plot to entrap Morrison, he would have explained in the strongest possible terms that he was not – but he was never asked.[51]

On its face, MI5's reluctance to assist James and Surtees made no sense. Would it not have been in their interest to help explode Morrison's conspiracy theory of a pre-planned plot to entrap him as a republican myth? On the other hand, since Stevens 3 had found the evidence that showed Scappaticci's alibi to be bogus, perhaps MI5 feared first Stevens then Kenova might seek to use Lynch to re-open the prosecution of Scappaticci for kidnapping and conspiracy to murder.

In January 2009, the Court of Appeal gave its reasons for quashing the convictions of Morrison and his seven co-defendants the previous October, although that rather exaggerates what happened. In the face of the Crown's continued submissions about the criticality of preserving NCND, the court's reasoning was very brief and utterly opaque, despite having initially adjudged that there was nothing in the secret annexures that would have caused the 'public interest or the interests of justice' to have been 'infringed' by disclosure. In the absence of any input from Lynch, the CCRC is understood to have taken quite seriously Morrison's argument that he was the victim of an entrapment plot,[52] and presumably so did their lordships. In a critique of the CCRC, Kenova 'forensically pulled that case apart', although this was not a criticism of Detective Superintendent James' investigation. Because of MI5's refusal to facilitate James' access to Lynch, 'Phil had been operating with one arm tied behind his back,' said a former colleague.[53] The convictions were highly likely to have been quashed anyway, irrespective of whether entrapment was regarded as a credible defence argument, since the RUC's decision to withhold Scappaticci's status as a police agent from the DPP at Morrison's trial was terminal. It was a fundamental breach of legal procedure and justice.

Because NCND required the annexures to be secret, the public never learned exactly what weight (if any) the Court of Appeal gave to the entrapment theory. All that was said was that, had the withheld 'evidence' been given at trial, 'that evidence would almost certainly have led to the acquittal of the appellants on all charges.'[54] As a consequence, Morrison and his seven co-defendants were collectively enriched by a reported £1.6m in compensation,[55] despite the fact that Lynch had quite clearly been held against his will and was utterly convinced his execution was imminent.

Meanwhile, Detective Superintendent James had informed the CCRC of a real conspiracy – an extremely serious one – which five members of the FRU and the head of Belfast CID, Detective Chief Superintendent Caskey, are alleged to have cooked up after Scappaticci took refuge in Dublin in 1990.[56] This was the FRU–Caskey plot to ensure Scappaticci would not be prosecuted on his return to Belfast in late 1992 by voiding the evidence of his thumbprint on the bug detector with a false alibi.

Following the quashing of the convictions of Morrison and his seven co-accused, the DPP, Sir Alasdair Fraser, asked the PSNI to investigate any offences referred by the CCRC report to the Court of Appeal concerning Scappaticci's status as an agent. This included both the FRU–Caskey plot and the RUC's non-disclosure of Scappaticci's status as an agent. Police primacy meant that the disclosure obligation had been squarely on Special Branch. In deliberately withholding that information from the DPP and by conspiring to help Scappaticci evade prosecution, Special Branch, the FRU and Caskey appear to have perverted the course of justice. Sir Alasdair's referral to the PSNI for investigation was made under section 35(5) of the Justice (Northern Ireland) Act 2000, so this wasn't a polite request from the DPP – it was a statutory order with the full backing of Lord Chief Justice Kerr and his fellow justices in the Northern Ireland Court of Appeal.

Yet this seems to have had little impact. Under the Police (Northern Ireland Act) of 1998, following the Good Friday Agreement, legacy investigations into the military and the police were parcelled out between the PSNI and the Office of the Police Ombudsman (OPONI). The latter could only investigate the conduct of the police, and the former could only investigate the military. The fact that in this case, both the military (the FRU) and the police (Caskey) were involved allowed the PSNI and the OPONI to pass the parcel, even though both elements were part of the same conspiracy to pervert the course of justice. ACC Drew Harris insisted that the case was the OPONI's sole responsibility because the allegations concerned a retired police officer (Caskey), while Al Hutchinson, the then police ombudsman, complained that he had no funds. The result was that nothing happened for at least a year, and very little after that, despite Lord Chief Justice Sir Brian Kerr having very publicly endorsed Sir Alasdair's decision to refer the case for investigation, noting in the court's typically understated way that 'offences' may have been 'commission(ed) contrary to the law of Northern Ireland'.[57] Yet again, the legacy can was being kicked down the road.

Solicitor Kevin Winters, who was representing several relatives of victims of the IRA's nutting squad, was becoming ever more frustrated:

> We were going round and round in circles. The PSNI would say: 'We can't investigate this. It has to go to OPONI.' So, we'd go to Hutchinson who would say: 'I don't have the resources.' I remember him sitting smugly on the other side of the table saying, 'It will take me 50 years to investigate all the troubles-related cases in my office.' And I thought – you're getting a letter![58]

The paralysis came to a head in a fractious meeting in late January 2012 with Al Hutchinson, Drew Harris, the new DPP Barra McGrory, his soon to be deputy Pamela Atchison, Commander Dave Cox and Detective Superintendent Phil James, both representing the HET. 'What have you done about Caskey?' James asked of Hutchinson, now in his final days of office, having announced his resignation. When it became apparent that the answer was nothing, James was furious. 'Caskey was a Chief Superintendent, for Christ's sake,' he fumed. 'He's perverted the course of justice!'

'Hutchinson was utterly underwhelming,' recalls James, who'd also been chivvying the OPONI to investigate several ISU executions of alleged informers. These were cases that James' White Team at the HET had referred to the OPONI under Operation Chiggerhill. James specifically wanted to know whether Special Branch had responded to warnings from the FRU and other agents about agents suspected to be at risk of abduction and execution. 'McGrory was livid at the lack of progress,' said James, 'and everyone was handwringing.' The last straw came when Harris explained that part of the delay was down to the PSNI having lost the DPP's letter of referral. 'Dave and I were at our wits end, while Pamela [Atchison] was looking at me as if to say, "Please, don't say anymore!"'[59]

PSNI Chief Constable Baggott later wrote to McGrory to say that he would see if there was a need to investigate the FRU. This did not help the already tense relationship between the two men.[60] To McGrory, there could be no doubt that an investigation was needed: in 2008, his predecessor, Sir Alasdair Fraser, had referred to the PSNI for investigation all of the issues Detective Superintendent James had raised in his report to the CCRC, after the Court of Appeal expressed serious concern about potential criminal conduct on the part of state agencies in the concealment of Scappaticci's true status during the prosecutions of Morrison and his co-accused. Included in those issues was the FRU–Caskey plot to pervert the course of justice in the FRU's attempt to reinstate Scappaticci operationally as an agent north of the border after his near three-year refuge in the Irish Republic.

At McGrory's request, a progress-chasing letter was sent by his deputy, Pamela Atchison, to the PSNI. This was met with what McGrory regarded as unhelpful responses, and although he found Baggott personally to be supportive when they spoke, progress was still painfully slow. A judicial review of the OPONI, triggered by the letter from Kevin Winters to Hutchinson requiring the OPONI to fulfil its statutory obligation by investigating the RUC within a reasonable time, had finally got the wheels turning in May 2012,[61] but they were not turning fast enough, and the investigation limped on, making little progress.

In January 2013, Sir Declan Morgan, who had replaced Sir Brian Kerr as lord chief justice, necessitated a further 35(5) direction to the PSNI, this time requested by McGrory as DPP, to investigate Special Branch's failure to disclose Scappaticci's agent status in the prosecution of James Martin and Veronica Ryan for falsely imprisoning Joe Fenton at 124 Carrigart Avenue in February 1989.[62] When their convictions were finally quashed in October 2014, once more the reasons were not disclosed because, again, NCND held sway. The Crown issued another PII certificate preventing disclosure of the deception, which the court felt compelled to accept, albeit once again expressing its 'regret … acutely aware of the clear fact that justice is required to be conducted openly and in public and that exceptions to this should only occur in cases where there is indeed an overriding public interest'[63] – that 'overriding public interest' being the continued protection of Scappaticci's status as a state agent under NCND.

Instead of the PSNI and OPONI continuing to play pass-the-parcel, now, under the supervision of Detective Chief Superintendent Ricky Campbell, they were attempting to conduct an investigation in parallel. Yet Campbell, a dedicated and hard-working officer, was also frustrated by the slow pace, which again is said to have been partly due to MI5 obfuscation.[64] Caskey was interviewed by the OPONI,[65] while the FRU's former CO, Gordon Kerr, who had retired to France, declined to co-operate, referring the PSNI to his statements to and interviews with the three Stevens inquiries. Scappaticci was also interviewed but responded by sniggering and pretending at times to fall asleep.[66] By now, McGrory was seriously frustrated and tried to speed things along with George Hamilton, who had replaced Matt Baggott as PSNI chief constable. McGrory, with Atchison, was also meeting Campbell and OPONI investigators.[67]

Over at the OPONI, since taking office in July 2012, Michael Maguire – the police ombudsman who replaced Al Hutchinson – had embarked on a separate track, one which would eventually lead to the revival of the criminal investigation into Scappaticci under Operation Kenova. Detective Superintendent Phil James and his White Team at the HET had also not been idle. In August 2012, James sent the OPONI his detailed review of fifteen Scappaticci-linked cases. 'You need to look at these,' he urged, referring to the failure of the branch to act on intelligence warnings about a number of impending ISU abductions.[68] The thirty-two boxes of military and police files that Operation Waresley had shipped to the HET in 2006 had been supplemented by Operation Chiggerhill with new material. The 'evidence' was still overwhelmingly intelligence-based and fell short of what would be required for a prosecution against either Scappaticci or the intelligence services. Nonetheless, Maguire was struck by what appeared to be 'a pattern' in Scappaticci's regular involvement in nutting squad interrogations and abductions, which seemed to have been allowed by his FRU handlers and tolerated by Special Branch and MI5. So, while Maguire's specific remit was confined to reviewing the conduct of the police, it became clear this 'couldn't be pursued in isolation to other agencies'.[69]

Relatives of some of Scappaticci's victims were also putting pressure on Maguire to investigate Scappaticci's legacy. 'They were incredibly brave,' he said, given the opprobrium 'they'd suffered in their communities' for having relatives executed by the IRA for informing. Many families had never been given even 'the most basic and uncontroversial information about what happened to their loved ones'.[70]

As a former chief inspector with the Criminal Justice Inspectorate in Northern Ireland, Maguire evidently felt the prospect of criminal proceedings was not entirely forlorn, so he had the thirty-two boxes moved from the HET to the OPONI's office. 'We looked at those cases in a way they hadn't been looked at before,' he said. 'And we decided to take a more strategic view of the way in which these cases were linked together, both in terms of the individual concerned, but also the unit within the IRA in which he [Stakeknife] was operating.'[71]

Pamela Atchison has told me in email correspondence that in December 2014 she and McGrory were briefed by the ombudsman and the joint investigation team that Stakeknife was suspected of being involved in as many as fourteen murders. McGrory told me that the meeting was tense due to the lack of progress over the investigation into the Fenton murder that he'd required after James Martin's and Veronica Ryan's convictions had been quashed in January 2013. He said he'd pointed out to the investigation team that, in Stakeknife, they were 'potentially dealing with a serial killer and that he expected more progress by now'. To date, his office had not received 'as much as a sheet of paper by way of documented evidence despite two formal requests for information', first from his predecessor in 2009 and then by him in 2013 in relation to the Fenton murder.

In June 2015, McGrory was informed by Maguire that two analysts had now completed the OPONI's review of the thirty-two boxes, which had taken so long partly because the files were uncatalogued and not in any order.[72] Most of the victims had been Special Branch agents, and there was a pattern to the executions inasmuch as some followed within hours of Stakeknife having wrung confessions from them; opportunities to save them sometimes hadn't been taken.[73]

Meanwhile, the PSNI had still not completed its investigation into the FRU element of the FRU–Caskey conspiracy referred to them by Sir Alasdair Fraser six years earlier. The genial, pipe-smoking Fraser had died from throat cancer in 2011, and McGrory was by now extremely exercised that his predecessor's formal instructions had yet to be fulfilled. It 'just wasn't being acted upon,' he recalled. 'It's a pretty serious matter for the DPP … to have exercised that power of referral to the police. For that to be simply ignored by the PSNI was also a very serious matter, so, yes, I was furious about this, as I believed Alasdair Fraser would have been.'[74]

As head of the PPS's section dealing with terrorism and legacy cases, McGrory's deputy, Pamela Atchison, had been the lead lawyer dealing with Stakeknife since 2002 and throughout Stevens 3. She had also been progress-chasing the PSNI on McGrory's behalf on the two S35(5) referrals for investigation by him and his predecessor, Sir Alasdair Fraser, in respect of the murder of Fenton and the kidnapping of Lynch. According to McGrory, however, it was only when the ombudsman briefed him and Atchison in December 2014 about the potential scale of Stakeknife's criminal activities that he began to understand that he had been a rogue agent whose criminality extended well beyond Fenton and Lynch. Until then, he said, he had only been briefed about Stakeknife's role in those two cases. Atchison responded that this was 'not entirely correct', pointing out that in August 2012 the OPONI had briefed both of them about forty cases, 'many of which involved the activities of Stakeknife'.[75] McGrory, however, is clear that he had no sense of the scale of the issue until the end of 2014, which unsettled him, because by then he had been DPP for just over three years.[76] What unsettled him even more, he said, was the fact that it was only after the ombudsman had completed the intelligence analysis of the thirty-two boxes in June 2015 that Atchison disclosed to him the fact that Scappaticci had been investigated for perjury in 2007 and that she had concluded he should not be prosecuted. McGrory says he was both surprised and troubled by this given that Atchison had known how exasperated he'd been about the lack of progress in the investigations into Scappaticci's role in the Fenton and Lynch cases – investigations that both he and Sir Alasdair Fraser had ordered, and which had been publicly endorsed by two lord chief justices.[77]

When asked about his disagreement with Atchison over the perjury case, McGrory said he couldn't get into the detail because he was still bound by neither confirming nor denying Stakeknife's identity.[78] However, I understand that when he reviewed Atchison's written reasons for not prosecuting Scappaticci, McGrory didn't accept her view that he had a viable defence of necessity for having lied on oath. He is said to have argued that had Scappaticci genuinely felt his life to be at immediate risk, he could have accepted MI5's offer of resettlement. Instead, Scappaticci had chosen to stay in Belfast. Nor had Scappaticci's claim to be in imminent fear of his life been tested by Detective Chief Superintendent Wright, because he had not been interviewed under caution after MI5's psychological assessment advised that further criminal investigation would likely exacerbate his depression to the point of suicide. Also, as a matter of law, McGrory is said to have argued that the rarely used defence of necessity was something more appropriately determined by a court than the PPS. It was for these reasons that McGrory considered Atchison's decision not to prosecute Scappaticci to have been seriously flawed on the evidence available at that time.[79]

On 21 October 2015, McGrory announced that he had asked the PSNI to review Wright's perjury investigation. 'I have serious concerns in relation to this decision,' he said, which clearly extended to the PPS. 'Having reviewed all of the available evidence I consider that the original decision did not take into account relevant considerations and also took into account irrelevant factors.'[80] McGrory also referred the OPONI's analysis of the thirty-two boxes of Stakeknife files back to the PSNI to investigate 'the range of offences alleged to have been committed' by the agent – the third time in six years that a Northern Ireland DPP had felt compelled to exercise that power under Section 35(5) of the Justice (Northern Ireland) Act 2000. Included was 'any criminal activity that may have been carried out' by the intelligence services – in other words, a criminal investigation not just into Scappaticci, but also into how he was handled and managed by the FRU and any role played by MI5 and Special Branch.

While Atchison had concluded Scappaticci should not be prosecuted for perjury, she had reached this view in consultation with her superiors at that time.[81] To McGrory, however, the way that decision had been arrived at was in marked contrast to the PPS's approach six months earlier in its decision not to prosecute the ex-FRU CO Gordon Kerr and two of his officers for misfeasance in public office for how Brian Nelson had been handled. In Nelson's case, the PPS file contained a clear audit trail of the decisions taken, while for Scappaticci there was a thin file containing only Atchison's written opinion, setting out her reasoning as to why Scappaticci had a viable defence of necessity. The PPS appears to have felt obliged to comply with MI5's requirement that all the accompanying papers be stored elsewhere, even though the PPS had for decades stored equally sensitive material.[82]

I understand McGrory began a hunt for all papers linked to the perjury case, first by calling the PSNI, who contacted MI5, who said they'd given the papers to the PSNI, but the PSNI told McGrory they could not be located. Eventually, the PSNI managed to retrieve some of the papers, which included Detective Chief Superintendent Wright's handwritten report to Atchison in 2007 recommending no prosecution. He also retrieved papers relating to Scappaticci's 2003 judicial review of NCND and was appalled to discover that MI5, government law officers and Lord Chief Justice Carswell had all known not only that Scappaticci's affidavit was entirely false but that so too were his reasons for pursuing the review: an entirely performative ruse aimed at persuading the IRA and the wider Northern Ireland public that he wasn't Stakeknife, so that he could continue to live in Belfast a while longer.[83] McGrory says that while he is 'not at liberty to discuss the details' of the review, he was 'concerned that certain events that arose in the context of those proceedings had caused very considerable damage to the integrity of the administration of justice in this jurisdiction'.[84]

He also stated that two further differences between the Nelson and Scappaticci cases stood out. First, unlike Nelson, the PPS had chosen not to consult senior counsel before deciding Scappaticci had no case to answer. Second, while both cases involved significant issues relating to national security, unlike Nelson, there was no record of any referral of the Scappaticci file to the Attorney General's Office in London, as per the rules required in 2007 in cases of national security,[85] prior to the devolved post of attorney general for Northern Ireland being established in 2010. This was despite the fact that prior to the post being devolved, the attorney general's chief adviser on Northern Ireland, Kevin McGinty, often made weekly trips to Belfast to be briefed by the PPS. McGinty's job as deputy director of the Attorney General's Office was to advise his superior 'on all aspects' of their role 'as Attorney General for Northern Ireland'[86] – except, it seems, his advice was not sought on one of the most consequential decisions the PPS in Belfast had ever taken: the alleged perjury of a key British agent. The attorney general had been closely involved in all the Stevens 3 prosecutorial decisions, and those who know McGinty say it is inconceivable that he would not have involved the attorney general had he known Scappaticci was being considered for prosecution.[87]

The decision by the PPS not to consult the Attorney General's Office appears to have been taken above Atchison's head, and without consulting her, even though she had been tasked with considering the available evidence and coming to a conclusion about whether Scappaticci should be prosecuted. 'I am not aware of the nature or extent of any consultation that may have taken place' between the PPS and Attorney General's Office, she told me.[88] As I mentioned previously, at the time the PPS avoided publicly disclosing whether the decision not to prosecute Scappaticci had been on evidentiary or public interest grounds, despite the new code committing the PPS to at least that basic level of transparency.[89] McGrory says that when, as DPP, he sought an explanation for this in 2016, his 'efforts did not bear fruit'.[90] That too was in marked contrast to the Nelson case, where, over ten pages, the PPS had set out its reasoning for not prosecuting any member of the FRU.[91]

Much troubled by the perjury case, McGrory sought advice from several leading London-based QCs, whose prosecution credentials had given them insights into the workings of the security establishment. He was recommended to seek a formal opinion from Jonathan Laidlaw QC, a former Treasury counsel and head of 2 Hare Court Chambers. Having read the papers supplied by McGrory, Laidlaw advised that he found Atchison's perjury decision 'significantly and troublingly flawed' and confirmed McGrory in his view that further investigation was required.[92] Acting on Laidlaw's advice that, for the matter to be properly investigated, Atchison should be interviewed under caution during the course of any such investigation, McGrory also considered it necessary to alert Northern Ireland Attorney General John Larkin, who had responsibility for any disciplinary issues concerning the office holders of both the director and deputy DPP. Meanwhile, McGrory told Atchison he had advised the chief constable that the s35(5) referral he'd made the previous October should also 'consider the possibility of criminal misconduct on the part of those in the PPS who had carriage of the case'.[93] Atchison was then put on gardening leave.[94]

This was a heavy blow for a lawyer widely respected for her experience in legacy cases. The disciplinary case was never resolved, as she reached the statutory retirement age while the attorney general was still considering the matter. McGrory told me that he acknowledges how hard this must have been for his deputy, but says he'd been 'dumbstruck' by what he alleges was her failure to inform him of the perjury decision, having known for many years that the same individual may also have been involved in many murders and abductions.[95] He also said the fact that the perjury decision had not been referred to the Attorney General's Office by the PPS concerned him greatly, although Atchison says that was nothing to do with her. Nevertheless, McGrory reiterates that the Northern Ireland DPP, unlike his counterpart in England and Wales, was subject to superintendence and direction by the attorney general. The PPS was therefore required to consult the attorney general on all decisions pertaining to national security. During the Stevens 3 investigations into Stakeknife, the Attorney General's Office had been consulted every step of the way, and the fact that this had not happened in the perjury case led him to suspect that MI5 had put pressure on the PPS to 'keep the lid on it' in order to keep NCND intact, or to avoid scrutiny from the most senior UK law officer into how the investigation had been managed. He also felt that the failure to prosecute meant a suspected multiple murderer had again been protected. 'I was determined that would not happen again. Not on my watch,' he said.[96]

In light of the legal advice given to him that Atchison should be interviewed under caution, he did not consider his treatment of her to be disproportionate. 'Had evidence emerged of prosecutorial complicity in a conspiracy to prevent this individual from being prosecuted over perjury, that would have been utterly catastrophic for the PPS,' he said. 'Fortunately, it didn't, but on the basis of the available evidence at the time, I didn't know that.'[97]

As mentioned, Atchison has emphasised that had she felt MI5 was trying to keep 'a lid' on Scappaticci's prosecution for perjury, she would have had no part of that. Her former PPS colleague, Stephen Herron, who succeeded McGrory as DPP, has said he found 'no evidence of any bad faith or impropriety in terms of how' she'd 'sought to fulfil' her 'responsibilities'. Herron also found her decision not to prosecute Scappaticci to have been 'correct, or at the very least, a decision that could reasonably have been taken on the evidence available at that time'.[98] Herron acknowledged that, by acting as decisionmaker in Atchinson's case, his role 'clearly raised an issue of an actual or perceived conflict of interest' since she and he had been colleagues, but he said he'd 'sought to address' the 'risk of any potential perception of impartiality' by getting outside counsel's advice 'as regards the prospects of conviction' after consulting the Northern Ireland attorney general.[99]

Asked by me why she had not informed McGrory of the perjury investigation and her role in it until after June 2015, when the ombudsman had shown McGrory the full extent of Scappaticci's criminality, Atchison told me she did not intend to reopen the perjury issue.[100]

The disagreement between McGrory and his deputy soured what, up to then, is understood to have been a close and amicable working relationship. McGrory had held Atchison in high regard as a conscientious and able criminal lawyer.[101] In correspondence with me, Atchison questioned whether McGrory had acted in good faith when he referred her role to the police for investigation of potential misconduct. 'I question whether there was a proper and sufficient basis for the bona fide exercise of the Director's statutory powers,' she told me.[102] In earlier correspondence, she said she would 'refrain from speculating as to why' McGrory had referred her to the police.[103] McGrory responded that, in the light of Laidlaw's advice that she should be interviewed under caution, he felt he had no choice.[104]

Atchison's wounding intimation that McGrory had acted out of some unspecified motive is reflective of how bitterly divisive legacy can become. What exactly she had in mind, she has declined to say. For his part, McGrory said his only motive was to uphold the rule of law and to protect the integrity and reputation of the PPS he'd been appointed to lead following the much-delayed devolution of justice powers under the terms of the Good Friday Agreement. By the time of his appointment in 2011, justice powers had been devolved to the Northern Ireland institutions, and the NI DPP was no longer subject to superintendence and direction from the attorney general of England and Wales. He said he was 'determined to establish a prosecution service that was robustly independent'. While he was 'very relieved' that, upon investigation, no evidence of misconduct emerged, he said he was still at a loss to understand why much fuller disclosures about Stakeknife had not been made to him while he was director – the explanation for which has never been given to him.[105]

Meanwhile, in PSNI Chief Constable George Hamilton, McGrory found a supportive partner in his desire to get to the bottom of Stakeknife's crimes and the extent to which the intelligence service turned a blind eye to them. Following McGrory's referral back to the PSNI for a full-scale criminal investigation, Hamilton began the search for an outside police force prepared to take on the job – the eleventh occasion when a police officer, judge or barrister had been called in to review the legacy of the 1981 Walker doctrine, whose murky depths seemed to have no bottom. Although McGrory didn't know it then, as things turned out, his decision to reopen the criminal investigation into Scappaticci was to have a profound influence on attempts to open the doors that NCND had kept so firmly shut for decades. For one thing, the police officer who responded to Hamilton's request would come to believe just as firmly as McGrory that the time to let in more light on the lawless elements of Northern Ireland's counter-insurgency was long overdue.

Chapter Seventeen

6126 – Operation Kenova v MI5

JON BOUTCHER WAS MEETING FELLOW chief constables at a Surrey hotel in late spring 2016 when George Hamilton invited him for a walk to discuss a sensitive matter. There Hamilton set out the Stakeknife story. 'Could you take it on?' he asked.

Having spent much of his thirty-three years in covert policing in the Metropolitan Police fighting gangland crime and al-Qaeda and Islamic State-inspired terrorists, there was no dispute about his qualifications for the job. But Boutcher was also chief constable of Bedfordshire. 'How will you manage both jobs?' his wife asked him. That wasn't the issue for the workaholic Boutcher, who tends to mask a searing ambition for challenges behind a casual aside that he's just as happy walking his much-loved dog. The main question was, would he actually succeed?

Canvassing opinion from police colleagues, he was told firmly that there was not a chance. Only Lord Stevens urged him to accept the challenge, mindful of the obstruction he had faced investigating Brian Nelson, the murder of Patrick Finucane and Scappaticci. The rest were 'bleak depressives', with one ex-PSNI chief constable reminding Boutcher that Northern Ireland had been a career graveyard. 'That's why I took the job,' said Boutcher, 'because everyone but John Stevens told me not to.'[1]

Before definitely signing up, he flew to Belfast to meet the family of one of Freddie Scappaticci's victims. Hearing at first hand the intimate pain of their loss and how they had endured decades of community stigma, he returned to England, mind made up. 'Someone has got to fix this,' he told his wife. 'I'd like to try.'[2] Boutcher would come to see such families as the 'bravest, most humble, gracious, resilient, deserving and wronged group of victims' he had met in almost forty years of policing.[3] Today, no one doubts his empathy, nor his contempt for the many former members of the IRA approached by his officers to assist the families in finding the truth only to be referred to their lawyers who stated that they were unwilling to help.[4]

Much of the second half of 2016 was spent organising the complex logistics for Operation Kenova, recruiting a team of some sixty detectives, despite a national shortage, reading them in and devising a strategy for trying to open doors that had been firmly closed to previous inquiries. The investigation began in earnest in January 2017.[5]

Boutcher chose as Kenova's SIO Keith Surtees, a colleague from their days in the Metropolitan Police's Anti-Terrorist Branch, forerunner of the Counter Terrorism Command, SO15. Surtees was a Metropolitan Police commander, and like Boutcher he had worked closely with MI5 when he was head of investigations at SO15 during the 2012 London Olympic Games and the Queen's Diamond Jubilee celebrations.[6] Now MI5 was potentially in their sights, because Kenova's terms of reference spanned not just the criminality of the agent known as Stakeknife, but also 'any criminal activity that may have been carried out by Security Service personnel.'[7]

'We're not old school,' were Surtees' opening words when I met him and Boutcher for a drink soon after Kenova's press conference launch.[8] They were seeking my impressions of the obstacles confronting John Stevens' previous inquiries, on which I'd reported extensively. The problem was that several of the institutions with which Boutcher and Surtees would have to deal *were* rather old school.

The first in a series of culture shocks was their encounter with the PPS in Belfast. The outgoing DPP, Barra McGrory QC – whose referral of the Stakeknife case to the PSNI had led to Operation Kenova – was about to hand over to his deputy, Stephen Herron.[9] McGrory had made a start in trying to align the PPS more closely with its counterparts in the rest of the UK. Old habits die hard, however. Boutcher had urged the PPS to bring in counsel at an early stage to work alongside Surtees and his team, advising how best to maximise evidential leads as they developed. That was what

Boutcher and Surtees had been used to in London in similarly complex anti-terrorist cases. They found that the PPS in Belfast, by contrast, treated outside counsel's advice as confidential and had a tendency to exclude investigators from key conversations. The PPS listened politely to Boutcher's reasons as to why he considered this approach to be dated and how it led generally to a 'disjointed and transactional process with prosecutors, counsel and investigators each operating on the basis of different assumptions and understandings'.[10] As the investigation wore on, it became clear the PPS was not yet ready to leave its comfort zone entirely, content with its traditional, more standoffish view, summarised by one seasoned Belfast lawyer as: 'No, you're the police, we're the prosecutor, we'll wait till you do your job, then we'll do our job. And then *we'll* decide, thank you very much.'[11] Critics of this approach say it has its roots in an old class-bound culture that saw the lawyers at one level and the police below, an attitude that faded away years ago in the rest of the UK.

Another surprise was the discovery that what had been presented to Operation Kenova as the definitive legacy intelligence database held by the PSNI, turned out not to be fully available to them. Called MACER, this database had been created by the MoD for the army's use in the late 1980s, and it was handed over to the PSNI in 2007, when 'Operation Banner', the army's deployment in Northern Ireland, finally came to a close. The login the PSNI supplied to Kenova gave detectives access to two 'drawers' – the first to RUC/PSNI material and the second to the military. However, Kenova discovered there was a third drawer which had never been disclosed to any previous legacy inquiry.

This discovery was made when Surtees sent two of his officers to search through the crates of Operation Banner files that had been shipped from Belfast to the MoD's deep underground storage facility in Derbyshire. A two-day rummage showed that the most sensitive material had gone into crates marked 'Miscellaneous', including all of the files relating to the army's covert 14 Intelligence Company, the 'Det', which conducted surveillance operations. The officers also found the design blueprint for MACER, which revealed the third drawer. This Aladdin's cave held ten times the number of MISRs relating to Stakeknife as the other drawers,[12] none of which had seen the light of day during Stevens 3.

The MoD had promised Boutcher that he would get everything – an undertaking which the Kenova team still regards as having been given in good faith,[13] since there appeared to be no one left in the MoD with the institutional memory of a third MACER drawer or who knew the system's design. That wasn't entirely the case for the PSNI, however. One senior PSNI officer did know but didn't tell.[14]

Having retained much of the conflict-related material it had received from both the FRU and Special Branch,[15] MI5 chiefs also promised to cooperate by agreeing an information-sharing protocol, pledging that all material relevant to Kenova would be disclosed.[16] It was a promise which Boutcher and Surtees initially had high hopes the security service would fulfil, not least since both men had worked closely with MI5 on Islamist terrorism investigations. But that was not how things worked out, says Boutcher, with the Kenova–MI5 relationship enduring some 'extremely fractious spells' where the 'process of extracting information … sometimes felt like a hard-fought uphill battle'.[17] An early hint of problems came when MI5 remarked to Boutcher that Scappaticci was in protective custody, the inference being that he should be treated differently from the way suspects under criminal investigation were normally treated. Boutcher pointed out the obvious: protective custody didn't mean he was above the law.[18]

An issue also arose over who would ultimately decide what documents were 'relevant' to Kenova's investigation. MI5 appointed two officers to service requests for information from two retired but experienced detectives on the Kenova staff embedded at MI5's headquarters, Thames House, as 'Single Points of Contact' (SPOCs).[19] While the SPOCs were furnished with documents from which they could decide what was relevant, they had no way of knowing if those documents represented the full range of relevant material under MI5's control.[20] And although both ex-detectives were vetted to the highest level, they found the answers they were getting tended to be strictly limited to the precise question asked, with no elaboration. This 'narrow transactional approach'[21] was reminiscent of the Stevens 3 Inquiry's experience with MI5, whereby 'if you didn't get the question right you didn't get the answer'.[22] It provoked 'constant verbal spats' between the Kenova SPOCs and their two MI5 interlocutors, one of whom had apparently served in Northern Ireland when Scappaticci was operational. 'Why do you need this? Why do you need that?' the SPOCs would be asked as they began to uncover material not previously available to Stevens 3 and other legacy inquiries, including previous RUC investigations.[23] These middle-ranking MI5 officials seemed to have a lot of autonomy, despite MI5's leadership having pledged full support. Curious as to whether both interlocutors might have been operationally involved with Stakeknife in their younger days, Kenova sought their CVs, but the request went unanswered.[24] Trust was also not enhanced by the discovery that MI5 had accessed the secure safe where the two Kenova SPOCs stored their papers in a room set aside for them. Kenova had understood the combination code to be theirs alone, and it had to be changed as a result.[25]

From the outset, MI5 insisted to Kenova that it had had no supervisory or operational role over Scappaticci, and that its involvement with him was peripheral,[26] limited to handling his periodic flirtations with resettlement. 'The service kept telling us they weren't on the pitch.'[27] This proved to be untrue, and particularly disconcerting to Kenova was the fact that these claims came mostly from MI5's legal department.[28]Also inaccurate was an internal assessment of Scappaticci drawn up by MI5, which was shared with Kenova and contained false assumptions about his value as an agent, repeating 'inaccurate and unreliable FRU figures about lives saved by Stakeknife'. As Boutcher would later explain, 'the report set out a position … that MI5 had seen and heard nothing to suggest that Stakeknife had been personally involved in any serious criminality'.[29] The service also claimed that the assessment covered the entirety of their files; that too would prove to be spectacularly untrue, with a large tranche of files conveniently discovered by MI5 only *after* the Northern Ireland (Legacy and Reconciliation) Act 2023 came into force prohibiting the continuation or commencement of any conflict-related criminal investigation, civil action, inquest or police complaint.[30] This is further addressed in the next chapter.

While Kenova was becoming sceptical about MI5's initial pledges of full co-operation, some of the families of Scappaticci's victims were sounding sceptical about Kenova's ability to get to the truth. As Boutcher himself acknowledged, some assumed Kenova would be 'nothing more than a puppet of the British establishment and would not investigate their cases properly'.[31] In January 2018, a decision was made that Kenova hoped would send a clear signal demonstrating the opposite.

'Frank Conway', the alias MI5's resettlement department had given Scappaticci, was whiling away his days comfortably in exile, if a little bored, in a white detached house protected by a high hedge in Guildford, Surrey. To his neighbours in the semi-rural Worplesdon Road, he seemed to occupy his days gardening and walking his cocker spaniel.[32] To those who enquired, 'Frank' said he'd been in 'construction', both cover name and occupation (Freddie/Frank; bricklayer/construction) being minor variations on Scappaticci's true identity to enable him to adapt more credibly to his new false persona. His wife, Sheila, would occasionally visit, but, having always fancied himself as something of a ladies' man, he had also found a girlfriend,[33] reportedly in a dog-walking group, and he would take her occasionally to Pizza Express in Guildford before returning to his silver Mercedes 'parked around the corner for a fumble'.[34] This wasn't sufficient to satisfy his sexual appetite, however. Surveillance showed that, alone in his house, extreme pornography with animals beat Netflix for Scappaticci when it came to his viewing habits.

Then, one day in January 2018, to the astonishment of his neighbours, police surrounded the house and arrested 'Frank'. The raid served a dual purpose: one, it sent a signal to Kenova's sceptics in Belfast that it was serious; and two, Kenova suspected that Scappaticci may have hidden in the house an insurance policy that evidentially might serve as a confession and also demonstrate complicity by his handlers – something similar to the journal Nelson had written on remand in Crumlin Road Gaol intended as his defence should he be charged with murder. An extensive search, however, drew a blank.

The raid infuriated Scappaticci and MI5, upending their resettlement arrangements and necessitating a search for a new safe abode. In the custody suite at the Metropolitan Police's Southwark police station, Scappaticci projected an air of entitlement, as if this was not at all where an important state asset expected to find himself. He was particularly incensed at the response to his enquiry about the fate of his dog. In view of the extreme nature of the pornography he'd been watching, the animal had been taken into custody to be checked by a vet to see if it had been interfered with. It hadn't.

During interrogation under caution, Scappaticci stayed silent, except when the tape was off. In one breath he cursed Surtees as a 'c***', while in another he attempted to strike up a friendly banter with a female Kenova interrogator.[35] When questioned about the executions of Vincent Robinson, Seamus Morgan and Anthony McKiernan, he remained silent but showed flickers of emotion.[36] Was he perhaps reflecting back to when Robinson and McKiernan had been family friends, and the fact that Morgan – with whom he spent his last hours – was in emotional pieces as he waited for the executioner's bullet?

Scappaticci was eventually charged with possession of extreme pornography, to which MI5 raised strong objections. On the eve of his appearance at Westminster magistrates court, the list for the following day's hearings was unusually absent. The computer link had apparently – perhaps suspiciously – failed. Nonetheless, a reporter was in court to hear that the British Army's 'golden egg' had watched 329 sexually extreme images on his computer. Although Chief Magistrate Baroness Emma Arbuthnot sentenced Scappaticci to three months suspended for a year, she struck an unworldly note by commenting: 'You have not been before the court for 50 years – and that's good character in my book.'[37] Perhaps she hadn't read the newspapers.

In asking the PSNI to launch a criminal reinvestigation of Freddie Scappaticci, in 2015 the then DPP, Barra McGrory, had spoken of what he feared had become the 'potential complete corruption of the judicial and legal process' in the favourable way the spy and his ISU associates had been dealt with.[38] What McGrory particularly had in mind was not just the suspicion that some agents had been sacrificed to preserve Scappaticci's cover, but also the reluctance and sometimes outright refusal of Special Branch to assist the CID in investigating him and the ISU following an execution, and also the FRU's attempts to prevent the risk of that happening. The Kenova investigation bore out that concern. Boutcher says it established that other agents were 'actively involved or implicated in kidnappings, unlawful imprisonment, assaults and murders and that the unit withheld information that could have prevented these crimes.'[39]

Kenova's remit included investigating whether there was evidence of anyone having committed a criminal offence 'in respect of allegations of perjury connected to the alleged agent.'[40] The basis of Scappaticci's alleged perjury was the false affidavit he'd sworn on 21 May 2003 in support of his bogus judicial review of the government's refusal to neither confirm nor deny that he was Stakeknife. As previously seen, that exercise had been a sham.

Scappaticci himself had acknowledged to MI5 that his real agenda was to give judicial credence to his vociferous public denials that he was Stakeknife in the hope that he could continue to live securely in Belfast. Since MI5 and government law officers, including Attorney General Lord Goldsmith and Lord Chief Justice of Northern Ireland Lord Carswell, did not appear to have raised any objection to this sham, it fell to Boutcher and Surtees to interview them. It was an unusually delicate task for the police.

To borrow British comedian Catherine Tate's catchphrase, requests for police interviews with these two pillars of the legal establishment were greeted with a barely suppressed 'how-very-dare-you' response from their lordships.[41] Still, they needed to provide answers to Kenova's questions. Carswell had, after all, decided to take over Scappaticci's judicial review from the judge rostered to hear the case with only four days to go, after Philip Sales, the government's senior legal advisor, had explained to Carswell that Scappaticci was indeed Stakeknife and did not actually want the public relief he was pretending to seek. When Boutcher and Surtees sat down to question Carswell, there was a tangible froideur from the former lord chief justice. Carswell told the officers that he had informed Sales curtly, 'You didn't need to tell me that!', apparently on the basis that whether Scappaticci had lied on oath would not be material to the legal issue before the court, which was whether the government had been right to apply NCND, irrespective of the truth of Scappaticci's affidavit.[42]

A week after the hearing, Carswell issued his judgment that the government had been quite correct to apply NCND to Scappaticci on the grounds that the public interest lay in strictly maintaining the principle of neither confirming nor denying whether someone was an agent to ensure future recruitment and retention of agents. There was no mention of Scappaticci's fraudulent affidavit, which had kicked the whole thing off.

Puzzled by Carswell's reasoning in the face of the facts, Surtees pressed him as to why exactly he had considered Scappaticci's alleged perjury to be immaterial? After all, without Scappaticci's false affidavit, there would have been no proceedings in the first place. Carswell bristled.[43] Surtees pressed on. Surely the proceedings became 'material' the moment Scappaticci had used the false affidavit to secure permission from the lower court under Mr Justice Kerr to have the full hearing before Carswell himself? Back came a frozen look that seemed to say, 'I, a former Lord Chief Justice, really shouldn't have to account for myself to a couple of coppers.'[44]

No more satisfactory were Kenova's interviews with the two principal MI5 officers who had withheld from the PSNI's 2007 perjury investigation the fact that Scappaticci had sworn not one but four affidavits. Kenova judged that the MI5 officers – one of whom was a lawyer in MI5's legal department – had misconducted themselves in public office and had conceivably attempted to pervert the course of justice. Prosecution files were sent to the PPS. At the very least, Kenova argued, as public servants with a law enforcement role, they had a duty of candour to police officers conducting a criminal investigation.

According to Boutcher, MI5 was also limiting Kenova's ability to question 'former security force personnel' (presumably ex-FRU personnel) properly by providing them with 'greater and unorthodox access to MI5 materials' than that being supplied to Kenova. The Security Service had also upgraded the classification of documents previously marked 'Secret' to 'Top Secret'.[45] This, said Boutcher, was impeding 'analytical and investigative examination and comparison work', because Kenova's HOLMES computer was only accredited to hold material classified up to 'Secret'.[46] Other obstacles included claims that witness statements made by MI5 personnel belonged to MI5 and could not be disclosed to the DPP or referred to in other Kenova interviews without its permission. [47] At one stage, the level of impediments MI5 was putting in Kenova's way caused Boutcher to consider applying for a search warrant of its headquarters,[48] a step the Stevens 3 Inquiry had also contemplated over a decade earlier.

There were also what Boutcher perceived as attempts to undermine Kenova's work generally and him personally. In November 2019, at a face-to-face meeting with MI5, Boutcher was told Kenova had breached national security and that he'd colluded with a BBC Northern Ireland *Spotlight* documentary that was critical of the Security Service. The BBC had broadcast a clip in which the former FRU handler Ian Hurst had covertly recorded a Kenova detective chief inspector telling him that Kenova had found MI5 'documents that Stevens never found which are very telling about the role that our man [Stakeknife] played in certain things'. The MI5 documents 'tree' was what 'we keep shaking', said the officer. 'A little bit more comes out all the time.'[49]

In fact, the broadcast recording shows that the detective chief inspector stuck strictly to NCND protocol by not identifying Scappaticci as Stakeknife – referring simply to 'our man' – despite knowing that Hurst, as an ex-member of FRU, knew exactly who he was. It was, after all, Hurst's accusations that Scappaticci had repeatedly committed perjury that had led to the PSNI's 2007 investigation in the first place. The detective chief inspector had met Hurst to arrange taking a statement from him and also to update him on the general progress of the inquiry, a courtesy that Hurst did not reciprocate when he secretly recorded him and then passed the recording to the BBC. Boutcher told MI5 he'd had no prior knowledge of the *Spotlight* programme before transmission, because the BBC had not sought his response. It was a storm in a teacup, yet it didn't stop MI5's then deputy director general, Ken McCallum, from sending a letter of complaint to the NIO and the deputy national security advisor, despite Boutcher having rebutted each of MI5's allegations by letter.[50]

These shenanigans were interpreted by Boutcher as an attempt to shake his confidence.[51] In January 2020, he was confronted with an even more lurid allegation: he was accused of having breached the Official Secrets Act by passing the names of agents to former members of the PIRA. Invited to PSNI headquarters to give a general update on Kenova, Boutcher found Chief Constable Simon Byrne and ACC George Clarke poised to ask him a series of questions, informing him his answers would be forwarded to MI5.

The allegations related to a meeting Boutcher had had with a lawyer acting for the relatives of two armed, balaclava-wearing brothers in the IRA who were shot by the SAS as they were about to murder an unarmed off-duty soldier in 1988 in Drumnakilly, County Tyrone. The lawyer wished to know if there was evidence of Scappaticci having set up the SAS ambush? Clear that this theory was 'misconceived', Boutcher suggested that if the lawyer wished to pursue the matter, he should take it up with the PSNI. The ex-IRA members to whom Boutcher was falsely said to have leaked the names of agents were not present at the meeting and Boutcher said he'd never met them.[52] Byrne never told Boutcher whether the attempted smear had originated from an MI5 or PSNI agent.[53]

Coincidence or otherwise, both confrontations happened shortly after Kenova had attempted – and failed – to submit the first tranche of thirty-five prosecution files to the PPS in Belfast. They failed because, on the day the files were due to be submitted, MI5 intervened to say the PPS's Belfast offices' security accreditation, allowing the PPS to hold the files there, had expired.[54] To speed things up, Boutcher offered to make the files available to the PPS at a suitably accredited PSNI location, but they declined.[55]

This initial tranche was particularly sensitive as far as MI5 was concerned because it contained evidence against the two MI5 officers relating to misconduct in public office – the two who had not disclosed three of Scappaticci's sworn affidavits to the PSNI's perjury investigation.[56] It also included the evidence against Scappaticci for perjury, as well as evidence covering mostly IRA suspects involved in five murders and three abductions.[57] The tranche also contained evidence against six FRU members and former Detective Chief Superintendent George Caskey for conspiring to pervert the course of justice through their joint plot to prevent Scappaticci from being charged with abducting and falsely imprisoning Sandy Lynch in 1990 on Scappaticci's return to Belfast nearly three years later.[58]

Kenova's prosecution files were, of course, classified, but there was nothing unprecedented about their sensitivity where the PPS was concerned. They'd been in receipt of equally sensitive material for decades and, so far as is known, no objection to their security arrangements had been raised previously. In truth, that same office had probably reviewed more sensitive national security cases than any other part of the UK.[59] In February 2020, MI5 finally approved the PPS's security accreditation and the tranche was submitted.[60] The four-month delay from the initial attempt at submission was only the start of a process that would see PPS lawyers take another four years to reach a conclusion on all thirty-five of Kenova's prosecution files.

None of this is to suggest that Kenova got only crumbs of information from a permanently obstructive MI5: by February 2020, the service had responded to 1,500 requests, provided access to hundreds of files, and facilitated interviews with thirty current and former staff, although Kenova complained that too much of it had been like pulling teeth. A 'potentially relevant' MI5 file, which Kenova initially reported as having gone 'missing within MI5',[61] was also found. And, in fairness to McCallum, he responded to Boutcher's complaints by commissioning a review, after which Boutcher acknowledged the information-sharing process improved significantly.[62]

The sniping did not entirely cease, however. In November 2019, Boutcher had been formally asked by the PSNI to review another legacy case, that of the so-called 'Hooded Men', whose treatment by the army in 1971 after being arrested during internment has been determined by the Supreme Court to amount to torture by today's standards. Interrogated at Ballykelly army base, fourteen men were 'hooded; beaten, deprived of sleep, food and water; and forced to stand in the stress position'.[63] Out of the blue, in March 2021, the PSNI told Boutcher to cease his review, after an affidavit sworn by a PSNI superintendent accused him of having 'acted on my own initiative (or words to that effect)' by drawing up his own terms of reference rather than using the PSNI's. Boutcher emphasised to the PSNI that this was untrue, and, after a solicitor for the hooded men intervened, the PSNI accepted Boutcher's denial[64] and the affidavit was amended.[65] To Kenova, however, it was another example of attempted control by what Boutcher has referred to as the 'self-appointed guardians' of the conflict's history.[66]

In October 2020, the PPS ruled there should be no prosecution of Scappaticci for perjury, or of the two MI5 officers for misconduct in public office for withholding information relevant to the PSNI's 2007 criminal investigation into his alleged perjury.[67] DPP Stephen Herron agreed with his former colleague Pamela Atchison's 2007 decision that Scappaticci had a 'defence of duress of circumstances', which allows a false statement on oath in the face of an imminent and unavoidable threat of death or serious bodily harm. This decision puzzled some lawyers, as Scappaticci, who had declined to be interviewed by Kenova about the matter, had provided no tangible evidence about his 'necessity' to lie.[68] As explained earlier, Scappaticci could reasonably have accepted MI5's offer of resettlement, removing the risk to his life from a possible IRA attack. Instead, in the full knowledge of MI5, government lawyers and the judiciary, he chose to take his chances. How Scappaticci could successfully have availed himself of a defence of duress in those circumstances was not explained by Herron, who said he was prevented from doing so by NCND.[69]

As to Herron's rejection of Kenova's case against the two MI5 officers, he ruled the three affidavits they had withheld from the PSNI were irrelevant because they 'contained no false statement'.[70] It is true that none of these affidavits repeats in precise terms Scappaticci's false statement sworn on 21

May 2003 that he was not a security force agent, 'whether known as Stakeknife or by any other name'.[71] Yet it is also true that, for example, the third affidavit, sworn in February 2004, stated, 'I have strenuously denied this allegation and have already attempted to clear my name of this allegation through the courts.' The get-out here appears to be that he was merely reporting the fact of his previous denial, as distinct from *reiterating* that denial. But as Boutcher emphasised, all three undisclosed affidavits were grounded in Scappaticci's first affidavit,[72] and Herron acknowledged there was a 'reasonable prospect' of proving Scappaticci knew that first affidavit to be false.[73] A 'reasonable prospect'? Who better to know for certain that he was the agent known as Stakeknife than the agent himself?

Nonetheless, Herron concluded this didn't amount to perjury because, although the affidavit was sworn and signed for the purpose of court proceedings, it wasn't strictly 'material' to the precise legal issue to be determined by Carswell – which was whether the government had been correct to apply NCND in Scappaticci's case. Carswell had ruled that that issue was about judging where the balance of public interest lay, between the risk to Scappaticci's life by continuing to neither confirm nor deny he was Stakeknife, against making an exception in his case. To the man on the Clapham omnibus, these serpentine legal weavings must have seemed quite baffling in the face of the simple facts, which are that Scappaticci swore a false oath for the purpose of legal proceedings, knowing it to be false and exploiting the judicial system with his legal charade, while continuing to perpetuate that falsehood with three further affidavits.

Herron, it should be emphasised, was relying largely on a lengthy written opinion from the Treasury's former go-to counsel David Perry QC. Boutcher had relied on the opinion of Jonathan Laidlaw QC.[74] Both are highly experienced criminal barristers. Laidlaw had previously advised McGrory that the PPS's 2007 decision not to prosecute Scappaticci for perjury hadn't provided sufficient basis to conclude that he had a viable defence of necessity. In fact, Laidlaw had concluded that a court would likely have rejected that defence. On the question of whether Scappaticci's lie on oath was material to the legal issue to be determined by Carswell, I understand Perry accepted that might be arguable; Laidlaw thought the issue should be decided by the court. Herron, however, judged there would be 'significant difficulty' in proving materiality and therefore it was not worth putting to the court, but that even had it been, the prosecution would still be unable to 'disprove beyond a reasonable doubt any defence of duress of circumstances' – a position with which Laidlaw and Boutcher fundamentally disagreed.[75]

As mentioned, Herron declined to elaborate further on the reasoning behind his decision not to prosecute Scappaticci for perjury, apparently prevented by government lawyers from giving any further details. The client of those lawyers was, of course, MI5. Once again, the strict application of the NCND policy required the public to have only limited information. Boutcher disagreed that Herron was unable to provide a fuller explanation: 'I am quite certain that DPP(NI) could quite properly have gone into more detail about the facts and the rationale for his decision not to prosecute' with no impact on national security through any potential 'negative impact on agent recruitment or activity'.[76] However, MI5 was adamant – Herron could not go further. They even insisted on major redactions on the perjury case in Boutcher's interim report. Boutcher responded by making it clear that if they persisted with this demand, he would take them to court, saying this was 'not about national security but about national embarrassment'.[77] In respect of Pamela Atchison, however, Kenova agreed with Herron that there was no evidence that she had acted in bad faith or with impropriety in reaching her decision in 2007 not to prosecute.[78]

When Boutcher set foot in Belfast in 2016, he had privately expressed confidence that Kenova would secure prosecutions, at least against Scappaticci and some members of the IRA, but this early rejection from the PPS marked a turning point in his expectations. Following the decision not to prosecute, he said, 'Legacy should not be judged simply through the prism of prosecutions. It must be considered as a process which provides the truth to those families who have lost loved ones.'[79] The change of emphasis from prosecutions to truth recovery as the litmus test of Kenova's success confirmed – at least in Boutcher's mind – his early misgivings about the PPS's dated approach to legacy cases.

The PPS wasn't entirely to blame. One of the few things that Northern Ireland's tribal politicians appear to agree on is that legacy victims come first – with 'appear' being the operative word. When Barra McGrory KC was DPP, the devolved Department of Finance cut his funding from £37m to

£32m despite the increasing demands that legacy cases were making on his budget. When his successor, Stephen Herron, asked the department for a £2m increase in his budget, he was refused. The PPS is an easy target to sideline because it isn't represented by a minister competing for the Minister of Finance's attention, and ministers get preferential treatment.

As a consequence, in 2021 Herron informed Boutcher that he could not promise a prosecutorial decision on the twenty-five files Kenova had submitted by May that year until well into 2022.[80] A further ten files were submitted in 2022. In the event, the decisions didn't start coming until December 2023 and weren't completed until 29 February 2024. Meanwhile justice delayed was justice denied. In February 2022, ex-Detective Chief Superintendent George Caskey died, well before Herron's lawyers got round to reviewing Kenova's evidence against him. In March 2023, the same fate befell the majority of Kenova's files on Freddie Scappaticci linking him to thirteen murders and fifteen abductions including torture.

Boutcher was informed by MI5 of Scappaticci's death on 6 April, Maundy Thursday, 2023. He had died of a stroke on 20 March.[81] The fetishised strictures of NCND would prevent Kenova from disclosing the date of his death in Jon Boutcher's interim report, published in March 2024,[82] presumably lest it led to the unravelling of his cover name 'Frank Cowley' by a nosey journalist tracking down his death certificate. 'Cowley' had been the alias he'd been living under since changing his name by deed poll from 'Frank Conway' after Kenova's raid on his house in Guildford in January 2018. More immediately, NCND posed a dilemma about how to actually announce his death. Clearly the relatives of his victims would wish to know, but if Boutcher announced his death, they would naturally ask how he knew. Any attribution by Boutcher to MI5 being the source of news of his demise would be tantamount to an admission that Freddie Scappaticci was indeed the agent known as Stakeknife. Otherwise, why would MI5 have anything to do with the matter? It was a connection NCND forbade Boutcher from making. The relatives would also probably ask if Boutcher had satisfied himself that Scappaticci really was dead. The slightest uncertainty in answering would feed Belfast's voracious appetite for conspiracy theories, which, at times, was not entirely without reason, given some well-established historical instances of the darker arts.

Within days, word of the death was spreading from parts of Belfast, apparently triggered by the disclosure from a Scappaticci family relative. Already Boutcher was getting calls from relatives of his victims: were reports of his death really true? Urgent discussions about the wording of any official announcement took place between the NIO, the PSNI and the PPS. Of course, Scappaticci's death also meant the PPS would no longer have to make a determination on the majority of the Kenova files still awaiting a decision.

The solution finally agreed on was for Boutcher to announce Scappaticci's death without attribution to MI5 and for Kenova to do its own due diligence on establishing that he had actually died, there being no body to identify because he had been cremated. Surtees dispatched officers to St Peter's Hospital in Chertsey, Surrey, where 'Frank Cowley' had finally succumbed to the stroke he'd suffered on 16 February at his new rented home called 'Homeleigh', in the Surrey village of West End,[83] six miles from the home he'd had to abandon in January 2018. Both properties were notable for being far larger than a single person would have needed, and both were obscured behind a high hedge. Although while resettled in England Scappaticci had had limited contact with his family, one of his sons appears to have been with him when he suffered his stroke. Alerted by four unmarked cars containing armed police descending on the house after Scappaticci pressed a panic button, a neighbour telephoned Homeleigh's owner Simon Meaney. 'I don't know what's going on at your house, mate, but you better get back here sharpish,' reported the neighbour. 'There's cops with guns everywhere.' Meaney asked 'Frank's' son what had happened but was told 'his Dad had become confused and dialled 999 by accident'. Then he sat on the sofa, turned on the TV and 'just wouldn't look me in the eye. I remember coming and saying to my wife, "I don't believe a word of what I've been told."'[84]

'Frank Cowley' entered hospital under his new alias, so to satisfy themselves that he was indeed Freddie Scappaticci, Kenova officers recovered the CCTV of the former being wheeled on a trolley from the ambulance into A&E. They also got a statement from the doctor who pronounced Cowley dead.[85] Satisfied that the agent known as Stakeknife was no more, on 11 April Boutcher made the announcement, emphasising Kenova's continued commitment to 'providing families with the truth of what happened to their loved ones'.[86]

'Frank Cowley' died a wealthy man, although how wealthy we will not know for another seventy years, because he shares with the royal family the distinction of a High Court ruling that his will should be sealed, in his case until 2095 – a practice that was challenged as legally questionable in relation to the royals by the last Conservative government.[87] The hearing to decide whether the 'Estate of Frank Cowley Deceased' should be sealed was held in private on 21 July 2025. The application was made by a 'Michael Johnson', who had said he was prepared to act as 'Cowley's' representative only on condition that the will was sealed. No clue as to 'Johnson's' real identity was given, save that the Security Service is understood to have said he was nothing to do with them,[88] in which case he was presumably a relative or friend of the family. The attorney general supported his application.

This was the first ever application for the sealing of a non-royal's will under the 1987 Non-Contentious Probate Rules, which allow this 'if in the opinion of a District Judge or Registrar, such inspection would be undesirable or inappropriate'. The judge, Sir Julian Flaux, Chancellor of the High Court, so considered 'Johnson's' application, yet neither the applicant nor Sir Julian gave any concrete rationale as to why disclosing Cowley's will would be 'undesirable' or 'inappropriate'. Sir Julian simply said there was a need to protect from 'the real risk of physical harm, or even death' the 'beneficiaries' of 'Frank Cowley', lest they be thought 'guilty by association with the Deceased'.[89] Yet 'Frank Cowley's' children have not changed their names by deed poll, so far as is known, so how disclosing what Scappaticci bequeathed to them in any way elevates that notional risk was not explained. It also begs the question as to whether disclosing the full extent of Freddie Scappaticci's wealth, thanks to the British taxpayer, was what was really considered by 'Michael Johnson' to have been 'undesirable'.

The lost opportunity to prosecute Scappaticci was a bitter blow for some relatives, though it is by no means certain that the PPS would have pressed a single charge against him, even had he lived. That much became clear to Kenova after a high voltage afternoon session at the PPS's Belfast office, where Surtees made the case for reopening the prosecution against Scappaticci for kidnapping and conspiracy to murder Sandy Lynch – the case the FRU–Caskey plot had scuppered in October 1992. Although Scappaticci had been told Lynch's death sentence had been confirmed, and he had properly relayed this to his handlers, he also knew his rescue was far from certain. Surtees explained to the PPS that not only had Kenova recovered a fragment of Scappaticci's eyelash from a glove at the crime scene, corroborating his presence that weekend at 124 Carrigart Avenue, but they'd also found 'extremely sensitive' witness testimony (undisclosed due to its sensitivity), so this was not an evidential rehash. It was new and important evidence. Furthermore, they'd reinterviewed Lynch without allowing him to refer to his original deposition. The statement was some fifty pages and 'almost word for word matched what Lynch had said thirty years earlier'.[90] Back in 1991, Lord Justice Hutton had dismissed Lynch as a man of no moral worth – a verdict that at the time had force because Lynch was a member of a proscribed organisation, albeit a police agent. Yet, since then, explained Surtees, Lynch had been a man of good character – 'he hasn't even been through a red traffic light in thirty years'. Before Surtees sat the impassive faces of DPP Stephen Herron, his deputy and other staff. Could he at least put Lynch before them with counsel questioning him so they could judge for themselves, asked the former Metropolitan Police commander? To Surtees and his fellow officers, a successful prosecution was likely. The PPS didn't agree and his request was refused.

Other relatives were more sanguine about the PPS's failure to bring a single charge against Scappaticci. They were more concerned about just getting to the truth and nothing but the truth, which Boutcher and Surtees were still endeavouring to do while navigating the restrictions imposed by MI5's dogmatic application of NCND, which prevented Kenova from clearly identifying Scappaticci's full role in the deaths of their loved ones. Instead, the Kenova team had to talk in semi-code to relatives by referring to Scappaticci as, for example 'Suspect A, B, or C', when identified by witnesses in a particular incident, and to the 'agent' when referring to intelligence reports about his role in the same incident, so it was not always clear in Kenova family briefings when the suspect and the agent were one and the same.

The legacy of NCND as bequeathed by the 1981 recommendation of Sir Patrick Walker had also by now become glaringly apparent to Kenova. By adopting Walker's recommendation, Chief Constable Sir Jack Hermon and his successors had prioritised intelligence gathering over the criminal justice system, which had left a void in the rule of law and bestowed the unintended consequence of mounds of high-grade intelligence left unexploited at the expense of criminal justice – the so called 'building pictures' syndrome. In not a single murder case involving Scappaticci and his ISU associates was a police investigation file even submitted to the PPS, let alone prosecuted,[91] because in those cases the priority was protection of sources over prosecution of the crime. 'The criminal justice system was basically parked,' observed Boutcher. 'I call it the COVID of its day.'[92]

Kenova's investigation into Scappaticci had concluded well before he died, and by that point Boutcher had also completed his 207-page interim report, which he'd dispatched to the Cabinet Office for vetting. But he couldn't publish it until the PPS had concluded its deliberations on all of Kenova's prosecution files – and that would take almost another year. In the meantime, Boutcher carried on with the three other legacy inquiries the PSNI had asked him to complete: Operation Mizzenmast (the investigation into the 1972 murder of Jean Smyth-Campbell); Operation Turma (the 1982 IRA murder of three RUC officers); and Operation Denton (the UVF's so-called 'Glenanne Gang', which was less a gang and more an alliance of two dozen rogue soldiers and police officers in cahoots with the UVF who, between them, were responsible for some 127 murders in the mid-1970s in Mid Ulster).[93]

The Kenova model of legacy investigation had attracted significant support, not only from relatives and victims' groups, but also MPs on the Northern Ireland Affairs Committee and a growing number of Northern Ireland politicians. It was not popular, however, with the Conservative government, which was determined to draw a line under the past with a clear end to legacy prosecutions and criminal investigations, replacing these with information recovery and reconciliation. In September 2023, the government published its Northern Ireland Legacy Bill. Running to almost a hundred pages, it sought an end to further Kenova-type inquiries and uncompleted inquests into legacy killings.[94] Ministers made it clear the bill had more to do with ending what they referred to as 'vexatious claims' than fostering reconciliation.[95] Boutcher was not alone in suspecting it had more to do with putting a lid on further embarrassing disclosures about state-run agents involved in murder and other serious criminality, and also ending the prosecution of army veterans (there had only been a handful).

Meanwhile a vacancy had opened up for the post of PSNI chief constable. On 4 September 2023, Simon Byrne resigned after weeks of pressure over several controversies, including being reprimanded by a judge for pandering to political pressure from Sinn Féin over the unfair disciplining of two junior constables and an extremely serious data breach involving the personal information of more than 10,000 officers and support staff.[96] The Police Federation for Northern Ireland said the force was 'in dire need of clear and strong leadership'.[97]

Several politicians, as well Byrne's predecessor (by now Sir) George Hamilton, urged Boutcher to apply.[98] 'Kenova is the most important job I've ever done,' Boutcher told colleagues, vowing not to accept the invitation unless Sir Iain Livingstone, the ex-Police Scotland chief constable then chairing Kenova's governance board, agreed to take over as officer in overall command of Kenova. Livingstone was on holiday with his wife in Sorrento when Boutcher called him, but he immediately agreed.

On 4 October 2023, the Northern Ireland Policing Board (NIPB) picked Boutcher from a selection of several candidates as their preferred candidate for interim chief constable.[99] In previous appointments, NIO approval for the NIPB choice was automatic. This time the NIO was not so keen, so the board had to wait a further eight days before Secretary of State for Northern Ireland Chris Heaton-Harris finally gave his approval.[100] The delay was a measure of the distance that had opened up between the NIO and Boutcher. In the months ahead, the secretary of state and the new chief constable would clash very publicly over the disclosure at inquests of intelligence summaries (gists), in cases where state agents had been involved in a murder. Boutcher's attempts to reverse what he has referred to as Northern Ireland's 'disclosure blind spot' was unwelcome to the NIO, which took its cue, as ever, from the MI5 gatekeepers who 'hated to be challenged'.[101]

Finally passed for publication by the Cabinet Office, Boutcher had signed off his interim report on the day the NIPB chose him as interim chief constable. His report didn't mince its words. It said the claim by FRU senior personnel, that if confronted with a choice between protecting a source's identity and saving a person's life they would always choose the latter, was 'not accurate'.[102] He referred to 'evidence implicating Stakeknife and others in very serious criminality';[103] he spoke of 'agents … regularly involved in inciting and committing serious criminal acts',[104] and of 'serious criminality' having been 'tolerated and left unchecked and families from all sections of the conflict have been let down and ignored'.[105] And he had promised that everything in his report would be 'provable'.[106]

The PPS decided otherwise – in its opinion the cases were not provable, at least to a criminal standard. On 29 February 2024, the PPS announced the last of its prosecutorial decisions on Kenova's thirty-five files covering thirty-two individuals: twelve FRU, two MI5, fifteen IRA, two RUC and one prosecutor.[107] Not a single prosecution had been authorised. High on the list of the reasons given for rejecting charges against the ex-IRA members was that most of the evidence Kenova had gathered would have been inadmissible because it was hearsay, sometimes multiple hearsay, or its provenance was unclear, based on statements from witnesses who were dead, or contradictory.[108] Because Scappaticci had died, the PPS was silent on its assessment of the prospects of a conviction had he lived, so its opinion on that will never be known. However, judging by the PPS's reasoning as to why there was no case against his FRU handlers, it seems unlikely Scappaticci would have been charged.

To Lord Stevens, this was all déjà vu, following the PPS's 2007 decision to bring no charges of misconduct in public office against any member of the FRU for turning a blind eye to Brian Nelson's rampant criminality. The public was now being invited to believe that two marathon criminal inquiries – Stevens 3 and Operation Kenova – staffed by hand-picked detectives, collectively costing over £50m and spanning some eleven years, had failed to turn up anything that was likely to result in even a single prosecution. Not only that. Just three weeks earlier, the PPS had acknowledged there had been a 'wilful and abject failure' by successive UK governments to ensure agent handling operated within the law.[109]

Kenova thought there was sufficient evidence to charge up to five members of the FRU (two officers and three handlers) for misconduct in public office in relation to two murders and abductions (McKiernan and Fenton) and two abductions in which Scappaticci was involved. The PPS gave seven reasons why it considered Kenova's evidence fell short of what would have been required for a conviction. The reasons were set up like a row of skittles – when the first one fell, it knocked down the next, until they'd all fallen down:

1) As intelligence reports, the surviving MISRs were insufficient to prove that Scappaticci had participated in any of the incidents because they were summaries of the original CFs, which no longer existed; also, there was no certainty as to which handler had been present at each debrief, and anyway …
2) Even if the content of the MISRs could be proved, it might be argued that Scappaticci hadn't behaved criminally since it had been in aid of providing the security forces with intelligence to frustrate his IRA associates, and anyway …
3) Since Scappaticci's handlers weren't lawyers, it couldn't be proved they were sufficiently clear that his participation in interrogations couldn't be permitted, particularly since …
4) They'd never been given clear guidance as to what was acceptable at the time when running agents in the IRA, and anyhow …
5) The FRU *did* generally pass on Scappaticci's intelligence to senior army officers and Special Branch, and anyway …
6) Senior branch officers and MI5's director and co-ordinator of intelligence had known the FRU was running an agent in the ISU so the FRU could have argued there was nothing potentially unlawful about running an agent in the IRA's nutting squad that executed fellow suspected agents, and anyway …
7) There was no evidence that Scappaticci had ever shot any victims or was present when they were shot.[110]

No evidence? Kenova had a witness statement from the man who said Scappaticci had shot him eight times in his ankles, knees and elbows in 1987 because he had refused to hand over his car for an IRA operation. He had the scars to prove it. The 9mm Parabellum Browning Scappaticci had used to fire into his limbs had also been used in the executions of Anthony McKiernan and Thomas Wilson in which intelligence reports – credible because there were so many of them – showed Scappaticci had been deeply involved.

It is, of course, true that intelligence files come with none of the safeguards of sworn witness statements or statements made under caution. Kenova argued, however, that in this particular case the question of their admissibility should not be seen in isolation. If the bare intelligence turned out to be corroborated by other facts, or even trends, at some point it could become admissible evidence. Kenova also argued that the MISRs showed discernible trends, for example of Scappaticci generally passing on intelligence, but his handlers choosing when and how much they would pass on to the police, the priority 'time and again' being his protection as a valued source over protecting life or bringing perpetrators to justice.[111] Furthermore, Kenova recovered two verbatim transcripts of debriefs Scappaticci had dictated into a portable cassette recorder after an incident,[112] in which he openly admitted his role in an execution or an abduction. Scappaticci was 'often very frank with handlers concerning his direct involvement in serious criminality including many murders,' says Kenova. 'On occasions these confessions resulted in handlers creating an official record of that confession on MISRs' consistent with their 'advanced training ... not to embellish or diminish the information they received'.[113]

And what about the FRU flying Scappaticci to England for some R&R between 1990 and 1992 while knowing he was a fugitive from justice for the Sandy Lynch kidnapping? The problem there was that the FRU had top cover from their bosses and also from MI5 and Special Branch, all of which were 'fully aware that FRU continued to meet and engage with the agent whilst he was wanted'.[114] Whichever case Kenova turned to, any possibility of prosecuting Scappaticci seemed caught in a Catch-22 situation. Cynics observe that with an average charging rate of 69.9 per cent over the last five years,[115] the PPS in Belfast gets fewer people to court than the Crown Prosecution Service in England and Wales. Had the PPS adopted the more collaborative approach Boutcher had urged from the outset of Kenova, working hand in hand with independent counsel to iron out evidential challenges, might some prosecutions at least have been pursued?[116] Certainly Kenova thinks so. Prospects for a prosecution were 'literally just thrown away', according to one senior officer. 'They should have heeded Boutcher.'[117] Still, it is not considered wise for police officers to blame prosecutors for failing to prosecute. The system is the system; the law is the law.

The PPS's decision was certainly a bitter blow, but worse was to come.

Chapter Eighteen

NCND: The Anchor that Holds Northern Ireland Back

TUESDAY, 23 APRIL 2024: AS Jon Boutcher headed to Parliament to answer MPs questions about his recently published interim Operation Kenova report, he was reportedly 'furious'.[1] Although he'd written that extracting information from MI5 had 'sometimes felt like a hard-fought uphill battle',[2] he'd also given MI5 the benefit of the doubt: on balance, he said he didn't believe anything had been 'intentionally withheld, or that there has been a deliberate attempt to frustrate my investigation'.[3] Not only that, he'd written that Kenova and MI5 had developed a 'constructive relationship' and had commended Director General Ken McCallum for getting his staff to respond 'in full to our requests'.[4]

That view no longer held. Barely had the ink dried on his report when Boutcher and his Kenova team began to suspect that they might have been double-crossed. A fortnight earlier, Kenova's two detectives serving as SPOCs in MI5's London headquarters at Thames House had made urgent calls to Boutcher and Sir Iain Livingstone, who'd replaced Boutcher as head of Kenova since Boutcher's appointment as PSNI chief constable in November 2023.[5] They said MI5 had found 'a significant quantity' of previously undisclosed material. Over the months to come, the material just 'kept bleeding in', said Livingstone.[6]

Under the 'Information Sharing Protocol' Boutcher thought he'd secured with MI5 early in 2020, MI5 had undertaken that 'all potentially relevant MI5 material' would be available to Kenova and that Kenova would also be 'informed of any new acquisition of potentially relevant MI5 material'.[7] Of course, MI5 would argue that is exactly what it was now delivering.

In opposition to this argument was the fact that Kenova's two SPOCs, selected by SIO Keith Surtees for their diplomatic as well as their sleuthing skills, had been in Thames House for much of the previous seven years. Moreover, MI5 had previously assured Kenova that their disclosure process was complete.[8] And it was not as if the files had been found down the back of a sofa. They'd been sitting in MI5's Northern Ireland 'legacy archive' in Thames House.

So, it is little surprise that when Boutcher and Livingstone sat down to be quizzed by MPs that Tuesday morning on the Northern Ireland Affairs Committee, they were quietly furious. Nonetheless, they held back, waiting for the fuller picture to emerge. It would be late October 2024 before the last of the files was handed over.[9] Only by then had all the 'missing' MI5 files been unearthed. In all, six tranches of documents were disclosed, which included two packed A4 lever arch files covering almost the entirety of the period during which Stakeknife had operated as an agent. These two bulky files had been recorded on MI5's central file index, but somehow their existence had not been identified by the two MI5 officers tasked by the service with handling disclosure requests from Kenova's two SPOCs.

The discovery of new files required several amendments to Kenova's final report, published in December 2025 by Sir Iain Livingstone, on what Boutcher had written in his interim report. For example, Kenova had been assured that MI5 did not have a specific file on Stakeknife. All it had, allegedly, were disparate intelligence reports.[10] The two lever arch files gave the lie to that.[11] Kenova had also been assured by MI5 that they 'didn't know much about Stakeknife',[12] and that they had not performed 'any leadership, controlling or authorisation role' in relation to the FRU.[13] The new material showed that to be untrue as well. MI5 *had* been involved in briefing and tasking Stakeknife via the FRU 'throughout his operation as an agent and received debriefs on all his intelligence and was involved in discussions with FRU and RUC SB about his role, importance and use'.[14] Not only that, MI5 had also supported Stakeknife's operation by providing 'technical support' to the FRU (typically visual and audio monitoring).[15] Occasionally, both MI5 and Special Branch had 'offered or sought' to take over the running of Stakeknife from the FRU,[16] just as MI5 had tried to do with Brian Nelson.

The extent to which MI5 appears to have been disingenuous in its dealings with Kenova shook the investigators to the core. The interim report had already shown that a review conducted by the Security Service of its material had 'repeated inaccurate and unreliable FRU figures about lives saved by Stakeknife' and had maintained it had neither 'seen' nor 'heard' anything 'to suggest that Stakeknife had been personally involved in any serious criminality'.[17] The new files emphatically showed the opposite. As mentioned, from the hundreds of MISRs recovered by Kenova, Stakeknife appears to have been 'very frank with his handlers concerning his direct involvement in serious criminality including murder'.[18] MI5 would have known this because, at the FRU's request, it maintained an accurate filing record of FRU intelligence, including that derived from Stakeknife.[19] Furthermore, every four to six weeks, the FRU CO personally briefed MI5's most senior officer in Northern Ireland, the director and co-ordinator of intelligence, about the FRU's most significant cases, of which Stakeknife was probably *the* most significant.[20] Yet Kenova found 'no evidence of MI5 personnel escalating any concerns about Stakeknife or his handling to more senior personnel within MI5 or any other member of the security forces'.[21]

Like all FRU personnel interviewed under caution by Kenova, its CO, Colonel Gordon Kerr, stayed silent, while visibly 'seething' at being questioned again by the police.[22] It seems he had a point. Despite MI5's earlier categorical denials, Kenova came to the view that the new files broadly validated the claims Kerr had made 'on numerous occasions' to the Stevens inquiries over Brian Nelson that MI5 had 'oversight of FRU's operations'. He'd emphasised that this, and the fact that there was operational co-operation between the FRU and Special Branch, gave the lie to any suggestion that FRU operations hadn't been officially sanctioned.[23] As with Nelson, Kenova concluded that 'everything done in respect of Stakeknife had been done with MI5's knowledge and consent', and, moreover, 'MI5 had an influential role'.[24]

A particular source of mistrust was MI5's assurance to Boutcher at the outset of his investigation that MI5 had no awareness of Stakeknife until it had responsibility for resettling him. The new files showed it had known about Scappaticci right from the start, when he was recruited by the army in 1978,[25] which was unsurprising since, as Kerr had pointed out, MI5 had 'regular access to the (FRU) files' on all their agents 'and it was their role to keep an eye on that'.[26]

And so, to the 64-million-dollar question: was the timing of the unearthed files convenient or coincidence? The timing of events had been undeniably fortuitous for the intelligence services and for Scappaticci. The previous February, the PPS had finally ruled out prosecutions against any FRU operatives; as for Scappaticci, the PPS hadn't got round to reaching a decision before he died. Now, suddenly, a whole raft of new files had apparently been unearthed which – according to Livingstone – revealed 'significant' new lines of criminal inquiry 'not previously known'.[27] Yet Kenova was powerless to do anything about them. A new law that would no longer allow Kenova to pursue new evidence was just about to come into force. At the stroke of a pen, from 1 May 2024, the Northern Ireland Legacy and Reconciliation Act meant the DPP could no longer refer any more legacy cases to the police for criminal investigation in the way that Sir Alasdair Fraser and Barra McGrory had over the two previous decades. As the act said, 'no criminal investigation of any Troubles-related offence may be continued or begun'.[28] So, from 1 May, any intelligence service operatives who'd been involved in running Stakeknife – even if they'd been complicit in what Boutcher described as his 'very serious and wholly unjustifiable criminality, including murder'[29] – were in the clear.

MI5 insists all this was entirely coincidental and not an attempt to restrict Kenova's criminal inquiries or prosecutions by running down the clock. They claim the files' existence was only discovered during a routine digitisation of old hard copy files that had been brought over from Belfast for this purpose[30] and that they just happened to surface a few days after 8 March, when Kenova's interim report had been published.[31] They'd informed Kenova about this on 8 April and handed over the two key lever arch files on 7 May. When the material came to light, MI5 bosses were 'as shocked' as Kenova, said Sir Iain Livingstone. They could also anticipate the embarrassment this would cause and yet they owned up to it, so Livingstone has given them the benefit of the doubt.[32] They 'also 'recognise that … the conduct of that agent was outrageous'.[33]

But was it just coincidence that the files had only surfaced *after* the two MI5 officers with whom Kenova and their two SPOCs at Thames House had sometimes had to fight 'uphill battles' to extract information had retired?[34] The two large lever arch files had been prepared by MI5 in response to Stevens 3, some fifteen years earlier. Not that they were disclosed to Stevens 3 either. Still, the two MI5 officers dealing with Kenova from 2017 should, at the very least, have been aware of their existence, because they'd been listed in MI5's central file index.[35] One might have thought they'd have been the very first set of files to be disclosed to Kenova. Had the two MI5 officers not been able to lay their hands on them immediately, at the bare minimum they could surely have notified Kenova's SPOCs that they were aware of their existence and were looking for them.

MI5's Director General Ken McCallum asked former Metropolitan Police Assistant Commissioner Helen Ball to conduct an 'independent review in order to establish the facts' about why the files had not been disclosed at any time in the previous seven years of Kenova's existence. Ball, an ex-senior national co-ordinator for Counter-Terrorism Policing, gave MI5 a clean bill of health. She said she had 'not seen evidence of a deliberate attempt to withhold' the files, either at 'an individual or an organisational level'.[36] I understand she reached that conclusion without having interviewed the two MI5 individuals who liaised with Kenova's SPOCs. The terms of reference given to Ball by MI5 strangely appear not to have permitted her to interview retired staff.[37]

The fact that Ball could not interview the two retired MI5 officers seems an extraordinary omission. The obvious questions an investigator would have asked them were: did they know the files existed by reference to MI5's central index, and if not, why not? If they did, why didn't they look for them?

There is also a question about what happened to two files containing what appear to have been some of Stakeknife's CFs, which had survived the MoD's cull intended to destroy all of these post-Brian Nelson. Kenova says that their fate is 'unclear', save that they were acquired by Stevens 3.[38] My understanding is that there was 'a huge quantity'.[39] If so, they have disappeared, which is fortuitous from the FRU's point of view, since it was the absence of original CFs that contributed significantly to the PPS's decision not to prosecute any FRU members.

These were among the many questions that ideally should have been directed at the two MI5 officials, since they were amongst those whom Boutcher complained had taken a 'narrow transactional approach to interactions with Kenova'[40] – meaning they'd allegedly responded to Kenova's questions without always disclosing material that provided wider relevance and context, or potential leads.[41] Ball did allude elliptically to MI5's narrow approach by suggesting that had the service conducted a 'broader assessment of its own position in relation to Operation Kenova's investigative remit and the material it might hold', the files might have been identified earlier. This failed to satisfy Kenova sceptics, including some of Ball's former Metropolitan Police colleagues, who pointed out that there was 'a sequence' to the undisclosed documents because they covered Stakeknife's 'entire career as an agent', key aspects of which MI5 had failed to tell Kenova about: specifically MI5's direct involvement from 1979 in his 'assessment, direction and tasking' whereas the service had maintained they'd had only limited involvement, and only from 1983.[42] The two, bulging, undisclosed lever arch files weren't 'just odd bits of paper that had been mislaid,' as one Kenova officer put it.[43] So, while Sir Iain Livingstone exonerated MI5's leadership of any involvement in the non-disclosure, he was less forthcoming about other members of MI5. 'Do I have reservations about some individuals in MI5?' he asked on the publication of Kenova's final report. 'Yes. I do. Are there issues within the service about misguided loyalty? Yes.'[44]

According to its website, MI5 prides itself on maintaining the '[h]ighest standards of integrity, objectivity' and its 'commitment to the rule of law, ethical conduct [and] accountability'.[45] Yet these admirable sentiments have sometimes borne no relationship to reality, which may come as a shock to many on the English side of the Irish sea, but not so much on the Irish side. MI5 has form for deliberately withholding relevant material from both non-criminal and criminal inquiries into agent running in Northern Ireland.[46] In 2014, for example, the Court of Appeal found that MI5's conduct over a contested 1982 fatal shooting arguably 'amounted to a perversion of the course of justice'.[47] A senior member of MI5[48] had ordered the destruction of the covertly recorded tape showing that police officers from a Headquarters Mobile Support Unit had lied when they claimed in court to have shouted a warning before shooting two young men in a hayshed in Lurgan in November 1982, killing Michael Tighe and wounding Martin McCauley.

MI5 rightly deploys duplicitous tactics when investigating individuals and organisations that genuinely pose a threat to national security, but clearly it should not extend these tactics to legal proceedings. Yet that is what it did in what has been described as an example of MI5's 'institutional defensiveness'[49] when it misled the public inquiry into the 2017 murder of twenty-two people by the suicide bomber Salman Abedi at the Ariana Grande concert in the Manchester Arena. In closed sessions, Witness J, representing MI5's 'corporate' position, said the service had assessed two pieces of intelligence on Abedi as relating to 'possible non-nefarious activity or to non-terrorist criminality', essentially drugs and organised crime, whereas the four MI5 officers who'd actually handled that intelligence assessed it more likely terrorism related. MI5 had not presented an 'accurate picture' concluded the inquiry chairman, Sir John Saunders.[50] In a letter to Sir Keir Starmer, the families of the dead have asked: 'How many times must MI5 show that it cannot be trusted before something is done?'[51]

While misleading the Manchester Arena statutory inquiry in London, MI5 was arguably committing contempt of court in its own dogmatic defence of NCND. The Security Service has been found to have given false evidence on three occasions to two different courts. In early 2022, the then attorney general, Suella Braverman, attempted to stop the BBC from revealing that a neo-Nazi working as an MI5 agent on far-right extremism was a violent misogynist using his MI5 role to coercively control his ex-partner, whose alias the BBC gave as 'Beth'. Agent X was alleged to have physically and sexually abused 'Beth' and had been filmed threatening to kill her and attacking her with a machete. He was also alleged to have abused another partner whose child he'd threatened to kill, to have harboured cannibal fantasies about eating children and to have paedophilic tendencies. The BBC had a valid public interest story going to the heart of the moral maze over agent running: what level of criminality is acceptable in exchange for intelligence gathering?[52] Braverman won an order to prevent Agent X from being named but failed to stop the BBC from broadcasting the abuse story.

On oath, a senior MI5 official denied having breached NCND to BBC reporter Daniel De Simone. MI5 again denied this when 'Beth' took her case to the Investigatory Powers Tribunal (IPT), an independent court which adjudicates complaints about the misuse of covert powers by the

UK intelligence services.[53] But this was untrue: MI5 had repeatedly told De Simone that X was an agent when trying to get him to drop the story. Only after the BBC produced a tape of MI5's conversations with De Simone, in which it abandoned NCND, did MI5 hold up its hands.[54] Two inquiries – one internal by MI5, the other by the government – have both subsequently been shown to be so flawed, including by failing to interview key witnesses, that the High Court has ordered a third 'robust and independent inquiry'.[55]

At the heart of the BBC's public shaming of MI5 is the latter's duty, as a public body, to be open and honest in disclosing relevant information in legal proceedings, particularly since it plays a key role in law enforcement. That is what is expected of every other organisation and citizen in the country, and MI5's Director General Sir Ken McCallum has said, 'We take our duty to provide truthful, accurate and complete information very seriously …'[56] But is that actually the case? There have been a number of instances that raise legitimate questions about the extent to which what MI5 says – either in its public pronouncements or in legal proceedings – can be taken at face value and relied upon, nowhere more so than in relation to the legacy of the Northern Ireland conflict.

While Jon Boutcher and Sir Iain Livingstone have made it clear that they 'massively' support the application of NCND when national security is genuinely at risk, they argue that its application in Northern Ireland has been far too 'broad',[57] and the question is why. As two of the UK's most senior police officers, both have spent much of their professional careers marinated in the security establishment. Subversives in uniform they are not. Their private conclusion to that question is therefore sobering: in their view, MI5's 'implacable' NCND dogma has 'as much to do with preventing further national embarrassment' about how the covert arm of the counter-insurgency was conducted as any legitimate concerns the service may have about protecting national security.[58] That is the conclusion these two police chiefs have come to, having been so deeply immersed through their Kenova work in so much of the legacy of the covert conflict.

The cover-up of the brutal murder of Sean Brown – now in its twenty-ninth year – is a case in point. It speaks volumes about how divisive the decades-long attritional war over legacy disclosure has become: the courts and Chief Constable Boutcher have firmly lined up behind the relatives of the dead still seeking answers, while the state has fought all three groups ever more tenaciously to retain control of the narrative bequeathed by the legacy of Sir Patrick Walker's 1981 recommendations prioritising intelligence gathering over law enforcement.[59] The resistance to scrutiny that this arrangement led to explains why the state has so deliberately hidden its role from the Brown family for so long, only adding to their enduring distress about the manner in which Sean was murdered. For the details are indeed chilling.

At 11.30 p.m. on 12 May 1997, the sixty-one-year-old father of six, who was chairman of the Wolfe Tone GAA Club in Bellaghy, County Antrim, was locking the gates to the training ground when he was abducted by gunmen from the Loyalist Volunteer Force (LVF), an even more extreme group than the UVF from whom they had split. There was, in all likelihood, a ferocious struggle. A shot was fired and Brown was dragged into the boot of his car, presumably still alive. By 2.30 a.m., when he still hadn't come home, his wife, Bridie, ventured out to the club with a torch but could find no sign of him or his car. A sleepless night followed.

Sean Brown's body was found the next morning next to his burning car, ten miles away in a laneway off the main Belfast to Derry Road at Randalstown. He'd been shot six times in the head. 'Was he conscious?' asks his daughter Clare, about that ten-mile journey. 'Did he know what was going to happen? And what was going through his head? This was not an easy death. This was a horribly violent death. And that's even more torturous to think about.'[60]

At 6 a.m. the following morning two RUC officers arrived at the Brown home and stood outside, a clear signal to Bridie that something dreadful had happened to her husband. So, she went outside to ask the officers if they had found his body. They were non-committal and instead asked her if her husband often didn't come back at night.[61] After his death became public, both the NIO and local RUC paid tribute to Brown, reflective of the esteem in which he was held in Bellaghy. 'He walked with both sides of the community,' said Bridie.[62] A close friend was the Nobel Laureate Seamus Heaney, who wrote that Brown 'represented something better than we have grown used to, something not quite covered by the word reconciliation, because that word has become a policy word – official and public.'[63] The stain on a society disfigured by so many blatantly sectarian murders had long since numbed the rest of a baffled UK, and it's easy to see why. 'Sean Brown was the softest of targets,' said the family's lawyer, Niall Murphy. 'He had no association whatsoever with any paramilitarism or criminality. His murder was just a dirty, stinking, targeted assassination.'[64]

A report in January 2004 by the police ombudsman into the original RUC investigation recounted a litany of familiar failings: 'no earnest effort' had been made to identify the perpetrators; no proper forensic analysis had been conducted on cigarette butts found close to Brown's body; there had been no proper search for witnesses at the location and no proper attempts to identify vehicles which had passed near to the scene of the abduction. In practice, there had been no police investigation at all. Yet again, Special Branch had withheld intelligence from the CID,[65] consistent with the practice arising from the Walker review. In May 2004, a further police investigation, under the auspices of a senior detective from Britain, was overseen by a board of management with representatives from North and South. No new leads emerged.[66]

That left an inquest into Brown's death as the only way for the state to discharge its obligation under Article 2 of the European Court of Human Rights, which requires the full facts of any killing, especially one involving the state, to be brought to light through, *inter alia*, full disclosure of relevant documents, the compellability of witnesses, and such full family or next-of-kin participation as is practicable.[67] The state, in the form of the Crown Solicitor's Office, as instructed by the PSNI and the NIO, and as advised by MI5, was under a statutory obligation to supply the coroner, the late John Leckey with any material relevant to Sean Brown's death. However, the state engaged in a peacetime version of the 'slow waltz' strategy deployed by Special Branch during the conflict to delay 'downward dissemination' of time-sensitive intelligence that it considered might compromise a source.[68]

The result was that, for a full fifteen years, the Brown family endured no fewer than forty preliminary hearings, the state apparently paying little heed to the forceful criticism first by Leckey and, after he retired, by the new coroner on the case, Patrick Kinney, who is also a High Court judge. Kinney said that state agencies had failed 'to comply with disclosure obligations'.[69] Questions from him had gone 'unanswered for an inordinate period' and these disclosure failings had been 'deplorable and frankly inexcusable'.[70] Yet Kinney's experience was not unusual. As of May 2024, inquests into the deaths of seventy-four people killed in the conflict were still waiting to be heard.[71]

In 2021, their patience exhausted, the Brown family's lawyers successfully judicially reviewed the state for its failure to convene an inquest. The opening hearing of the inquest finally commenced in March 2023, twenty-six years after Sean Brown's murder. By this time the state had nowhere left to hide. Ultimately it had no choice but to share with Kinney all the intelligence it had on Brown's murder. When this intelligence finally arrived – it having been withheld from the original RUC investigation, the OPONI's investigation of that failed investigation, the subsequent PSNI investigation and from Bridie Brown's civil case which was settled in 2022[72] – Kinney described it as 'highly important and relevant material'.[73]

The question Kinney, as coroner, was required to address was this: how had Sean Brown come by his death? From the classified material now in front of him (but inaccessible to Brown's family or their lawyers because it had all been classified as 'Secret'), Kinney attempted to answer that question by posing three further questions: 1) What relevant state agencies had known – if anything – about the plot to kill Sean Brown? 2) What had the state's agents told these agencies about who his killers were? 3) What had the agencies done about this?

The state insisted there should be no disclosure whatsoever of any part of the classified material finally shared with Kinney, claiming that such disclosure would be a breach of the government's NCND policy and would pose a risk to national security.[74] So on the last working day before Christmas 2023, the first of several ministerially signed PII certificates – three relating to intelligence gathered by MI5, one to the RUC (presumably Special Branch) and one to the Crown – landed on Niall Murphy's desk.[75] Signed by Minister of State for Northern Ireland Steve Baker and a junior defence minister, Dr Andrew Morrison, these PII certificates argued that the contents of the seventy-six redacted pages given to Murphy and stamped with PII on every page should not be disclosed to anyone except the coroner. Four days of closed hearings followed, attended only by the coroner, his counsel and the counsel for the Crown Solicitor's Office and the NIO.

Kinney considered this disclosed material to be highly relevant to the questions he had decided the inquest had to address, but he agreed with the assessment that most of the secret material, if disclosed, would pose a risk to national security. Typically, such risks would cover anything tending to reveal an agent's identity, the information the agent was disclosing and to whom, how they operated, various technical details and so on. So, Kinney came up with a compromise whereby a summary (gist) should be disclosed to all interested parties, including the Brown family, without disclosing any details that risked harming national security. This, he considered, would strike the right balance between disclosing what was in the public interest and what the relatives had a right to know, while mitigating any risk of harm to the national interest.

On 27 February 2024, Kinney convened yet another hearing without disclosing his intention to publish a gist. To Niall Murphy, the Brown family's solicitor, this sounded like just another routine procedural hearing, so he advised the family there was no need to attend, since they were unlikely to hear anything that they hadn't already heard and he didn't want Sean Brown's elderly widow Bridie to have another wasted journey. In the event, the hearing turned out to be one of the most eventful in Murphy's career as a criminal defence lawyer. It was the day that the decades-long attritional war over NCND moved into its final phase.

Settling into his seat, Murphy was astonished to hear Kinney authorise the release of what he termed a short 'global gist' of the relevant classified material – a few dry lines within which was the bombshell admission that amongst at least twenty-five suspects linked to Brown's murder by intelligence, were 'state agents' (plural). More astonishing still was the revelation that this gist had been agreed by the barrister representing the Crown Solicitor's Office, Mark Robinson KC. Until now, MI5 had made much of never having conceded NCND in open court. Had a new and enlightened dawn broken?

It had not. When word reached the Northern Ireland secretary's MI5 and NIO advisers that Kinney's decision had gone unchallenged by Robinson, there was consternation.[76] It seems inconceivable that Robinson would have gone rogue, in which case whoever in the Crown Solicitor's Office was responsible for instructing him would seem to have badly misjudged the sacrosanctity in which NCND is still held by the NIO. Either that, or there is some other unfathomable explanation.

The mood of the secretary of state's advisers darkened when they learned that Chief Constable Jon Boutcher had co-operated with Kinney in drafting the gist. He and his senior officers in the PSNI's intelligence branch had assessed that the gist had no adverse impact on operational policing or, for that matter, on the 'recruitment or retention of civilian agents in particular'[77] – the mantra MI5 most commonly cites to justify the strict and consistent application of NCND, and the pillar upon which the government's NCND case has rested since the former Lord Chief Justice Carswell ruled in support of the government in Scappaticci's bogus judicial review of the policy in 2003. In other words, the gist had not in any way posed a risk to national security. The sky had not fallen in.

Nevertheless, MI5 and the NIO saw the Brown gist as the start of a slippery slope, an end to business as usual, when previous PSNI chief constables had deferred to advisers to secretaries of state (in other words MI5) over whether sensitive material should be subject to PII. No previous chief constable had acted unilaterally like this. Officials in the NIO and MI5 – pejoratively known as 'securocrats' – advised Secretary of State for Northern Ireland Chris Heaton-Harris to quash the decision their own counsel had approved, never mind that the horse had already bolted since the gist had been published in practically every Irish newspaper.

Kinney had also thrown down another challenge to the status quo. Even though his plan to disclose his 'global gist' had been an advance, he made it clear it was still too limited to enable him to address one of the four statutory questions the inquest had to answer: how and in what circumstances had Sean Brown come by his death? The rest of the sensitive intelligence material relevant to that question still covered by PII certificates could not be disclosed by him and could not be taken into account when he made his findings at the conclusion of the inquest. 'I am sorry I cannot complete my work,' Kinney concluded, saying he intended to ask Heaton-Harris to establish a public inquiry as the only satisfactory alternative for the state to meet its Article 2 obligation, since, unlike an inquest, a public inquiry would allow the secret intelligence to be heard in closed session.[78]

There was no need for a public inquiry, responded Heaton-Harris. He invited Kinney to refer Sean Brown's case to the Conservative government's newly established Independent Commission for Reconciliation and Information Recovery (ICRIR) for investigation.[79] The ICRIR was the sole body created under the government's controversial Legacy Act to investigate conflict-related deaths.[80] But Kinney appears to have had little faith that the ICRIR would fully investigate the state's role in Brown's death, following a 200-page ruling by Mr Justice Colton the previous month that the ICRIR was not fully compliant with human rights legislation, particularly since it was due to grant perpetrators immunity from prosecution.[81] The perpetrators the government mostly had in mind were former members of the security forces, Conservative ministers having promised legislation to 'see the end of repeated and vexatious prosecutions of our service men, including in Northern Ireland'.[82] In fact there have been only ten prosecutions brought against veterans since the Good Friday Agreement twenty-eight years ago, with just one conviction.[83] This is not a high number bearing in mind that the security forces are rightfully held to a much higher standard than the PIRA.

'I do not regard the ICRIR as the appropriate mechanism to deal with the investigation of his death, or matters connected to it,' Kinney told Heaton-Harris in a letter.[84] He also emphasised the sheer quantity of 'highly important' material directly relevant to the circumstances of Brown's death that he'd had to exclude from the inquest because it was covered by PII certificates. This, he said, had 'resulted in an inquest that was incomplete, inadequate and misleading'.[85] The only option left for a 'full and fearless' investigation, said Kinney,[86] was a forum where the classified material could be examined and tested in 'closed proceedings', which were 'only available through a public inquiry'.[87] Kinney asked Heaton-Harris to confirm by 10 April that he was committed to establishing one. To the NIO's further annoyance, Boutcher supported Kinney by pledging 'unfettered and unredacted access' to PSNI files about the murder, saying the Brown family had been 'failed by the establishment'.[88] No RUC/PSNI chief constable had ever spoken so frankly.

In his letter to Heaton-Harris, Kinney emphasised the seriousness of the situation. 'Highly important and relevant' material had been withheld, he said, first from the RUC's initial investigation, then from the OPONI and yet again from the PSNI reinvestigation. He believed these were 'matters that would be, and should be, of very great concern to the public'. The fact it had taken twenty-seven years for there to be *any* acknowledgement of the state's role in Sean Brown's murder was also 'a matter that should be of real concern to *all* [author's emphasis] citizens of the United Kingdom'.

It is doubtful that it was. Kinney's letter got barely any coverage outside Northern Ireland. As for Heaton-Harris, he appears to have been more concerned by the fact that Boutcher had acted unilaterally and, moreover, had told the policing board that he supported a public inquiry into Sean Brown's murder, knowing it would inevitably delve into the 'conduct of the organisation he heads'.[89] What especially seems to have perturbed Heaton-Harris and his NIO advisors was the fact that Kinney had emboldened other coroners overseeing inquests into deaths at the hands of loyalist murder gangs in which the state appears to have had some kind of involvement.

Twenty-five-year-old Liam 'Topper' Thompson was shot dead in April 1994, as he sat in the front seat of a taxi at 11.30 p.m. in Springfield Park, separated by a 'peace line' (a wall built to minimise inter-communal violence) from the adjoining loyalist Springmartin estate. The taxi driver appears to have been lured to Springfield Park by the UDA with a bogus call to the taxi firm 'Grab-a-Cab' to collect a passenger there. Seeing no one waiting for the taxi, it turned round to leave, and as it did so, gunmen appeared, firing multiple shots into it, hitting Thompson in the chest and wounding the driver. The gunmen had got access to Springfield Park through a hole in the 'peace line'. The area was subject to regular attacks by loyalist gunmen, which is why, several hours before Thompson was murdered, the security breach had been urgently reported to both the RUC and NIO, yet no action had been taken. Thompson's family suspected there was collusion between the UDA and police elements.[90]

What hardened that suspicion was the fact that intelligence files from the police, MoD and the Crown covered by ministerially signed PII certificates had been disclosed to the coroner, Louisa Fee, conducting the much-delayed inquest into Thompson's murder. Inspired by the fact that Patrick Kinney, who'd released his global gist in Sean Brown's inquest, was also a High Court judge, on 6 March 2024 Fee produced a gist from one of seven intelligence folders belonging to the police. When Boutcher saw Fee's proposed gist, he agreed with Heaton-Harris that it shouldn't be disclosed. He thought it went too far in giving details that posed a risk to national security, thereby breaching NCND.[91] It also demonstrated that his opposition to the government's 'dogmatic' application of NCND in legacy cases was not doctrinal but evidential.

However, to the mounting exasperation of Heaton-Harris, Boutcher proposed a compromise. The hearing was set for 22 March. Boutcher suggested Fee redraft her initial gist (Gist 1) to mitigate any risk to national security. He acknowledged that the revised version, Gist 2, was not 'particularly revealing' but said it nevertheless 'would be of some value to the (Thompson) family'.[92] Since the intelligence referenced events that had happened over three decades earlier, reasonable people might struggle to see how disclosing its key points, albeit abridged, posed even the remotest risk to national security. Yet, in conceding a partial and anodyne gist of the folder, Boutcher seems again to have committed the cardinal sin of breaking with the practice of his predecessors, who had automatically offered the NIO the choice of whether they wanted a ministerially signed PII certificate when it came to decisions about disclosing sensitive legacy material.

From March 2024, Boutcher had instructed the PSNI to issue its own PII certificates, accompanied by an affidavit from him, instead of one signed by a minister. From then on, the NIO would only be consulted if the PSNI considered there was a legitimate national security issue. So, in effect, Boutcher was now saying to MI5:

> I am the Chief Constable. This is *my* material to disclose if I assess that by gisting it, there is no risk to national security. In those circumstances, my judgement is that the public interest lies in letting those whose lives have been affected by this material know about it. I am also independent of ministers and MI5 so I do not believe I need to seek your approval or ministerial approval.[93]

Boutcher soon found that the courts were not standing in his way. On 25 March, he learned that if anything, he'd been too conservative in his opposition to Gist 1 in the Thompson inquest. Mr Justice Humphreys dismissed Boutcher's initial support for Heaton-Harris' claim that Louisa Fee had disregarded the risk to national security. Any reasonable coroner would have done what Fee had done, ruled the judge.[94] Boutcher immediately issued a statement saying the PSNI 'accepted the judgment' and 'welcomed the clarity it provided',[95] making it clear that, whatever Heaton-Harris decided, he, as chief constable, would not be appealing the decision. Boutcher's response marked, in the clearest possible terms, an end to the chief constable's traditional automatic support for the secretary of state on the vexed question of transparency and accountability over PII on intelligence matters. Nothing like this had ever happened before.

The next day, Heaton-Harris fired off a letter to Boutcher making it clear that he regarded the latter's comments as 'unwelcome' and expressing his 'deep concern' about what he described as a 'developing trend' towards departures from the NCND policy. He asked Boutcher to revert to the practice of his predecessors by consulting the NIO before deciding whether sensitive information qualified for PII.[96] Boutcher hit back the following day by reminding Heaton-Harris that while he had no intention of disclosing information harmful to national security, he was nonetheless 'independent of the executive and not subject to the direction or control of government ministers, departments or agencies'.[97]

This led to Home Secretary James Cleverly pointing out to the advocate general for Northern Ireland how the NCND policy was now under 'considerable pressure' from coroners gisting sensitive material.[98] Cleverly was certainly right about that. A third coroner was about to propose a gist of PII-covered intelligence files relating to the inquest of another victim of an LVF murder gang. In January 1998, the body of twenty-eight-year-old Fergal McCusker, who had been shot in the head, was found behind the back wall of a youth club in Maghera, County Londonderry. He'd only recently returned from working in the US. Like Patrick Kinney, the coroner, Patrick McGurgan, was confronted with a Catch-22 situation: he was in possession of secret material relevant to how McCusker had come by his death but was not able to conduct a proper investigation due to the sensitive nature of that self-same material. Heaton-Harris objected to McGurgan's plan to produce a gist. 'This is an unprecedented intervention by the British government in this inquest to curtail very important information being provided to the McCusker family,' Barra McGrory KC – now back in private practice and representing the family – told the inquest.[99] So, like Coroner Kinney in the case of Sean Brown's murder, McGurgan asked the secretary of state to establish a public inquiry into McCusker's death as the only way of resolving the deadlock.[100]

To the NIO, an appalling vista was unfolding: ministerial PIIs were being replaced by gists of intelligence drawn up at the chief constable's discretion. With the NIO – and therefore MI5 – at risk of losing control of the legacy narrative, it upped the ante. On 13 March, Coroner Kinney had set 10 April as the deadline by which he wanted a response from Heaton-Harris to his request for a public inquiry into the murder of Sean Brown. Heaton-Harris made it his business to reply to Kinney that very day, but not by answering the question Kinney had asked him. Instead, Kinney was sent a pre-action letter, served with salt: a notice that his decision to publish a gist was to be judicially reviewed, a reprisal which seemed likely to fail. After all, Heaton-Harris had already lost his judicial review of Coroner Fee's Gist 1 on Thompson,[101] and the Sean Brown gist he was now judicially reviewing had long since been published and was being quoted liberally. As Niall Murphy put it, 'the milk had already been spilt'.[102]

What troubled the relatives of Scappaticci's victims about the government's refusal to move on by disapplying NCND to Stakeknife was not that they were still unsure whether he was actually Freddie Scappaticci – they knew for a fact he was; the issue was: what else might the government be hiding? 'For me personally and I am presuming for a lot of families, NCND has ended any hopes of truth,' said Paul Wilson, whose father Thomas was murdered after Scappaticci interrogated him.[103]

Boutcher, meanwhile, was just getting into his reformist stride. 'I am at odds here with the Secretary of State,' he told MPs on the Northern Ireland Affairs Committee. '[W]e cannot breach NCND where we will give the details of who an agent is. We can't put anybody's life at risk. But this iron curtain approach leads to a lack of trust and confidence towards the security forces. It is unnecessary and the world has moved on from there.'[104] He also took a swipe at the stranglehold on criminal justice that the 1981 Walker doctrine had exerted by prioritising source protection and keeping agents in place, irrespective of the level of criminality they'd engaged in: 'Saying that you cannot investigate a crime any further because there is an agent involved is poppycock. That is not right.' The way that NCND had been applied as a mantra in the past was 'an anchor that holds us back', he said. 'Nobody who commits murders should be protected by the policy of NCND. I don't think anybody could disagree with that.'[105] Yet that is what has happened with Freddie Scappaticci. At the time of going to press, the government was still refusing to say if it will formally identify him as Stakeknife. If ministers do finally concede the pantomime that this refusal has become, will NCND continue to be strictly applied in a blanket fashion to other legacy inquests and civil proceedings involving state agents? Or will discretion be used, with each case judged on its merits? Boutcher hopes for the latter in time, but lawyers acting for Scappaticci's victims fear the former.

The sobering fact is that protecting state murderers during the conflict was precisely the unwritten rule that the intelligence agencies and successive British governments had reconciled themselves to applying. And those who saw themselves as the rightful custodians of that legacy were not prepared to share its details with the relatives of its victims or the wider public, a position with which the Conservative government appeared content. The problem for that government was that the Northern Ireland Court of Appeal didn't agree. It was not opposing Boutcher or Fee over Thompson, nor was the High Court opposing Kinney over Brown. On 30 April 2024, the Court of Appeal said it was 'not convinced' that either of the two Thompson gists had breached the government's NCND policy.[106] That decision was the climax of increasingly frenzied government attempts to overturn a succession of judgments in favour of disclosure in the course of more than a dozen court proceedings.[107] When an amendment to the Legacy and Reconciliation Bill by Parliamentary Under-Secretary of State at the NIO Lord Jonathan Caine meant that all inquests where evidence had still to be heard by 1 May would be dissolved,[108] Northern Ireland's judiciary – today respected for its robust independence – appears to have seen this as an interference with their legislative independence. And while there wasn't a chance of the Brown, Thompson or McCusker inquests being completed by 1 May, it seems the courts were anxious to provide as much legal clarity over 'gisting' as possible by then, acutely conscious of the fact that the decades-long attritional war over disclosure was being propelled across the Irish Sea and into the final court of appeal, the Supreme Court in London.

The stage was now set for the Supreme Court to be the ultimate arbiter of who would end up controlling the darker side of the historical narrative of the Northern Ireland conflict. No one could have imagined how the years of attritional warfare over disclosure would redraw the battle lines: arraigned against the state and its praetorian guard of MI5 lawyers was now a once unthinkable insurgent alliance of relatives of the unresolved dead, the full force of the Northern Ireland judiciary and Northern Ireland's chief constable, no less. They were not just lined up against a state under the Conservative government either. Whatever else about their differences over the Legacy Act, the new Labour government elected in July 2024 shared their predecessors' misgivings on the two key constitutional issues thrown up by the Brown and Thompson inquests. Hilary Benn, the new secretary of state for Northern Ireland, was deeply concerned about the precedent that would be set were judges able to order ministers to hold public inquiries.

There was a serious prospect of that happening. A few days before Christmas 2024, to the NIO's intense irritation, Mr Justice Humphreys had again been upsetting the securocratic applecart. This time he'd endorsed Kinney's ruling that only a public inquiry – not the ICRIR – could deliver an Article 2 compliant investigation into the murder of Sean Brown.[109]

Benn appealed Humphreys and lost in April 2025,[110] but he won leave to appeal to the Supreme Court.[111] He was unapologetic. 'Look, I want there to be a full, independent, rigorous investigation into the murder of Sean Brown,' he said. 'That is not the issue at hand in the appeal. The appeal relates to a constitutional principle: who orders public inquiries in the United Kingdom, and the long-standing convention is it is governments and not the court.'[112] Benn had a point. Ministers – not chief constables – are ultimately accountable to Parliament and have discretion over whether to initiate an inquiry under the Inquiries Act 2005, which typically provides a breadth of inquiry not available in legal proceedings. Also, public inquiries are often aimed at investigating policy failures not failures of the law. Then there is the fact that they can be costly and suck in vast amounts of civil service resources.

Benn had also pressed on with his Conservative predecessor's appeal to the Supreme Court on Thompson on the question of gisting, a 'very important court case', he said, affecting the future use of NCND, which was a 'very important policy, for reasons that are long established and well set out'.[113] It certainly was a very important case – and not just because a judgment in the chief constable's favour would leave the government finally free to abandon the delusional ambiguity MI5 had sought to foster for a quarter of a century by refusing to neither confirm nor deny if Scappaticci was the agent known as Stakeknife. More consequentially, the outcome would determine who was the final arbiter over whether an enlightened, reform-minded chief constable was free to open up more of his own PSNI files, which the NIO and MI5 had so successfully kept closed. And with some 1,200 unsolved legacy killings and 700 claims for damages still going through the civil courts,[114] a vast potential for disclosure remained.

The law of the land was about to be settled by the most senior jurists in the land – in London. It is doubtful that, unlike their Northern Ireland counterparts, their lordships will have appreciated just how much murders, such as those of Sean Brown, Liam Thompson and Fergal McCusker – which appear to have been covered up for decades in the service of 'national security' – touch the soul of wider Irish nationalism. It is also doubtful their lordships will have spent time in places like Bellaghy, where, on 16 May 2025, in the week of the twenty-eighth anniversary of Sean Brown's murder, at just forty-eight hours' notice, 10,000 people marched holding 'Walk for Truth' banners. Sean Brown's frail widow, Bridie (87), was cheered loudly as she was driven through the crowds. Her husband's murder had rekindled nationalist Ireland in a way that few other recent incidents have. 'So many people have approached me to express their admiration for Bridie's stoicism and dignity,' Niall Murphy said. 'She reminds people of their own grandmother, and they immediately feel: is that how I would expect my grandmother to be treated?'[115] In essence, that was what the Supreme Court would have to decide.

Epilogue

11 June 2025: The Supreme Court of the United Kingdom

A SPARKLING JUNE DAY GREETED the barristers, their instructing solicitors and government officials packed into Courtroom One of the Supreme Court's magnificent Grade 2 listed building on the south-west corner of Parliament Square. 'Yes, Sir James,' said Lord Robert Reed breezily, the Supreme Court president, inviting Sir James Eadie KC, the government's first Treasury counsel, to begin his opening submission.

Eadie has been entrusted by successive British governments to defend its positions on every kind of predicament they've found themselves in, no matter how awkward or embarrassing, from Boris Johnson's prorogation of Parliament in 2019 to securing a two-year super-injunction preventing the disclosure of a massive government data leak that caused thousands of Afghans to be brought secretly to the UK to prevent Taliban reprisals.[1]

At Eadie's side was his Belfast-based counterpart, Tony McGleenan KC, whose failed attempts to stop the Northern Ireland judiciary from breaching NCND by permitting Boutcher and the coroners from gisting decades of dusty intelligence files had led to this seminal moment in the attritional war of disclosure. McGleenan appears to have been extremely exasperated by having lost every application he'd made on behalf of the government in the Northern Ireland courts in respect of Thompson and Brown. Professionally, if for no other reason, he was eagerly anticipating vindication from the highest court in the land. He would not be disappointed.

Also eagerly awaiting the judgment was the Operation Kenova chief, Sir Iain Livingstone. Ten months earlier he'd sent the first tranche of Kenova family reports outlining Stakeknife's role in a loved one's murder to the Cabinet Office for security checking. Surely, argued Livingstone, after all the families had been through, the least they deserved was to have the agent's real identity officially confirmed? But the government was relying on the 2003 ruling by Lord Justice Carswell on Scappaticci's bogus judicial review of NCND, that to admit someone was an agent could discourage the recruitment and retention of agents.

Livingstone argued that there was no conceivable way any actual or potential agent would be deterred from providing intelligence if Scappaticci's status was officially confirmed. They would already know that he was credibly alleged to have been an agent and had to be resettled under a new identity. Livingstone firmly believes that persisting with this 'rigid dogma that flies in the face of reality' has become 'wholly contrary to the public interest'. Confirming Stakeknife's identity would serve as a useful reminder to state agents that lifetime secrecy can never be guaranteed 'where an individual has clearly gone beyond any sense of humanity'. In such a case 'you have to say to them, "There are limits on how you can conduct yourself"' and 'grotesque murdering, terrorist torture and criminality certainly go past those limits'.[2]

The Cabinet Office was in no hurry to respond to Livingstone's appeal on behalf of the families. It was five months before he got a reply, and even then it was more can kicking: there would be no security checking of the family reports until ministers had decided whether Stakeknife should be named. A further four months passed before Livingstone was finally told that the decision would depend upon the outcome of the Thompson case. In the meantime, he should assume the answer would be no.[3] The omens were not good. One of the two lead justices on the case before the Supreme Court was Lord Sales – who, in 2003, as a barrister, had played a central role in securing that judgment from Carswell (see Chapter 16).

What the Thompson case had to do with Livingstone's request on Stakeknife was unclear. Thompson was about three issues: whether the coroner, Louisa Fee, had been right to propose that a gist of intelligence received from an agent in connection with his murder should be disclosed; whether the Northern Ireland courts had been correct in rejecting the secretary of state's appeal against Fee's decision; and whether the chief constable was right to have proposed a revised gist that could be disclosed without having consulted the secretary of state. Of course, common to both Thompson and Stakeknife were questions about national security, but there the difference ended. Thompson was pre-eminently about whether the correct decisions in law had been applied by Fee and the reviewing courts, whereas the decision over whether to finally confirm Stakeknife's identity was more straightforwardly about government policy, although in 2023 the Cabinet Office under the Conservatives had also sought to make it about the law by rather absurdly implying that Boutcher risked breaching the Official Secrets Act if he confirmed Stakeknife was Freddie Scappaticci.[4]

With Labour's arrival, not much changed. While its 2024 manifesto had accused the last government of 'denying justice to the families and victims of the Troubles', Hilary Benn, the successor to Heaton-Harris, seemed to be fully on board with the latter's blanket use of NCND. Boutcher had begun to worry that Benn might have fallen prey to persuasive government lawyers on the need to hold the line, just like one of Benn's predecessors, immediately upon his appointment. This 'impressive former Secretary of State … described to me how … he was visited by Whitehall lawyers regarding a matter of national security,' explained Boutcher. 'The meeting resulted in him feeling somewhat overawed with a sense of having to go along with what they had said as this was a matter of national security, of which he had no experience, and his visitors were particularly persuasive.'[5]

Meanwhile, over the two-day hearing at the Supreme Court, a majority of the five justices would show themselves to be sympathetic to Eadie's arguments that it should be the secretary of state who decides what information touching on national security should be disclosed, not the PSNI chief constable, or coroners for that matter, and that the Northern Ireland courts should pay heed to that. There was a 'how-very-dare-you!' whiff in Eadie's criticism of Boutcher's support for the gisting of intelligence classified by ministerially certified PII certificates by the coroners Kinney and Fee. The chief constable, of all people, had had the effrontery to think he was 'entitled to act solo in these cases,' said Eadie.

Eadie was not entirely wrong, but one could also see Boutcher's point. The single intelligence file he was happy to gist in Liam Thompson's inquest was his force's property, not the MoD's or MI5's; its content pertained directly to the death of Thompson, and Boutcher and his officers who had assessed the gist were confident it posed no risk to national security.[6]

Eadie was having none of this. 'The chief constable is a regional chief constable in a devolved jurisdiction,' he boomed, his fluent baritone resonating around the chamber. 'He does not have the breadth of view that His Majesty's government has on issues of national security across the UK and further afield. Nor does he have access to the same degree or breadth of expertise and advice on such matters as is available to UK government ministers.' Boutcher had 'no business making judgments' about gisting, said Eadie. And if the 'regional' chief constable didn't like the system, why, he could always resign.[7]

Aside from the fact that Boutcher had spent much of his career dealing with real contemporary threats to national security from the world's most lethal terrorists in the shape of Al-Qaeda, it might be asked who – if not he and his own PSNI officers – was most expert in judging any theoretical risk to national security that might conceivably arise from disclosing intelligence about a murder gang in Northern Ireland from three decades ago? Not the chief constable according to Lord Sales. 'Isn't it necessarily the case that the secretary of state has access to a wider range of expertise?' he cut in.[8] Sales would intervene many more times than any of his fellow M'lords.

The bench so warmed to the silken advocacy of Sir James that he and Lord Reed would sometimes finish each other's sentences. The contrast with Lord Reed's curt putdowns of counsel representing Boutcher, Oliver Sanders KC, was striking. 'If you want to persist with your submissions on this, that's the matter for you,' the court president chided Sanders. 'But there's a saying that if you're in a hole, stop digging!'[9]

Sanders had been trying to explain why Boutcher had ceased the PSNI's practice of his predecessors, who'd simply left it to the NIO (usually meaning MI5) to decide if sensitive information whose disclosure was being sought by, for example, lawyers representing relatives of a murder victim, should be subject to a ministerial PII certificate. Now the PSNI did their own assessment of whether disclosure would harm national security and only shared this with the NIO if they considered it did. 'I think we've heard enough about this point,' said Lord Reed five minutes after Sanders had been advised to 'stop digging'. 'I hope you can make more productive use of the remainder of your time. We'll adjourn now and hear what you have to say next at 2 o'clock.'[10] All rise.

The Supreme Court president's mood hadn't improved after lunch. When Sanders completed his submissions, Ian Skelt KC, representing Coroner Fee, stood up. Lord Reed appears to have deemed Skelt's presence irrelevant. This was despite the fact that amongst the matters to be determined by the Supreme Court was whether Fee had acted *ultra vires* (beyond her powers) by ordering the disclosure of a gist, given that Liam Thompson's inquest had no prospect of being completed since it was about to be dissolved by the Legacy Act. A short and rather fractious exchange followed in which the justices showed no interest in hearing Skelt. 'Why should we pay any attention whatsoever to anything the coroner has to say?' asked Lord Reed tartly.

The beef the justices had with Skelt was that Coroner Fee was the equivalent of a judge of first instance and, in adversarial court hearings, the original trial judge is never allowed to appear at an appeal in her or his own defence. On the other hand, the inquest into Liam Thompson was an inquisitorial process and it is common for the 'judge' in such proceedings to be represented, as, indeed, Skelt had represented Fee in all the proceedings in the Northern Ireland courts that had led up to this Supreme Court hearing. Skelt tried to explain that he was 'mindful' of the rule about first instance judges not appearing before a court of appeal, but asked if he could 'just point very briefly–'

He was not allowed to finish.

> Lord Reed: 'Well, if you're mindful of that, why don't you sit down?
> Ian Skelt: 'I will. Thank you.'
> Lord Reed: 'Thank you. Next up?'[11]

Eadie's strongest argument in the case was the constitutional one: when it comes to matters of national security, the elected government of the day has the whip hand over an unelected chief constable since governments are accountable to Parliament.[12] So far, so true. Yet Boutcher's argument was that while that may generally apply, like all legacy cases, Liam Thompson was killed when the police had the national security lead in Northern Ireland, and on these specific localised cases, the secretary of state should respectfully entrust him with disclosure decisions.[13]

Eadie dismissed this as Boutcher 'playing politics with national security', leading to the only time any of the justices intimated a hint of disagreement.[14] To many, this will have felt like a cheap shot unworthy of the First Treasury Counsel. The idea that a chief constable might risk national catastrophe by playing politics with national security certainly struck Lord Hodge as unlikely. 'I wonder if that's a fair characterisation,' he interjected. 'I mean, presumably, the chief constable is wanting to do as much as he can to reassure all the communities in Northern Ireland about the fairness of policing ...'[15] Presumably, yes.

Reassurance has indeed been the driving force behind Boutcher's quest to liberate Northern Ireland from decades of paralysing MI5 secrecy. Policing in Northern Ireland is not like policing in any other part of the UK. Boutcher is the chief of a police service still recovering from a raging conflict lasting thirty years. Policing is, in fact, at the heart of the reconciliation part of the peace process, yet the PSNI continues to be nowhere near to meeting its target of half its recruits coming from republican/nationalist communities to more fairly reflect Northern Ireland's shifting demography. Ever since Archbishop Robin Eames and the former priest Denis Bradley launched their legacy consultation in 2007, a narrative war over legacy has raged in Northern Ireland. To this day, the three protagonists – the IRA, loyalists and the British government – still fight to own the truth of what happened, and who ultimately was to blame. The IRA and loyalists have made it clear they intend to protect their narrative with bland 'corporate responses' to unresolved questions. To maintain their 'truth', answers are carefully vetted with no individual accountability. Northern Ireland's politicians have failed to break that conflict mould, being either incapable or perhaps unwilling to do so. Mutual condemnation persists, whether about the past, identity or cultural issues.

'The PSNI still does not have the trust and support it needs within communities,' explained Boutcher in his affidavit to the proceedings. In fact, trust has gone into reverse – latest figures show Catholics as a declining percentage of applicants – just 26.7 per cent,[16] the lowest since 2013,[17] whereas in the wider population, Catholics now outnumber Protestants.[18] 'The issue here is not about the recruitment and retention of covert agents,' says Boutcher, 'rather it is about ordinary overt policing and community relations. It is about members of the public reporting issues and telling us what they have seen and heard and what is going on around them, rather than turning a blind eye.'[19] Boutcher and Livingstone have attempted to change the legacy weather in Northern Ireland, where all other efforts have so miserably failed. As exemplars of modern policing, they have rather valiantly tried to consign the word 'securocrat' to the dustbin of history by bringing a breath of fresh air to stale thinking in pursuit of greater reconciliation, not, as Eadie implied, by playing politics to garner popular support.

On 9 December 2025, the Supreme Court issued its long-awaited judgment. The government won on all counts. The verdict was unanimous – and withering: they found no less than six errors in Fee's decision in the Liam Thompson inquest to disclose the two gists; they said that both the High Court and the Court of Appeal had erred by having merely reviewed whether Fee's decisions were within proper legal boundaries, whereas ministerial claims about risks to national security covered by PII constituted the substantive evidential question. That, said the justices, meant both Northern Ireland courts should have gone back to square one and re-taken the decision. As for Boutcher, they ruled it was wrong for him to have made submissions about matters of national security to Coroner Fee – only the secretary of state, they said, could do that, because the latter's view on matters of national security would always take precedence over that of the chief constable,[20] although Boutcher was free to make representations of his own.[21]

From the court's lengthy written judgment, it would seem that Fee did err significantly in law, while senior lawyers who might have preferred the decision to go in her favour have also quietly acknowledged the force of the court's criticism of the two Northern Ireland reviewing courts.[22] The bottom line, however, is that the ruling has ensured that families wanting to know about the state's involvement in their relative's murder will continue to be constrained by MI5's purist interpretation of national security, limiting what they can be told about the fate of a loved one from decades ago. That interpretation is increasingly seen, not only in the republican and nationalist community, as might be expected, but also now by the likes of Boutcher and Livingstone, as having as much to do with retaining control of the conflict's historical narrative and protecting reputations as it has about protecting the UK from harm.

Whatever about the legal merits of the Supreme Court judgment, it has done nothing to break the conflict mould. The reverse, in fact. Sizeable chunks of the population – not just nationalists but many in the political centre ground that's opening up, wearying of Belfast's political dysfunctionality – will see the judiciary as having reinforced the state's dogmatic use of NCND to protect its truth, inhibiting Boutcher in his ability to build public confidence in the PSNI. As he says, 'Nobody who commits murders should be protected by the policy of NCND.'[23] Yet it protected Freddie Scappaticci for the whole of his life and, thanks to the judgment, will continue to be deployed in other legacy inquests and civil court proceedings as a way of guarding the past.

The Supreme Court's judgment may be the final word on the question of who is the ultimate arbiter of legacy disclosure, but it is insentient to the raw nerve that cases like Thompson, Brown and McCusker touched in the one of the realm's most distant parts. In particular, the high-handed tone of some of Eadie's remarks reminds us of the tone-deafness that Englishmen can unwittingly bring to arguments about Ireland. It reminds us, too, that England and many parts of Northern Ireland are two very different places. 'You gave Boutcher a bloody nose,' Tony McGleenan KC was heard congratulating Eadie after putting a 'regional chief constable' in his place over the superior assessments of the MI5.[24]

So yes, it was a good day for the Treasury Bar. But for reconciling Northern Ireland to the legacy of the moral maze in which Britain lost itself for three decades? Not so much.

ENDNOTES

PREFACE

1 The Rt Hon Sir Desmond de Silva QC, *The Report of the Patrick Finucane Review* (hereafter De Silva Review), December 2012, Vol. II, pp. 282–3: https://assets.publishing.service.gov.uk/media/5a7c2313e5274a25a9140ac8/0802.pdf.

2 Cabinet Office, Guidance Note on NCND Principle, October 2017: www.kenova.co.uk/41.%20D5371%20Guidance%20Re%20NCND%202017.pdf.

3 *Operation Kenova Northern Ireland 'Stakeknife' Legacy Investigation, Interim Report of Jon Boutcher QPM*, March 2024 (hereafter Operation Kenova Interim Report), para. 48.7: www.kenova.co.uk/Kenova%20Report%202024%20Digital%20(002).pdf.

4 Hilary Benn, written ministerial statement, House of Commons, Hansard, Vol. 777, 9 December 2025: https://hansard.parliament.uk/Commons/2025-12-09/debates/25120914400019/NorthernIrelandTroublesOperationKenova?highlight=kenova#contribution-6F5CF04D-9898-4AE8-91D7-5063749A7BF8.

5 Author interview, confidential source, December 2025.

6 *Kenova Final Report, Northern Ireland Legacy Investigations and Reviews*, December 2025 (hereafter Operation Kenova Final Report), p. 7: www.kenova.co.uk/FINAL%20Kenova%20Report.pdf.

CHAPTER 1

1 'Army (FRU SOURCE) Code 6137', summary of Nelson Force Research Unit (hereafter FRU) engagement, as seen by author, para. 6.

2 Brian Nelson, statement to Stevens 1 Inquiry led by John Stevens, January 1990, as seen by author.

3 FRU Contact Form (hereafter CF), 25 August 1984. Copies of all contact forms in this chapter seen by author.

4 FRU CF, 11 October 1984.

5 FRU CF, 8 May 1984.

6 Operation Kenova Interim Report, para. 9.11: www.kenova.co.uk/Kenova%20Report%202024%20Digital%20(002).pdf. See also: *Report on the Interchange of Intelligence between Special Branch and C.I.D., and on the R.U.C. units involved, including those in Crime Branch (C1)*, 31 March 1980: www.kenova.co.uk/6.%20D13484%20Walker-Report-1980.pdf.

7 Brian Nelson statement to Stevens 1 Inquiry.

8 Ibid.

9 Interview with Elaine Higgins in 'Agent 6137', *Bed of Lies* podcast, Series 3, Episode 3, 13 February 2025: www.youtube.com/watch?v=CIQ2I9wBaaM.

10 Author interview with Nelson's sister, Carole Creighton, June 1992.

11 FRU summary of Brian Nelson's career as FRU agent from 8 May 1984 to his arrest on 12 January 1990.

12 Brian Nelson statement to Stevens 1 Inquiry.
13 Ibid.
14 David McKittrick, Seamus Kelters, Brian Feeney and Chris Thornton, *Lost Lives: The Stories of the Men, Women and Children who Died as a Result of the Northern Ireland Troubles* (Mainstream Publishing, 1999), Table 2, p. 1553.
15 Brian Nelson statement to Stevens 1 Inquiry.
16 Interview with Elaine Higgins in 'Agent 6137', *Bed of Lies*.
17 Paddy Topping, court report, 4 July 1973, as seen by author.
18 Brian Nelson before Lord Justice Kelly, Belfast Crown Court, 29 January 1992, author's court transcript.
19 Author interview with Brian Nelson, Crumlin Road Gaol, April 1991.
20 '£1000 for man in false imprisonment case', *Belfast News-Letter*, 17 August 1973.
21 '"Blind" man brutally tortured, court told', *Belfast Telegraph*, 4 July 1973.
22 'Why my daddy: UDA spy's forgotten victim', *Belfast Telegraph*, 15 February 2004.
23 De Silva Review, December 2012, para. 6.5: https://assets.publishing.service.gov.uk/media/5a7c2313e5274a25a9140ac8/0802.pdf.
24 '"Blind" man brutally tortured, court told', *Belfast Telegraph*, 4 July 1973.
25 Brian Nelson statement to Stevens 1 Inquiry.
26 FRU CF, 4 June 1984.
27 Ibid.
28 FRU CF, 11 October 1984.
29 FRU CF, 15 February 1985.
30 FRU CF, 27 March 1985.
31 FRU CF, 3 January 1985.
32 FRU CF, 1 August 1985.
33 Ibid.
34 See De Silva Review for multiple references to Adair's role as a UFF military commander and gunman under the acronym L/05, to Kincaid's role as a UFF military commander and gunman under the acronym L/03, and to Dodds' role as a UFF military commander and gunman under the acronym L/22.
35 FRU CF, 12 April 1985.
36 FRU CF, 13 March 1985.
37 FRU CF, 2 May 1985.
38 FRU CF, 15 February 1985.
39 Statement Soldier A to Stevens 2 Inquiry, as seen by author, 20 January 1994.
40 Brian Nelson journal, 1990–91, p. 30, copy held by author.
41 Statement Soldier A, Stevens 2 Inquiry.
42 Brian Nelson journal, p. 28.
43 Ibid., p. 31.
44 Author interview, confidential source, May 2015.
45 De Silva Review, para. 6.39. See also *Cory Collusion Inquiry Report, Patrick Finucane*, 1 April 2004 (hereafter Cory Collusion Inquiry Report), para. 1.53: https://cain.ulst.ac.uk/issues/collusion/cory/cory03finucane.pdf.
46 FRU CF, 16 May 1985.
47 Ibid.
48 Author interview, confidential source, November 2001.
49 Author interview, Kevin Sheey, November 2001.
50 Brian Nelson journal, p. 16.
51 Ibid.
52 Ibid., p. 17.
53 FRU CF, 13 March 1985.

54 Author interview, confidential source, June 2016.
55 1985 Belfast City Council election: https://en.wikipedia.org/wiki/1985_Belfast_City_Council_election.
56 FRU CF, 1 August 1985.
57 Stevens 1 Interim Report to the Northern Ireland Director of Public Prosecutions (hereafter DPP), as seen by author.
58 David Lister and Hugh Jordan, *Mad Dog* (Mainstream publishing, 2003), p. 55.
59 Ibid.; see also De Silva Review, para. 6.31.
60 Brian Nelson journal, p. 34.
61 De Silva Review, para. 6.17.
62 Brian Nelson journal, p. 37.
63 'UFF shoot and wound Harry Fitzsimmons Sinn Fein in Unity Flats Belfast, 27th September 1985', *Northern Ireland Conflict Videos*, 22 January 2022: www.youtube.com/watch?v=DfvVuyO5SIQ.
64 Brian Nelson journal, p. 35. See also De Silva Review of L/28's role in the targeting of Harry Fitzsimmons, paras 6.8–6.26.
65 De Silva Review, para. 6.33.
66 Ibid., para. 9.47.
67 Operation Kenova Interim Report, p. 30, also para. 50.
68 Her Majesty's Court of Appeal, *The Queen v Martin McCauley*: www.judiciaryni.uk/files/judiciaryni/decisions/R%20v%20McCauley%20%28Martin%29.pdf, para. 15.
69 Author interview, Jon Boutcher, October 2025.
70 Operation Kenova Interim Report, para. 50.1. See also Operation Kenova Final Report, December 2025, para. 7.5: www.psni.police.uk/sites/default/files/2025-12/Operation%20Kenova%20Final%20Report%202025.pdf.
71 Operation Kenova Interim Report, para. 50.6.
72 Author interview, confidential source, June 2016.
73 'Britain's Secret Terror Deals', *Panorama*, BBC, 28 May 2015.
74 Operation Kenova Interim Report, p. 30.
75 Author interview, Ray White, February 2017.
76 Margaret Thatcher said on BBC Radio 4, 6 March 1981: 'We all have a common interest in creating a society where the gunman has no place … the rule of law must apply to everyone.'
77 'Dirty War', *Panorama*, BBC, June 1992.
78 'Home Office Circular No. 97/169 Informants who take part in crime', Letter from Sir Philip Allen, Permanent Under-Secretary, Home Office, to Chief Constables, 12 May 1969, as referenced in De Silva Review, para. 4.25.
79 'Directive for the Force Research Unit (Northern Ireland)', 26 July 1986, as referenced in De Silva Review, para. 4.20.
80 'Instructions for Source Control and Handling in Northern Ireland', 25 July 1986, as referenced in De Silva Review, paras 4.21–4.23.
81 Author interview, confidential source, 17 February 2015.
82 Operation Kenova Interim Report, 20–24 March, para. 67.5.
83 Minute, Security Service Director General to Deputy Director General, 13 July 1989, as referenced in De Silva Review, para. 4.33.
84 De Silva Review, para. 4.34.
85 Brian Nelson journal, p. 36.
86 De Silva Review, para. 6.25.
87 Brian Nelson journal, p. 41: 'The Fitzsimmons affair, the circumstances of which prompted my leaving in the first place.'
88 Ibid., p. 36.
89 FRU CF, 7 October 1985.
90 FRU CF, 10 October 1985.
91 FRU CF, 3 January 1986.

92 FRU CF, 26 December 1985.

93 'Ian Paisley: In quotes', *BBC News*, 12 September 2014: www.bbc.co.uk/news/uk-northern-ireland-29171017.

94 'Wednesday 20 November 1985', CAIN Web Service: https://cain.ulster.ac.uk/events/aia/chron.htm.

95 FRU CF, 26 December 1985. The CF noted that Tommy Lyttle had sought Brian Nelson's return because the Anglo-Irish Agreement had been announced. Nelson also told his handlers that the UDA wanted him back because he had changed the password on the computer and they couldn't retrieve the intelligence information. The report also states: 'It would appear that 6137's main motivation factors are a strong sense of idealism, a dislike of paramilitaries and a very strong sense of affinity with his handlers. These factors became apparent during the debrief when 6137 was asked to give up his job in Germany and return to work for the office.'

96 FRU CF, 17 October 1985.

97 FRU CF, 26 December 1985.

98 FRU CF, 30 December 1985.

99 FRU CF, 4 October 1985.

100 Ibid.

101 Ibid.

102 Ibid.

CHAPTER 2

1 East Detachment, FRU, 'Note to file – Summary of Telecon' (hereafter FRU Summary of Telecon), 9 April 1986, as seen by author.

2 FRU CF, 18 February 1989. Copies of all CFs in this chapter seen by author.

3 Statement of Ronnie Anderson to Stevens 2 Inquiry, 19 August 1993, as seen by author.

4 Ibid. See also, FRU Summary of Telecon, April 1986, para. 5.

5 FRU Summary of Telecon, April 1986, para. 6.

6 Ibid., para. 8.

7 'Violence Unionist Strike', RTÉ Archives, 3 March 1986: www.rte.ie/archives/collections/news/21213392-violence-unionist-strike/.

8 'Monday 3 March 1986, Unionist "Day of Action"', CAIN Web Service: https://cain.ulster.ac.uk/events/aia/chron.htm.

9 Colonel Gordon Kerr, written statement to Stevens 2 Inquiry, 9 October 1990, as seen by author.

10 Ibid.

11 FRU 'Account of meeting', 22 May 1986, as seen by author.

12 Ibid.

13 Brian Nelson journal, p. 41.

14 Author interview, Carole Creighton, 'Dirty War', *Panorama*, BBC, June 1992.

15 Colonel Gordon Kerr, written statement to Stevens 1 Inquiry, 9 October 1990, as seen by author.

16 Hugh Jordan, 'Cop turned writer reveals story of ex-RUC detective's war against the IRA and UVF', *Sunday World*, 17 May 2025: www.sundayworld.com/news/northern-ireland-news/cop-turned-writer-reveals-story-of-ex-ruc-detectives-war-against-the-ira-and-uvf/a812581808.html.

17 Author interview, George Caskey, November 2001.

18 Author interview, confidential source, July 2001.

19 Neil Mackay, 'The secret wars of a spymaster', *The Sunday Herald*, 26 November 2000: https://mail.patfinucanecentre.org/fru/fru22022k1c.html.

20 Author interview, Eric Anderson, November 2001.

21 Author interview, confidential source, undated.

22 Author interview, Sir Jack Hermon, February 1992.

23 Author interview, ACC Brian Fitzsimons, May 1992.

24 Author interview, confidential source, April 1992.

25 Author interview, Lee Platts, January 2002.
26 Author interview, Phil Smith, December 2001.
27 Author interview, Nigel Wylde, April 2002.
28 Interview with Phil Smith, 'Handlers', *Bed of Lies* podcast, Series 3, Episode 5, 20 February 2025: www.youtube.com/watch?v=jnC_znUpS48.
29 Author interview, Steve Pyrnne, November 2001.
30 Author interview, Kevin Dodd, February 2002.
31 Author interview, confidential source, January 2002.
32 Interview with Ian Hurst, 'Handlers', *Bed of Lies* podcast, Series 3, Episode 5, 20 February 2025: www.youtube.com/watch?v=jnC_znUpS48.
33 Stevens 1 submission to DPP(NI), September 1990.
34 FRU, '6137 Update for ACOS G2/ASP', undated, para. 3 and para. 5, as seen by author.
35 FRU CF, 14 January 1987.
36 FRU, '6137 Update for ACOS G2/ASP', para. 1. See also, Soldier Q statement to Stevens 2 Inquiry, 17 August 1993, as seen by author.
37 Brian Nelson journal, p. 38.
38 Ibid.
39 FRU CF, 14 January 1987.
40 Ibid.
41 Brian Nelson journal, p. 41.
42 Ibid.
43 Ibid.
44 Ibid., p. 42.
45 FRU CF, 14 January 1987.
46 FRU, '6137 Update for ACOS G2/ASP', February 1987, para. 11.
47 Ibid., para. 7.
48 Ibid., para. 5.
49 De Silva Review, Vol. II, p. 301: https://assets.publishing.service.gov.uk/media/5a7c2313e5274a25a9140ac8/0802.pdf.
50 Ibid, para. 8.173.
51 FRU, '6137 Update for ACOS G2/ASP', para. 5, as seen by author.
52 Ibid., para. 7.
53 Ibid., para. 12.
54 Ibid., para. 15.
55 Ibid., para. 16.
56 Ibid., para. 18.
57 Ibid., para. 19.
58 Ibid., para. 20.
59 Ibid., para. 21.
60 Ibid.
61 Ibid., para. 22.
62 De Silva Review, para. 9.63.
63 FRU, '6137 Update for ACOS G2/ASP', para. 23.
64 Ibid., para. 29.
65 Ibid., para. 22.
66 Ibid., para. 27.
67 Ibid., para. 29.
68 Ibid., para. 31.
69 Ibid., paras 31 and 32.
70 Colonel Gordon Kerr written statement to Stevens 1 Inquiry, 9 October 1990.
71 John Deverell, Director and Co-ordinator of Intelligence, Northern Ireland, statement to Stevens 2 Inquiry, 21 June 1993, as cited in De Silva Review, para. 6.72.

72 De Silva Review, para. 7.240.
73 WhatsApp from Brian Feeney to author, February 2026.
74 Brian Nelson journal, p. 44.
75 FRU CF, 18 February 1987.
76 FRU CF, 25 February 1987.
77 Interview with Martin Callan, 'Holding the Line', *Brits*, BBC Two, 31 May 2000.
78 FRU CF, 18 February 1987.
79 FRU CF, 29 May 1987.
80 Brian Nelson journal, pp. 45 and 46.
81 FRU CF, 18 February 1987.
82 Brian Nelson journal, p. 44. Nelson records this as 6 May. FRU CF for 18 May 1987 indicates it was 25 May.
83 Martin Callan, statement to Stevens 1 Inquiry, 8 March 1990, as seen by author.
84 Ibid.
85 Brian Nelson journal, p. 48.
86 FRU CF, 4 October 1985.
87 FRU CF, 30 April 1987.
88 FRU CF, 29 May 1987.
89 FRU CF, 10 June 1988.
90 Author interview, David Creighton, 1992.
91 FRU CF, January 1988.
92 FRU CF, 6 April 1988.
93 FRU CF, 3 May 1988.
94 FRU CF, 2 June 1988.
95 FRU CF, 15 August 1988.
96 FRU CF, 5 September 1988.
97 FRU CF, 1 November 1988.
98 FRU CF, 7 April 1989.
99 Martin Callan statement to Stevens 1 Inquiry, 5 December 1990.

CHAPTER 3

1 De Silva Review, p. 178, para. 7.293: https://assets.publishing.service.gov.uk/media/5a7c2313e5274a25a9140ac8/0802.pdf.
2 DPP(NI), note on Stevens 1 Inquiry, as seen by author.
3 Ronnie Anderson, statement to Stevens 3 Inquiry, 19 August 1993, as seen by author.
4 De Silva Review, para. 6.80.
5 Author interview, confidential source, December 1992.
6 De Silva Review, para. 24.55.
7 Note from Colonel Gordon Kerr to ACOS G2/ASP, February 1987, para. 22.
8 Colonel Gordon Kerr, written statement to Stevens 1 Inquiry, 9 October 1990.
9 ACOS G2 (Soldier AA), interview with Stevens 1 Inquiry, 25 October 1990.
10 Brian Nelson journal, p. 48.
11 Ibid., pp. 51–2.
12 Martin Callan, statement to Stevens 1 Inquiry, 8 March 1990, as seen by author.
13 Brian Nelson journal, p. 51.
14 Martin Callan, statement to Stevens 1 Inquiry, 8 March 1990, as seen by author.
15 Ibid., p. 52.
16 Author interview, confidential source, April 2016. See also Security Service, telegram, 21 May 1987, De Silva Review, Vol. II, pp. 302–4, para. 4.
17 Martin Callan, statement to Stevens 1 Inquiry, 8 March 1990, as seen by author.

18 Brian Nelson journal, p. 56.
19 Author interview, Vincent McFadden, January 2002.
20 Author interview, confidential source, October 2001.
21 Brian Nelson journal, p. 58.
22 De Silva Review, para. 7.264.
23 FRU CF, 10 January 1989.
24 Brian Nelson journal, p. 152.
25 FRU CF, 23 May 1988.
26 FRU Telephone Contact Form (hereafter TCF) 20 May 1988: 'It's because you are involved. Had you not been, then you would not know about it and would go ahead.'
27 Security Service, telegram, 21 May 1987, De Silva Review, Vol. II, pp. 302–4, para. 4.
28 Ibid., para. 3.
29 MI5 section F8 to Head of agent-running section, 27 May 1987, as referenced in De Silva Review, paras 8.198–8.200.
30 Author interview, ACC Brian Fitzsimons, May 1992.
31 Brigadier Gordon Kerr, written statement to Stevens 3 Inquiry, 2 December 2002, as cited in De Silva Review, para. 6.59.
32 De Silva Review, para. 8.59.
33 'Examination of Military Files Relating to Nelson', Stevens 1 Inquiry, September 1990, as seen by author.
34 Transcript of author interview with Nicholas Benwell from 'A Licence to Murder – part 2', *Panorama*, BBC, June 2002, in reference to the murder of Gerard Slane: http://news.bbc.co.uk/hi/english/static/audio_video/programmes/panorama/transcripts/transcript_23_06_02.txt.
35 Note from ACOS G2 to GOC undated, as referenced in De Silva Review, para. 8.15.
36 De Silva Review, paras 8.13, 8.53, 8.60, 8.121.
37 Cory Collusion Inquiry Report, para. 1.247: https://cain.ulster.ac.uk/issues/collusion/cory/cory03finucane.pdf.
38 De Silva Review, para. 8.43.
39 Author interview, confidential sources, April 2002.
40 De Silva Review, para. 7.268.
41 Ibid., para. 8.57.
42 Ibid., paras 9.20 and 9.42.
43 Ibid., para. 42.
44 Ibid., para. 8.59.
45 Author interview, Ray White, April 2015.
46 De Silva Review, para. 61.
47 Ibid., para. 9.8.
48 Author interview, confidential source, June 2016.
49 Statement of Detective Superintendent Joseph Meeke, 13 December 1990, as seen by author.
50 De Silva Review, para. 8.19.
51 Cory Collusion Inquiry Report, para. 1.251.
52 Security Service telegram, 1 June 1990, as cited in De Silva Review, para. 8.207.
53 Author interview, confidential source, December 2016.
54 Ibid., February 2015.
55 De Silva Review, para. 9.33.
56 Ibid., para. 9.34.
57 Ibid., paras 9.23–9.34.
58 Ibid., paras 8.114, 9.14, 9.48, 9.64, 16.34, 16.43, 24.91.
59 Ibid., para. 43.
60 Author interview, confidential source, February 2015.
61 De Silva Review, paras 9.67, 8.71, 8.77.

62 Brian Nelson statement as quoted by Lord Justice Kelly in his judgment at Nelson's trial, 3 February 1992.
63 FRU CF, 4 August 1988.
64 'Pat Finucane assassination: Who did know in Whitehall?', *An Phoblacht*, 6 January 2013: www.anphoblacht.com/contents/22627.
65 FRU CF, 6 April 1988.
66 Author interview, confidential source, January 2002.
67 Author interview, confidential source, February 2002.
68 Gordon Kerr, written submission to De Silva Review, para. 7.285.
69 Brigadier Gordon Kerr, prepared statement given in interview to Stevens 3 Inquiry, 2 December 2002, as cited in De Silva Review, para. 8.86.
70 De Silva Review, para. 8.94.
71 Ibid., paras 8.98 and 8.99.
72 Ibid., para. 8.101.
73 Ibid., paras 8.102 and 8.104.
74 Ibid., para. 8.105.
75 FRU CF, 6 February 1989.
76 De Silva Review, para. 7.270.
77 Author interview, Nicholas Benwell, June 2002.
78 Terence McDaid, 10 May 1988; Brendan 'Ruby' Davison, 25 July 1988; Gerard Slane, 23 September 1988; James Craig, 15 October 1988; Patrick Finucane, 12 February 1989; Loughlin Maginn, 26 August 1989.
79 Brian Nelson journal, pp. 169–71.
80 Colonel Gordon Kerr evidence at Nelson trial, January 1992, transcript held by author.
81 Param Cumaraswamy, 'Report on the mission of the Special Rapporteur to the United Kingdom of Great Britain and Northern Ireland', 5 March 1998: https://digitallibrary.un.org/record/251350?v=pdf.
82 De Silva Review, para. 7.247.
83 'Holding the Line', *Brits*, programme 3, BBC Two, May 2000.
84 FRU CF, August 1988.
85 Martin Callan statement to Stevens 1 Inquiry, 5 November 1990.
86 De Silva Review, para. 11.111.

CHAPTER 4

1 Brian Nelson, statement to Stevens 1 Inquiry, January 1990.
2 FRU CF, 30 August 1989.
3 FRU CF, 14 October 1987.
4 Brian Nelson journal, pp. 62, 63.
5 Brian Nelson journal, p. 64.
6 De Silva Review, para. 24.55.
7 Author interview, Vincent McFadden, January 2002.
8 FRU CF, 20 October 1987.
9 FRU CF, 7 July 1989.
10 FRU CF, 16 August 1989.
11 Author interview, Vincent McFadden, May 2002.
12 Based on FRU CFs available to author.
13 FRU CF, 7 April 1989.
14 Soldier Z interview with Detective Chief Superintendent Arthur Mandry, 6 December 1990.
15 De Silva Review, paras 7.40–7.46: https://assets.publishing.service.gov.uk/media/5a7c2313e5274a25a9140ac8/0802.pdf.

16 Martin Callan statement to Stevens 1 Inquiry, 6 November 1990, as seen by author.
17 Author analysis of ninety-seven murders and attempted murders between September 1985 and February 1992 of individuals whose names appeared in Brian Nelson's intelligence files.
18 Brigadier Gordon Kerr, prepared statement to Stevens 3 Inquiry, 2 December 2002, as cited in De Silva Review, para. 7.6.
19 Colonel Gordon Kerr, written statement to Stevens 1 Inquiry, 9 October 1990, as seen by author.
20 De Silva Review, para. 7.27.
21 Ibid., para. 7.31.
22 Transcript of meeting between Gordon Kerr and Sir Desmond de Silva QC, 7 September 2012, para. 8.88.
23 'Holding the Line', *Brits*, programme 3, BBC 2, May 2000.
24 For a summary of Brendan Hughes' life in the IRA, see 'Looking Back in Anger', *Socialist Review*, 1 September 2006: https://socialistworker.co.uk/socialist-review-archive/looking-back-anger/.
25 De Silva Review, paras 7.88–7.107.
26 FRU TCF, 22 March 1988.
27 De Silva Review., para. 7.212.
28 FRU TCF, 17 July 1988.
29 Ibid.
30 'Conspiracy to murder Alex Maskey', Stevens 1 Interim Report to DPP(NI), September 1990.
31 Brian Nelson journal, p. 92.
32 Author interview with Brian Nelson, 13 June 1991.
33 FRU TCF, 12 August 1988.
34 Brian Nelson journal, p. 80.
35 FRU CF, 17 November 1988.
36 FRU TCF, 11 May 1988.
37 Author interview, Maura McDaid, June 1992.
38 Author interview, Tracy McDaid, December 2014.
39 FRU CF, 11 May 1988.
40 Ibid.
41 Inquest statement, 11 September 1989, from author 2002 notes.
42 Author interview, confidential source, 14 August 2001.
43 Wendy Robbins, interview with Maura McDaid, May 1992.
44 Brian Nelson statement to Stevens 1 Inquiry, 18 January 1990, as seen by author.
45 Author interview, Nicholas Benwell, November 2001.
46 Terence McDaid, Gerard Slane, Patrick Finucane, Loughlin Maginn
47 Author interview, confidential source, 7 June 2016.
48 Author interview, Sarah Bynum, February 2002.
49 Cory Collusion Inquiry Report, para. 1.261: https://cain.ulst.ac.uk/issues/collusion/cory/cory03finucane.pdf.
50 David McKittrick, Seamus Kelters, Brian Feeney and Chris Thornton, *Lost Lives: The Stories of the Men, Women and Children who Died as a Result of the Northern Ireland Troubles* (Mainstream Publishing, 1999), pp. 1146–7.
51 Author interview, Sean Slane, March 2002.
52 John Ware and Geoff Seed with Alasdair Palmer, 'Assassination by Proxy', *The Sunday Telegraph*, 29 March 1989.
53 McKittrick et al., *Lost Lives*, p. 1146.
54 Brian Nelson, statement to Stevens 1 Inquiry, 15 January 1990, as seen by author. See also De Silva Review, para. 7.148, where Spence is referred to by his acronym L/20.
55 MISR, 23 September 1988, as cited in De Silva Review, para. 7.156.
56 MISR, 3 October 1988, as cited in De Silva Review, para. 7.158.
57 De Silva Review, para. 7.162, where Spence is referred to as L/20.

58 Cory Collusion Inquiry Report, para. 1.15.
59 De Silva Review, para. 12.9.
60 Author interview, Michael Finucane, 'A Licence to Murder', Part 2, *Panorama*, BBC, 23 June 2002.
61 Email to author from Kevin Winters, the instructing solicitor for the case, July 2025.
62 Instructions taken by Madden & Finucane, solicitors from former client of Pat Finucane; De Silva Review, para. 18.18.
63 John Ware, 'Time to come clean over the army's role in the "Dirty War"', *New Statesman*, 24 April 1998.
64 De Silva Review, para. 18.12.
65 FRU CF, 10 January 1989.
66 FRU CF, 5 January 1988.
67 FRU CF, 10 January 1989.
68 Ibid.
69 FRU CF, 25 January 1989.
70 The attempted murders of Patrick Monaghan (9 November 1988), James Morgan (14 November 1988) and Joe O'Donnell (17 January 1989).
71 Brian Kerr QC, prosecution opening facts, *Crown v Brian Nelson*, Crumlin Road court, 22 January 1992.
72 FRU CF, 23 August 1988.
73 FRU CF, 4 January 1989.
74 Brian Nelson 'undoubtedly did the recce on the solicitor, Pat Finucane', Head of Security Service operational section, General Assessment, 24 May 1989, para. 10, as cited in De Silva Review, Volume II, p. 201.
75 FRU CFs, 2 and 9 March 1989.
76 Brian Nelson, statement to Stevens I Inquiry, 15 January 1990, as seen by author.
77 De Silva Review, para. 12.7
78 Ibid., para. 21.190.
79 Operation Kenova Family Report, 'Murder of Thomas Emmanuel Wilson, July 2025', p. 30, copy held by author.
80 Author interview, Nicholas Benwell, June 2002.
81 FRU CF, 14 February 1989.
82 Transcript of de Silva meeting with Gordon Kerr, 7 September 2012, referenced in De Silva Review, para. 21.188.
83 De Silva Review, paras 21.185 and 21.186.
84 Detective Superintendent Alan Simpson, deposition at the inquest of Patrick Finucane, 6 September 1990.
85 Sir Ronnie Flanagan, 'Careless Talk', *Panorama*, BBC, 21 June 1999; 'Orde pressured over Finucane IRA claims', *Belfast Telegraph*, 18 April 2004: www.belfasttelegraph.co.uk/news/orde-pressured-over-finucane-ira-claims/28189491.html.
86 'Former RUC chief stands by Finucane claim', *BBC News*, 11 May 1999: https://newsimg.bbc.co.uk/1/hi/uk_politics/341084.stm.
87 De Silva Review, paras 66–68.
88 Ibid., paras 14.33 and 14.34.
89 Ibid., para. 1.37.
90 Prime Minister David Cameron statement on Patrick Finucane, 12 December 2012: www.gov.uk/government/speeches/prime-minister-david-cameron-statement-on-patrick-finucane.
91 FRU, '6137 Update for ACOS G2/ASP', para. 21, as seen by author.
92 FRU CF, 29 November 1989.
93 'Pat Finucane's widow calls de Silva report "a whitewash"', *The Guardian*, 12 December 2013: www.theguardian.com/uk/2012/dec/12/pat-finucane-de-silva-report.
94 Author interview, Phil James, 22 January 2025.

95 FRU CF, 16 June 1989.
96 MoD, 'Problem Areas' document, as cited in De Silva Review, para. 7.115.
97 FRU CF, 16 August 1989.
98 FRU CF, 16 June 1989.
99 Ibid.
100 FRU CFs, 27 June and 19 June 1989.
101 Statement of Ronnie Anderson to Stevens 2 Inquiry, 19 August 1993, as seen by author.
102 Security Service telegram, 21 May 1987, as cited in De Silva Review, para. 7.255.
103 Security Service telegram, 11 July 1988, as cited in De Silva Review, para. 7.291.
104 FRU CF, 6 July 1988.
105 Statement of Martin Callan to Stevens 1 Inquiry, 6 November 1990, as seen by author.
106 FRU CF 6 April 1988.
107 FRU CF, 15 August 1988.
108 De Silva Review, para. 8.121.
109 Ibid., para. 8.199.

CHAPTER 5

1 Gerry Adams, 'Celebrating 40 years of the Conway Mill (oh, yes, and Bono too)', 28 October 2022: https://belfastmedia.com/gerry-adams-40-years-of-the-conway-mill-oh-yes-and-bono-s-new-book.
2 'Fógraí bháis Tom Cahill', 8 February 2001: www.anphoblacht.com/contents/7168.
3 Jim Gibney, 'The "Mill": A threat to Britain's national security', 8 April 2004: www.anphoblacht.com/contents/11505.
4 'Scappaticci: The Wilsey Tape', *The Broken Elbow*, 7 April 2017: https://thebrokenelbow.com/2017/04/07/scappaticci-the-wilsey-tape/.
5 Author interview, confidential source, June 2025.
6 Ian Hurst, WhatsApp to author, July 2025.
7 Author, WhatsApp with Ian Hurst, December 2025.
8 Operation Kenova Final Report, December 2025, para. 9.26: www.psni.police.uk/sites/default/files/2025-12/Operation%20Kenova%20Final%20Report%202025.pdf.
9 Ibid., para. 9.28.
10 Transcript of Scappaticci covert interview with *The Cook Report*, ITV, 28 August 1993: https://thebrokenelbow.com/2019/01/11/remembering-freddie-scappaticci/.
11 FRU CF, 18 November 1987.
12 Author interview, Anthony McIntyre, December 2016.
13 Ibid.
14 Author interview, Sean O'Callaghan, May 2016.
15 Adams was credited as the 'architect of the IRA's re-organised system' by Major General James Glover in his secret but leaked assessment 'Northern Ireland: Future Terrorist Trends', November 1978.
16 'Ivor Bell: The former IRA leader who split with Sinn Féin', *BBC News*, 17 October 2019: www.bbc.co.uk/news/uk-northern-ireland-50068277.
17 Bernard Teggart (13 November 1973).
18 William Martin (22 August 1977).
19 Jean McConville (7 December 1972).
20 Author interview, Anthony McIntyre, December 2016.
21 Author interview, confidential source, May 2016.
22 'Stakeknife flies home', *The People*, 14 March 2004: https://web.archive.org/web/20150927062542/http://www.nuzhound.com/articles/Sunday_People/arts2004/mar14_stakeknife_flies_home.php.
23 Author interview, confidential source, November 2016.

24 Author interview, confidential source, February 2015.
25 Author interview, confidential source, May 2017.
26 Certified copy of birth certificate, registered 18 January 1946, held by author.
27 Richard O' Rawe, *Stakeknife's Dirty War: The Inside Story of Scappaticci, the IRA's Nutting Squad and the British Spooks who Ran the War* (Merrion Press, 2023) p. 5.
28 Author interview, confidential source, May 2016.
29 Author interview, Richard O'Rawe, May 2025.
30 O'Rawe, *Stakeknife's Dirty War*, pp. 6–7.
31 Author interview, Jim Davison, July 2016.
32 The Sunday Times *Insight team, Ulster* (Penguin, 1972), pp. 114, 117.
33 Author interview, Anthony McIntyre, December 2016.
34 Ibid.
35 Author interview, confidential source, December 2016.
36 O'Rawe, *Stakeknife's Dirty War*, p. 7.
37 Ibid., p. 8.
38 Ibid., p. 9.
39 Ibid.
40 Author interview, confidential source, April 2016.
41 Ibid.
42 'Freddie Scappaticci threatens BBC reporter', *BBC News*, 7 March 2024: www.bbc.co.uk/news/av/uk-northern-ireland-68493626.
43 Author interview, Anthony McIntyre, December 2016.
44 O'Rawe, *Stakeknife's Dirty War*, p. 24.
45 Author interview, confidential source, November 2016.
46 Ibid.
47 Author interview, Anthony McIntyre, December 2016.
48 Author interview, Tommy Gorman, November 2016.
49 Ibid., November 2016.
50 Ibid., December 2016.
51 Ibid., November 2016.
52 'Four people were kneecapped and once again no A or B list men were arrested although a sighting of SCAPPATICCI occurred', extract from 39 Brigade intelligence summary for 13–19 July 1974, as seen by author.
53 Author interview, confidential source, November 2016.
54 Author interview, Anthony McIntyre, December 2016.
55 'Shadow of a Gunman: Interview with Anthony McIntyre', *The Pensive Quill*, 1 May 2019: www.thepensivequill.com/2019/05/shadow-of-gunman.html.
56 O'Rawe, *Stakeknife's Dirty War*, p. 35.
57 Author interview, confidential source, August 2016.
58 O'Rawe, *Stakeknife's Dirty War*, p. 37.
59 Operation Kenova Final Report, December 2025, para. 9.22.
60 Author interview, confidential source, April 2016.
61 O'Rawe, *Stakeknife's Dirty War*, p. 27.
62 Author interview, confidential source, June 2016.
63 Author interview, confidential source, June 2016.
64 Author interview, confidential source, and email, February 2004.
65 Author interview, confidential source, May 2016; also interview with separate confidential source, October 2025.
66 Author interview, confidential source, October 2025.
67 Author interview, confidential source, December 2025.
68 Author interview, confidential source, April 2016.

69 Operation Kenova Final Report, December 2025, para. 9.22.
70 Author interview, confidential source, April 2016.
71 Operation Kenova Final Report, December 2025, para. 9.22.
72 Ibid., para. 9.24.
73 John Wilsey, 'The Source Handler's Tale', *The Ulster Tales* (Pen & Sword Military, 2011), p. 57.
74 Author interview, confidential source, April 2016.
75 Author interview, confidential source, November 2016.
76 Author interview, confidential source, November 2016.
77 'Belfast murder: Who was ex-IRA man "Jock" Davison?', *BBC News*, 5 May 2015: www.bbc.co.uk/news/uk-northern-ireland-32590286.

CHAPTER 6

1 Author interview, confidential source, November 2025.
2 Author interviews, Phil James, June 2016 and June 2025.
3 Author interview, confidential source, February 2016.
4 Operation Kenova briefing to author, June 2025. The list is: Michael Kearney – July 1979; Eugene Simons – January 1981; Patrick Trainor – February 1981; Vincent Robinson – June 1981; Anthony Braniff – September 1981; Seamus Morgan – March 1982; James (Jas) Young – February 1982; Patrick Murray – August 1986; David McVeigh – September 1986; Charles McIlmurray – April 1987; Emmanuel Wilson – June 1987; Anthony McKiernan – January 1988; Joe Fenton – February 1989.
5 Operation Kenova, briefing to author, February 2025.
6 PPS, 'Murder of Victim C – 1993', Operation Kenova – Summary of Decisions Not to Prosecute, 6 December 2023, para. 9.9: www.ppsni.gov.uk/files/ppsni/2023-12/Public%20Statement%206%20December%2023%20_0.pdf.
7 Author interview, several confidential sources in the IRA and PSNI, 2016.
8 Statement of Mervyn Bishop for civil proceedings (undated), as seen by author.
9 Ibid.
10 Ibid.
11 Operation Kenova Family Report, 'The murder of Michael Kearney, 12 July 1979', July 2025, p. 17, as shared with author.
12 Michael Kearney written debrief to the IRA, as shared with author in July 2016.
13 Operation Kenova Family Report, 'The murder of Michael Kearney, 12 July 1979', July 2025, p. 18.
14 Statement of Mervyn Bishop for civil proceedings (undated), as seen by author.
15 Operation Kenova Family Report, 'The murder of Michael Kearney, 12 July 1979', July 2025, p. 33.
16 Author interview, Séamus Kearney, November 2016.
17 Operation Kenova Family Report, 'The murder of Michael Kearney, 12 July 1979', July 2025, pp. 26 and 27.
18 Ibid., p. 20.
19 Author interview, Séamus Kearney, July 2016.
20 Operation Kenova Family Report, 'The murder of Michael Kearney, 12 July 1979', July 2025, p. 29.
21 Operation Kenova briefing to Séamus Kearney, 5 March 2024.
22 Author interview, Séamus Kearney, July 2016, reading from Michael Kearney's debrief.
23 Author interview, Séamus Kearney, July 2016.
24 Operation Kenova Family Report, 'The murder of Michael Kearney, 12 July 1979', July 2025, p. 28.
25 Ibid., p. 29.
26 Ibid. For details of the General Army Orders see IRA, *Green Book*: https://cain.ulster.ac.uk/othelem/organ/ira/ira_green_book.htm.
27 Author interview, Séamus Kearney, July 2016.
28 Operation Kenova briefing to Séamus Kearney, 5 March 2024.
29 Ibid.

30 Author interview, Séamus Kearney, July 2016.
31 Ibid., December 2016.
32 Operation Kenova Family Report, 'The murder of Michael Kearney, 12 July 1979', July 2025, pp. 7, 11–12.
33 Ibid., p. 10.
34 Ibid., p. 25.
35 Ibid., pp. 7, 29.
36 Ibid., pp. 27–9, 33.
37 Ibid., p. 8.
38 IRA statement to Kearney family, 28 January 2003, held by author.
39 Author interview, Séamus Kearney, July 2016. See also 'IRA Probe Clears Name of Executed Volunteer', *Saoirse*, 32, 26 September 2003: https://saoirse32.wordpress.com/2003/09/.
40 Operation Kenova Final Report, December 2025, reference to Case 8 (Michael Kearney), p. 67: www.psni.police.uk/sites/default/files/2025-12/Operation%20Kenova%20Final%20Report%20 2025.pdf.
41 Operation Kenova Family Report, 'The murder of Michael Kearney, 12 July 1979', July 2025, p. 27.
42 Author interview, confidential source, December 2016.

CHAPTER 7

1 Interview with Angela Donnelly, 'Bonus Episode with Angela Donnelly, Sister of Eugene Simons', *Stakeknife*, Episode 12, BBC Sounds, 20 June 2025: www.bbc.com/audio/play/p0lk8q6c.
2 Mark Urban, *Big Boys' Rules: The SAS and the Secret Struggle Against the IRA* (Faber and Faber, 1992), p. 107. Also, Angela Donnelly, 'Bonus Episode with Angela Donnelly', *Stakeknife*, 20 June 2025.
3 'Who were the Disappeared?', *BBC News*, 27 November 2024: www.bbc.co.uk/news/uk-northern-ireland-27235088.
4 'Authorities lost skull of man shot dead by IRA more than 40 years ago', *The Irish News*, 8 August 2025: www.irishnews.com/news/northern-ireland/authorities-lost-skull-of-man-shot-dead-by-ira-more-than-40-years-ago-FI6PGFGWZRHN7NV23ZMYLJFJRM/.
5 Author interview, confidential source, July 2025.
6 'Grisly secrets of the "disappeared" of Anglo-Irish war uncovered by research', *The Guardian*, 11 February 2024: www.theguardian.com/world/2024/feb/11/grisly-secrets-of-the-disappeared-of-anglo-irish-war-uncovered-by-research.
7 Interview with Angela Donnelly, 'Bonus Episode with Angela Donnelly', *Stakeknife*, 20 June 2025.
8 'Authorities lost skull of man shot dead by IRA more than 40 years ago', *The Irish News*, 8 August 2025.
9 Operation Kenova Final Report, December 2025, Case 9 (Eugene Simons), p. 68: www.kenova.co.uk/FINAL%20Kenova%20Report.pdf.
10 Author interview, confidential source, October 2025. See also 'Simons and the family friends now suspected of his abduction', *The Irish News*, 30 June 2025: www.irishnews.com/news/northern-ireland/scappaticci-kenova-disappeared-victim-eugene-simons-and-the-family-friends-now-suspected-of-his-abduction-QSKQPAYAHBDRRIS75ZXHNZNAPM/.
11 'Authorities lost skull of man shot dead by IRA more than 40 years ago', *The Irish News*, 8 August 2025.
12 Operation Kenova Final Report, December 2025, para. 7.23.
13 Moira Todd speaking at a press conference, Stormont Hotel, Belfast, 9 December 2025.
14 Operation Kenova Final Report, December 2025, Case 9 (Eugene Simons), pp. 67, 68.
15 Interview with Angela Donnelly, 'Bonus Episode with Angela Donnelly', *Stakeknife*, 20 June 2025.
16 Urban, *Big Boys' Rules*, p. 107.
17 'Authorities lost skull of man shot dead by IRA more than 40 years ago', *The Irish News*, 8 August 2025.

18 Interview with Angela Donnelly, 'Bonus Episode with Angela Donnelly', *Stakeknife*, 20 June 2025.
19 '"I'm not going to hide again": Stakeknife report met with relief by victims' families', *The Guardian*, 9 December 2025: www.theguardian.com/uk-news/2025/dec/09/stakeknife-report-relief-victims-families.
20 Operation Kenova Family Report, 'The murder of Patrick Trainor, 22 February 1981', pp. 15, 16.
21 Ibid., p. 21.
22 Eamon Collins with Mick McGovern, *Killing Rage* (Granta Publications, 1997), p. 237.
23 Operation Kenova Family Report, 'The murder of Patrick Trainor, 22 February 1981', in which 'Suspect I' is Scappaticci, p. 19.
24 Ibid.
25 Ibid., p. 16.
26 KRW-Law report of Operation Kenova meeting with Eileen Hughes, 29 May, p. 3, as briefed to author.
27 David McKittrick, Seamus Kelters, Brian Feeny and Chris Thornton, *Lost Lives: The Stories of the Men, Women and Children who Died as a Result of the Northern Ireland Troubles* (Mainstream Publishing, 1999), pp. 1466, 1467.
28 Author interview, confidential source, November 2016.
29 Transcript of Scappaticci covert interview with *The Cook Report*, ITV, 26 August 1993: https://thebrokenelbow.com/2019/01/11/remembering-freddie-scappaticci/.
30 Ibid.
31 Operation Kenova Family Report, 'Murder of Thomas Emmanuel Wilson, 24 June 1987' in which 'Suspect I' is Scappaticci and the man he shot is 'Victim 3', p. 26, copy held by author.
32 Thomas Wilson: June 1987 and Anthony McKiernan: January 1988, as referenced in above report respectively as 'Victim 2' & 'Victim 5', p. 14.
33 Author interview, confidential source, May 2025.
34 Author interview, Eileen Hughes, July 2016.
35 In September 1995, Tony Kane was shot in the head as he sat in his car after a funeral, see McKittrick et al., *Lost Lives*, p. 1383.
36 Operation Kenova Family Report, 'The murder of Patrick Trainor, 22 February 1981', p. 14.
37 Ibid., p. 20.
38 Ibid., p. 26.
39 KRW-Law report of Operation Kenova meeting with Eileen Hughes, 29 May 2024, p. 2, as seen by author.
40 Author interview, Eileen Robinson, December 2015.
41 Operation Kenova Family Report, 'Murder of Vincent Robinson, 26 June, 1981', in which 'Suspect C' is Scappaticci, 2025, p. 5, copy held by author.
42 Ibid., p. 29.
43 Ibid., p. 5.
44 KRW-Law attendance note of Operation Kenova meeting with Eileen Robinson, January 2024, p. 3.
45 Operation Kenova Family Report, 'Murder of Vincent Robinson, 26 June, 1981', in which 'Suspect C' is Scappaticci, 2025, p. 23.
46 HET, 'Review Summary Report concerning the death of Vincent Robinson, 26 June 1981', postmortem examination, p. 9, as seen by author.
47 Ibid., p. 6.
48 McKittrick et al., *Lost Lives*, p. 868.
49 KRW-Law attendance note of Operation Kenova meeting with Eileen Robinson, January 2024, p. 7.
50 Operation Kenova Family Report, 'Murder of Vincent Robinson, 26 June 1981', in which 'Suspect C' is Scappaticci, 2025, p. 19.
51 Ibid., p. 28.
52 Ibid., p. 30.

53 KRW-Law attendance note of Operation Kenova meeting with Eileen Robinson, January 2024, p. 7.
54 Author interview, confidential source, June 2016.
55 Operation Kenova Family Report, 'Murder of Vincent Robinson, 26 June 1981', in which 'Suspect C' is Scappaticci, 2025, p. 24.
56 HET, 'Review Summary Report concerning the death of Vincent Robinson, 26 June 1981', postmortem examination, pp. 14, 15.
57 Author interview, confidential source, December 2025.
58 HET, 'Review Summary Report concerning the death of Vincent Robinson, 26 June 1981', postmortem examination, p. 17. See also KRW-Law attendance note of Kenova meeting with Eileen Robinson, January 2024, p. 4; Operation Kenova Family Report, 'Murder of Vincent Robinson, 26 June 1981', in which 'Suspect' D is Joe McKee, 2025, p. 5.
59 KRW-Law attendance note of Kenova officers meeting with Eileen Robinson, January 2024, p. 4.
60 Ed Moloney, *Voices from the Grave* (Faber and Faber Ltd, 2010), pp. 280 and 281.
61 Operation Kenova Family Report, 'The murder of Anthony McKiernan, 19 January 1988', 2025, p. 18.
62 Author interview, confidential source, October 2025.
63 Author interview, confidential source, December 2025. See also 'Dirty fighting', *The Guardian*, 13 January 2009: www.theguardian.com/uk/2009/jan/13/northernireland-northernireland.
64 Author interview, confidential source, December 2025.
65 Gerry Bradley, *Insider* (O'Brien Press Ltd, 2009), p. 159 (eBook edition).
66 Author interview, Brian Feeney, June 2016.
67 'PIRA claim of responsibility', *Downtown Radio*, 24 June 1987, as cited in HET family report, July 2025, p. 31.
68 Archive BBC News, 'Frank', *Stakeknife*, Episode 10, BBC Sounds, 1 February 2025: www.bbc.co.uk/sounds/play/p0km0vdx.
69 Operation Kenova Family Report, 'The murder of Thomas Emmanuel Wilson, 24 June 1987', in which 'Suspect I' is Scappaticci, p. 31.
70 Ibid., p. 22.
71 Operation Kenova Family Report, 'The murder of Anthony McKiernan, 19 January 1988', p. 26.
72 Ibid., in which Scappaticci is referred to as 'the informant'.
73 Ibid.
74 Ibid., p.18.
75 Operation Kenova Final Report, December 2025, Case 3 (Anthony McKiernan), p. 64: www.psni.police.uk/sites/default/files/2025-12/Operation%20Kenova%20Final%20Report%202025.pdf.
76 Operation Kenova Family Report, 'The murder of Anthony McKiernan, 19 January 1988', in which Scappaticci is referred to as 'the informant', p. 27.
77 Author interview, confidential source, May 2025.
78 PPS, 'Operation Kenova – summary of decisions not to prosecute', 29 February 2024, p. 8, para. 27: www.ppsni.gov.uk/files/ppsni/2024-02/Operation%20Kenova%20Public%20Statement%2029%20February%202024.pdf.
79 Author interview, confidential source, June 2025.
80 Operation Kenova Family Report, 'The murder of Anthony McKiernan, 19 January 1988', p. 27.
81 Ibid., p. 9. See also McKittrick et al., *Lost Lives*, p. 1108.
82 Operation Kenova Family Report, 'The murder of Anthony McKiernan, 19 January 1988', in which Scappaticci is referred to as 'the informant', p. 18.
83 Ibid.
84 McKittrick et al., *Lost Lives*, p. 1108.
85 Author interview, confidential source, July 2025.
86 Operation Kenova Family Report, 'The murder of Anthony McKiernan, 19 January 1988', p. 27.
87 Ibid., p. 31.
88 Ibid., p. 16.
89 Ibid., p. 27.

90 Ibid., p. 31.
91 Author interview, confidential source, November 2011.
92 Author interview, Sharon Murtagh, August 2016.
93 'Family of alleged IRA informer launch bid for police files on his death', *The Irish Times*, 25 April 2016: www.irishtimes.com/news/crime-and-law/family-of-alleged-ira-informer-launch-bid-for-police-files-on-his-death-1.2623992.
94 Operation Kenova Family Report, 'The murder of Anthony McKiernan, 19 January 1988', p. 25.
95 Author interview, confidential source, October 2025.
96 Jon Boutcher, press conference, Stormont Hotel, Belfast, 9 December 2025.
97 'Seamus Morgan: IRA shot Co Tyrone man dead after he "broke" under RUC interrogation', *The Irish News*, 12 March 2024: www.irishnews.com/news/northern-ireland/seamus-morgan-ira-shot-co-tyrone-man-dead-after-he-broke-in-ruc-station-TBXQPRZJXVEE7O75MNNWU4UM54/.
98 Author interview, confidential source, July 2025.
99 Author interview, confidential source, May 2025.
100 Author interview, confidential source, August 2025.
101 PPS, 'Operation Kenova – summary of further decisions not to prosecute', 6 February 2024, para. 55: www.ppsni.gov.uk/files/ppsni/2024-02/PPS%20Public%20Statement%206%20February%202024.pdf.
102 Author interview, confidential source, October 2025.
103 Operation Kenova Interim Report, March 2024, para. 3.8: www.kenova.co.uk/Kenova%20Report%202024%20Digital%20(002).pdf.
104 Operation Kenova Final Report, December 2025, Case 1 (Seamus Morgan) p. 63.
105 PPS, 'Operation Kenova – summary of further decisions not to prosecute', 6 February 2024, para. 54.
106 Author interview, confidential source, May 2025.
107 Ed Moloney, *A Secret History of the IRA* (Penguin, 2007), p. 582.
108 Author interviews, confidential sources, November 2016 and July 2025.
109 PPS, 'Operation Kenova – summary of further decisions not to prosecute', 6 February 2024, para. 53, p. 18.
110 'IRA Offer Informers Amnesty', *An Phoblacht*, 28 January 1982, copy held by author.
111 Moloney, *A Secret History of the IRA*, p. 582.
112 McKittrick et al., *Lost Lives*, p. 896.
113 Author interview, confidential source, August 2025.
114 'John Joe McGirl commemoration', *Irish Republican News*, 8 August 2024: https://republican-news.org/current/news/2024/08/john_joe_mcgirl.html.
115 'IRA Informers', BBC *Spotlight*, 26 March 1982.
116 Author interview, confidential source, December 2016.
117 Author interview, confidential source, December 2025.
118 Operation Kenova Final Report, December 2025, para. 12.20 (6).
119 Witness statement, Detective Constable Kenneth Hayes, 26 February 1991, statement held by author.
120 Author interview, confidential source, December 2025.
121 Author interview, confidential source, December 2016.
122 'Provo torture boss was ex-army!', *Belfast Telegraph*, 29 December 2002: www.belfasttelegraph.co.uk/news/provo-torture-boss-was-ex-army/28128409.html
123 As told by Billy McKee to Dr Anthony McIntyre, confirmed to author, September 2025.
124 Ed Moloney and Dr Anthony McIntyre, 'The Security Department: IRA Defensive Counterintelligence in a 30 year war against the British', April 2006, p. 30, copy held by author.
125 Author interview, confidential source, December 2016.
126 PPS, 'Operation Kenova – summary of further decisions not to prosecute', 6 February 2024, para. 57.
127 Ibid., para. 58.
128 Operation Kenova Final Report, December 2025, Case 2 (Jas Young), p. 64.
129 Ibid.

130 'Stakeknife – The Case of Jimmy Young', *The Pensive Quill*, 24 April 2023: www.thepensivequill.com/2023/04/stakeknife-case-of-jimmy-young.html.
131 Ibid.
132 Author interview, confidential source, May 2025.
133 Ibid., January 2025.
134 Author interview, confidential source, May 2025.
135 PPS, 'Operation Kenova – summary of further decisions not to prosecute', 6 February 2024, para. 56. See also Urban, *Big Boys' Rules*, pp. 119–121; 'Stakeknife – The Case of Jimmy Young', *The Pensive Quill*, 24 April 2023.
136 This individual is referred to only as 'Victim K' in the PPS statement of 6 February 2024 summarising some of its no prosecution decisions related to Scappaticci, see paras 58 and 60.
137 Author interview, confidential source, May 2025.
138 Ibid.
139 Author interview, confidential source, December 2016.
140 Operation Kenova Final Report, December 2025, Case 11 (Patrick Murray), p. 68.
141 Author access to confidential document, September 2024.
142 Ibid.
143 Gerry Bradley, *Insider* (O'Brien Press, 2009), pp. 178–9.
144 Author access to confidential document, September 2024.
145 Bradley, *Insider*, pp. 178–9.
146 Author access to confidential document, September 2024.
147 Bradley, *Insider*, pp. 178–9.
148 Author access to confidential document, September 2024.
149 Bradley, *Insider*, pp. 178–9.
150 Operation Kenova Final Report, December 2025, Case 11 (Patrick Murray), p. 69.
151 Author access to confidential document, September 2024.
152 Ibid.
153 Operation Kenova Final Report, December 2025, Case 11 (Patrick Murray), p. 69.
154 Operation Kenova Interim Report, paras 67.3 and 72.5.
155 Author interview, Gerard Hodgins, April 2016.

CHAPTER 8

1 David McKittrick, Seamus Kelters, Brian Feeney and Chris Thornton, *Lost Lives: The Stories of the Men, Women and Children who Died as a Result of the Northern Ireland Troubles* (Mainstream Publishing, 1999), p. 1148.
2 '"They Killed the Ice Cream Man": an extraordinary story of the Troubles', *Belfast News-Letter*, 10 October 2016: www.newsletter.co.uk/news/politics/they-killed-the-ice-cream-man-an-extraordinary-story-of-the-troubles-1192108.
3 Operation Kenova Final Report, December 2025, para. 9.45: www.psni.police.uk/sites/default/files/2025-12/Operation%20Kenova%20Final%20Report%202025.pdf.
4 Archive interview, Patrick Fenton, 'The (Estate) Agent', *Stakeknife*, Episode 4, BBC Sounds, 6 December 2024: www.bbc.co.uk/programmes/p0k8ymkb.
5 Author interview, Michelle Fenton, October 2016.
6 Author interview, confidential source, August 2025.
7 Belfast Brigade, IRA statement on the execution of Joe Fenton, 28 February 1989, transcript held by author; see also Ed Moloney, *A Secret History of the IRA* (Penguin, 2002), pp. 28–9.
8 Author interview, confidential source, May 2025.
9 RUC Source Report 'SB 50', 6 June 1988: https://cryptome.wikileaks.org/scap-file.htm.
10 Author interview, confidential source, December 2025.
11 McKittrick et al., *Lost Lives*, p. 1071.

12 Ibid., p. 1072.
13 Operation Kenova Final Report, December 2025, Case 7 (Charles McIlmurray), pp. 66, 67.
14 Ibid.
15 Author interview, confidential source, May 2025.
16 RUC Source Report, 'SB 50', 6 June 1988.
17 Author interview, confidential source, August 2025.
18 Ibid.
19 Author interview, confidential source, October 2016.
20 Author interview, confidential source, November 2024.
21 PPS statement 'Operation Kenova – Summary of decisions not to prosecute', 29 February 2024, para. 34: www.ppsni.gov.uk/files/ppsni/2024-02/Operation%20Kenova%20Public%20Statement%2029%20February%202024.pdf.
22 Ed Moloney, *Voices from the Grave* (Faber and Faber, 2010), p. 283 and *A Secret History of the IRA*, p. 31.
23 Moloney, *Voices from the Grave*, p. 283.
24 Martin Dillon, *The Dirty War* (Hutchinson, 1990), p. 325.
25 Author interview, Anthony McIntyre, July 2025.
26 Author interview, confidential source, November 2015.
27 Author interview, confidential source, November 2024.
28 PPS statement, 'Operation Kenova – Summary of decisions not to prosecute', 29 February 2024, para. 35.
29 Assessment of confidential source who has seen the surviving intelligence, June 2025.
30 Moloney, *Voices from the Grave*, p. 283.
31 Dillon, *The Dirty War*, p. 325.
32 Operation Kenova Interim Report, para. 67.3: 'Some Kenova victims who survived PIRA mistreatment have named those responsible for violence against them and I have established that some of them were agents when they committed acts of torture, including shootings. There is no information about these agents' criminal activities in their contact records with their handlers and it has not always been possible to tell whether they told their handlers about their criminal acts.': www.kenova.co.uk/Kenova%20Report%202024%20Digital%20(002).pdf.
33 Author interview, confidential source, June 2016.
34 PPS statement 'Operation Kenova – Summary of decisions not to prosecute', 29 February 2024, para. 40.
35 Author interview, confidential source, May 2025.
36 Ibid.
37 Michelle Fenton, witness statement to RUC, 27 February 1989, copy held by author.
38 Detective Constable George Fletcher, witness statement re interview with James Martin, 19 September 1990, copy held by author.
39 PPS statement, 'Operation Kenova – Summary of decisions not to prosecute', 29 February 2024, para. 42.
40 PPS statement, 'Operation Kenova – Summary of decisions not to prosecute', 29 February 2024, para. 36.
41 Ibid.
42 Michelle Fenton, witness statement to RUC, 27 February 1989.
43 Detective Constable George Fletcher, witness statement re interview with James Martin, 19 September 1990.
44 James Martin, written statement, 11 January 1990, copy held by author.
45 Detective Constable Gary Kirkpatrick, witness statement re interview with Veronica Ryan, 4 February 1990, copy held by author.
46 Detective Constable George Fletcher, witness statement re interview with James Martin, 19 September 1990.

47 Patrick Fenton, statement to RUC on the content of the tape of his son's confession, 13 March 1990, copy held by author.
48 Detective Constable Gary Kirkpatrick, witness statement re interview with Veronica Ryan, 4 February 1990.
49 Ali Watkins, *The Next One Is For You: A True Story of Guns, Country, and the IRA's Secret American Army* (Icon books, 2025), p. 362.
50 Detective Constable George Fletcher, witness statement re interview with James Martin, 19 September 1990.
51 James Martin, written statement to the RUC, 11 January 1990.
52 Detective Constable George Fletcher, witness statement re interview with James Martin, 19 September 1990.
53 Report of Professor Thomas Marshall, state pathologist, 27 February 1989, copy held by author.
54 Author interview, confidential source, January 2025.
55 Report of Professor Thomas Marshall, state pathologist, 27 February 1989.
56 Detective Constable George Fletcher, witness statement re interview with James Martin, 19 September 1990.
57 Sandy Lynch statement to RUC, 9 September 1990, copy held by author.
58 PPS statement, 'Operation Kenova – Summary of decisions not to prosecute', 29 February 2024, para. 41.
59 James Martin, written statement to RUC, 11 January 1990.
60 Author interview, confidential source, June 2025.
61 Operation Kenova Final Report, Case 4 (Joe Fenton), p. 65.
62 Author interview, confidential sources, November 2024 and December 2025.
63 Moloney, *Voices from the Grave*, pp. 283–4.
64 Danny Morrison 'Terence "Cleeky" Clarke – Death of a hero', June 2000: www.dannymorrison.com/wp-content/dannymorrisonarchive/115.htm#.
65 'Adams' "minder" dies', *Belfast Telegraph*, 14 June 2000: www.belfasttelegraph.co.uk/news/adams-minder-dies/28263302.html.
66 'Our Unique Friend. A tribute from Gerry Adams', *An Phoblacht*, 23 June 2000: www.anphoblacht.com/contents/6388.
67 Moloney, *Voices from the Grave*, p. 285.
68 Author interview, confidential source, May 2025.
69 Dillon, *The Dirty War*, interview by 'senior IRA member', p. 324. Brendan Hughes was that 'senior IRA member' as confirmed by his friend Dr Anthony McIntyre to author, July 2025.
70 Author interview, confidential source, May 2016.
71 Author interview, confidential source, August 2025.
72 Mark Urban, *Big Boys' Rules* (Faber and Faber, 1992), p. 122.
73 Operation Kenova Final Report, December 2025, para. 3.4.
74 Alasdair Palmer, 'The ECHR compromises British agents', *The Spectator*, 16 March 2024: https://spectator.com/article/the-echr-is-compromising-british-agents/.
75 Author interview, Ray White, September 2016.
76 De Silva Review, para. 4.48: https://assets.publishing.service.gov.uk/media/5a7c2313e5274a25a9140ac8/0802.pdf.
77 Margaret Thatcher Speech to Conservative Party Conference, 'Margaret Thatcher Foundation', October 1988: www.margaretthatcher.org/document/107352.
78 Operation Kenova Interim Report, March 2024, para. 71.8.
79 Operation Kenova Final Report, December 2025, para. 3.4.
80 Author interview, confidential source, May 2025.
81 'Met spy admits relationship was "open secret"', *BBC News*, 18 December 2025: www.bbc.co.uk/news/articles/cpvdxv3vv9yo.
82 Handwritten note, Solicitor General, 11 August 1992, as cited in De Silva Review, para. 4.56.

83 Desmond Boal QC, in his plea for sentence mitigation to Lord Justice Kell in the *Crown v Brian Nelson*, Crumlin Road court, February 1992, transcript held by author.

CHAPTER 9

1 FRU CF, 30 August 1989.
2 Ibid.
3 Jenny Maginn, interview 'A Licence to murder', Part 1, *Panorama*, BBC, transcript, June 2002: http://news.bbc.co.uk/hi/english/static/audio_video/programmes/panorama/transcripts/transcript_19_06_02.txt.
4 Brian Nelson journal, p. 166.
5 Rory McShane, Maginn family lawyer, interviewed by *Panorama*, BBC, February 1990: www.youtube.com/watch?v=lu9_XrQWs9Y.
6 FRU CF, 4 January 1989.
7 'MoD Problem Areas' document, De Silva Review, para. 11.75: https://assets.publishing.service.gov.uk/media/5a7c2313e5274a25a9140ac8/0802.pdf.
8 'Security Service intelligence report', De Silva Review, para. 11.72.
9 FRU CF, 30 August 1989.
10 Author interview, confidential source, April 1992.
11 Report of Stevens 1 Inquiry, May 1990, para. 1, copy held by author.
12 Bobby Philpott interview, *Loyalists*, Part 3, BBC Two, 7 March 1999: www.youtube.com/watch?v=PnZFB59Lpa4.
13 Report of Stevens 1 Inquiry, May 1990, para. 41, copy held by author.
14 John Stevens, *Not for the Faint-hearted: My Life Fighting Crime* (Phoenix, 2005), p. 176.
15 De Silva Review, para. 11.23.
16 Ibid., para. 11.43.
17 FRU CF, 30 August 1989.
18 FRU CF, 22 September 1989.
19 Martin Callan witness statement to Stevens I inquiry, 5 December 1990, as seen by author.
20 Stevens, *Not for the Faint-hearted*, p. 177.
21 Sara Bynum interview, 'A Licence to Murder', Part I, *Panorama*, BBC, transcript, June 2002: http://news.bbc.co.uk/hi/english/static/audio_video/programmes/panorama/transcripts/transcript_19_06_02.txt.
22 De Silva Review, para. 3.18.
23 Ibid., para. 24.43.
24 Ibid., para. 24.27. See also, General Waters, submission to de Silva, para. 24.30.
25 Colonel Gordon Kerr written statement to Stevens 1 Inquiry, 9 October 1990.
26 De Silva Review, para. 24.28.
27 Ibid., para. 24.33.
28 Ibid., para. 24.31.
29 De Silva Review, DHSB briefing paper to Sir John Stevens, 27 September 1989, Vol. II, pp. 318–22.
30 De Silva Review, OC East Det FRU, statement to Stevens 2 Inquiry, 9 December 1993, para. 24.55.
31 De Silva Review, para. 24.49.
32 De Silva Review, Brian Fitzsimons, statement to Stevens 2 Inquiry, 25 November 1993, para. 24.62.
33 De Silva Review, RUC SB, Daily Intelligence Book, 22 September 1989, para. 24.65.
34 Author interview, ACC Brian Fitzsimons, May 1992.
35 Colonel Gordon Kerr, written statement to Stevens 1 Inquiry, 9 October 1990.
36 De Silva Review, Brian Fitzsimons, statement to Stevens 1 Inquiry, 17 October 1990, para. 24.75.
37 De Silva Review, Gordon Kerr submission, para. 24.70.
38 De Silva Review, para. 24.46.

39 De Silva Review, MI5 HAG (Head of Assessments Group) letter to DHSB, 11 October 1989, para. 24.78.
40 De Silva Review, para. 24.79.
41 FRU CF, 22 September 1989.
42 FRU CF, 25 September 1989.
43 De Silva Review, Figure 10, 'Origin of security force leaks 1987–1989', para. 11.20.
44 De Silva Review, HAG to DCI, 3 October 1989, Vol. II, p. 328, para. 5.
45 De Silva Review, para. 8.23.
46 Author interview, confidential source, April 2002.
47 Author interview, confidential source, July 2001.
48 Author interview, George Caskey, November 2001.
49 Author interview, Vincent McFadden, April 2003.
50 Stevens, *Not for the Faint-hearted*, p. 176.
51 Author interview, Vincent McFadden, May 2002.
52 John Lyttle, 'In the name of my father', *The Independent*, 30 March 1996: www.independent.co.uk/arts-entertainment/in-the-name-of-my-father-1344885.html.
53 FRU CF, 22 September 1989.
54 FRU CF, 12 October 1989.
55 FRU CF, 2 November 1989.
56 FRU CF, 8 November 1989.
57 Woodvale Working Men's Club; 195 Crimea Street; 135 Cambrai Street; Glencairn Community Centre – as cited in Stevens 1 Interim Report to the DPP(NI), 27 September 1990.
58 Stevens, *Not for the Faint-hearted*, p. 180.
59 FRU CF, 22 September 1989.
60 David McKittrick, Seamus Kelters, Brian Feeney and Chris Thornton, *Lost Lives: The Stories of the Men, Women and Children who Died as a Result of the Northern Ireland Troubles* (Mainstream Publishing, 1999), p. 1176.
61 Brian Nelson journal, p. 14.
62 Author's note of visit to Nelson's house, 5 December 1989.
63 FRU CF, 30 November 1989.
64 FRU CF, 1 December 1989.
65 Ibid.
66 FRU CF, 6 December 1989.
67 FRU CF, 19 December 1989.
68 FRU CF, 6 December 1989.
69 FRU CF, 11 December 1989.
70 Stevens, *Not for the faint-hearted*, pp. 183–4.
71 De Silva Review, para. 11.78 (L/45 is the cypher for Bobby Philpott).

CHAPTER 10

1 Prisoner's Aid Committee, *Irish Political Prisoners in English Jails*, December 1980, p. 11: https://share.google/3eMRqWHvfxoRfwd1i
2 'EYE ON THE PAST – June 1983: High turnout in North and West Belfast for general election', *Belfast Media*, 7 June 2024: https://belfastmedia.com/eye-on-the-past-june-1983-high-turnout-in-north-and-west-belfast-for-general-election.
3 Detective Constable Angela Coleman, witness statement, 21 September 1990, copy held by author.
4 Ibid.
5 James Martin, written statement, 11 January 1990, copy held by author.
6 Alexander Lynch criminal record, RUC, 8 January 1990, in trial bundle, *R v Morrison & Others*, Belfast Crown Court, November 1990, copy held by author.

7 Transcript of interview with friend of Alexander Lynch, undated.
8 'Biography of S Lynch' by a friend signed only as 'J' from North Belfast.
9 Recollections of a friend of Lynch who was in Magilligan jail with him from 1983–86.
10 Ibid.
11 Alexander Lynch, deposition, 29 October 1990, p. 3, copy held by author.
12 Author interview, confidential source, January 2025.
13 Martin Ingram and Greg Harkin, *Stakeknife: Britain's Secret Agents in Ireland* (O'Brien Press, Dublin, 2004) p. 139.
14 Witness statement, Alexander Lynch, 9 September 1990, p. 2, copy held by author.
15 Ibid.
16 Author interview, confidential source July 2025.
17 Witness statement, Alexander Lynch, 9 September 1990, pp. 3–4.
18 Alexander Lynch, witness statement, 9 September 1990, p. 4.
19 'It is likely that the deplorable treatment to which the Hooded Men were subjected at the hands of the security forces would be characterised today, applying the standards of 2021, as torture.' UKSC/2020/0100, judgment, 15 December 2021, para. 186: https://supremecourt.uk/uploads/uksc_2020_0019_judgment_4c858a008e.pdf.
20 Transcript of Scappaticci covert interview with *The Cook Report*, ITV, 26 August 1993, as broadcast by UTV's *Insight* programme on 15 March 2004: https://cryptome.wikileaks.org/scap-clive.htm.
21 Alexander Lynch, witness statement, 9 September 1990, p. 6.
22 Operation Kenova Interim Report, March 2024, para. 67.3: www.psni.police.uk/sites/default/files/2024-03/Operation%20Kenova%20Interim%20Report%202024.pdf.
23 'Man "shocked" at agent claims', *BBC News*, 3 August 2003: http://news.bbc.co.uk/1/hi/northern_ireland/3120901.stm.
24 Author interview, confidential source, April 2023.
25 'Sinn Fein's Seán Mag Uidhir – five decades of republican activism ends in resignation', *Irish News*, 30 September 2024: www.irishnews.com/news/politics/sinn-feins-sean-mag-uidhir-five-decades-of-republican-activism-ends-in-resignation-XD7BOUGR25A2JFSGUICIDWBKLQ/
26 Detective Constable, Angela Coleman, witness statement, 21 September 1990.
27 'Revealed: five British spies inside IRA', *The Guardian*, 18 May 2003: www.theguardian.com/politics/2003/may/18/uk.northernireland1.
28 Eamon Collins, *Killing Rage* (Granta, 1998), pp. 233–43.
29 Author interview, confidential source, December 2016.
30 Alexander Lynch deposition, 29 October 1990, p. 5.
31 Ibid., p. 6.
32 Transcript of Scappaticci covert interview with *The Cook Report*, ITV, 26 August 1993, as broadcast by UTV *Insight* programme on 15 March 2004: https://cryptome.wikileaks.org/scap-clive.htm.
33 Alexander Lynch deposition, 29 October 1990, p. 7.
34 Ibid., p. 6.
35 Ibid.
36 IRA, *Green Book* (Books I and II): https://cain.ulster.ac.uk/othelem/organ/ira/ira_green_book.htm.
37 Alexander Lynch, witness statement, 9 September 1990, p. 11.
38 Ibid.
39 Ibid., p. 13.
40 Transcript of Scappaticci covert interview with *The Cook Report*, ITV, 26 August 1993: https://thebrokenelbow.com/2019/01/11/remembering-freddie-scappaticci/.
41 Transcript of Scappaticci covert interview with *The Cook Report*, ITV, 26 August 1993, as broadcast by UTV's *Insight* programme on 15 March 2004: https://cryptome.wikileaks.org/scap-clive.htm.

42 Alexander Lynch, witness statement, 9 September 1990, p. 14.
43 Ibid.
44 Alexander Lynch, deposition, 29 October 1990, p. 12.
45 Alexander Lynch, witness statement, 9 September 1990, p. 15.
46 Ibid.
47 Alexander Lynch, witness statement, 9 September 1990, p. 16.
48 Alexander Lynch, deposition, 29 October 1990, p. 15.
49 'Dirty fighting', *The Guardian*, 13 January 2009: www.theguardian.com/uk/2009/jan/13/northernireland-northernireland.
50 Alexander Lynch, witness statement, 9 September 1990, p. 16.
51 Police Constable Ivan McKelvey, witness statement, 9 January 1990, copy held by author.
52 'Dirty fighting', *The Guardian*, 13 January 2009.
53 Privates Simon Flower and Christopher Cairns, witness statements, 8 January and 7 January 1990 respectively, copies held by author.
54 Private Simon Flower, witness statement, 10 January.
55 Constable Keith Nugent, witness statement, 17 January 1990, copy held by author.
56 Sergeant Edwin Potter, witness statement, 11 January 1990, copy held by author.
57 Sergeant Adam McKinley, witness statement, 11 January 1990, copy held by author.
58 Alexander Lynch, salvaged tape N '… can't tell you how much I hope my family, my wife can be shown the sympathy as I don't deserve that I don't deserve. Although if there is a way to let me live with this guilt, then I can tell you that it is far more punishment …', copy held by author.
59 Author interview, confidential source, June 2025.
60 Chief Inspector William Brown, witness statement, 7 January 1990, copy held by author.
61 Author interview, confidential sources, April 2016 and December 2025.
62 Alexander Lynch, deposition, 29 October 1990, p. 12.
63 Ed Moloney, *Voices from the Grave* (Faber and Faber, 2010), pp. 280, 281.
64 Author interview with victim, June 2016.
65 Danny Morrison, 'The story of Stakeknife is full of holes', *The Guardian*, 16 May 2003: www.theguardian.com/politics/2003/may/16/northernireland.northernireland.
66 Danny Morrison evidence, as cited in Hutton LCJ, judgment, Belfast Crown Court, *The Queen v Daniel Morrison and Others*, 8 May 1991.
67 Hutton LCJ, judgment, Belfast Crown Court, *The Queen v Daniel Morrison and Others*, 8 May 1991.
68 Danny Morrison blog, 'No 10's Murderer – Scap', 30 January 2016: www.dannymorrison.com/the-times-of-no-10s-main-murderer/.
69 Author interview, confidential source, May 2016.
70 Tim McGregor interview, 'The Spy in the IRA', *Panorama*, BBC, April 2017.
71 Author interview, confidential source, October 2025.
72 Author interview, confidential source, December 2025.
73 'We lost agents plural because the army had an informant in the IRA security unit': author interview with Special Branch officer, March 1991.
74 Author interview, confidential source, September 2024.
75 Detective Constable Kenneth Hayes, witness statement, 26 February 1991, statement held by author.
76 Danny Morrison, *Then the Walls Came Down: A Prison Journal* (Mercier Press, 1999), p. 15.

CHAPTER 11

1 Stevens 1 Interim Report to the DPP(NI), 27 September 1990.
2 John Stevens, *Not for the Faint-hearted: My Life Fighting Crime* (Phoenix, 2005), p. 8.
3 De Silva Review, para. 24.82: https://assets.publishing.service.gov.uk/media/5a7c2313e5274a25a9140ac8/0802.pdf.
4 FRU CF, 10 January 1990, copies of all CFs in this chapter seen by author.

5 Stevens 1 Interim Report to the DPP(NI), 27 September 1990, p.11, citing Brian Nelson statement to Stevens 1 Inquiry.
6 'Dirty War', *Panorama*, BBC, June 1992.
7 FRU CF, 10 January 1990.
8 Ibid.
9 Stevens, *Not for the Faint-hearted*, p. 1.
10 Author interview, Sarah Bynum, June 2002.
11 Detective Superintendent Alan Simpson, fire report, January 1990, para. 20.
12 Author interview, Sarah Bynum, June 2002.
13 The reserve constable's witness statement, 11 January 1990.
14 Detective Constable Stephen Lodge, witness statement, 11 January 1990, copy held by author.
15 Detective Constable Sarah Bynum, witness statement, 11 January 1990, copy held by author.
16 Stevens, *Not for the Faint-hearted*, p. 4.
17 Ibid.
18 Stevens 1 Interim Report to DPP(NI), 27 September 1990.
19 Stevens, *Not for the Faint-hearted*, p. 179.
20 Detective Superintendent Alan Simpson, fire report, January 1990, para. 20.
21 Letter from K.J. Arnold of the NI Forensic Science Laboratory to Detective Superintendent Simpson, 18 January 1990, copy held by author.
22 Detective Superintendent Alan Simpson, fire report, para. 1.
23 'Stevens' office fire "not arson"', *The Irish Press*, 9 February 1990.
24 Author interview, Sarah Bynum, June 2002.
25 Stevens, *Not for the Faint-hearted*, p. 11.
26 Summary report of Stevens 1 Inquiry, May 1990, para. 15, copy held by author.
27 Author interview George Caskey, 15 November 2001.
28 Stevens, *Not for the Faint-hearted*, p. 8.
29 'What will the Stevens report bring?', *BBC News*, April 2003: http://news.bbc.co.uk/1/hi/programmes/panorama/2953705.stm.
30 Author interview, Laurie Sherwood, June 2002.
31 Author interview, confidential sources, 2025.
32 Author interview, Alan Simpson, April 2002.
33 Ibid.
34 'Alan Simpson: An RUC detective colleague told me the Finucane murder would follow me to my grave ... I don't believe we've heard the last of it yet', *Belfast Telegraph*, 8 October 2019: www.belfasttelegraph.co.uk/opinion/news-analysis/alan-simpson-an-ruc-detective-colleague-told-me-the-finucane-murder-would-follow-me-to-my-grave-i-dont-believe-weve-heard-the-last-of-it-yet/38574748.html.
35 Author interview, Alan Simpson, June 2002.
36 Detective Superintendent Alan Simpson, fire report, January 1990, para. 35.
37 Author interview, Alan Simpson, April 2002.
38 Detective Sergeant Nicholas Benwell, witness statement, 12 January 1990, held by author.
39 Police Constable Patricia Tosney, witness statement, 11 January 1990, held by author.
40 Witness statements of Detective Constable Roberto Rizzo, 11 January 1990 and Detective Sergeant Thomas Bradley, Detective Superintendent Arthur Mandry, 12 January 1990 – copies held by author.
41 Geoff Seed interview, Arthur Mandry, March 1994.
42 Police Constable Alan Jackson, witness statement, 11 January 1990.
43 Detective Superintendent Alan Simpson, fire report, January 1990, para. 38.
44 Ibid., para. 37.
45 'Stevens blaze "caused by cigarette"', *Belfast News-Letter*, 23 January 1990.
46 'Cigarette started leaks fire', *Daily Mirror*, 23 January 1990.

47 Detective Superintendent Alan Simpson, fire report, January 1990, para. 23.
48 Author interview, Vince McFadden, June 1991.
49 Letter from K.J. Arnold of the NI Forensic Science Laboratory to Detective Superintendent Simpson, 18 January 1990.
50 Author interview, Alan Simpson, April 2002.
51 Author interview, Sarah Bynum, June 2002.
52 Author interview, Nicholas Benwell, November 2001.
53 Detective Superintendent Alan Simpson, fire report, para. 21.
54 Police Constable William Corry, witness statement, 11 January 1990.
55 Detective Superintendent Alan Simpson, fire report, paras 27 and 28.
56 Author interview, confidential source, November 2001.
57 Detective Superintendent Alan Simpson, fire report, paras 6 and 10.
58 Letter from N. Newell, Northern Ireland Forensic Laboratory, to Detective Superintendent Simpson, 13 February 1990.
59 Ibid.
60 Detective Superintendent Alan Simpson, fire report, para. 27.
61 Terence Hack, Principal of Safeguard Security Consultants, report for *Panorama*, BBC, January 2002, para. 3.2.
62 Ibid., para. 3.4.
63 Colin Roberts, senior fire engineer, Arup Fire, January 2002.
64 Letter from N. Newell, Northern Ireland Forensic Laboratory, to Detective Superintendent Simpson, 13 February 1990.
65 Terence Hack, Principal of Safeguard Security Consultants, report for *Panorama*, BBC, January 2002, para. 3.4.
66 Detective Superintendent Alan Simpson, fire report, para. 30.
67 Author interview, confidential source, March 1994.
68 Detective Superintendent Alan Simpson, fire report, para. 3.
69 Ibid. para. 32.
70 NAO: 'The Estate Strategy of the Police Service of Northern Ireland', December 2006: www.nao.org.uk/wp-content/uploads/2006/12/0607101.pdf.
71 Author interview Vincent McFadden, February 1994.
72 *Stevens Enquiry: Overview and Recommendations, 17 April 2003*: https://cain.ulster.ac.uk/issues/collusion/stevens3/stevens3summary.htm.
73 De Silva Review, para. 24.85.
74 FRU CF, 10 January1990.
75 Stevens 2 Inquiry: Casual conversation with Brian Nelson at HMP (not named) on 17 February 1993, as cited in De Silva Review, Vol. II, p. 60, para. 10.
76 'Dirty War', *Panorama*, BBC, June 1992.
77 Ibid.
78 Author interview, Brian Nelson, Crumlin Road Gaol, 18 April 1991.
79 Desmond Boal QC, plea for sentence mitigation before Lord Justice Kelly, *Crown v Brian Nelson*, Crumlin Road court, February 1992, transcript held by author.
80 Brian Kerr QC, submission on sentencing, Crumlin Road Courthouse, 22 January 1992.
81 Author interview, Lynn Evans, June 2002.
82 Written statement, Colonel Gordon Kerr, 9 October 1990.
83 Author interview, Lynn Evans, June 2002.
84 Author interview, Sir John Stevens and Laurie Sherwood, April 2001.
85 Author interview, Lynn Evans, June 2002.

CHAPTER 12

1 John Stevens, *Not for the Faint-hearted: My Life Fighting Crime* (Phoenix, 2005), p. 186.
2 Ibid., p. 192.
3 De Silva Review, December 2012, para. 24.68: https://assets.publishing.service.gov.uk/media/5a7c2313e5274a25a9140ac8/0802.pdf.
4 Ibid.
5 Ibid., paras 24.62–24.63.
6 Ibid., para. 24.59.
7 Ibid., paras 24.60–24.61.
8 Ibid., para. 24.56.
9 Ibid., para. 24.63.
10 Ibid., para. 24.62.
11 'To be economical with the actualité': meaning and origin', *World Histories*: https://wordhistories.net/2024/03/20/economical-with-actualite/.
12 Author interview, ACC Brian Fitzsimons, May 1992.
13 De Silva Review, December 2012, paras 24.70–24.71.
14 Ibid., para. 24.71.
15 Ibid., para. 24.73.
16 Ibid., para. 24.75.
17 Ibid., para. 24.79.
18 Ibid., para. 24.80.
19 Ibid., para. 24.88.
20 Author interview, ACC Brian Fitzsimons, May 1992.
21 De Silva Review, para. 11.92. See also para. 11.20, Fig. 10.
22 Ibid., para. 11.23.
23 Stevens 1 Report, para. 38, May 1990, as cited by Lord Stevens in his evidence to the Billy Wright Inquiry, 11 May 2009, accessed by Jane Winter of British Irish Rights Watch.
24 Stevens 1 Report, para. 41.
25 De Silva Review, para. 24.87.
26 Operation Kenova Interim Report, March 2024, para. 55.9: www.kenova.co.uk/Kenova%20Report%202024%20Digital%20(002).pdf.
27 House of Lords, 'Liversidge Appellant; and Sir John Anderson and other Respondents', *The Law Reports (Appeal Cases)* 1941, September 18, 19, 22; November 3: www.bailii.org/uk/cases/UKHL/1941/1.html.
28 Operation Kenova Interim Report, March 2024, paras 54.9 and 57.7.
29 Ibid., p. 7.
30 Author interview, Nicholas Benwell, *Panorama*, BBC, June 2002.
31 Author interview, Sarah Bynum, June 2002.
32 Author interview, confidential source, August 2001.
33 Author interview, confidential source, June 2002.
34 'Examination of Military Files Relating to Nelson', p. 1, Stevens Inquiry, 1990.
35 Stevens, *Not for the Faint-hearted*, p. 190.
36 De Silva Review, para. 8.185.
37 Ibid., paras 8.187–8.188.
38 Ibid., para. 8.189.
39 Ibid., para. 3.19.
40 Author interview, former senior MI5 officer in Northern Ireland, February 2015.
41 De Silva Review, para. 8.184.
42 Ibid., para. 24.95.
43 Stevens 1 reports submitted to the Northern Ireland DPP, 1990.

44 Author interview Brian Nelson, Crumlin Road Gaol, 12 April 1991.
45 Ibid., 23 May 1991.
46 Ibid., 5 July 1991.
47 Ibid., 18 April 1991.
48 De Silva Review, para. 24.97: 'A Shawcross exercise broadly refers to the established convention by which Government Ministers can raise public interest considerations with the Attorney General regarding a proposed prosecution.'
49 Martin Callan, statement to Stevens 1 Inquiry, 6 November 1990, as seen by author.
50 De Silva Review, para. 24.111.
51 Ibid., para. 7.264.
52 Ibid., para. 24.137.
53 Ibid., para. 24.131.
54 Ibid., para. 24.102.
55 Ibid., para. 11.43.
56 Ibid., paras 7.115, 11.91, 11.92, 24.70, 24.71.
57 Ibid., para. 24.107.
58 Ibid., paras 24.169, 24.165, 24.133, 24.175.
59 Ibid., para. 24.116.
60 Ibid., para. 24.118.
61 Ibid., para. 8.23.
62 Ibid., para. 24.121.
63 Ibid., para. 24.123.
64 Ibid., para. 24.170.
65 House of Lords, Liversidge Appellant; and Sir John Andreson and Another Respondents, 1941, September 18, 19, 22; November 3: www.bailii.org/uk/cases/UKHL/1941/1.html.
66 Letter from Sir Patrick Mayhew, Attorney General letter to Secretary of State for Defence, 25 April 1991. See De Silva Review, Vol. II, pp. 279–83.
67 Sir Patrick Mayhew, HC Deb., 25 January 1988, vol. 126, c21: https://api.parliament.uk/historic-hansard/commons/1988/jan/25/royal-ulster-constabulary-stalker.
68 Author interview, confidential source, July 2016.
69 Brian Kerr QC, submission on sentencing, Crumlin Road court, 22 January 1992, transcript held by author.
70 De Silva Review, para. 24.175.
71 Ibid., para. 24.102.
72 Ibid., para. 24.144.
73 Ibid., para. 24.129.
74 Author interview Sir Patrick Mayhew, February 2015.
75 Author interview, confidential source, September 2025.
76 De Silva Review, para. 24.180.
77 *R v Anderson* [1986] AC 27 [1985] Crim. L.R. 651.
78 Desmond Boal QC, plea in mitigation, Crumlin Road court, February 1992, transcript held by author.
79 Sir Brian Kerr QC, submission on sentencing, Crumlin Road court, 22 January 1992.
80 FRU CF, 11 May 1988. See also De Silva Review, para. 7.133.
81 Colonel Gordon Kerr, examination in chief, Crumlin Road court, 29 January 1992, transcript held by author.
82 Cory Collusion Inquiry Report, para. 1.288: https://cain.ulst.ac.uk/issues/collusion/cory/cory03finucane.pdf. Justice Cory said that Colonel Kerr's evidence was misleading and based on 'highly dubious numerical analysis that cannot be supported on any basis'.
83 De Silva Review, para. 8.60.
84 Ibid., para. 24.212.

85 Ibid., para. 7.248.
86 Author interview, Vincent McFadden, February 2002.
87 De Silva Review, para. 9.67.
88 Northern Ireland Gallantry Awards: OBE (Military) Lieutenant Colonel James Gordon Kerr, *The Times*, 14 May 1991; MBE (Military), Captain Geoffrey Peter Herbert Gillion, *The Times*, 14 May 1991; BEM (Military), Sergeant (now Staff Sergeant) Margaret Jones, *The Times*, 7 November 1990.
89 Barney Rowan, *Living with Ghosts: The Inside Story from a 'Troubles' Mind* (Merrion Press, 2022), p. 150.
90 John Creaney's comment to author after Nelson trial.
91 Cory Collusion Inquiry Report, para. 1.169.
92 Author interview, Ray White, December 2016.
93 De Silva Review, para. 8.161.
94 Ibid., para. 8.164.
95 Ibid., para. 8.163.
96 Interview by Barney Rowan with member of Brian Nelson family, as referenced in the documentary 'Collusion', RTÉ, 15 June 2015.
97 Cory Collusion Inquiry Report, paras 1.167 and 1.168.
98 Stevens, *Not for the Faint-hearted*, p. 197.

CHAPTER 13

1 Author interview, confidential source, January 2025.
2 Author interview, confidential source, December 2016.
3 'Dirty fighting', *The Guardian*, 13 January 2009: www.theguardian.com/uk/2009/jan/13/northern ireland-northernireland.
4 'Collusion and double standards', *The Irish Times*, 15 August 2003: www.irishtimes.com/opinion/collusion-and-double-standards-1.369739.
5 Danny Morrison blog, 'No 10's Murderer – Scap', 30 January 2016: www.dannymorrison.com/?p=3620.
6 'Ex-IRA man disputes claims Stakeknife was "stood down" in 1990', *The Irish News*, 4 February 2016: www.irishnews.com/news/2016/02/04/news/former-ira-disputes-claims-stakeknife-was-stood-down-in-1990-405354/.
7 Operation Kenova Interim Report, March 2024, para. 72.7: www.kenova.co.uk/Kenova%20Report%202024%20Digital%20(002).pdf.
8 'Wilson held power "over life and death of IRA volunteers if they transgressed"', *Irish Independent*, 15 March 2015: www.independent.ie/irish-news/wilson-held-power-over-life-and-death-of-ira-volunteers-if-they-transgressed/31067402.html.
9 Author interview, confidential source, November 2016.
10 'Two killers in IRA funeral mob jailed for 25 years' *The Herald*, 2 June 1989: www.heraldscotland.com/news/11917656.two-killers-in-ira-funeral-mob-jailed-for-25-years/.
11 Author interview, Anthony McIntyre, July 2025.
12 Author interview, confidential source, April 2016.
13 'Particulars of cases for trial at the Crown Court', *The Queen v Daniel Morrison and Others*, 29 October 1990, copies held by author.
14 Neutral Citation No. [2014] NICA 72, *Ryan (Veronica) and James Martin v Regina*: www.judiciaryni.uk/judicial-decisions/2014-nica-72.
15 Hutton LCJ, judgement, Belfast Crown Court, *The Queen v Daniel Morrison and Others*, 8 May 1991, held by author.
16 Ibid.; sentence hearing, 9 May 1991.
17 Author interview, confidential sources, October 2025 and December 2025.
18 Author interview, confidential source, February 2017.

19 Author interview, confidential source, December 2025.
20 Ibid.
21 Operation Kenova Final Report, para. 12.28, December 2025: www.psni.police.uk/sites/default/files/2025-12/Operation%20Kenova%20Final%20Report%202025.pdf.
22 Author interview, confidential source, December 2016.
23 Author interview, Phil James, June 2016.
24 Author interview, confidential source, November 2024.
25 Author interview, confidential source, June 2016.
26 Chris Moore, *Kincora Britain's Shame: Mountbatten, MI5, the Belfast Boys' Home Sex Abuse Scandal and the British Cover-Up* (Merrion Press, 2025), pp. 114–20.
27 Author interview, confidential source, November 2025.
28 Ibid.
29 'Death of Con McHugh', *An Phoblacht*, 3 July 2003: www.anphoblacht.com/contents/10210.
30 Author interview, confidential source, December 2016.
31 Ibid.
32 Author interview, Kevin Winters, July 2025.
33 Author interview, Tim McGregor, April 2017.
34 Author interview, confidential sources, January 2025 and December 2025.
35 Author interview, confidential source, December 2025.
36 Ibid.
37 Ibid.
38 Author interview, confidential sources, May and December 2025.
39 Author interview Tim McGregor, January 2026.
40 Authur interview, Tim McGregor, April 2017.
41 Author interview Tim McGregor, January 2026.
42 Tim McGregor RUC diary, *Detention Schedule R v Scappaticci*, 21 October 1992, content held by author.
43 Ibid.
44 Author interview, Tim McGregor, April 2017.
45 Author interview, confidential source, December 2025.
46 Ibid.
47 Author interview, confidential source, May 2025.
48 Author interview, confidential source, December 2025.
49 Author interview, Tim McGregor, January 2026.
50 Author interview, confidential source, May 2025.
51 Author interview, confidential sources, April 2016 and December 2025.
52 Author interview, Tim McGregor, January 2026.
53 Ibid.
54 Northern Ireland Gallantry Awards, MBE, (Military) Warrant Officer Moyles, *The Times*, 14 May 1991.
55 Author interview, confidential source, April 2016 and January 2026.
56 PPS, 'Operation Kenova – Summary of decisions not to prosecute', 6 December 2023, para. 11.5: www.ppsni.gov.uk/files/ppsni/2023-12/Public%20Statement%206%20December%2023%20_0.pdf.
57 Author interview, confidential source, October 2025.
58 Operation Kenova Interim Report, March 2024, para. 44.10.
59 Author interview, confidential source, October 2025.
60 'Former RUC officer who oversaw Kincora Inquiries passes away', *The Irish News*, 26 February 2022: www.irishnews.com/news/northernirelandnews/2022/02/26/news/former-ruc-officer-who-oversaw-kincora-inquiries-passes-away-2599165/.
61 PPS, 'Operation Kenova – summary of decisions not to prosecute', 6 December 2023, paras 11.1–11.18.
62 Author interview, confidential source, December 2016.

63 'The IRA told me that Scappaticci was redundant after 7th January 1990' – Danny Morrison, 'No 10's Murderer – Scap', 30 January 2016: www.dannymorrison.com/the-times-of-no-10s-main-murderer/.
64 Barney Rowan, *Living With Ghosts: The Inside Story From A 'Troubles' Mind* (Merrion Press, 2022) p. 203
65 'Scappaticci: The Wilsey Tape', *The Broken Elbow*, 7 April 2017: https://thebrokenelbow.com/2017/04/07/scappaticci-the-wilsey-tape/.
66 Author interview, confidential source, April 2016.
67 Operation Kenova Interim Report, March 2024, paras 63.4 and 63.7.
68 Operation Kenova Final Report, December 2025, para. 9.43.
69 Author interview, confidential source, December 2025.
70 Sir Iain Livingstone, press conference, Stormont Hotel, 9 December 2025.
71 'Scappaticci: The Wilsey Tape', *The Broken Elbow*, 7 April 2017.
72 Author interview, confidential information, December 2016.
73 Author interview, confidential source, July 2025.
74 Ibid.
75 Transcript of Scappaticci covert interview with *The Cook Report*, ITV, 28 August 1993: https://thebrokenelbow.com/2019/01/11/remembering-freddie-scappaticci/.
76 Operation Kenova Final Report, December 2025, para. 9.35.
77 Author interview, confidential source, December 2016.
78 *Confession*, ITV Network First television documentary series, 18 March 1995: www.youtube.com/watch?v=rsfM_kXUU5c.
79 Author interview, confidential source, December 2025.
80 Operation Kenova Final Report, December 2025, para. 9.58.
81 Ibid., para. 9.54.
82 Ibid., para. 9.55.
83 Ibid., para. 9.56.
84 Author interview, Tommy Braniff, July 2016.
85 Operation Kenova Final Report, December 2025, Case 6 (Anthony Braniff), p. 66.
86 Author interview, Tommy Braniff, July 2016.
87 Author interview, confidential source, December 2016.
88 'Anthony Braniff – IRA Statement', *An Phoblacht*, 25 September 2003: www.anphoblacht.com/contents/10570.
89 PPS, 'Operation Kenova – Summary of further decisions not to prosecute', 6 February 2024, paras 49–51: www.ppsni.gov.uk/files/ppsni/2024-02/PPS%20Public%20Statement%206%20February%202024.pdf.
90 'Anthony Braniff – IRA Statement', *An Phoblacht*, 25 September 2003.
91 Author interview, confidential source, December 2016.
92 Author interview, confidential source, June 2016.

CHAPTER 14

1 Brian Nelson statement under caution, interviewed by Detective Sergeant Benwell, 19 April 1993, as cited in De Silva Review, Vol. II, p. 63: https://assets.publishing.service.gov.uk/media/5a7c2313e5274a25a9140ac8/0802.pdf.
2 Brian Nelson journal, pp. 62–3.
3 Author interview with Brian Nelson whilst on remand in Crumlin Road Gaol, July 1991.
4 Brian Nelson journal pp. 84–6.
5 Ibid., p. 70.
6 Author interviews with Brian Nelson whilst on remand in Crumlin Road Gaol,18 April and 13 June 1991.

7 *Panorama*, BBC, transcript of recorded meeting with Kenneth Barrett, 3 September 2001, copy held by author.
8 Brian Nelson journal, p. 65b.
9 Brian Nelson journal, p. 65c.
10 Brian Nelson journal, p. 65d.
11 FRU CF, 8 October 1987.
12 Brian Nelson journal, p. 65d.
13 FRU CF, 2 November 1987.
14 De Silva Review, para. 21.91.
15 Ibid., para. 21.8.
16 Brian Kerr QC cross-examination of Colonel Gordon Kerr, *Regina v Brian Nelson*, before Lord Justice Kelly, Crumlin Road court, 29 January 1992, transcript held by author.
17 De Silva Review, para. 21.58.
18 Author's notes of interview with 'Tucker' Lyttle, December 1993.
19 Lord Stevens, WhatsApp to author, June 2025.
20 De Silva Review, para. 21.33.
21 Assistant Treasury Solicitor, P. Whitehurst, letter to author, 14 August 1992.
22 Assistant Treasury Solicitor, D. Brummell, letter to author, 29 March 1993.
23 Press release, Northumbria Police. See also European Court of Human Rights, Case of *Finucane v. The United Kingdom*, application 29179/95, judgment, Strasbourg, 1 July 2003, para. 26: https://hudoc.echr.coe.int/eng#{%22itemid%22:[%22001-61185%22]}.
24 Detective Sergeant Nicholas Benwell, statement of interview with Soldier G, 18 August 1993, as seen by author
25 Brian Nelson statement to Detective Sergeant Benwell, 28 June 1993, De Silva Review, Vol. II, p. 70.
26 UKSC/2017/0058: In the matter of an application by Geraldine Finucane for Judicial Review (Northern Ireland), Judgment, 27 February 2019, para. 12: https://supremecourt.uk/uploads/uksc_2017_0058_judgment_d29fee2774.pdf.
27 De Silva Review, para. 1.80.
28 Author interview, Nicholas Benwell, November 2001.
29 Detective Sergeant Nicholas Benwell, statement of interview notes of interview with Soldier G, 18 August 1993, as seen by author.
30 Statement of Soldier C, 22 July 1993, as seen by author.
31 Statement of Soldier Q, 17 August 1993, as seen by author.
32 Statement of Soldier D, 17 August 1993, as seen by author
33 Statement of Soldier C, 22 July 1993, as seen by author
34 As referenced as soldier 'A/02' in De Silva Review, para. 7.70.
35 De Silva Review, paras 7.18–7.39.
36 FRU CF, 26 October 1987.
37 Brian Nelson, statement to Stevens 1 Inquiry, 15 January 1990, as cited in De Silva Review, Vol. II, p. 45.
38 Brian Nelson statement, HMP Bristol, 17 February 1993, De Silva Review, Vol. II, pp. 55–8.
39 'Note of casual conversation with Brian Nelson, as cited in De Silva Review, Vol. II, pp. 58–60.
40 De Silva Review, para. 21.32.
41 Brian Nelson statement, HMP Bristol, 19 April 1993, De Silva Review, Vol. II, p. 63.
42 Ibid., pp. 63–6.
43 De Silva Review, para. 21.42.
44 Author interview with Tommy Lyttle, June 1994.
45 De Silva Review, para. 21.58.
46 Brian Nelson statement to Stevens 2, HM Prison, 19 April 1993, cited in De Silva Review, Vol. II, p. 66.
47 Brian Nelson, statement to Stevens 1 Inquiry, January 1990, as cited in De Silva Review, Vol. II, p. 43.
48 De Silva Review, para. 21.11. See also Brian Nelson journal, pp. 167–8.

49 FRU CFs 2 and 9 March 1989. See also De Silva Review, para. 21.103.
50 Brian Nelson journal, p. 64.
51 Author interview, ACC Brian Fitzsimons, May 1992.
52 'Notes of Casual Conversation with Brian Nelson', signed by Detective Sergeant Benwell and another (unnamed) detective sergeant, 28 June 1993, as cited in De Silva Review, Vol. II, p. 75.
53 Author interview, Nicholas Benwell, June 2002.
54 FRU CF, 11 May 1989.
55 Inquest statement of Detective Chief Inspector Kieran Lagan, 11 September 1989: 'Terence McDaid was working as a bricklayer in various building sites in the Belfast area prior to his death. He had no paramilitary connections, and it is not known why he was singled out for this attack', note held by author.
56 De Silva Review, para. 21.18.
57 Ibid., paras 21.25 and 21.34.
58 David McKittrick, Seamus Kelters, Brian Feeney and Chris Thorton, *Lost Lives: The Stories of the Men, Women and Children who Died as a Result of the Northern Ireland Troubles* (Mainstream Publishing, 1999), pp. 1112–16.
59 De Silva Review, para. 15.01.
60 Ibid., para. 15.20.
61 Ibid., para. 15.14.
62 Ibid., paras 15.49–15.51.
63 John Ware, 'Finucane: Who knew of this deniable murder?' *The Sunday Telegraph*, 15 December 2012: www.telegraph.co.uk/news/uknews/northernireland/9747132/Finucane-Who-knew-of-this-deniable-murder.html.
64 De Silva Review, para. 15.50.
65 Ibid., paras 16.60–16.61.
66 De Silva Review, para. 16.62. See also Cory Collusion Inquiry Report, para. 1.176: https://cain.ulst.ac.uk/issues/collusion/cory/cory03finucane.pdf.
67 De Silva Review, paras 16.63–16.66.
68 Ibid., para. 18.29.
69 John Ware, 'Plot to kill Belfast lawyers revealed', *The Guardian*, 2 August 2002: www.theguardian.com/uk/2002/aug/02/northernireland.northernireland.
70 De Silva Review, para. 14.49.
71 Ibid., para. 23.13.
72 The Rosemary Nelson Inquiry Report, 23 May 2011, witness statement of Oliver Kelly, p. 196, footnote: https://cain.ulster.ac.uk/issues/collusion/docs/nelson_230511.pdf.
73 De Silva Review, para. 23.11, where Kincaid, McKee and Spence are referred to by their respective acronyms L/03, L/28 and L/20.
74 Cory Collusion Inquiry Report, para. 1.104. Note that Cory wrongly attributes these source reports to the FRU. De Silva makes clear they were Special Branch SB50s, see para. 23.10.
75 De Silva Review, para. 23.9.
76 Ibid., para. 15.51.
77 Ibid., para. 23.15; see also Vol. II, p. 28.
78 Cory Collusion Inquiry Report, 1 April 2004, para. 1.105.
79 *Deadly Intelligence*, report by British Irish Rights Watch, February 1999, para. 18.1, copy held by author.
80 Author interview with Sir John Stevens, February 2002.
81 Operation Kenova Interim Report, March 2024, Recommendation 7, p. 40: www.kenova.co.uk/Kenova%20Report%202024%20Digital%20(002).pdf.
82 De Silva Review, paras 8.137 and 8.144.
83 Ibid., paras 8.137–8.152.
84 Ibid., para. 8.155.
85 Directive for the FRU (Northern Ireland), 26 July 1986, as cited in De Silva Review, paras 4.20 and 4.23.

86 De Silva Review, para. 4.21.
87 Ibid., para. 8.167.
88 Ibid., para. 8.163.
89 Ibid., para. 8.164.
90 Ibid., para. 8.170.
91 Ibid., paras 8.174–8.175.
92 Ibid., paras 8.183–8.191.
93 Ibid., para. 8.178.
94 Ibid., paras 8.221–8.222.
95 John Stevens interview with MI5's Assistant Secretary Political, October 1990, as seen by author.
96 De Silva Review, para. 8.223.
97 Ibid., para. 89.
98 John Ware and Geoff Seed, with Alasdair Palmer, 'Army Set Up Ulster Murders', *The Sunday Telegraph*, 22 March 1998.
99 'Deadly Intelligence – State Involvement in Loyalist Murder in Northern Ireland – Summary', February 1999: https://cain.ulster.ac.uk/issues/violence/birw0299.htm.
100 Letter to the Secretary of State for Northern Ireland Mo Mowlam, 'An Assessment of the report by British Irish Rights Watch' p. 2, 13 April 1999, copy held by author.
101 De Silva Review, para. 1.86.
102 Madden & Finucane, 'Justice Delayed – State Collusion in the murder of Patrick Finucane and Others', para. 4.4: https://madden-finucane.com/2000/02/01/justice-delayed-state-collusion-in-the-murder-of-patrick-finucane-and-others/.
103 Author interview, confidential source, Dublin, April 1999.
104 Meeting between Eamonn McKee of the Anglo-Irish Secretariat, Geraldine Finucane, Seamus Finucane, Eamon McMenamin, Wellington Park Hotel, 21 April 1999.
105 Letter from John Stevens to British Irish Rights Watch, 17 January 1995, copy held by author.
106 Parliamentary Question, Douglas Henderson, Minister of State for the Armed Forces, replying to Kevin McNamara MP, 16 April 1999: https://hansard.parliament.uk/commons/1999-04-16/debates/f6482a93-6a0d-48a4-9d7d-3fdbc2f9dbcf/MrNicholasDavies.
107 Letter from John Stevens to Peter Madden, 23 April 1999, as cited in 'Beyond Collusion: The UK Security Forces and the Murder of Patrick Finucane', Lawyers Committee for Human Rights, 2002, Section IV 'The Stevens Investigations', Part D: https://madden-finucane.com/2002/02/12/beyond-collusion-the-uk-security-forces-and-the-murder-of-patrick-finucane/.
108 Affidavit of Sir Kevin Tebbit, permanent under-secretary for the Ministry of Defence, 20 May 1999, copy held by author.
109 De Silva Review, para. 23.100.
110 Ibid., 23.132.
111 Johnston Brown, *Into the Dark: 30 Years in the RUC* (Gill & Macmillan, 2005), p. 247.
112 De Silva Review, para. 23.132.
113 'Licence to murder', Part 1, *Panorama*, BBC, transcript, June 2002: http://news.bbc.co.uk/hi/english/static/audio_video/programmes/panorama/transcripts/transcript_19_06_02.txt.
114 'Finucane killer gets 22 years', *BBC News*, 16 September 2004: http://news.bbc.co.uk/1/hi/northern_ireland/3662452.stm.
115 Author interview, confidential source, April 2025.

CHAPTER 15

1 Guidance Note on NCND, 'The NCND Principle – its use, importance and effectiveness', Cabinet Office, 2017: www.kenova.co.uk/41.%20D5371%20Guidance%20Re%20NCND%202017.pdf.
2 Operation Kenova Interim Report, March 2024, para. 48.7: www.psni.police.uk/sites/default/files/2024-03/Operation%20Kenova%20Interim%20Report%202024.pdf.

3 Sir Iain Livinsgtone, press conference at the launch of Operation Kenova Final Report, Stormont Hotel, Belfast, 9 December 2025.
4 Cabinet Office Guidance Note on NCND, para. 8.
5 Affidavit of Jon Boutcher, Chief Constable of PSNI, 17 March 2025, paras 7.3–8.3; 'In the matter of an application by the Secretary of State for Northern Ireland for Judicial Review (Appellant), Supreme Court', 11 June 2025, copy held by author.
6 MI5, 'Centenary History Policy on Disclosure', *Security Service*: www.mi5.gov.uk/history/mi5-the-authorised-centenary-history/centenary-history-policy-on-disclosure.
7 Author interview, Jon Boutcher, October 2025.
8 CAJ annual lecture by Jon Boutcher, 10 December 2025: https://caj.org.uk/wp-content/uploads/2025/12/CAJ-Lecture-CC-Jon-Boutcher-NCND-10.12.25-Public.pdf.
9 Jon Boutcher, press conference at launch of Operation Kenova Final Report, Stormont Hotel, Belfast, 9 December 2025.
10 James Eadie KC, 'In the matter of an application by the Secretary of State for Northern Ireland for Judicial Review (Appellant), Supreme Court', 11 June 2025: www.supremecourt.uk/cases/uksc-2024-0083.
11 Operation Kenova Family Report, 'The murder of David McVeigh, September 1986', p. 17.
12 Operation Kenova Final Report, Case 12 (David McVeigh), p. 69: www.psni.police.uk/sites/default/files/2025-12/Operation%20Kenova%20Final%20Report%202025.pdf.
13 Operation Kenova Family Report, 'The murder of David McVeigh, September 1986', p. 21.
14 Ibid., where 'Suspect A' is Scappaticci, p. 13.
15 Ibid., p. 20.
16 Office of Government Information Services, 'NCND/Glomar: When Agencies Neither Confirm Nor Deny the Existence of Records', 29 March 2024: www.archives.gov/ogis/resources/foia-ombuds-observer/2024-01.
17 *Wind of Change*, podcast, Spotify, April/May 2020: https://open.spotify.com/show/3vikAuFxKVNe2GBZC61IYD.
18 CIA, X post, 6 June 2014: https://x.com/CIA/status/474971393852182528?lang=en
19 Author interview, Sir Iain Livingstone, February 2025.
20 'Intelligence "UFF Targeting", 24 August 1981', as cited in De Silva Review, Vol. II, p. 188: https://assets.publishing.service.gov.uk/media/5a7c2313e5274a25a9140ac8/0802.pdf.
21 De Silva Review, paras 16.52–16.58.
22 Author interview, Ian Hurst, September 2025.
23 Liam Clarke, 'The British spy at heart of IRA', *The Sunday Times*, 8 August 1999.
24 Author interview, confidential source, February 2025.
25 Operation Kenova Final Report, December 2025, para. 9.24.
26 'The chilling sound that signalled death for IRA "informers"', *BBC News*, 5 March 2024: www.bbc.co.uk/news/uk-68424617.
27 Operation Kenova Final Report, December 2025, para. 9.52.
28 Author interview, Ian Hurst, September 2025.
29 British Irish Rights Watch, 'Submission to UN Special Rapporteur on Freedom of Expression & Opinion Concerning Reporting of State Collusion in NI', *Rights and Security International*, 1 May 2000: www.rightsandsecurity.org/impact-post/submission-to-un-special-rapporteur-on-freedom-of-expression-opinion-concerning-reporting-of.
30 Letter from John Stevens to Peter Madden, 23 April 1999.
31 Author interview, Sir Hugh Orde, February 2025.
32 Author interview, Phil James, February 2025.
33 Operation Kenova Final Report, December 2025, para. 9.39.
34 Ibid., para. 9.37.
35 Author interview, Phil James, February 2025.
36 Author interview, confidential source, March 2017.

37 Author interview, confidential source, January 2025.
38 Author interview, Barney Rowan, December 2025, referencing his conversation with PSNI officers at the meeting.
39 Author interview, Sir Hugh Orde, February 2025.
40 Author interview, confidential source, February 2026.
41 Author interview, confidential source, November 2024.
42 Operation Kenova Interim Report, 4 March 2024, paras 49.2 and 49.4.
43 Author interview, confidential source, November 2024.
44 Author interview, Phil James, June 2016.
45 Author interview, confidential source, November 2024.
46 Author interview, confidential source, December 2025.
47 Peter Cory died in April 2020.
48 Sam McBride, 'Tony Blair worked behind scenes to thwart Pat Finucane public inquiry after discussion with MI5 boss', *Belfast Telegraph*, 9 April 2024: www.belfasttelegraph.co.uk/news/politics/tony-blair-worked-behind-scenes-to-thwart-pat-finucane-public-inquiry-after-discussion-with-mi5-boss/a1324106581.html.
49 Cory Collusion Inquiry Report, para. 1.293: https://cain.ulster.ac.uk/issues/collusion/cory/cory03finucane.pdf.
50 'Desmond de Silva: Flamboyant barrister with a client list to rival them all', *The Independent*, 21 June 2018: www.independent.co.uk/news/obituaries/desmond-de-silva-dead-barrister-footballers-charles-taylor-war-crimes-a8398896.html.
51 John Ware, 'Finucane: Who knew of this deniable murder?', *The Telegraph*, 15 December 2012: www.telegraph.co.uk/news/uknews/northernireland/9747132/Finucane-Who-knew-of-this-deniable-murder.html.
52 Oral statement to parliament, 'Statement by the Secretary of State for Northern Ireland on the murder of Patrick Finucane', 11 September 2024: www.gov.uk/government/speeches/statement-by-the-secretary-of-state-for-northern-ireland-on-the-murder-of-patrick-finucane.
53 Renee M. Pomerance, 'Dispatches from the Collusion inquiry: a tribute to the Honourable Peter Cory', *Fordham International Law Journal*, 2020, Vol. 44:1, pp. 245–56: https://ir.lawnet.fordham.edu/cgi/viewcontent.cgi?article=2806&context=ilj.
54 Author interview, Peter Cory, February 2003.
55 Pomerance, 'Dispatches from the Collusion inquiry', pp. 245–56.
56 Operation Kenova Interim Report, March 2024, para. 60.7.
57 Author interview, Renee Pomerance, April 2025.
58 'How MI5 piled falsehood on falsehood in the case of neo-Nazi spy who abused women', *BBC News*, 6 July 2025: www.bbc.co.uk/news/articles/c3w4nwdwywno.
59 Author interview, confidential source, September 2025.
60 Author interview, Renee Pomerance, April 2025.
61 Author interview, confidential sources, November 2024.
62 Martin Ingram and Greg Harkin, *Stakeknife: Britain's Secret Agents in Ireland* (The O'Brien Press, 2004), p. 243.
63 Author interview, confidential source, April 2025.
64 Author interview, Neil Mackay, September 2025.
65 Gerry Kelly, Sinn Féin statement 'Scappaticci allegations', 12 May 2003: www.sinnfein.org/releases/03/pr031202.html.
66 Author interview, confidential source, July 2016.
67 'Scappaticci Allegations', Sinn Féin press release, 12 May 2003: www.sinnfein.org/releases/03/pr031202.html.
68 Press statement issued by Michael Flanigan on 13 May 2003, as cited in Kerr J., 'In the matter of an application by Freddie Scappaticci for leave to apply for judicial review', High Court, Belfast, 17 June 2003: www.judiciaryni.uk/files/judiciaryni/decisions/In%20the%20matter%20of%20

an%20Application%20by%20Freddie%20Scappaticci%20for%20Leave%20to%20apply%20for%20Judicial%20Review.pdf.

69 Author interview, Barney Rowan, April 2025.

70 Author interview, confidential source, April 2016.

71 'The Spy in the IRA', *Panorama*, BBC, 11 April 2017: www.bbc.co.uk/programmes/b08l636g.

72 'Scappaticci says he never left Belfast', *The Irish Times*, 15 May 2003: www.irishtimes.com/news/scappaticci-says-he-never-left-belfast-1.359000.

73 'Adams: Scappaticci innocent until proven guilty', *The Guardian*, 16 May 2003: www.theguardian.com/uk/2003/may/16/northernireland.northernireland.

74 Danny Morrision, 'No 10's Murderer – Scap', 30 January 2016: www.dannymorrison.com/the-times-of-no-10s-main-murderer/.

75 Jane Kennedy, HC Deb, 14 May 2003, vol. 405, cc90: https://api.parliament.uk/historic-hansard/westminster-hall/2003/may/14/stevens-inquiry.

76 Author interview, confidential source, July 2016.

77 Author interview, confidential sources, November 2024.

78 Carswell, LCJ, 'In the matter of an application by Freddie Scappaticci for Judicial Review', 18 August 2003: www.judiciaryni.uk/files/judiciaryni/decisions/In%20the%20matter%20of%20an%20application%20by%20Freddie%20Scappaticci%20for%20Judicial%20Review.pdf.

79 Author interview, confidential sources, November 2024.

80 Ibid.

81 Kerr J, 'In the matter of an application by Freddie Scappaticci for leave to apply for judicial review', High Court, Belfast, 17 June 2003.

82 Author interview, confidential sources, November and December 2024.

83 Ibid.

84 Ibid.

85 Author interview, confidential sources, November 2024.

86 Author interview, confidential sources, July 2016, September 2024, November 2024.

87 Author interview, confidential source, November 2024.

88 Maura Kalthoff, Communications Manager Supreme Court of the United Kingdom, email to author, 6 March 2025.

89 Steven Fifer, deputy head of communications, Attorney General's Office, email to author, 4 March 2025.

90 Letter to Lord Woolf, 27 February 2025.

91 Operation Kenova Interim Report, March 2024, para. 65.3.

92 Author interview, confidential sources, November 2024.

93 Carswell LCJ, 'In the matter of an application by Freddie Scappaticci for Judicial Review', 18 August 2003.

94 Author interview, confidential source, November 2024.

95 Ibid.

96 Rosie Cowan, 'Stakeknife "told TV crew that McGuinness ordered killings"', *The Guardian*, 14 July 2003: www.theguardian.com/media/2003/jul/14/pressandpublishing.northernireland.

97 Transcript of Scappaticci covert interview with *The Cook Report*, ITV, 26 August 1993: https://thebrokenelbow.com/2019/01/11/remembering-freddie-scappaticci/.

98 Sylvia Jones, 'Scappaticci told me IRA secrets before cop told me he was an agent called Stakeknife', *The People*, 20 July 2003.

99 'Freddie Scappaticci threatens BBC reporter', *BBC News*, 7 March 2024: www.bbc.co.uk/news/av/uk-northern-ireland-68493626.

100 Operation Kenova Final Report, December 2025, para. 9.10 1(b).

101 'Loose Talk', *Insight*, UTV, 15 March 2004: https://cryptome.wikileaks.org/scap-clive.htm.

102 Author interview, confidential sources, November 2024.

103 Author interview, Phil James, December 2024.

104 Operation Kenova Final Report, December 2025, para. 8.9.
105 Author interview, confidential sources, November 2024.
106 Author interview, Phil James, December 2015.
107 Author interview, confidential source, November 2024.
108 Ibid.
109 Author interview, Phil James, June 2016.
110 John Ware, 'Northern Ireland: No more answers', *Prospect*, 15 October 2014: www.prospectmagazine.co.uk/politics/46846/northern-ireland-no-more-answers.

CHAPTER 16

1 Application by Michael Flanigan on behalf of Freddie Scappaticci to quash 'the decision by the Ministry of Defence not to apply for an injunction against the *Sunday Life* and Martin Ingram', 3 February 2004, copy held by author.
2 ACC Sam Kinkaid letter to Ian Hurst's lawyer Peter Binning, 20 February 2006, copy held by author.
3 Jane Winter, British Irish Rights Watch, letter to ACC Peter Sheridan, 16 June 2006, copy held by author.
4 Operation Kenova Interim Report, March 2024, para. 65.14: www.kenova.co.uk/Kenova%20Report%202024%20Digital%20(002).pdf.
5 *Freddie Scappaticci v MGN Limited, Independent News & Media Limited*, 'Order for an injunction' before the Honourable Mr Justice Weir, 29 June 2006, copy held by author.
6 Author interview, confidential source, March 2025.
7 Operation Kenova Interim Report, para. 65.13.
8 Author interview, confidential source, October 2025.
9 Operation Kenova Interim Report, para. 65.11.
10 Ibid., para. 65.15.
11 Barney Rowan, 'Castlereagh break-in: Who was behind it?', *BBC News*, 5 September 2002: http://news.bbc.co.uk/1/hi/northern_ireland/2238298.stm.
12 Author interview, confidential source, November 2016.
13 Author interviews, confidential sources, January 2017, November 2024, December 2024.
14 Pamela Atchison, email to author, 7 March 2025.
15 Author interview, confidential source, November 2024.
16 Author interview, (separate) confidential source, November 2024.
17 No response to emails from author to Philip Wright on 19 and 21 September 2025.
18 Author interview, confidential source, November 2024.
19 *Regina v Hasan* [2005] UKHL 22, 17 March 2005, pp. 9–11: https://publications.parliament.uk/pa/ld200405/ldjudgmt/jd050317/hasan.pdf.
20 Andrew Parker, MI5 Director for Northern Ireland terrorism advice to the Northern Ireland Office, May 2003, as disclosed to author by confidential source.
21 Author interview, confidential source, November 2024.
22 Pamela Atchison, email to author, 13 March 2025.
23 Author interview, confidential source, December 2024.
24 Author interview, confidential source, November 2024.
25 Author interview, (separate) confidential source, November 2024.
26 Miss M. Lavery, Policy and Information Section, PPS, Belfast, letter to Jane Winter, 9 January 2008, copy held by author.
27 'Statement by the DPP for Northern Ireland in relation to decisions as to prosecution arising out of the Stevens III Investigation', 'The policy of the Public Prosecution Service in relation to the giving of reasons for decisions, which is set out in the Code for Prosecutors issued by the Service, is to give reasons in the most general terms', 25 June 2007: www.ppsni.gov.uk/news/statement-director-public-prosecutions-northern-ireland-relation-decisions-prosecution-arising.

28 Author interview, Jane Winter, February 2025.
29 Author interview, confidential source, January 2025.
30 Pamela Atchison, email to author, 7 March 2025.
31 Ibid.
32 Author interviews, confidential sources, September and November 2024.
33 Author interview, confidential source, November 2024.
34 Ibid.
35 'Morrison conviction is quashed', *BBC News*, 24 October 2008: http://news.bbc.co.uk/1/hi/northern_ireland/7688669.stm. See also Neutral Citation No. [2009] NICA 1, *The Queen v Daniel Morrison and Others*, 9 January 2009: www.judiciaryni.uk/files/judiciaryni/decisions/Queen%20v%20Daniel%20Morrison%20and%20Others%20%5B2009%5D%20NICA%201.pdf.
36 Author interview, Kevin Winters, January 2026.
37 'Dirty fighting', *The Guardian*, 13 January 2009: www.theguardian.com/uk/2009/jan/13/northernireland-northernireland.
38 Danny Morrison, 'Dirty Fighting', *The Guardian*, 13 January 2009: www.theguardian.com/uk/2009/jan/13/northernireland-northernireland.
39 Author interview, confidential source, September 2025.
40 'Morrison conviction is quashed', *BBC News*, 24 October 2008, 9 January 2009.
41 Peter Baker, 'I am afraid I cannot explain the matter any further', *Slugger O'Toole*, 16 November 2008: https://sluggerotoole.com/2008/11/16/i-am-afraid-i-cannot-explain-the-matter-any-further/comment-page-1/.
42 Danny Morrison, 'No. 10's Murderer – Scap', 30 January 2016: www.dannymorrison.com/the-times-of-no-10s-main-murderer/.
43 Danny Morrison, 'Dirty Fighting', *The Guardian*, 13 January 2009.
44 Martin Ingram and Greg Harkin *Stakeknife: Britain's Secret Agents in Ireland* (The O'Brien Press, 2004), p. 139.
45 Author interview, confidential source, January 2025.
46 Author interview, (separate) confidential source, January 2025.
47 Operation Kenova Interim Report, March 2024, para. 71.7.
48 LCJ Hutton, *The Queen v James Martin, Veronica Mary Martin (née Ryan), Liam James Martin, Daniel Caldwell, Gerard Hodgins, James O'Carroll, John Anthony Murray, Daniel Gerard Morrison*, judgment, 8 May 1991, copy held by author.
49 Author interview, Phil James, September 2025.
50 Ibid.
51 Author interview, confidential source, January 2026.
52 Author interview, confidential source, October 2025.
53 Author interview, confidential source, December 2025.
54 Neutral Citation No. [2009] NICA 1, *The Queen v Daniel Morrison and Others*, 9 January 2009, para. 6.
55 '£1.6million pay-out for IRA kidnap gang leaves victims outraged', *The Irish Post*, 1 February 2016: www.irishpost.com/news/1-6million-pay-out-for-ira-kidnap-gang-leaves-victims-outraged-79425.
56 Author interview, confidential source, December 2025.
57 Neutral Citation No. [2009] NICA 1, *The Queen v Daniel Morrison and Others*, 9 January 2009, para. 7.
58 Author interview, Kevin Winters, April 2023.
59 Author interview, Phil James, December 2024.
60 Author interview, confidential source, August 2012.
61 Neutral Citation No. [2012] NIQB 89, Martin's (James) Application, 26 October 2012: www.judiciaryni.uk/files/judiciaryni/decisions/Martin%E2%80%99s%20%28James%29%20Application.pdf.
62 Operation Kenova Interim Report, para. 1.7 (2).
63 Neutral Citation No. [2014] NICA 72, *Ryan (Veronica) and James Martin v Regina*, 10 October

2014, para. 15: www.judiciaryni.uk/files/judiciaryni/decisions/Ryan%20%28Veronica%29%20%26%20Martin%20%28James%29%20%20v%20R.pdf.

64 Author interview, confidential source, September 2025.

65 Author interview, confidential source, November 2015.

66 Author interview, confidential source, December 2015.

67 Email to author from Bara McGrory KC, January 2026.

68 Author interview, Phil James, February 2025.

69 Author interview, Michael Maguire, January 2017.

70 Operation Kenova Final Report, December 2025, para. 7.1.

71 Author interview, Michael Maguire, January 2017.

72 Author interview, confidential source, November 2024.

73 Ibid.

74 Written response to author from Barra McGrory KC, 29 December 2025.

75 Pamela Atchison, email to author, 18 December 2025.

76 Barra McGrory KC, email to author, 30 December 2025.

77 Ibid.

78 Barra McGrory KC, email to author, 26 February 2026.

79 Author interview, confidential source, February 2025.

80 PPS, 'DPP requests in-depth investigation into Stakeknife allegations', 21 October 2015, copy held by author.

81 Author interview, confidential source, October 2025.

82 Author interview, confidential source, November 2024.

83 Author interview, confidential sources, November and December 2024.

84 Barra McGrory KC, email to author, 26 February 2025.

85 Ibid.

86 Kevin McGinty, CV: www.gov.uk/government/people/kev.

87 Author interview, confidential source, November 2024.

88 Emails to author from Pamela Atchison, 7 March and 19 December 2025.

89 'Statement by the Director of Public Prosecutions for Northern Ireland in relation to decisions as to prosecution arising out of the Stevens III Investigation', 25 June 2007.

90 Barra McGrory KC, email to author, 26 February 2025.

91 'Statement by the Director of Public Prosecutions for Northern Ireland in relation to decisions as to prosecution arising out of the Stevens III Investigation', 25 June 2007.

92 Author interview, confidential source, November 2024.

93 Text of letter from Barra McGrory KC to George Hamilton, April 2016.

94 'Step back over Stakeknife, PPS deputy asked', *BBC News*, 11 April 2017: www.bbc.com/news/uk-northern-ireland-39561180.

95 Barra McGrory KC, telephone conversation with author, 3 January 2026.

96 Barra McGrory KC, email to author, 22 January 2026.

97 Barra McGrory KC, telephone conversation with author, 3 January 2026.

98 PPS, 'Public statement as PPS issues four decisions in connection with Operation Kenova files', para. 21: www.ppsni.gov.uk/files/ppsni/publications/PPS%20Public%20Statement%2029.10.20.pdf.

99 Public statement as PPS issues four decisions in connection with Operation Kenova files', para. 9, 29 October 2020.

100 Pamela Atchison, email to author, 18 December 2025.

101 Author interview, confidential source, April 2016.

102 Pamela Atchison, email to author, 18 December 2025.

103 Ibid., 7 March 2025.

104 Author interview, confidential source, March 2025.

105 Barra McGrory KC, email to author, 29 December 2025.

CHAPTER 17

1 Author interview, Jon Boutcher, October 2025.
2 Ibid.
3 Operation Kenova Interim Report, March 2024, para. 16.27: www.kenova.co.uk/Kenova%20Report%202024%20Digital%20(002).pdf.
4 Operation Kenova Final Report, December 2025, para. 7.29: www.psni.police.uk/sites/default/files/2025-12/Operation%20Kenova%20Final%20Report%202025.pdf.
5 Operation Kenova Interim Report, March 2024, p. 23.
6 'Keith Surtees recognised in King's Honours list': www.kenova.co.uk/keith-surtees-recognised-in-kings-honours-list.
7 DPP requests in-depth investigation into 'Stakeknife' allegations', PPS news release, 21 October 2015, copy held by author.
8 Author meeting with Keith Surtees and Jon Boutcher, June 2016.
9 'Biographies – Senior Management: Stephen Herron, the Director of Public Prosecutions': www.ppsni.gov.uk/biographies-senior-management.
10 Operation Kenova Interim Report, March 2024, para. 44.4.
11 Author interview, confidential source, November 2024.
12 Author interview, confidential source, October 2025.
13 Operation Kenova, family reports section under 'Ministry of Defence', 2025: 'The first step taken by Operation Kenova was to secure a high-level agreement for full cooperation from the British Army General responsible for Home Command. This was further supplemented by a dedicated team of lawyers and military personnel to service Operation Kenova requests for information.'
14 Author interview, confidential source, October 2025.
15 Operation Kenova Interim Report, March 2024, para. 41.2.
16 Operation Kenova Final Report, December 2025, para. 8.19.
17 Operation Kenova Interim Report, March 2024, para. 41.1.
18 Author interview, confidential source, June 2016.
19 Operation Kenova Interim Report, March 2024, p. 25.
20 Author interview, confidential source, December 2025.
21 Operation Kenova Interim Report, March 2024, para. 41.24.
22 Author interview, confidential source, November 2025.
23 Operation Kenova Final Report, December 2025, para. 7.10.
24 Author interview, confidential source, October 2025.
25 Operation Kenova Final Report, December 2025, para. 12.5.
26 Operation Kenova Interim Report, para. 41.3.
27 Author interview, confidential source, October 2025.
28 Ibid.
29 Operation Kenova Interim Report, March 2024, para. 41.8.
30 Northern Ireland Troubles (Legacy and Reconciliation) Act 2023, Part 3: www.legislation.gov.uk/ukpga/2023/41/part/3.
31 Operation Kenova Interim Report, March 2024, para. 14.6.
32 Interview with Paul Wilson, 'Frank', *Stakeknife*, Episode 10, BBC Sounds, 1 February 2025: www.bbc.co.uk/sounds/play/p0km0vdx.
33 Author interview, confidential source, October 2025.
34 'The IRA scoured the world hunting for Stakeknife the British spy who'd double-crossed them for 22 blood-stained years … The one place they didn't look? A quiet corner of suburban Surrey', *Daily Mail*, 17 June 2023: www.dailymail.co.uk/news/article-12206261/The-IRA-scoured-world-hunting-Stakeknife-British-spy-whod-double-crossed.html.
35 Author interview, confidential source, October 2025.
36 Author interview, confidential source, December 2025.

37 '"Stakeknife" accused Scappaticci pleads guilty to having extreme porn', *Belfast Telegraph*, 5 December 2018: www.belfasttelegraph.co.uk/news/courts/stakeknife-accused-scappaticci-pleads-guilty-to-having-extreme-porn/37597176.html.
38 Barra McGrory interview, 'The Spy In the IRA', *Panorama*, BBC, April 2017.
39 Operation Kenova Interim Report, March 2024, para. 55.5.
40 Ibid., p. 18.
41 Author interview, confidential source, September 2024.
42 Ibid.
43 Author interview, confidential source, January 2025.
44 Ibid.
45 Operation Kenova Interim Report, March 2024, para. 41.10.
46 Ibid., para. 41.15.
47 Ibid., para. 41.22.
48 Author interview, confidential source, March 2025.
49 'Detective in Stakeknife probe says new MI5 documents found', *The Irish News*, 23 October 2019: www.irishnews.com/news/northernirelandnews/2019/10/23/news/detective-in-stakeknife-probe-says-new-mi5-documents-found-1745925/.
50 Operation Kenova Interim Report, March 2024, paras 41.11–41.19.
51 Author interview, confidential source, October 2025.
52 Operation Kenova Interim Report, March 2024, paras 38.1–38.8.
53 Author interview, confidential source, October 2025.
54 Operation Kenova Interim Report, March 2024, p. 29.
55 Ibid., para. 44.11.
56 PPS, 'Public statement as PPS issues four decisions in connection with Operation Kenova files', 29 October 2020, paras 19 and 20: www.ppsni.gov.uk/files/ppsni/publications/PPS%20Public%20Statement%2029.10.20.pdf.
57 Operation Kenova Interim Report, March 2024, para. 44.10.
58 PPS, 'Operation Kenova – summary of decisions not to prosecute Part A – General Matters', 6 December 2023, para. 11.1: www.ppsni.gov.uk/files/ppsni/2023-12/Public%20Statement%206%20December%2023%20_0.pdf.
59 Author interview, confidential source, October 2025.
60 Operation Kenova Interim Report, March 2024, p. 29.
61 Ibid., para. 41.6.
62 Ibid., paras 41.23–41.26.
63 'Hooded Men: Police apologise over 1971 interrogations', *BBC News*, 13 June 2023: www.bbc.co.uk/news/uk-northern-ireland-65892145.
64 Operation Kenova Interim Report, March 2024, paras 39.6–39.7.
65 Author interview, confidential source, October 2025.
66 Author interview, (separate) confidential source, October 2025.
67 PPS, 'Public statement as PPS issues four decisions in connection with Operation Kenova files', 29 October 2020, paras 10–20.
68 Author interview, confidential source, March 2025.
69 Operation Kenova Interim Report, March 2024, para. 65.28.
70 PPS, 'Public statement as PPS issues four decisions in connection with Operation Kenova files', 29 October 2020, para. 13.
71 Operation Kenova Interim Report, March 2024, para. 65.2.
72 Ibid., para. 65.14.
73 PPS, 'Public statement as PPS issues four decisions in connection with Operation Kenova files', 29 October 2020, para. 13.
74 Author interview, confidential source, September 2024.
75 Author interview, confidential source, September 2024.

76 Operation Kenova Interim Report, March 2024, para. 65.28.
77 Author interview, confidential source, February 2025.
78 PPS, 'Public statement as PPS issues four decisions in connection with Operation Kenova files', 29 October 2020, para. 21.
79 Kenova statement following PPS announcement, 29 October 2020: www.kenova.co.uk/kenova-statement-following-pps-announcement.
80 Author interview, confidential source, May 2021.
81 Sir Julian Flaux, 'In the High Court of Justice Chancery Division Business and Property Courts of England and Wales Property Trusts and Probate List: In the Estate of Frank Cowley Deceased', 28 July 2025, para. 1: www.serlecourt.co.uk/images/uploads/news-and-events/Michael_Johnson_v_His_Majesty%E2%80%99s_Attorney-General-_2025__EWHC_1943_%28Ch%29.pdf.
82 Operation Kenova Final Report, December 2025, para. 9.10 (1)a.
83 'Final days of Freddie Scappaticci, the IRA killer hidden in Surrey', *The Times*, 5 December 2025: www.thetimes.com/uk/defence/article/freddie-scappaticci-army-ira-spy-lbf3799hg.
84 Ibid.
85 Author interview, confidential source, October 2025.
86 'Stakeknife: Alleged Army agent in IRA Freddie Scappaticci dies', *BBC News*, 11 April 2023: www.bbc.co.uk/news/uk-northern-ireland-65244928.
87 'Secrecy of royal wills questioned by senior officials, documents reveal', *The Guardian*, 19 July 2022: www.theguardian.com/uk-news/2022/jul/19/secrecy-of-royal-wills-questioned-by-senior-officials-documents-reveal.
88 Author interview, confidential source, November 2025.
89 Sir Julian Flaux, 'In the High Court of Justice Chancery Division Business and Property Courts of England and Wales Property Trusts and Probate List: In the Estate of Frank Cowley Deceased', 28 July 2025, para. 60.
90 Author interview, confidential source, December 2025.
91 Operation Kenova Interim Report, March 2024, para. 68.4.
92 Author interview, Jon Boutcher, May 2021.
93 Operation Kenova Interim Report, December 2025, para. 1.11 (3).
94 'What is the Northern Ireland Legacy Bill?', *BBC News*, 5 September 2023: www.bbc.co.uk/news/uk-northern-ireland-66648806.
95 James Cartlidge, shadow Secretary of State for Defence, 'Defending our veterans', 7 October 2025: www.conservatives.com/news/defending-our-veterans.
96 'Simon Byrne: What went wrong for the PSNI's chief constable?', *BBC News*, 4 September 2023: www.bbc.co.uk/news/uk-northern-ireland-66679018.
97 'PSNI: Jon Boutcher picked as interim chief constable', *BBC News*, 4 October 2023: www.bbc.co.uk/news/uk-northern-ireland-67006063.
98 Author interview, confidential source, October 2025.
99 'PSNI: Jon Boutcher picked as interim chief constable', *BBC News*, 4 October 2023.
100 'Policing Board confirms appointment of Interim Chief Constable', *BBC News*, 12 October 2023: www.nipolicingboard.org.uk/news-centre/policing-board-confirms-appointment-interim-chief-constable.
101 Author interview, confidential source, October 2025.
102 Operation Kenova Interim Report, March 2024, para. 55.3.
103 Ibid., para. 63.1.
104 Ibid., para. 67.8.
105 Ibid., p. 8.
106 Author interview, confidential source, February 2020.
107 Operation Kenova briefing to author, October 2025.
108 PPS, 'Operation Kenova – Summary of decisions not to prosecute', 29 February 2024, para. 98–119.
109 PPS, 'Operation Kenova – Summary of further decisions not to prosecute', 6 February 2024, para. 20

(viii): www.ppsni.gov.uk/files/ppsni/2024-02/PPS%20Public%20Statement%206%20February%20 2024.pdf.

110 PPS, 'Operation Kenova – Summary of decisions not to prosecute', 29 February 2024, paras 79–88.

111 Operation Kenova, Final Report, December 2025, para. 9.50.

112 Ibid., para. 10.8.

113 Operation Kenova Family Report, 'The murder of Thomas Emmanuel Wilson', 24 June 1987, p. 30.

114 Operation Kenova Final Report, December 2025, para. 12.28.

115 For NI see PPS statistical bulletin: www.ppsni.gov.uk/pps-statistical-bulletin. For GB see CPS data summary Quarters 1-4 (2020–21 to 2024–25) under 'charging' for 'all legal decisions'.

116 Northern Ireland Affairs Committee, Oral evidence: Operation Kenova, HC 671, Q 20, 23 April 2024: https://committees.parliament.uk/oralevidence/14669/pdf/.

117 Author interview, confidential source, August 2025.

CHAPTER 18

1 Author interview, confidential source, February 2025.

2 Operation Kenova Interim Report, March 2024, para. 41.1: www.kenova.co.uk/Kenova%20 Report%202024%20Digital%20(002).pdf.

3 Ibid., para. 41.6.

4 Ibid., para. 41.26.

5 Author interview, confidential source, February 2025.

6 Note of Iain Livingstone meeting with KRW-Law, August 2024, held by author.

7 Operation Kenova Interim Report, March 2024, para. 41.25.

8 'Kenova Disclosure – External Review, Unclassified Summary', Helen Ball QPM, February 2025: www.kenova.co.uk/Kenova%20External%20Review%20by%20H%20Ball%20Feb%202025%20 (002).pdf.

9 Operation Kenova Final Report, December 2025, para. 4.6 (5): www.psni.police.uk/sites/default/ files/2025-12/Operation%20Kenova%20Final%20Report%202025.pdf.

10 Author interview, confidential source, September 2024.

11 Author interview, confidential source, February 2025.

12 Ibid.

13 Operation Kenova Interim Report, March 2024, para. 8.4.

14 Operation Kenova Final Report, December 2025, para. 12.20 (2).

15 Ibid., para. 12.20 (3).

16 Ibid., para. 12.20 (5).

17 Operation Kenova Interim Report, March 2024, para. 41.8.

18 Operation Kenova Final Report, December 2025, para. 10.9.

19 Ibid., para. 9.26. This continued until at least 1986.

20 Ibid., para. 12.22.

21 Ibid., para. 12.21.

22 Author interview, confidential source, August 2025.

23 PPS, 'Operation Kenova – Summary of decisions not to prosecute', 29 February 2024, para. 72: www.ppsni.gov.uk/files/ppsni/2024-02/Operation%20Kenova%20Public%20Statement%20 29%20February%202024.pdf. See also Operation Kenova Final Report, December 2025, para. 12.26.

24 Operation Kenova Final Report, December 2025, para. 12.26.

25 Ibid., para. 12.20 (1).

26 De Silva Review, December 2012, para. 8.139: https://assets.publishing.service.gov.uk/media/5a7c 2313e5274a25a9140ac8/0802.pdf.

27 Letter from Sir Iain Livingstone to Hilary Benn, 6 August 2024: www.kenova.co.uk/Sir%20Iain%20 Letter%20to%20SOSNI%20070824.pdf.

28 Northern Ireland Troubles (Legacy and Reconciliation) Act 2023, S.38 (1): www.legislation.gov.uk/ukpga/2023/41/part/3/crossheading/criminal-investigations-and-proceedings.
29 'Government and Republican leadership urged to apologise', Operation Kenova, March 2024: www.kenova.co.uk/government-and-republican-leadership-urged-to-apologise.
30 Author interview, confidential source, August 2024.
31 Operation Kenova Final Report, December 2025, para. 4.4.
32 Sir Iain Livingstone, oral evidence to Northern Ireland Affairs Committee, Q22, 14 January 2026: https://committees.parliament.uk/oralevidence/17001/pdf/.
33 Ibid., Q4.
34 Author interview, confidential source, November 2025.
35 Author interview, confidential source, December 2025.
36 'Kenova Disclosure – External Review Unclassified Summary', Helen Ball QPM, February 2025.
37 Operation Kenova Final Report, December 2025, para. 12.12; also confidential source.
38 Operation Kenova Final Report, December 2025, para. 9.41.
39 Author interview, confidential source, April 2016.
40 Operation Kenova, Interim Report, March 2024, para. 41.24.
41 Author interview, confidential source, November 2025.
42 Author interview, confidential source, January 2026.
43 Author interview, confidential source, July 2025.
44 Sir Iain Livingstone, press conference, Stormont Hotel, Belfast, 9 December 2025.
45 MI5 website, 'Purpose and Values': www.mi5.gov.uk/about-us/purpose-and-values.
46 Operation Kenova Interim Report, reference to Judge Cory's experiences with MI5, March 2024, p. 32.
47 Neutral Citation No. [2014] NICA 60, 10 September 2014, para. 20: www.judiciaryni.uk/files/judiciaryni/decisions/R%20v%20McCauley%20%28Martin%29.pdf.
48 Author interview, confidential source, 5 September 2024.
49 'MI5 "institutionally defensive" after Arena bomb', *BBC News*, 5 November 2024: www.bbc.co.uk/news/articles/c7v37g41jddo
50 'Manchester Arena Inquiry Volume 3: Radicalisation and Preventability', paras 24.53–24.58: https://assets.publishing.service.gov.uk/media/63ff865ae90e0740dc92d1d8/MAI_Final_PDF_Volume_3.pdf.
51 'Manchester Arena families say MI5 must be fully included in new law on cover-ups', *BBC News*, 5 January 2026: www.bbc.co.uk/news/articles/crkr0r6lrdjo.
52 'How MI5 piled falsehood on falsehood in the case of neo-Nazi spy who abused women', *BBC News*, 6 July 2025: www.bbc.co.uk/news/articles/c3w4nwdwywno.
53 The IPT, 'Who are we?': https://investigatorypowerstribunal.org.uk/about-the-tribunal/.
54 'How I exposed MI5's lie about its violent abusive agent', *BBC News*, 12 February 2025.
55 'PM orders investigation into MI5 over false evidence', *BBC News*, 16 September 2025.
56 Ibid.
57 'Uncovered Day 2: Boutcher, Scappaticci and the secretive world of MI5', *The Irish News*, 25 March 2025: www.irishnews.com/news/northern-ireland/uncovered-day-2-boutcher-scappaticci-and-the-secretive-world-of-mi5-V3PE6YDBUFARJDDAI5IAVDYWAY/.
58 Author interview, confidential source, February 2025.
59 Operation Kenova Interim Report, March 2024, p. 30.
60 'Murder Without Answers', *Spotlight*, BBC Northern Ireland, 10 June 2025: www.bbc.co.uk/iplayer/episode/m002dg8l/spotlight-murder-without-answers.
61 Author interview, Niall Murphy, November 2025.
62 'Sean Brown's widow "wants answers" 28 years after murder', *BBC News*, 21 May 2025: www.bbc.co.uk/news/articles/ckg7785lljro.
63 'Heaney says Brown's murder "shocking"', *The Irish Times*, 16 May 1997: www.irishtimes.com/news/heaney-says-brown-s-murder-shocking-1.72648.
64 Author interview, Niall Murphy, February 2025.

65 'Significant failures in investigation of 1997 Sean Brown murder', OPONI News release, 19 January 2004: www.policeombudsman.org/news/significant-failures-in-investigation-of-1997-sean-brown-murder.
66 Author interview, Niall Murphy, February 2025.
67 Niall Murphy, 'Inquests and the Failure by the State to discharge its international legal obligations and comply with the Lord Chief Justice's Concept Plan', KRW-Law, December 2016, copy held by author.
68 William R. Matchett, 'The RUC Special Branch: How Effective was it at Defeating an Insurgency?', PhD thesis, University of Ulster, July 2014, copy held by author.
69 Neutral Citation No. [2024] NIKB 109, 17 December 2024, para. 8: www.judiciaryni.uk/files/judiciaryni/2024-12/Brown%27s%20%28Bridie%29%20Application.pdf.
70 Neutral Citation No. [2024] NICoroner 18, 4 March 2024, paras 20 and 24: www.judiciaryni.uk/files/judiciaryni/2024-03/In%20the%20matter%20of%20an%20inquest%20touching%20the%20death%20of%20Sean%20Brown.pdf.
71 'Northern Ireland inquests involving 74 deaths during Troubles will not go ahead after Legacy Act takes effect', *The Irish Times*, 1 May 2024: www.irishtimes.com/ireland/2024/05/01/ni-inquests-involving-74-deaths-during-troubles-sidelined-after-legacy-act-takes-effect/.
72 Email to author from Niall Murphy, 27 February 2025.
73 Letter from Mr Justice Kinney to Chris Heaton-Harris, 13 March 2024, copy held by author.
74 Neutral Citation No. [2024] NICoroner 18, 4 March 2024, para. 13.
75 PII Bundle as disclosed to KRW-Law in December 2023 and January 2024.
76 Author interview, confidential source, February 2025.
77 Affidavit of Jon Boutcher, 17 March 2025, paras 6.4–6.5, as seen by author.
78 Neutral Citation No. [2024] NICoroner 18, 4 March 2024, paras 30–40.
79 Letter from Secretary of State for Northern Ireland to coroner Patrick Kinney, 8 March 2024.
80 Neutral Citation No: [2024] NIKB 11, 28 February 2024, paras 33–52: www.judiciaryni.uk/judicial-decisions/2024-nikb-11.
81 Ibid.
82 Defence minister, Johnny Mercer, tweet, 24 February 2020: https://x.com/JohnnyMercerUK/status/1232026832150679552.
83
- Soldiers A and C, acquitted for murder of IRA man Joe McCann in 1972 (May 2021): www.bbc.co.uk/news/uk-northern-ireland-56942056
- Dennis Hutchings, dies during trial for attempted murder of John Pat Cunningham in 1974 (October 2021): www.bbc.co.uk/news/uk-northern-ireland-58960262
- David Holden, convicted of manslaughter of Aidan McAnespie in 1988 (November 2022): www.bbc.co.uk/news/uk-northern-ireland-63754980
- Soldier B, dies while awaiting trial for murder of Daniel Hegarty in 1972 (September 2023): www.bbc.co.uk/news/uk-northern-ireland-63290028
- Soldier F, charged with murder, and soldiers F, B, C, D, charged with attempted murder in 1972 (February 2024): www.bbc.co.uk/news/uk-northern-ireland-68238984
- Soldier F, acquitted of murder and attempted murder over Bloody Sunday shooting in 1972 (October 2025): www.bbc.co.uk/news/articles/c993nlken18o

84 Letter from Mr Justice Kinney to Chris Heaton-Harris, 13 March 2024, copy held by author.
85 Ibid.
86 Ibid.
87 Neutral Citation No. [2024] NICoroner 18, 4 March 2024, para. 42.
88 'Chief constable pledges "unfettered access" to police files on Sean Brown', *The Independent*, 7 March 2024: www.independent.co.uk/news/uk/police-service-of-northern-ireland-chris-heatonharris-government-ministry-of-defence-belfast-b2508847.html.
89 Letter from Mr Justice Kinney to Chris Heaton-Harris, 13 March 2024.
90 'Terminally ill brother of Catholic man killed by loyalists appeals to British government for truth', *The Irish News*, 7 June 2025: www.irishnews.com/news/northern-ireland/seriously-

ill-brother-of-catholic-man-killed-by-loyalists-appeals-to-british-government-for-truth-NGI2HWQ6F5A7LH2WV3PH5ZRMXY/.

91 Neutral Citation No. [2024] NIKB 18, 25 March 2024, para. 5: www.judiciaryni.uk/files/judiciaryni/2024-04/The%20Chief%20Constable%20of%20The%20Police%20Service%20of%20Northern%20Ireland%27.pdf.

92 Affidavit of Jon Boutcher, 17 March 2025, para. 1.5 in the matter of an application for judicial review by the Secretary of State for Northern Ireland (Appellant) and Coroner Louisa Fee, Eugene Thompson (Next of Kin), Chief Constable of the Police Service of Northern Ireland, UK Supreme Court (Respondents).

93 Author interview, confidential source, October 2025.

94 Neutral Citation No. [2024] NIKB 18, 25 March 2024, para. 36.

95 'Belfast: High Court rules on Liam Paul Thompson inquest disclosure', *BBC News*, 25 March 2024: www.bbc.co.uk/news/uk-northern-ireland-68657029.

96 Affidavit of Jon Boutcher, 17 March 2025, para. 12.2.

97 Letter from Jon Boutcher to Chris Heaton-Harris, 27 March 2024.

98 Neutral Citation No. [2024] NIKB 32, 25 April 2024, para. 7 (xii): www.judiciaryni.uk/files/judiciaryni/2024-04/Chief%20Constable%20PSNI%20%20and%20Secretary%20of%20State%20for%20NI%E2%80%99s%20Applications.pdf.

99 'Exclusive: Chris Heaton-Harris accused of "unprecedented political intervention" in legacy inquest', *The Irish News*, 10 April 2024: www.irishnews.com/news/northern-ireland/exclusive-chris-heaton-harris-accused-of-unprecedented-political-intervention-in-legacy-inquest-G5HBSNUMQ5EUNFRFXVI7577Y4Y/.

100 Neutral Citation No. [2024] NICoroner 24, 24 April 2024, paras 43 and 44: www.judiciaryni.uk/files/judiciaryni/2024-07/In%20the%20matter%20of%20an%20Inquest%20into%20the%20death%20of%20Fergal%20McCusker%20-%20Provisional%20Ruling%20on%20the%20viability%20of%20the%20inquest%20proceeding.pdf.

101 Pre-action papers for leave to apply for judicial review in respect of the coroner's decision in the inquest of Sean Brown, 10 April 2024, copy held by author.

102 Author interview, Niall Murphy, February 2025.

103 Interview with Paul Wilson, 'Frank', *Stakeknife*, Episode 10, BBC Sounds, 1 February 2025: www.bbc.co.uk/sounds/play/p0km0vdx.

104 Jon Boutcher, oral evidence to Northern Ireland Affairs Committee, Q23, 23 April 2024: https://committees.parliament.uk/oralevidence/14669/pdf/.

105 Ibid.

106 Neutral Citation No. [2024] NICA 39, 30 April 2024, para. 63: www.judiciaryni.uk/files/judiciaryni/2024-05/The%20Secretary%20of%20State%20NI%20and%20Coroner%20Fee%20And%20Inquest%20into%20the%20death%20of%20Liam%20Paul%20Thompson.pdf.

107 Neutral Citation No. [2024] NICA 82 (McCloskey LJ, dissenting judgment), 30 May 2024, Appendix 1: www.judiciaryni.uk/files/judiciaryni/2024-12/%5B2024%5DNICA82Final%20-%20Typed.pdf. See also the pre-action letter served on Coroner Kinney on 10 April with hearing on 16 April.

108 Government introduces amendments to NI Troubles legacy legislation, 8 June 2023: www.gov.uk/government/news/government-introduces-amendments-to-ni-troubles-legacy-legislation.

109 Neutral Citation No. [2024] NIKB 109, para. 85, 17 December 2024: www.judiciaryni.uk/files/judiciaryni/2024-12/Brown%27s%20%28Bridie%29%20Application.pdf.

110 Neutral Citation No. [2025] NICA 16, para. 159, 3 April 2025: www.judiciaryni.uk/files/judiciaryni/2025-04/In%20the%20matter%20of%20an%20application%20by%20Brown%20%28Bridie%29.pdf.

111 'In the matter of an application by Bridie Brown for Judicial Review', UKSC/2025/0091, 30 May 2025: www.supremecourt.uk/cases/uksc-2025-0091#previous-proceedings.

112 'Murder Without Answers', *Spotlight*, BBC Northern Ireland, 10 June 2025.

113 Hilary Benn, oral evidence to Northern Ireland Affairs Committee, Q224, 3 September 2025: https://committees.parliament.uk/oralevidence/16397/html/.

114 'In the matter of an application by Martina Dillon, John McEvoy, Brigid Hughes and Lynda McManus for Judicial Review (Respondents)', UKSC/2025/0013, 'Facts', 24 January 2025: www.supremecourt.uk/cases/uksc-2025-0013.

115 Author interview, Niall Murphy, November 2025.

EPILOGUE

1 Sir James Eadie, KC, Blackstone Chambers: www.blackstonechambers.com/barristers/james-eadie-kc/.

2 Sir Iain Livingstone, oral evidence to Northern Ireland Affairs Committee, Q3, 14 January 2026.

3 Ibid., paras 11.10–11.16.

4 Ibid., para. 4.13.

5 Jon Boutcher, CAJ 2025 annual lecture 'Neither Confirm Nor Deny Policy' and Legacy Investigations, 10 December 2025: https://caj.org.uk/publications/submissions-and-briefings/caj-2025-annual-lecture/.

6 Oliver Sanders KC, UK Supreme Court, morning and afternoon sessions, 11 June 2025: https://supremecourt.uk/cases/uksc-2024-0083; also, affidavit of Jon Boutcher, 17 March 2025.

7 Sir James Eadie KC, UK Supreme Court, morning session, 11 June 2025: https://supremecourt.uk/cases/uksc-2024-0083.

8 Lord Philip Sales, UK Supreme Court, afternoon session, 11 June 2025.

9 Lord Robert Reed, UK Supreme Court, morning session, 11 June 2025.

10 Ibid.

11 Lord Robert Reed, UK Supreme Court, afternoon session, 11 June 2025.

12 Sir James Eadie KC, UK Supreme Court, morning session, 11 June 2025.

13 Oliver Sanders KC, UK Supreme Court, afternoon session, 11 June 2025.

14 Sir James Eadie KC, UK Supreme Court, afternoon session, 11 June 2025.

15 Ibid., Lord Hodge.

16 'Over 4,000 applications to join the Police Service of Northern Ireland', PSNI, 18 February 2026: www.psni.police.uk/latest-news/over-4000-applications-join-police-service-northern-ireland

17 '"Fear and apprehension" of Catholic PSNI recruits needs tackled', BBC News NI, 19 February 2026: www.bbc.co.uk/news/articles/c24dqd558m5o.

18 'Statistics press notice, Ireland and Northern Ireland – A Joint Census Publication 2021–2022', Northern Ireland Statistics and Research Agency: www.nisra.gov.uk/system/files/statistics/2025-07/ireland-and-northern-ireland-a-joint-census-publication-2021-2022-statistics-press-notice-v2.pdf.

19 Affidavit of Jon Boutcher, 17 March 2025, para. 9.2.

20 UKSC/2024/0083, press summary, 17 December 2025: https://supremecourt.uk/uploads/uksc_2024_0083_press_summary_6c3ea3a0d2.pdf.

21 UKSC/2024/0083, judgment, 17 December 2025, para. 163: https://supremecourt.uk/cases/press-summary/uksc-2024-0083.

22 Author interview, several confidential legal sources, December 2025.

23 Jon Boutcher, oral evidence to Northern Ireland Affairs Committee, Q25, 23 April 2024: https://committees.parliament.uk/oralevidence/14669/pdf/.

24 Author interview, confidential source, June 2025.

INDEX